Research Comes Alive!

A Guidebook for Conducting Original Research with Middle and High School Students

Gina D. Schack
Alane J. Starko

Creative Learning Press, Inc.
P.O. Box 320 • Mansfield Center • Connecticut 06250

Book Layout & Design
Siamak Vahidi

Cover & Graphic Design
David J. Jernigan

Editors
Debra L. Briatico
Rachel A. Knox

Printed in the United States of America
ISBN 0-936386-75-4

Creative Learning Press, Inc.
P.O. Box 320
Mansfield Center, CT 06250
Phone: 888-518-8004 • 860-429-8118
Fax: 860-429-7783
www.creativelearningpress.com

Acknowledgments

We would both like to acknowledge and thank the many people who encouraged us to write this book, particularly after the publication of **Looking for Data**. We also appreciate the many teachers who piloted the lessons and ideas in this book. Credit is also due Deb Briatico and Rachel Knox, our editors at Creative Learning Press, for helping increase the clarity of writing and consistency of format in the book. We once again thank Dr. Joseph Renzulli for his vision of children as practicing professionals and his encouragement while writing this book. Gina appreciates Brenda Overturf for all she has taught her about authentic assessment in particular and inspired teaching of adolescents in general. Alane thanks her husband Bob for his patience and support during many hours at the computer and many years of adventures.

Further, we are grateful to the Literary Executor of the late Sir Ronald A. Fisher, F.R.S., Dr. Frank Yates, F.R.S., and the Longman Group Ltd., London, for permission to reprint the tables for the Critical Values for the Chi Square Distribution, Correlation Coefficient, and Distribution from their book **Statistical Tables for Biological, Agricultural and Medical Research** (6th Edition, 1974), as well as the Iowa State University Press for the Table of Random Numbers.

Table of Contents

List of Figures

List of Activities

Introduction

Where We're Heading

In West Virginia, a group of high school students investigates water quality in a nearby stream. Using water quality analysis techniques and observation data, they monitor pollution levels from year to year, reporting their results to county officials. In the same school, other students who had heard that younger students were afraid of nuclear war interview elementary students to see if the same is true for their own town. In Kentucky, 8th graders survey a random sample of fellow students to see what their concerns are about moving to the nearby high school. In Connecticut, middle school students design and conduct experiments to determine the effects of various types and volume levels of music on students' ability to do school work. What thread connects these adolescents working in different parts of the country? In each case, they are conducting authentic research-making hypotheses, gathering and analyzing data, and drawing conclusions, just like professional adult researchers.

Unfortunately, "research" at the middle and high school level often consists of paraphrasing facts from reference books located in the school library. Students who are fortunate enough to have the equipment and know-how can peruse the Internet for information. Ascertaining validity and reliability still remains a challenge to many learners. While these skills of locating information in libraries and through other media are both necessary and important, they do not come close to accurately representing the wide variety of techniques used by adults in the real world.

Defining Research

Although there are many types of research, they all share certain basic characteristics. According to the American Heritage Electronic Dictionary (1992), research is " 1. Scholarly or scientific investigation or inquiry. 2. Close, careful study." The focus of research is the discovery or production of new knowledge or understanding. This role is somewhat different for students who have traditionally been expected to consume information, not produce it. Researchers deal with questions without known answers, problems without effective solutions. Rather than re-examine what others have done, cutting-edge researchers add to the body of knowledge by producing new information. It is this approach to research, not traditional report-writing, that we encourage.

This role is new for us as teachers. Most of us were trained to help students understand and appreciate the collective wisdom of the ages and solve problems for which we knew the answers. We'll need to give that up if we are to help students identify unsolved problems and questions, which is the skill youngsters will need in the future. Students can't conduct research, in the sense that we use the word, to determine the capitals of countries in Europe and Africa, but they can survey their peers and teachers to see who has lived in or visited those countries. They can't do original research to find out the name of their city's first mayor, but they can try to analyze changes in housing patterns in various parts of the city with respect to socio-economic characteristics of the residents. The challenge of guiding students through authentic research is that no one knows ahead of time which resources are available or what the results will be. Assisting students in posing genuine research questions, questions to which there are no predetermined answers and for which data is available, is both the challenge and the key to success in facilitating authentic research with students.

Why Teach Research?

Teachers of gifted students have long used independent study as an important strategy for challenging their students. Along with this approach has been a focus on real-world problems (Maker, 1992; Renzulli, 1977a). In addition, Renzulli (1 977a) has long advocated programs that help students become producers of new knowledge, rather than consumers of existing knowledge. Others in the field of gifted education suggest that gifted students should be involved in more sophisticated and in-depth content and process skills and that they should study topics in greater depth. We hope teachers of the gifted will see how our approach to original research facilitates those curricular and instructional modifications and that this book facilitates this type of study.

We have also written this book for classroom teachers. Educators may wonder why we ask them to teach this type of research in the regular classroom, given all the other demands on teaching time. Why not simply tell students what pollution exists in waterways or how music affects concentration? As you probably have already realized, there is too much information in the world right now to teach students everything of importance. In fact, the speed at which this information is growing keeps increasing every day. So we need to focus on our ultimate goal of helping students gain the necessary skills and desire to become lifelong learners.

We can't even begin to know the kinds of challenges our students will face as adults. Twenty years ago, who would have anticipated the effects of cellular phones, computers, changing weather patterns, etc.? So how can we expect to give them the information necessary to become successful problem solvers, decision makers, and thinkers twenty and thirty years into the future? Obviously we can't. But we can give them the tools to think critically, frame questions, identify valid data, and discover, analyze, and organize information. Research methodology provides many of these tools.

Original research also fulfills the aims of authentic curriculum and performance assessment. When teaching is organized around real-world problems and involves not just the acquisition of information and skills but also their application, the resulting learning is more powerful, accessible, and permanent. When you think about the things you've learned and the things your ancestors have learned over the centuries, you will quickly notice that learning has taken place in order to do something valued by an individual or a society. Those learning activities may have involved survival skills like hunting and gathering, expressive activities like drawing and storytelling, or leisure activities like games and crafts. Unless you are one of the few winners of Jeopardy, you've probably rarely learned things in order to be able to tell them to someone else ... outside of school, that is. In the real world, the information we gain is used to solve problems, understand our world, communicate ideas, and become actively used.

In the past it has often been acceptable for students to repeat back information in order to pass tests and get good grades. Recent assessment techniques that require students to actually understand and use information and skills in context reveal that many students have difficulty doing this task. Teachers are in search of new curriculum, instruction, and assessment strategies that can facilitate more authentic learning. We feel original research serves these purposes by involving students in real-world questions as active investigators and inviting them to gather, analyze, and interpret data and present their results to authentic audiences using appropriate communication vehicles.

We also believe involving students in original research contributes to increased motivation. This motivation comes when students are encouraged to investigate questions of genuine interest to them. Students also see the value of what they are learning in school when they recognize that it helps them answer questions they find relevant and compelling. Structuring learning so that students are actively involved in designing and carrying out research also gives them a more active role as learners.

Finally, we feel it is important to help students understand not just the content of the school curriculum (knowledge about), but also how professionals expand what is known and contribute new knowledge to the world (knowledge how). Content has traditionally been presented as a set body of knowledge to be learned. If, instead, it is approached as the end result of someone's research and creative productivity, students can gain a whole new perspective on both content and their own potential as knowledge producers. They also can gain tools for critical understanding. If they know what constitutes acceptable research, they can better judge information they encounter in the media, school, among peers, etc.

What's in This Book?

We hope to share with you strategies for teaching students how to conduct original research. In order to do this, you'll need some information about research design, techniques, and some basic vocabulary. While you may be the exception, most teachers do not encounter this kind of learning in their teacher preparation programs. In fact, the first either of us ever had any formal training in research methodology was in our Ph.D. program. And even then, it was hard to wade through ponderous textbooks and sometimes daunting lectures.

Because research became interesting to us once we actively participated in the research process and investigated questions of our own, we began to think about how we could share this excitement and challenge with students. Our efforts to conduct research with students were fueled by library reading, trial and error, and seat-of-thepants efforts. Even after we graduated and were working in teacher education ourselves, we still had a hard time finding materials that discussed research techniques that might be used by young people or gave suggestions for student projects or training activities. Our first effort to remedy this difficulty, **Looking for Data in All the Right Places** (Starko & Schack, 1992), presented research techniques and activities for students in grades K-6.

In this book we have expanded on the research process introduced to elementary students by incorporating examples and activities appropriate for middle and high school students. In addition, we have included four additional research approaches in the "Types of Research" chapter, added a section on the research methodologies peculiar to academic disciplines, included more advanced data analysis methods, such as qualitative analysis, and added a chapter about assessing original research.

This book may not be sufficient for your graduate "Survey of Research" course, but it should help you understand, in a professional and non-threatening way, what you need in order to help students become original researchers. (Actually, we think it might help make that graduate textbook more understandable!) If we are to help students become more professional and sophisticated about research, we need to do so ourselves. In addition to explanations and examples, we have included practice activities, as well as suggestions for real-world projects students might want to pursue. We wrote the activities with students in mind, so you can use them as individual assignments or explorations. You can also use or adapt them for teacher-led activities or as resources and starting points for your own planning. You have complete permission to reproduce any activities for classroom use.

We want to be clear that this book will not be effective as a workbook, cookbook, or book you "do" with students. Asking students to complete the activities without prior instruction would be like asking them to do a book report without reading the book-and we've all seen at least one of those! Our goal is to share the information with you in an inviting and professional manner so you can decide how best to share these research techniques with your students. You know best what fits with your existing curriculum and teaching style, what your students have learned previously about data analysis, and what their interests might be with respect to research. We hope the sample activities are useful and provide adequate practice and inspiration for your students.

One way to include research activities in the regular curriculum is through a topic-based unit. Any unit on ecology, for example, can be enriched by conducting a study on the number of students who do and do not recycle. A unit about Congress can be enhanced by completing a survey about current issues.

Another approach to research inclusion involves teaching relevant research activities as a mini-unit. You can teach students to analyze primary documents for validity and reliability as a prelude to an historical study. We encourage you to do this with the entire class, but if you are convinced it would not be effective, you can offer it to a cluster group within the class.

Finally, you can use research methodology to assist high-end learners who want to conduct individual or small group projects. More authentic research techniques can enable such students to transform their individual efforts from just another school report to the knowledge production of adult researchers.

This book is organized to follow the stages of the research process. Chapters I and 2 provide information about finding, framing, and focusing research questions. Chapter 3 describes nine types of research and includes sample activities for each type. Chapter 4 discusses data gathering strategies that can be used in different types of research. Chapter 5 outlines procedures for sample selection, while Chapters 6 and 7 deal with analyzing data and sharing research results. Chapter 8 suggests procedures for assessing the original research efforts of students. Chapter 9 addresses the teaching of specific research methodologies used in academic disciplines and highlights the ways in which practicing professionals create new knowledge.

We hope you and your students enjoy the strategies and activities in this book and that you develop new research ideas for going beyond the scope of this text. Since researchers are creators of knowledge, we look forward to the contributions of you and your students in the coming years. Please consider sharing your efforts about teaching students to be original researchers through articles in professional journals (*Social Education, Mathematics Teacher, Mathematics Teaching in the Middle School, School Science and Mathematics, Science and Children, English Journal, Voices From the Middle, Middle School Journal, Educational Leadership, Kappan*, and *Instructor*). We would also be delighted to hear about your efforts and wish you many hours of happy, challenging research.

Getting Started

Chapter 1

Students as Researchers

How do your students respond when you mention doing research? For many middle and high school students, the reaction is a negative one. For some, research conjures up images of hours in the library laboring over encyclopedias, note cards, bibliographies, and report writing. Others may envision genetic engineers, nuclear physicists or other professionals far from the world of secondary schools. Each of these concepts of research limits students. If they perceive research as too sophisticated, too difficult, too tedious, or too remote, it is unlikely they will envision themselves as researchers. In truth, the essence of research can be found in ideas and events that are familiar to most adolescents.

A Broomhilda cartoon from several years ago portrayed one of Broomhilda's friends explaining at length why he thought she was crazy. Broomhilda listened for a while (four cartoon panels, to be exact), then said the friend's hunch may be right, but he was going to have to come up with some proof. In the real world, that is what research is about. Someone has a question or hunch about something and tries to come up with proof or evidence by gathering and analyzing data. Adolescents have many questions and ideas about their world, but often don't have the tools to pursue validating them.

Introducing students to a broadened conception of research entails opening their eyes to examples of research that surround them. Research on late model cars in **Car and Driver**, reader surveys in teen magazines, comparisons of movie attendance, and even the number of "hits" on a favorite web site represent data gathering in real-world contexts. Once you and your students begin to look for examples of research, you may find them in sources as diverse as magazine advertising, yearbook sales figures, and the ten most popular videos of the week.

Another way to help students think more broadly about research is to have them think about careers and the research various individuals might do as part of their job. For example, what questions might a professional athlete want to answer? A successful salesperson? A social worker working with the homeless? The player who investigates an opponents' style of play, the salesperson who charts the features and colors most frequently requested, and the social worker who keeps track of the strategies that are most effective in helping clients find employment not only do their jobs more effectively, but also become true researchers. You may want to invite people from the community to discuss the types of information they research on the job. You may also want to discuss with students the kinds of research you do on a daily basis—finding out what books students like to read, discovering the most effective yearbook sales techniques, or locating the best place in your garden to grow basil.

It is important to help students recognize their own researchable questions. For example, if Tamika claims that everyone else gets to date except her, you might suggest she gather data to find out if it is true. If Jacob wonders why the school building was constructed, you could encourage him to find out. Students may not always elect to investigate the questions they raise, but they should recognize the identification of questions as a valuable skill, one essential to a budding researcher.

In fact, one question teachers of research must ask themselves is "Is my classroom a problem-friendly place?" In other words, is the atmosphere in the classroom one in which it is safe for students to be unsure, to question, or to wonder? There are several strategies that can help make a classroom more problem-friendly. Perhaps the most important is for teachers to serve as a model of questioning. In a research-oriented classroom, the teacher cannot be the one with all the answers. Teachers can model their curiosity about ideas in their personal and professional lives. Comments such as "Last night as I was thinking about this assignment, I started to wonder why the author chose to . . ." or "My eight-year-old seems just as interested in the advertisements on Saturday morning TV as she is in the cartoons. I wonder how effective that type of advertising is in influencing toy sales?" are examples of the problem finding process that sparks interest in research. Like students, teachers do not always need to gather data to examine their questions, although doing so occasionally is also good modeling.

Teachers may find it necessary to teach students the difference between checking for understanding and actual questioning. In the first instance, the teacher knows the answer to the question, but asks it in order to gain information about the students' understanding. In the second instance, the teacher or other questioner is curious and genuinely wants to know the answer to the question. That distinction can help students understand that not all answers are found in the back of the book and that there are many questions to which they are not expected to know the answers. Activities, like some of those at the end of this chapter, in which students practice asking interesting questions simply for the sake of developing the skill of questioning can reinforce the idea that questioning is a valued ability.

One teacher encouraged students' questions by creating a bulletin board entitled "I Wonder . . . " Any time questions were raised in class or students suggested ideas that could not be investigated immediately, the questions were recorded and posted on the board. Students could later investigate or simply admire questions raised by their classmates. Once students begin to envision the potential variety and excitement in their role as researchers, the next step is to identify an interesting topic for investigation.

Finding a Research Topic

As teachers, we are probably most accustomed to seeking topics of interest within the regular curriculum. Certainly, those are the topics with which students will spend much of their time during the school day. The key to finding research topics within the curriculum is to transform the way we view the curriculum itself. Rather than viewing the content as a series of facts to be learned, it is helpful to think about the content as a collection of areas to be investigated. Finding those areas within the curriculum in which students can be authentic investigators can help in selecting areas of emphasis for content learning. For example, many science classes teach units on ecology that are full of potential research topics. If the unit is to cover air pollution, samples can be gathered from various places in the community. If it is to cover recycling, neighbors can be surveyed. Literature classes can gather data about students' favorite books. A study of colonial times could lead to an investigation of the local community during that period. Occasionally a topic notably missing from the curriculum can lead to a research project. What role did African Americans play in World War II? How many women are mentioned in the social studies texts at each grade level?

Sometimes topics may not come directly from the regular curriculum, but may branch off from topics studied. A drama class may investigate the clothing, furnishings or music of the period in which a particular play is set. A study of town government may lead to interest in a current local issue. Studies about nutrition may lead to questions about the snacking habits of fellow students.

There are also research topics that do not originate in the regular curriculum at all, but are rooted in students' current interests. Identifying topics based on students' interests presents a challenge to teachers who may not be familiar with students' interests or are faced with students who claim not to be interested in anything at all. Despite these difficulties, many teachers find that the motivation generated by ties to students' individual or group interests is worth the effort necessary to identify and, in some cases, develop student interests.

Interest Assessment

Teachers have many informal ways of identifying their students' interests. Certainly it would be difficult to miss the latest media/marketing craze on a student's T-shirt or the fact that every book Jesse takes out of the library is about medieval times. However, there may be times when you want to assess student interests in a more systematic manner. Your basic choice in interest assessment tools is between open-ended and closed-ended responses. An open response inventory asks students to provide responses to open-ended questions such as "I like to read books about __________" or "If I could invite anyone living or dead to visit our classroom, I would invite _________." By examining the answers to several such questions, it is possible to identify themes and trends in particular students' interests. Such analysis can provide a wealth of information and insight into the worlds of individual students. The parallel disadvantage is, of course, that open-ended questions are not easily tallied and may be time-consuming to analyze for large groups. If every student chooses a different book or a different dinner guest, you may find it difficult to use that information. If you decide to use an open response inventory, you may develop your own or purchase commercially available inventories such as the **Interest-A-Lyzer** (Renzulli, 1977b).

Another alternative for interest assessment is to present students with a more closed set of responses. One way to do this is to use a list of possible topics and ask students to circle the ones which they would most like to explore. We have provided one such list in Figure 1.1, excerpted from a longer list in **Pathways to Investigative Skills** (Burns, 1990). We have also provided expanded lists within each of the major disciplines for a more focused picture of students' interests within a subject area (see Figure 1.2). If you use the latter, we encourage you to use it in conjunction with the more general list. Some students who are convinced there is nothing at all interesting in your subject could indicate interests on the general list that you will be able to connect to your discipline. For example, a student who claims no interest in social studies, but has an interest in the impact of computers, may be interested in the social changes that accompanied other major changes in technology, particularly in the ways such changes may or may not parallel those to technology today.

Another possible source of information on student interests is a more systematic recording of the informal data that is part of everyday life with a room full of adolescents. It is not always easy to identify the interests, needs, or concerns of secondary students. If you are interested in maximizing the ties between research (and other curricular efforts) and students' worlds, it is helpful to keep written records of the clues to the mysteries of those lives. You can keep records of topics mentioned in journal writing, independent reading, or informal conversation. You may want to consider anecdotal records of class or informal comments or topics of library books. Whatever method you choose, the goal is to become as familiar as possible with students' interests and concerns that may provide the basis for a research topic.

You can also use student interests in a more "spur of the moment" fashion by linking students' interests and research types to identify possible topics for research. For some topics, such as food fads or current school controversies, the connections between interests and research areas can be fairly straight-forward. For others, it may become more of a challenge. A teacher once told us that it was difficult to make links to his students' interests because they weren't interested in much except pop culture and rock music. Together we proceeded to outline several researchable topics related to those interest areas. While the particular types of research may not yet be familiar to you, this list of research questions related to rock music should give you a sense of the possibilities.

1. Do children, parents, and record store owners feel record albums should contain ratings or warnings about record content? Do such warnings affect their buying habits? (descriptive)
2. How many middle/high school students watch MTV or other video channels? How often? (descriptive)
3. How are the lyrics of top 40 songs today similar to or different from those of a different decade? (historical)
4. How does playing rock music affect plant growth? Does the volume or type of rock matter? (experimental)
5. Does listening to rock music while doing school work reduce the quality of work? Are all subject areas affected similarly? (quasi-experimental)
6. Are there developmental stages in learning how to play an instrument or sing? (developmental)
7. Do students who like rock music do worse in school? Does it matter how much time they spend listening to music each day? (correlational)
8. Is there a relationship between the kinds of music students like and the kinds of music their parents like? (correlational)
9. How does a rock band go about creating songs, finding jobs, getting along, and publicizing themselves? (case study)
10. How are the backgrounds of more successful and less successful rock bands different? (causal-comparative)
11. How can we make our band more successful? (action)

Sample Interest Inventory

This year we want to include things that are interesting to you in our topics of study. On the list below, please circle the ten things that are most interesting to you. If you already know a lot about a topic, but are still interested in it, lightly shade in the circle. Mark the MOST interesting thing with a star. If you have interests that are not listed, fill them in.

SOCIAL SCIENCES
Archaeology
Careers/Jobs
Crime
Different Cultures
(Which ones?)
____
____
____
Disabilities
The Economy
Families
Family History
Foreign Countries
(Which ones?)
____
____
____
The Future
Geography/Maps
Native Americans
Local Government
Local History
Military
National Government
Politics
Prejudice
Race Relations
Religions
Social Problems
Your City
Your State
War
Women's Issues
World History
____
____
____

SCIENCE
Birds
Chemistry
Dinosaurs
Environment
Electricity/Electronics
Energy

SCIENCE (continued)
Fish
Fossils
Health/Medicine
Human Body
Insects
Nutrition
Oceanography
Plants
Pollution
Prehistoric Life
Recycling
Reptiles
Robots
Rocks/Minerals
Space/Stars/Planets
Weather
____
____
____

COMMUNICATION
Advertising
Authors
Book-Making
Foreign Languages
(Which ones?)
____
____
____
Games
Plays/Drama
Poetry
Magazines
Movies
Myths/Fables
Newspapers
Public Speaking
Short Stories
Sign Language
Songs
____
____
____

VISUAL and PERFORMING ARTS
Acting
Calligraphy
Cartooning
Clay/Pottery
Dance
Drawing
Movie-Making
Music
Painting
Pantomime
Photography
Puppetry
Putting on a Play
Radio
Sculpture
Television/Video
____
____
____

Figure 1.1. Sample interest inventory.

Social Sciences

Anthropology

Different Cultures (Which ones?)

____

____

____

____

Families/Family Structures

My Culture

Native Americans

Archaeology

Fossils

Dinosaurs

Early Humans

"The Missing Link"

Sociology

Crime

Disabilities

Ethnic Groups

Gangs

Prejudice

Race Relations

Religions

Social Problems

Women's Issues

Economics

Balance of Payments

Careers/Jobs

Credit/Debt

Health-Related

Economics (continued)

Imports/Exports

Inflation

Making Money

Starting a Business

Stock Market

Unemployment

U.S. Economy

Welfare Systems

Geography

Climate

Cultural Geography

Demographics

Foreign Countries (Which ones?)

____

____

____

____

Geography of Your State

Making Maps

Medical Geography

Natural Resources

Physical Features

Physical Geography

Political Geography

History

African History

African American History

Family History (Genealogy)

History of Buildings

Figure 1.2. Expanded interest inventory (social sciences).

Social Sciences
(continued)

History (continued)

History of Particular Countries

(Which ones?) ______________________

____

History of Particular Groups

(Which ones?) ______________________

____

History of Particular People

(Which ones?) ______________________

____

Local History

Oral History

U.S. History

Wars

Women's History

World History

Political Science

Campaigning

Corruption/Scandal

Elections

Interest Groups

Law-Making

Lobbyists

Local Government

National Government

Political Parties

State Government

Team/School Governance

Psychology

Behaviorism

Child Psychology

Cognitive Psychology

Counseling

Developmental Psychology

Experimental Psychology

Humanism

Learning

Mental Illnesses

Personality

Perception

Psychopharmacology

Miscellaneous

Futuristics/The Future

Military

____

____

____

____

____

____

Figure 1.2. Expanded interest inventory (social sciences *continued*).

Science

Biology

AIDS

Bacteria/Viruses

Biochemistry

Botany (Plants)

Chronobiology

Communicable Diseases

Dinosaurs

Entomology (Insects)

Fossils

Health/Medicine

Herpetology (Reptiles)

Human Body

Ichthyology (Fish)

Life on Other Planets

Marine Mammals

Microbiology

Nutrition

Oceanography

Ornithology (Birds)

Paleontology

Ecology/The Environment

Alternative Energy Sources

Animal Habitats

Endangered Species

Global Warming

Greenhouse Effect

Interdependence

Ozone Depletion

Ecology/The Environment (continued)

Pollution

The Rainforest

Recycling

Physical

Astronomy

Chemistry

Earthquakes

Electricity/Electronics

Energy

Meteorology (Weather)

Physics

Plate Tectonics

Robots

Rocks/Minerals

Volcanoes

Other

____

____

____

____

____

____

Figure 1.2. Expanded interest inventory (sciences).

Mathematics

Algebra

Arithmetic Patterns

Computer Programming

Geometric Patterns

Geometry

Logic

Number Systems

Number Theory

Packaging

Probability

Programming Languages

Statistics

Tessellations

____

____

____

____

____

____

Figure 1.2. Expanded interest inventory (mathematics).

Communication/Language Arts

Advertising
Internet
Magazine
Newspaper
Radio
TV

Writing
Authors (Which ones?)
____
____
____
Book-Making
Editing
Fiction
Genres
Journalism
Mysteries
Nonfiction
Novels
Play Writing
Plays
Poetry
Romance
Science Fiction
Script Writing
Short Stories
Song Writing
Technical Writing

Language
Etymology (Word origins)
Foreign Languages (Which ones?)
____
____
____
Grammar
Sentence Diagramming
Sign Language

Reading and Literature
Fiction
Literary Criticism
Mysteries
Myths/Fables
Newspapers
Nonfiction
Novels
Poetry
Science Fiction
Short Stories
Speed Reading

Speaking
Debate
Oral Interpretation
Persuasive Speaking
Public Speaking
Storytelling

Visual
Cartooning
Film Animation
Graphic Design
Movie-Making
Posters
Video Production

Other
____
____
____
____
____
____

Figure 1.2. Expanded interest inventory (communication/language arts).

Visual and Performing Arts

Visual Arts

Calligraphy

Cartooning

Charcoal

Clay/Pottery

Collage

Drawing

Glass Blowing

Graphic Design

Painting

Pastels (Chalk)

Photography

Sculpture

Stained Glass

Technical Drawing

Water Color

Audio/Visual

Computer Art

Movie-Making

Music

Radio

Television/Video

Theater

Acting

Box Office Aspects

Costume Design

Directing

Dramaturg

Theater (continued)

Lighting

Marketing/Advertising

Producing

Props

Puppetry

Putting on a Play

Set Design

Sound

Stage Makeup

Stage Manager

Movement

Dance

Pantomime

Other

____

____

____

____

____

____

Figure 1.2. Expanded interest inventory (visual and performing arts).

While these are not yet fully formed research questions, they are the beginning stages of finding a problem that can allow students to become actively involved in an area of personal interest.

It is possible to use similar brainstorming to generate research suggestions based on students' responses in class. If you are familiar with general types of research, you may find that you can quickly turn an offhand comment into a research opportunity. If students disagree over whether women really work more hours per day than men, you could suggest a way to find out. If the interest expressed is more general (e.g., "I think monster trucks are awesome!"), you might run through a quick mental checklist of subtopics or questions that might be suggested. The intention at this point is not to frame careful research questions, but to identify topics for further thought, discussion, and consideration.

You may find that students' responses to class assignments provide a similar interest "flag." The student who is asked to collect and organize ten rock samples for a collection and responds with thirty samples complete with information on source, hardness, and primary uses, may be signaling an interest in geology. Likewise, a student who reads several science fiction authors and is eager to discuss their differing views about the future may be alerting you to discuss further science fiction explorations. Still other research projects are suggested by a casual comment. Below we have highlighted some students' comments, actions, and suggested research topics.

- 8th grade students were complaining about how hard it was to find a good book to read for their required book reports. The teacher suggested they survey their peers about their favorite books and authors and compile a list of "peer-recommended" books so others might have a list from which to start.
- Several high school students were discussing a current events news item about how young children were very scared about nuclear war. They disagreed, saying their brothers and sisters didn't seem to be afraid. The teacher encouraged them to do a more systematic survey of the children in their community in order to find out.
- A group of middle school girls expressed disgust at the condition of the cafeteria tables and concern that putting food on them might be unsanitary. Their teacher suggested they think about how they could discover which cleaning supplies would do the best job in sanitizing the tables. That conversation was the impetus for a research project that involved growing bacteria cultures from tables cleaned with various substances.

You should be prepared if/when many of your invitations to further research are turned down. It is important for students to feel they can express interests without being obligated to pursue them. On the other hand, it is also highly unlikely that these three projects would have happened if the teachers had not made the suggestions they did.

Interest Development

Exploratory Activities

While it is important to identify students' current interests, developing enthusiastic student researchers also requires exposing students to new areas of potential interest. (After all, Sally Ride could not have become enthusiastic about space exploration if she had never been exposed to the subject.) Many portions of the secondary curriculum expose students to new ideas and skills, opening their worlds to new interests. An additional way to develop student interests is to provide regular opportunities that expose students to topics, questions, and issues not usually found in the regular curriculum. These enrichment experiences are not designed to provide students with extensive information or in-depth skills, but to help them become aware of new topics and offer the opportunity to follow up areas in which they develop an interest.

Think about areas in which you currently are interested. How did you first become aware of them? Did you read about them? Hear a speaker? See a display or exhibit? Watch a TV program? Talk with a friend? Exploratory activities can take a variety of forms including guest speakers, media presentations, trips, displays, or centers. They may be provided as part of the standard curriculum, as special exploratory classes or activities, or as extracurricular activities. A speaker on careers in design, a three week mini-course on creating hypertext documents, a hall display of local artifacts, or an after-school program in rocketry all provide students with the opportunity to be exposed to topics and ideas not usually found in the regular curriculum.

It is helpful to keep track of exploratory experiences presented to students so that you remember them for the next school year and check for balance among types and subjects of enrichment. The Enrichment Planning Guide can be helpful in organizing enrichment experiences (see Figure 1.3). Almost any topic can form the base for a research interest. In addition to topics within the regular curriculum, it is helpful to think about areas and disciplines that may not form a major part of your regular curriculum. The Enrichment Topic List in Figure 1.4 may get you started.

Debriefing

Debriefing is a term for activities following a learning experience that extend and transfer skills and concepts attained during formal instruction. Debriefing helps students process information, focus interests, and identify potential research questions. It builds a bridge between what students know or heard and what they still wonder about, while providing clues to possible avenues for further learning. Without debriefing, it is less likely that students will see the research possibilities in the content they learn. While debriefing may take several forms, the most common is a brief discussion following an enrichment or regular curricular activity. It may be conducted by a classroom teacher, resource teacher, parent, mentor, or guest speaker. A debriefing discussion should contain some or all of the following elements:

1. Ask students to identify areas in the presentation that were of particular interest.
2. Suggest specific resources students might want to pursue—books, videos, places to visit, people to contact, etc.
3. Point out opportunities for further training, especially in the investigative skills of related disciplines.
4. Make connections between the presentation and other topics of student interest.
5. Identify social or environmental issues related to the topic, with emphasis on those that might have a research component.
6. Identify literary or artistic themes students may want to investigate.
7. Identify research questions related to the topic or process.
8. Make plans for further study, if desired.

As is clear from the suggestions, the debriefer's role is somewhat different from that of a teacher or presenter. The debriefer issues invitations to learning, rather than demanding a command performance. The goal is to find students with an interest they might like to pursue or to help students see research possibilities in related topics. It takes creativity to make connections among student interests, the topic presented, and research methodology. However, these connections are necessary to help students see real research possibilities. The following suggestions may help you prepare effective debriefing discussions:

1. Think about the relationships between the content being presented and other subjects or disciplines.
2. Think about your students' interests. How might they relate to the presentation topic?
3. Locate other resources (books, periodicals, media, people, etc.) that might be useful to interested students.
4. Flip through the index of a basic adult book on the topic. Look for clues to interesting topics or questions.
5. Think about the types of research presented in Chapter 3. How might each relate to the topic?
6. Read as much as you can! You never know when those tidbits from **Time**, **National Geographic**, **Prevention**, or your local newspaper will come in handy.
7. Consult an expert, in person or through a "how to" book, in order to become familiar with basic research strategies or dilemmas associated with the topic.

Imagine that a class had just completed an enrichment experience with a lobbyist. The debriefing might begin with a brief discussion of the parts of the presentation the students found most interesting and continue as follows: (DBR=debriefer, ST=student)

DBR: Have you ever thought about problems related to lobbyists or lobbying? For instance, what problems might lobbyists cause for legislators?

ST1: Well, they may keep bothering them, wanting to talk to the legislator when he/she didn't have time.

DBR: Yes, that's certainly possible. I wonder how often legislators are contacted by lobbyists? That's something you could probably find out in a survey.

Enrichment Planning Guide—General

Record enrichment experiences in the appropriate column(s).

TOPICS

DELIVERY METHOD	Science/Math	Communication	Social Sciences	Arts
People Speaker				
Demonstration				
Performance				
Debate				
Panel Discussion				
Mini-Course				
Audio-Visual Film				
Filmstrip				
Slide Show				
Audiotape				

Figure 1.3. Enrichment planning guide (general).

Enrichment Planning Guide—General

(continued)

Record enrichment experiences in the appropriate column(s).

	TOPICS			
DELIVERY METHOD	Science/Math	Communication	Social Sciences	Arts
Audio-Visual (continued) Videotape				
TV Program				
Other Field Trip				
Display				
Museum Program				
Interest Development Center				
Newspaper/Magazine Article				
Books				
Simulation				

Figure 1.3. Enrichment planning guide (general *continued*).

Enrichment Planning Guide—Subject Specific

Discipline: ___________________________

Record enrichment experiences in the appropriate column(s).

	SUBDISCIPLINES			
DELIVERY METHOD				
People Speaker				
Demonstration				
Performance				
Debate				
Panel Discussion				
Mini-Course				
Audio-Visual Film				
Filmstrip				
Slide Show				
Audiotape				

Figure 1.3. Enrichment planning guide (subject specific).

Enrichment Planning Guide—Subject Specific
(continued)

Discipline: ____________________________

Record enrichment experiences in the appropriate column(s).

	SUBDISCIPLINES			
DELIVERY METHOD				
Audio-Visual (continued) Videotape				
TV Program				
Other Field Trip				
Display				
Museum Program				
Interest Development Center				
Newspaper/Magazine Article				
Books				
Simulation				

Figure 1.3. Enrichment planning guide (subject specific *continued*).

Possible Enrichment Topics

SOCIAL SCIENCE

Archaeology
Anthropology
Economics
Geography
History
Oral History
Political Science
Psychology
Sociology

MATHEMATICS

Algebra
Computer Programs
Geometry
Logic
Number Systems
Packaging
Probability
Statistics
Tessellations

SCIENCE

Astronomy
Biochemistry
Botany
Chemistry
Chronobiology
Ecology
Entomology
Geology
Herpetology
Ichthyology
Meteorology
Microbiology
Oceanography
Ornithology
Paleontology
Pathology
Physics

LANGUAGE ARTS

Cartooning
Debate
Editing
Etymology
Film Animation
Journalism
Linguistics
Literary Criticism
Movie Making
Play Writing
Poetry Writing
Public Speaking
Science Fiction
Screen Writing
Short Story Writing
Song Writing
Speed Reading
Storytelling
Technical Writing
Video Production

Figure 1.4. Possible enrichment topics.

ST2: They may get bribed by lobbyists and not know what to do about it or not be sure if it's even a bribe or not. There has been stuff like that in the paper recently.

DBR: Yes, after finding out what's considered ethical and unethical behavior, you could design a survey to see how often each occurs.

ST3: Well, one thing that's kind of a problem for legislators, but more of a problem for regular people like us, is that legislators may pay more attention to the interests of the people who can hire lobbyists than they do to our interests because we can't be there all the time talking to them.

ST4: Yeah, and buying them lunch and stuff.

DBR: Hmmm. You have several interesting ideas there. It sounds like you think legislators are indeed influenced in their voting by lobbyists. I wonder if that's true? There are ways to see if there is a relationship between lobbying efforts and legislator votes. It wouldn't prove that one caused the other, but it might give us more information. You could also use another kind of research called causal-comparative to look at legislation that passed and that didn't pass and look back to see the role of lobbyists, among other factors.

ST3: Could we focus on one or two legislators, maybe those from our area, and see how they go about making up their minds—what information they get and how they make decisions?

DBR: Excellent idea! A case study would give you an in-depth look at the life of a legislator—to whom he/she talks, how he/she decides on bills, and other aspects.

ST4: Or maybe we could see how lobbyists work, to see what they say and do. I think it would be cool to be always going out to dinner and on trips and have someone else pay for it.

DBR: Well, you may discover that their lives aren't quite that glamorous. How could you find out?

ST4: I guess you could do a case study on a lobbyist, too, if he/she would let you.

DBR: Yes, good idea. Let's expand on Lee's idea and think about problems lobbyists might have . . . .

The debriefing could continue as guided by student response and interest. An individual or group project might evolve from the discussion or it might not. In either case, students should be more aware that topics presented for enrichment can pose a variety of questions and that it is possible to investigate questions of interest.

This awareness is at the heart of "getting started" in research. We want students to become aware that research is a highly varied activity that can take place in almost all professions. It involves finding interesting questions to which we do not have answers. It involves gathering various types of data. Students may conduct research on almost any topic inside or outside the curriculum. We, too, may find questions that pique our curiosity and spur an investigation. In the beginning, we want to help students identify and develop interests in order to find research topics. Once the topic is selected, the questioning can begin.

Getting Started Activity 1

Question, Question, Who's Got the Question?

Albert Einstein once said that finding a good problem or asking a new question was the most important part of real advances in science. Good researchers are always asking questions about the world around them. They notice things that are interesting and wonder about the things they don't know. This exercise will help you practice being a good questioner. For each topic, think of as many interesting questions as you can. Try to think of some unusual questions, ones no one else will think of. For example, if the topic was athletic shoes, you might wonder

Do athletic shoes really improve sports performance?

Do you really need different kinds of shoes for different sports?

When did athletic shoes become popular with people who weren't professional athletes? Why? How?

You could also wonder

Which brands are most popular with athletes? Students at our school?

What is involved in celebrity endorsements of athletic shoes?

How many crimes involve the stealing of athletic shoes?

Now, what questions might you have about these topics?

Customs in your school:

Teenagers' eating habits:

Friendships:

Cars:

What other things do you wonder about?

Getting Started Activity 2

Searching for Researchers

Have you ever thought about a baseball coach doing research? How about the folks who make potato chips? People in all kinds of professions do research in order to gain the information they need to become successful at their jobs. Think about the kinds of questions these people might investigate. What questions might they ask?

PERSON	QUESTIONS
Writer for a teen magazine	
Veterinarian	
Volleyball coach	
Record store owner	
Cancer researcher	
History teacher	
Manager of a fast food restaurant	
Owner of an auto body shop	

Think of some people you know. What questions might they ask as part of their job?

Getting Started Activity 3

All Kinds of Questions

Just like newspaper reporters, researchers make use of key question words such as Who, What, When, Where, Why, and How. Using these key words, it is possible to think of interesting questions about just about anything. For example, take a look at these questions about ordinary classroom pencils.

Who *uses pencils?*
What *kind of pencil is easier for young children to use?*
When *did pencils become common household items?*
Where *are most pencils used?*
Why *do people choose to use a pencil instead of a pen?*
How *does the way you hold a pencil affect your handwriting?*
How *does a #2 pencil compare to a #3 pencil? How could you gather samples that would demonstrate the differences?*
How *many pencils are sold by the school store?*
What *if they advertised the pencils? Would sales go up?*
What *if someone didn't have a #2 pencil? Would anything else work in marking a standardized test?*

Pick a common item that seems interesting to you. Using the question stems, write the most interesting questions you can think of.

Who ____?

What ____?

When ____?

Where ____?

Why ____?

How ____?

How does ______________________________ compare to ___________________________?

How many ____?

What if ____?

What if someone didn't ____?

Focusing Your Problem

Chapter 2

Generating Subtopics

Finding an area of interest, either for a student or a group of students, is the first step in planning a research project. The next and probably most critical step is to focus the problem into a manageable research question. In most cases, however, the first interest areas generated by students or teachers are too broad to be effectively formed into clear research questions. Students may bring a general interest such as "I want to learn about rap music," "I like sports," or "I am interested in the Vietnam War." Teachers may think, "I'd like my student to research something about the way math is used in everyday life," or "I'd like them to investigate student food habits." In each of these cases, the researcher needs to narrow the focus into a more manageable subtopic before it will be possible to define a research question.

Probably the most common technique for generating subtopics is webbing. In webbing, a broad interest is placed in the center and subtopics branch off like strands of a spider's web. For example, in webbing the general topic of sports, a student might start with subtopics such as types, levels, injuries, salaries, or sports fans. Each of those topics can then be used to generate additional ideas (see Figure 2.1).

Another way to generate subtopics is to use key words or topics to generate ideas associated with various areas of study. A chart such as the one in Figure 2.2 can be useful in spurring more varied ideas. Each box provides a trigger that challenges the researcher to think about how a general interest area might relate to various topics or disciplines. For example, using the chart might help a student interested in sports think of additional subtopics including Hall of Fame players, the effects of technology on sports, sports as portrayed in art, laws regulating sports, the economics of professional sports, media coverage of sports, sports stories or movies, or sports equipment.

Another source of ideas for subtopics is the index of an introductory text on the subject—in this case, a book on sports or a particular sport. A quick check through the index or table of contents might add the following topics: injuries related to football, proper blocking and tackling techniques, classic lineups and plays, or the history of football. The task of identifying subtopics within a general interest may take several weeks.

While it is usually necessary to assist students in narrowing their topic, it is unwise to do so prematurely. In many cases, additional reading and information is necessary before the student is knowledgeable enough to generate subtopics. Library research to investigate what is currently known about a topic is an important part of the research process. This type of research is also known as a review of the literature. Some students may need help with this process, especially in gaining skills in reference materials beyond the encyclopedia. Many commercial materials are available to assist you in teaching students about library research. Problem Focusing Activities 1-3 can be used to help students practice generating subtopics as they prepare to focus a research question.

Research Questions

Even the richest web or longest list of topics is of limited value in beginning actual research. Within the chosen subtopic, it is still necessary to identify a research question. What is it about the subtopic that you really want to know? The research question is the key to a focused, well-organized, and manageable research study. It defines the variables to be investigated and gives direction to the research design. While there are many more technical definitions, it may be easiest to think of a research question as a clearly defined question which may be investigated through data gathering.

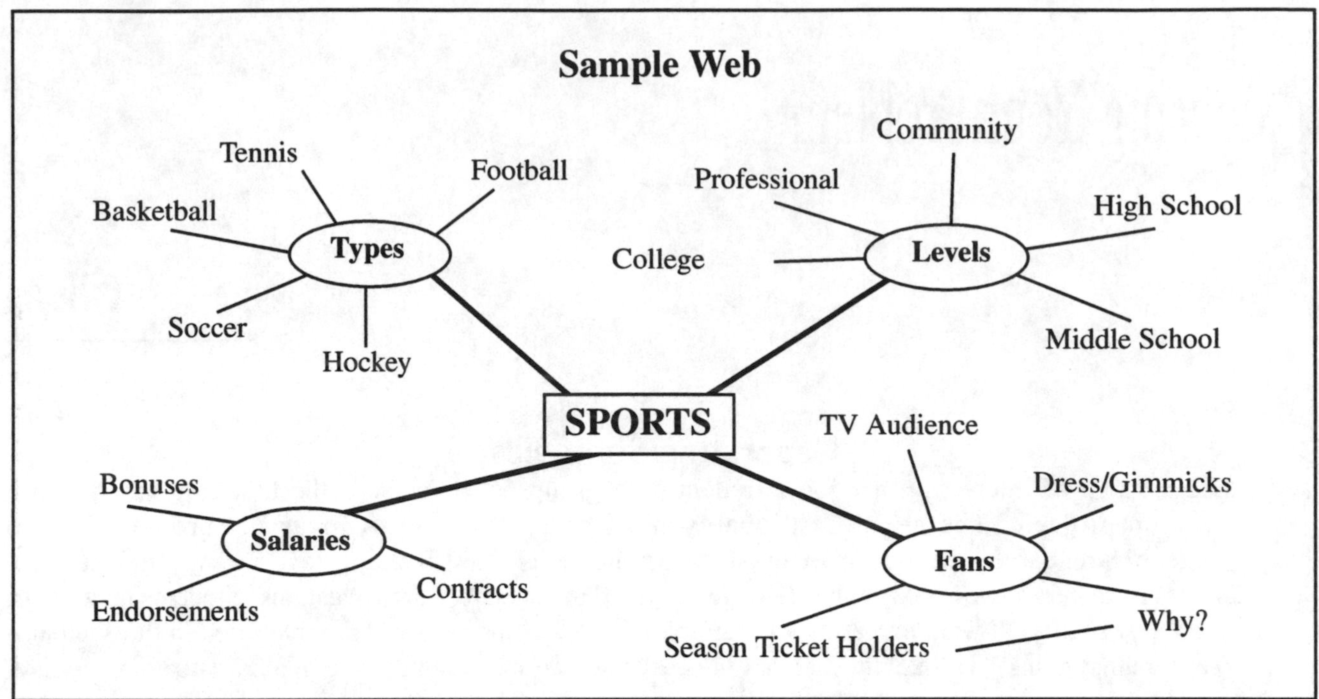

Figure 2.1. Sample web (sports).

This simple definition highlights several key features of an effective research question. A good research question is *clear*. Each term within the question should be unambiguously defined and give direction to the study. A research question *does not have a preset or clearly determined answer*—it needs to be investigated. A question such as "What do wolves eat?" is not a good research question for students because the answer can be quickly located in any encyclopedia. Finally, a good research question is *data driven*, that is, it can be answered or at least supported by gathering data from primary sources. A data driven question is not primarily an opinion or values question. For example, "What type of music is best?" is not a viable research question because there is no data we can gather to find a clear-cut answer. However, a question such as "What type of music is preferred by students in Smith Middle School?" can be investigated by gathering data. We cannot say that the music preferred by most students is the *best* music, but we can gather evidence of its popularity.

In order to conduct authentic research, we must also consider the types of data to be gathered. While using the library is an important skill, in this book we are not concerned with library research in which data are gathered from secondary sources. The question about wolves' food sources mentioned above would be most typically answered by reviewing secondary sources such as encyclopedias or books about wolves. (Though we must note that this question was originally answered using primary sources, as researchers observed wolves in the wild to see what they ate.) The research questions we will investigate entail the gathering of "raw" or primary data, either through observation, analysis of primary documents, surveys, or interviews. "How knowledgeable are Pine Forest citizens about wolves?" might form a beginning research question. Unless a local researcher has previously investigated this question, it is unlikely that the answer can be found in a reference book. It could, however, be studied through a survey or a series of interviews. In assessing potential research questions, your first three criteria should be: Is it clear? Does it have a predetermined answer? Could it be investigated though data gathering?

Finally, in beginning to define a research question, it is helpful to keep in mind the data that may be available. The availability of data relates to the final criterion you'll want to consider about a research question, "*Is it doable?*" The best research question is of limited value if the researcher has no access to the necessary data or if data gathering would take too long. For example, primary data on professional sports would be much more accessible near a city that had a professional team, while information on sports as portrayed in art would be available to anyone whose library contained art books or had access to interlibrary loans. Sometimes primary data is accessible, but beyond the technical expertise of students. For example, a group of students interested

The Topic Brainstormer

Topic: ______________________________	
Famous People	Technology
Fine Arts/Literature	History
Economy	Communication
Careers	Health/Medicine
Government/Politics/Laws	Geography
Education	Ecology/Natural Resources
Science	Problems/Controversy
Recreation	The Future

Figure 2.2. Topic brainstormer.

in emissions from a local factory might have difficulty collecting and analyzing the emissions. They might, however, collect data on the frequency of particular illnesses in the town surrounding the factory and compare them to those in surrounding towns.

Focusing a Research Question

Designing a research question entails identifying the variables to be studied and the aspects of the variables to be investigated. In most cases, students and teacher will work together to select among many possible research questions. Within a given subtopic, the key words who, what, where, when, why, and how may provide cues for generating questions. For example, the student interested in sports might investigate who likes books about sports and what are the most popular books. He or she might examine when injuries are likely to occur in a variety of sports or why students choose to play one sport rather than another. It is also possible to link a subtopic to other variables (What is the relationship between _____ and ____?) or to look at the way variables change over time. For example, a student might investigate the relationship between participation in college sports and graduation rate or the way college basketball has changed over time. The review of the literature can assist students in identifying variables that may serve as part of a research question.

Once an initial research question has been determined, it must be examined for clarity. One way to begin is to go back to the questions who, what, when, where, why, and how. Is it clear who the subjects are? Exactly what is being investigated? What are the geographical areas and time periods being studied? In addition, each word of the question must be clearly defined. In the question, "How many students in Ford High School wear expensive clothing?" it is not clear what is meant by "expensive." Some people may think a $20 silk shirt is expensive. Others may think a $20 shirt is a bargain and define a $100 silk shirt as expensive. If a definition is not obvious, either the word must be changed or an operational definition must be determined. An operational definition is one that will be used to clarify, define, or measure a variable during the course of a study. For example, researchers might decide on a list of designers or specific items of clothing that will be designated "expensive" for the purposes of the study.

Making Hypotheses

In most research studies, after the research question has been designed, researchers generate hypotheses. An hypothesis is an educated guess as to the results of the research. It asks, "Given what I know now, what do I think is likely to be the result of this study?" The more sophisticated the researcher, the more information can be taken into account in forming hypotheses. An 11th grade student who has reviewed the literature on homeless people might be ready to make hypotheses about the particular transient problems in Jefferson County, taking into account the influences of the local economy and social service agencies. Younger adolescents who have done less background research might make simpler hypotheses, based largely on their own experiences. They might hypothesize that food distribution is the greatest need of homeless people, based on their volunteer work in a soup kitchen.

It is important that students understand that hypotheses are not wild guesses, but are based on the best information available before gathering specific research data. It is also worthy to note that some qualitative research (see Chapter 3) does not begin with hypotheses, but allows the hypotheses to emerge from the data as they are gathered. However, such studies demand fairly sophisticated analysis skills and are most appropriate for students who have had practice in generating initial hypotheses. In most cases, beginning researchers identify variables, clarify research questions, and make hypotheses. When they reach this step in the research process, they are ready to select a research design.

Problem Focusing Activity 1

Spinning a Web

Have you ever had trouble trying to think of an idea for a story, report, or research project? Even professional authors can have difficulty choosing a topic for their next project. Webbing is a technique that can help you think of many ideas and choose the one that is right for you. In this exercise, you will think of ideas for a group web, then you will gather ideas for your own web.

Imagine you are working on a school health project with your friend, Jeremy. You are interested in learning more about physical fitness, but you can't decide what you want to learn about first. Jeremy has started a web of ideas, but needs some help completing it. With a partner, see how many branches you can add to Jeremy's web. After you look at all the branches, decide what your imaginary group might study.

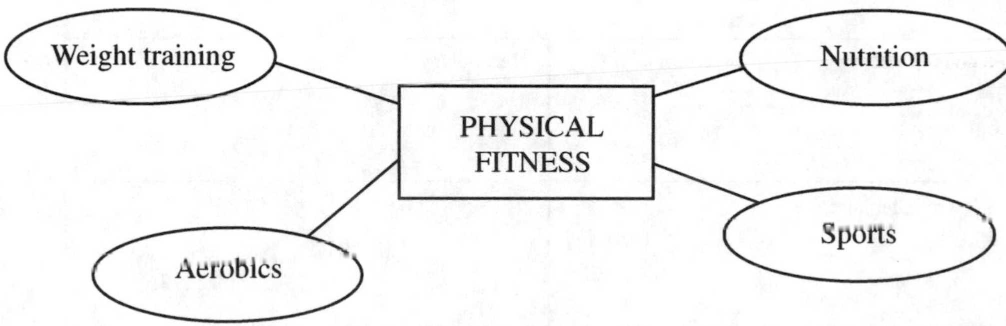

Now it is your turn. Think of a subject that interests you. It might be a topic related to school or an interest outside of school. Put your idea in the center of the web. Now see how many branches you can add to your web. You and your partner may want to help each other make your webs as full as possible. Which topic on your web seems most interesting?

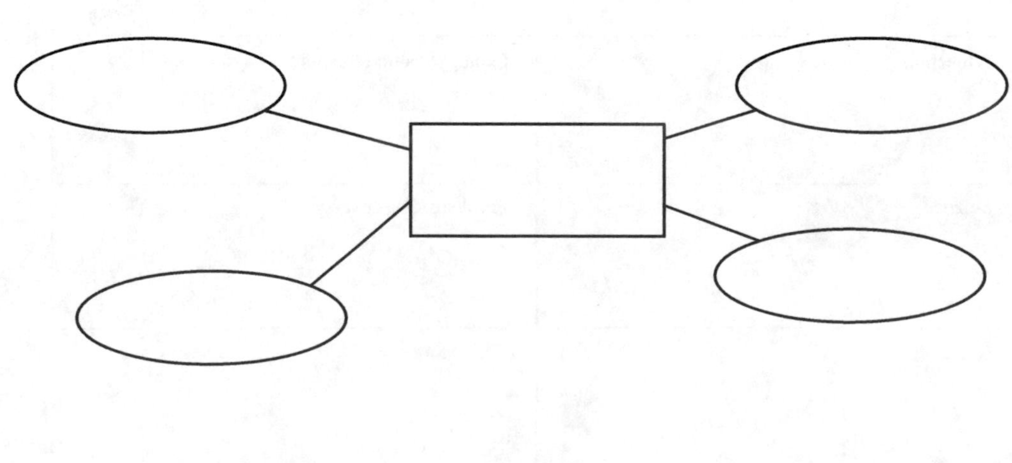

Problem Focusing Activity 2

Shaking Up a Brainstorm

When you are trying to think of a lot of different ideas, it can be helpful to have a tool to shake up your thinking and get your mind moving in different directions. The topic brainstormer can help you get new ideas by asking you how your first idea might fit with other ideas on the list. For example, if someone were looking for ideas about pond life and he/she saw the space for health/medicine, it might make him/her wonder about the levels of bacteria in local ponds or whether any pond life can be used for medicinal purposes.

Put a topic that interests you at the top of the Topic Brainstormer. Then, look at each box and think about how it might relate to your topic. See how many ideas you can find for each of the boxes.

THE TOPIC BRAINSTORMER

MY TOPIC: ______________________	
Famous People	Technology
Fine Arts/Literature	History
Economy	Communication
Careers	Health/Medicine
Government/Politics/Laws	Geography
Education	Ecology/Natural Resources
Science	Problems/Controversy
Recreation	The Future

Problem Focusing Activity 3

Searching an Index

Imagine you were interested in learning more about space exploration. You are trying to narrow your topic to a manageable size. You have been to the library and found a book that looks interesting. As you look through the index, you find several ideas that may be helpful. Look at the excerpt from the index below.* How many ideas for subtopics can you find? Underline them and circle the one that seems most interesting to you.

Index

*__Liftoff: The Story of America's Adventure in Space__ (1988). Written by Michael Collins and published by Grove Press in New York.

Problem Focusing Activity 4

Reducing the Size of the Problem

Newspapers are full of stories about problems that contain questions you might want to explore. Unfortunately, many of the problems in newspapers seem big and difficult to study. A good researcher must "trim" the problem down to size, looking for an idea that he or she can investigate. In this exercise, you will practice finding smaller ideas in giant problems. For example, the first box lists the large problem of teen violence. It would be very difficult for you to investigate teen violence across the country, but you could investigate the number of fights in your school. You could also survey students in your school or neighborhood to find out what they think about fighting. In many cases, you can trim the size of the problem by limiting your study to people or places near you. Now, try to find smaller sized problems for the rest of the listed topics.

Teen Violence	*Who gets into fights in our school? Document amount of verbal "violence" (threats, put-downs, etc.) in our school. Do people feel fighting is an appropriate way to deal with conflict?*
Teen Drug Use	
Pollution	
Unemployment	

Now, look in a newspaper from your town. List three large problems you find there. List at least one smaller sized problem for each one.

Problem Focusing Activity 5

A Question of Questions

One of the biggest tasks of any researcher is to develop good research questions. In a good research question, every word is clear and it is easy to tell exactly what the researcher wants to investigate. Many times, research questions must be rewritten several times to make them clear. Imagine that Pat had written the research question, "Are boys better than girls?" That question is a good start, but can you tell exactly what he will investigate? Which boys and which girls? Pat could change the question to "Are boys better than girls at Central High School?" since he will be interested in gathering primary data and his school population is accessible. That question is better, but it still is not clear. He can't investigate every possible thing boys and girls do. After webbing and focusing his question, Pat might choose "Are boys or girls at Central High School better students?" We're still not clear how he will determine "better" though. He could narrow it further in several different ways. Here are a few possibilities: "Are boys or girls at Central High School better musicians, determined by number of awards won at band competitions?" "Based on overall grade point average, are boys or girls at Central High School better academically?" "Based on teacher surveys, are boys or girls at Central High School more interested in learning?"

For each of the unclear questions below, write a new research question. Be sure your question is clear and answers the who, what, where, when, why, and how questions. When you're finished, show your questions to another student. Ask him/her to describe what he/she thinks each question means.

What kind of music do people like best?

Who does better in school, boys or girls?

What was this school like before we were here?

Types of Research

Chapter 3

There are many different approaches to research, each appropriate for particular kinds of questions. The best approach to choosing the right type is to first clarify the research question(s), then select the type of research that can best answer the question(s). Another approach, helpful for novice researchers, is to identify a topic of interest, then use information about the different types of research to identify several different angles on the topic. For example, if a student is interested in music, one way to help him/her identify possible research questions is to use each of the research types to think about how the topic of music might be explored. What kind of descriptive research might be conducted about music or a particular type of music? How might music be studied from an historical perspective? Could he/she design an experiment dealing with music? The more students know about available research designs, the easier it will be for them to match designs to their interests and questions.

This chapter describes nine types of research designs that we feel are appropriate for middle and high school students. The first three are broad categories that can be used to encompass most research types: descriptive, historical, and experimental. The last six types of research—quasi-experimental, correlational, developmental, case and field, causal-comparative, and action research—can be viewed as "subcategories" of one or more of the major headings. How one categorizes these types of research is less important than their value in focusing research ideas and matching questions and designs.

The format we'll use to discuss each type of research includes: (1) a description of the research design, (2) examples of both general and content-specific research questions, and (3) four possible research studies your students can do. The activities are arranged in order from less to more sophisticated, making them appropriate for middle and high school students with varying degrees of expertise. These activities are intended as springboards for research activities that are "custom-made" for your students, your curriculum, and your community. We also hope you will encourage your students to explore the research methodologies beyond the activities we provide and follow up on one of our research examples or one of their own.

Descriptive Research

Descriptive research is research that describes. It answers the question, "How are things now?" Its main purpose is to portray a current situation as systematically and accurately as possible. It doesn't attempt to explain causes or relationships among variables, but can suggest further studies to do so. Some real-world examples of descriptive research include market research, public opinion surveys, census reports, descriptive observations, consumer research, and analysis of current student test data. When the newspaper reports the test scores of all schools in your district and all districts in the state, that report contains descriptive research because it describes the current situation with respect to test scores. Newspaper rankings of customer satisfaction for various models of cars also provide a description of customers' feelings at a particular point in time. When a school district reports the number of students of varying ethnic groups in each school or in the gifted or special education program, that report is descriptive research. These are all considered descriptive research because they describe current situations. The researchers did not provide a treatment or manipulate any variables to see their effect. They just tried to describe a situation as clearly and accurately as possible. Students who survey peers regarding fast food consumption, conduct taste tests to determine the preferred brand of salsa, or observe peers to determine the most popular type of athletic shoe worn in school are also conducting descriptive research.

When doing descriptive research, students must first identify what they wish to describe. They can include items (different brands of jeans), behaviors (interrupting), attitudes (about capital punishment), preferences (brands of cola), living things (kind of pet owned), and most anything else they can count. It is important for students to define the things to be counted as precisely as possible, particularly if more than one person will be gathering the data. If one student surveys his/her friends about number of pets owned, he/she must decide whether to count each fish individually or just the number of fish tanks in a friend's house. Descriptive research is easier if student researchers create an easy way to record their data before they start. Creating a tally sheet with all possible items to be observed and a space to record tally marks is a good start. After gathering their data (see Chapter 4 for data gathering techniques), students should begin analysis. Descriptive research usually is reported using descriptive statistics such as mean, mode, median, standard deviation, frequency, and range. More information about data analysis can be found in Chapter 6.

Descriptive research is a good type of research to teach students first for several reasons. It is the easiest type of research to conduct and studies can often be completed quickly. It is less likely that students will need to review any literature to identify variables either. Descriptive research can use any of the four methods of data gathering we discuss later in the book: observation, surveys, interviews, and document analysis.

Think about how descriptive research can be used to enhance a current unit of study or build on an individual student's interest. If, for example, you are teaching driver education, you might plan a simple survey to determine how many students use seatbelts regularly or an observational study on how many drivers at a particular stop sign are wearing shoulder belts. If you are planning a unit on the federal government, your class might survey students or interview parents on their views about current issues facing legislators or how effective they feel government is. If an individual student is interested in censorship, he/she need not limit the study to library research, but may use interviews or surveys to gather information on community opinions.

Following the examples of research questions that lend themselves to descriptive research (see below), we have included four activities. These activities can be used as a framework for large or small group lessons on descriptive research or as individual student activities. You may find that students need review or instruction in data gathering techniques (see Chapter 4) before using these activities. You may also wish to plan additional activities around questions similar to those listed below.

DESCRIPTIVE RESEARCH EXAMPLES *

* Since many teachers are working on interdisciplinary teams with integrated units, we've included questions in each discipline related to the theme of power to illustrate how research can support such thematic teaching.

<u>General</u>

1. *How do students and parents feel about ratings on record album covers?*
2. *What is the most popular brand of athletic shoes in our school?*
3. *How do students and parents feel about school uniforms?*
4. *How many students have computers at home? Do they use them and, if so, for what purposes?*
5. *What percentage of students in our school want to go to college? Other kinds of post-secondary education?*
6. *Which are the most preferred musical groups among students?*
7. *What are the favorite books of middle school students?*
8. *What are the most and least favorite school subjects of students in my school?*
9. *How many students in my school work? What is the average number of hours worked?*
10. *Which soda is preferred by students in Ms. Jones class?*
11. *Which pens run out of ink fastest?*
12. *What brand of jeans is worn most frequently by students in my school?*
13. *How do students and faculty feel about having a dress code in my school?*
14. *How do students, parents, and teachers feel about the school choice issue?*
15. *Which candidate for office is preferred by students in this school?*
16. *How do people in this community feel about paid vs. volunteer fire fighters (or any other local issue)?*
17. *What are the most common hobbies of students in this school?*
18. *What is the average number of hours of TV watched by middle school students?*
19. *How much time do students spend on homework in the average week?*

20. *How do students, parents, and teachers feel about available recreation opportunities for teens in my community?*
21. *How many students always, sometimes, or never wear seat belts?*
22. *What time do most students go to bed on school nights?*
23. *How many teachers were born in this state?*
24. *What is the most common home grown vegetable?*

Science

1. *What insects (or animals) live on the school grounds?*
2. *How many boys and girls are interested in careers related to science?*
3. *How many grams of fat are consumed by students in a given week?*
4. *What soil types are found in our community?*
5. *To what extent are various forms of power (solar, nuclear, gas, coal, electric, etc.) used in our town?*

Social Studies

1. *What services are available for homeless children in my community?*
2. *What do people in my community think about U.S. involvement in Bosnia?*
3. *How do students in my school feel about relations among different racial/ethnic groups? Do feelings differ by age or racial group?*
4. *What do students in my school see as the most pressing problems in our community?*
5. *What do people in my community feel are the responsibilities of the United States as a world power?*

Language Arts

1. *What are the favorite books of students in the 7th grade?*
2. *How often and in what roles are people of racial and ethnic minorities portrayed in literature (during a particular time period, from a specific author, etc.)?*
3. *Of the short stories in my anthology, how often and in what roles are males and females portrayed?*
4. *Which products are advertised during different times of the day?*
5. *What piece of literature was most powerful (influential) in the lives of parents, teachers, and students?*

Mathematics

1. *How many students in my school feel confident about their ability to understand mathematics?*
2. *What percentage of students in our school take algebra? Geometry? Calculus? Are there race or gender differences in who takes each class?*
3. *What level of mathematical skill is needed for particular college majors? Careers?*
4. *Do students feel their math classes are too hard, too easy, or just right?*
5. *Are there gender differences in student use of computers?*

More often than being an area of study, mathematics is a process used to quantify data relevant to other content areas. Specific mathematical procedures that facilitate descriptive research include:

1. *Computing percentages.*
2. *Constructing graphs (bar, histogram, pie charts, etc.) and tables.*
3. *Range, frequency distribution, mean, mode, and median.*
4. *Measurement.*
5. *Any needed formulas, e.g., the formula for volume if students are investigating "What volume of recyclable material is discarded each day in this school?"*

Art and Music

1. *What is the favorite type of music of students in my school?*
2. *What works of art can be found in public spaces in our community?*
3. *How do students, parents, and teachers feel about the playing/singing of religious music at school events and programs?*

4. *How confident do students in my school feel about their artistic or musical abilities?*
5. *Which piece of art or music is considered most powerful by teachers, parents, or students?*
6. *What characteristics do "powerful" pieces share? What colors, instruments, etc. are identified as most powerful?*

<u>Foreign Language</u>

1. *How many languages are spoken in our community and by how many people?*
2. *What percentage of a sample of English words come from Latin, Greek, German, or other language roots?*
3. *To what degree do colleges require/prefer high school foreign language study of their applicants?*
4. *What languages would students in my school like to study?*
5. *What is the "power" of knowing a foreign language? Survey business owners about their responses to job applicants who speak more than one language.*

Descriptive Research Activity 1

What Do You Do in Your Spare Time?

In this activity you can find out about the hobbies and recreational interests of students at your grade level. You can use either interviews or surveys to answer the following research question: "What do you do in your spare time?" Why do you think it would be difficult to answer this question through observation?

In order to conduct this research, you will need to make several decisions. First, would you prefer to use written surveys or conduct interviews to get your data?

_______ Written Survey _______ Conduct Interview

Next, you must decide on the sample size you will use. How many people will you survey or interview?

How will you select the students for your sample in a way that will be fair?

Think about what you want to know and write the questions on a blank sheet of paper. To make it easier to record answers while you are interviewing people, figure out likely answers and create a response sheet on which you can easily mark off replies without having to do a lot of writing. If you think there may be differences in the answers of boys and girls, create a response sheet for each gender, so you can tally their answers separately. If asking about what sports students are involved in, create possible responses like those on the next page. If asking about hobbies, ask around to find out some of the more common ones and leave room to write in others that students might mention. The form on the next page includes some examples of questions related to hobbies and recreation. You can use it as is if it asks the kinds of questions in which you are interested. You can also use it as a starting point and create other questions related to the topic. Be sure to field test your questions on a few students who will not be in your final study. The reasons for doing this test are to find out if respondents understand the questions and if your response categories are appropriate and easy to use. If you have trouble, rewrite your questions before surveying or interviewing your sample.

(continued on next page)

Descriptive Research Activity 1

Sample Tally Sheet

Note gender of respondent: _______ female _______ male

Do you take part in any sports after school either at school, in a community league, or just with friends? _______ yes _______ no
(If the person says no, do not ask the following questions.)

What sports do you play?

Basketball ______________________________
Baseball ______________________________
Volleyball ______________________________
Football ______________________________
Soccer ______________________________
Softball ______________________________
Hockey ______________________________
Badminton ______________________________
Field Hockey ______________________________
Swimming ______________________________
Gymnastics ______________________________
Skiing ______________________________
Rollerblading ______________________________
Ice Skating ______________________________
Skateboarding ______________________________
Other: ______________________________

What other hobbies do you have?

Reading ______________________________
Board Games ______________________________
Electronic Games ______________________________
Computer Games ______________________________
Collecting ______________________________
Making Crafts ______________________________
Cooking ______________________________
Sewing ______________________________
Woodworking ______________________________
Playing a Musical Instrument ______________________________
Singing ______________________________
Playing Cards ______________________________
Watching Television ______________________________
Making Models ______________________________
Other: ______________________________

If you have been careful with this research, chosen your sample wisely, and asked clear questions, your results may be very important. Think about how this information might help teachers or other adults in your school plan for clubs or extracurricular activities. After completing your research, discuss the best way to share your results with them.

Descriptive Research Activity 2

The Cola Wars

This descriptive research activity will help you find out about something people like. You could find the answer to this research question in two different ways. The question is "Which kind of soda do students in this class like better—Coke®, Pepsi®, or a local brand of cola?" (Some students would probably appreciate your conducting a separate study for the diet or decaffeinated versions of each of these brands.)
What is your hypothesis? Which kind of soda do you think students in your class like best?

There are several ways to gather data about this question, and you may find differences in the results. The first way to get information is to take a short survey. This survey will only have one question, "Which kind of soda do you like best—Coke®, Pepsi®, or Shazam (our made-up name for a local brand of cola)?" You will need to create a tally sheet and then ask each person which one they like best. To make your survey more professional, vary the order of the cola names so you control for the possible influence of the order in which the person hears the names. Be sure one third of your sample gets asked each question.

"Which do you like best—Pepsi®, Shazam, or Coke®?"
"Which do you like best—Coke®, Pepsi®, or Shazam?"
"Which do you like best—Shazam, Coke®, or Pepsi®?"

Why do you think the order might matter?

You can record your results here using tally marks.

Prefers Coke®	
Prefers Pepsi®	
Prefers Shazam	

Another way to find out the answer to this question is to offer people in your class a sample cup of cola and see which brand they choose. All three brands should be identified, possibly by writing the name on the cup or by setting the cups in front of the bottle. Tell students they can have only one cup and ask which they would like. You should observe each student's choice and record the cola they choose. If you try this test, record the results here.

Chooses Coke®	
Chooses Pepsi®	
Chooses Shazam	

(continued on next page)

Descriptive Research Activity 2

A third way is to offer students tastes of all three (labeled K, L, and M) without their knowing which brand they are tasting. (Be sure to use clean cups for each student!) After they taste each cola sample, ask them which of the three they preferred and record that information.

If you tried all three methods of gathering data, do you think you would get the same results?________
Why or why not?

Which method would be best for cola manufacturers to use? ________________________________
Why?

Would the same method be best for all manufacturers? ________________________________
Why or why not?

Descriptive Research Activity 3

Who Interrupts Whom?

Descriptive research can be used to answer questions about what people like or things that they do. This study will help you answer a question about something people do. The question is "Do more boys or girls interrupt others while they are speaking?" Previous research has found gender differences with respect to this question. To see if your results confirm or contradict that research, you will need to observe people very carefully. Each day for one week, observe spoken interchanges in your classes. Because people sometimes change their behavior if they know they are being watched, try to do this in a class with students who don't know that you are making observations. It will also be important that they not realize you are tallying, so make your marks in a way that others won't see what you are doing. You'll tally by gender (boys or girls) only, so don't write down the names of individual students.

Before you start, make an hypothesis. Who do you think will do more interrupting of other speakers, _____ girls or _____ boys? Hypotheses are usually written in the form of a statement. Write yours below.

My hypothesis is that____

because____

____

Now, observe and find out. When you have finished, you may want to graph your results. For now, record a mark for each time a student interrupts another student during classroom time. Don't count interruptions during private conversations not related to the class. If there isn't much opportunity for discussion in your classes, you might have better luck observing interruptions at lunch or other informal settings. Be sure that others don't realize what you are doing because it might affect their behavior and your results. It will be easier to tally your results if your fifth tally mark is a cross through the previous four (~~IIII~~) so you can count by fives at the end.

Boys interrupt	
Girls interrupt	

This study might have raised additional questions that you could pursue with another related study. Do you think boys are more likely to interrupt boys or girls?

What about girls?

If your teacher interrupts students while they are talking, does he/she interrupt girls or boys more often?

You could do more descriptive research to find out.

Descriptive Research Activity 4

Working It Out

Who works after school? What do they do? How many hours per week do they work? This study will help you describe work commitments of students in your class by conducting interviews. First, you will need to decide what information you want to know regarding who works and what they do. You might want to know if more boys than girls work, how late students work on school nights, or if students feel work helps or hurts their achievement in school. You might also want to know what kinds of jobs students have. Think about what you want to know and, when you know the kinds of questions you want to ask, write them out on a blank sheet of paper. To make it easier to record answers while you are interviewing people, figure out likely answers and create a response sheet on which you can easily mark off replies without having to do a lot of writing. If you think there may be differences between boys and girls, create a separate response sheet for each gender so you can tally their answers separately. If you are asking about how many hours students work, create possible responses like those below. If you are asking about type of work, ask around to find out some of the more common jobs, then leave room to write in others that students might mention. The form below includes some examples of questions related to work.

Sample Tally Sheet

Note gender of respondent: _______ female _______ male

Do you work at jobs for which you are paid? _______ yes _______ no
(If the person says no, do not ask the remaining questions.)

What do you do?

Fast Food Restaurant __________
Retail Sales __________
Gas Station __________ ______
Other:______________________________

Baby-sit __________
Mow Lawns, Shovel Snow __________
Exercise Animals __________
____

What is the average number of hours you work on a school night?
_____ 0-1 _____ 1-2 _____ 2-3 _____ 3-4 _____ 4-6 _____ more than 6

What is the latest you would work on a school night?
_____ 9 p.m. ______ 10 p.m. ______ 11 p.m. _____ midnight _____ after midnight

What is the average number of hours you work on a weekend?
_____ 0-2 _____ 2-4 _____ 4-7 _____ 7-10 _____ 10-15 _____ more than 15

Field test your interview by asking three students from another class to answer the questions. Ask them if you left out anything important. If not, use your questions to interview 5-10 students from your class. You may want to add other questions to your interview. If so, be sure to field test them, too. Maybe a friend can interview other students and you can compare results.

Case and Field Research

The three main categories of research—descriptive, historical, and experimental—can be used to encompass all the research you or your students do. However, we will briefly discuss four subcategories of descriptive research that may be helpful in generating research ideas. The first subcategory is case and field research, in which the researcher takes a close and thorough look at one subject, either a person or setting. The advantage is learning a great deal about your subject and the context in which it operates. The disadvantage is that you can't really generalize to other people or settings, even though they may seem similar. However, case and field research can help identify hypotheses that students might want to investigate in more diverse settings in order to be able to make generalizations. This second phase of research would need to use other research methods.

Case and field research goes beyond the question of "what" to seek possible explanations for "why." When this type of research is done about a person, it is called a case study. When a group, institution, or event is studied, it is called field research.

In case studies, it is helpful to start with a general question that asks about what the researcher wants to know, such as "How did Ms. Janes come to be an assistant principal?" This question and its associated hypotheses serve as the starting point for data collection. Depending on the topic, case studies can include data from the subjects themselves as well as those who know the subjects and can include observations, interviews, and document analysis (both primary and secondary sources) related to the subject. The latter might include primary sources such as letters, diaries, report cards, resumes, and papers or stories the person has written and secondary sources like newsletter, magazine, and newspaper stories about the person.

Case and field studies are a form of qualitative research. Instead of counting and measuring variables, the researcher tries to identify the qualities of an experience and understand their meaning for the people involved. What makes case and field studies different from a traditional report is the use of primary sources. It is best if the researcher has direct access to the person or site in order to gather data through observation and interviews. Less desirable, but still acceptable, is direct access to primary sources (produced by the subject or people with direct knowledge of the subject). If the only data the researcher can access is secondary (others' synthesis of information), it is better to choose a different subject. What the student can produce with secondary sources only is more akin to a traditional report than a true case or field study.

Field research is related to ethnography, an area of anthropology that involves the accurate description of living cultures. Two main strategies used in ethnographic research are participant observation and interviewing. The observation skills used in both participant and nonparticipant observations are described in Chapter 4 along with interviewing skills.

In participant observation, researchers try to understand what the culture means *to the people in it* by participating as a member of the culture while they observe what's going on. This type of research is called field work and in anthropological studies includes learning the language, living in typical homes, eating the same food, doing the work, and taking part in the rituals and ceremonies of the people they are studying. While they take part in the culture, researchers also take notes to help them remember important information. Along the way, they'll also choose several people to interview, asking many questions in order to understand the culture from the point of view of the people in it. Participant observation can be done most easily when the group being studied is one in which the researcher can be a full participant. There are limits on the extent to which middle and high school students can do field work.

Nonparticipant observation is also a technique of field research. In this case, the researcher observes and interviews to gather data about the group, institution, or event under study, but does not participate directly in its activities.

Whether your students use participant or nonparticipant observation, they'll need to know about interviewing, since it is an important research method in qualitative research. Anthropologists do a special kind of interview called the ethnographic interview. This type of interview is different from traditional interviewing because the goal is to understand things from the point of view of the person who is talking, not from the researcher's point of view. For example, one student might think of report cards as a way for his/her parents to know how well he/she is doing in school. Another might think of report cards as a way for a teacher to get him/her in trouble at home or as a meaningless event. It's important for qualitative researchers to be able to set aside *their* view of things and see events the way the interview subject does. It is not as easy as it might sound!

Identifying Informants

One of the most important steps in qualitative research is to find the right people to interview. Ethnographers call these people informants because they are the ones who will inform the researcher or provide information about the culture. Good informants will have the following qualities:

1. They have been members of the group for quite a while. Someone who was raised as part of a religious group will probably know more about the group than someone who has recently joined it. A veteran teacher may know more about the school than a teacher in his/her first year.
2. They are still members of the group you are studying. Someone who used to be a troublemaker in school, but who has gone straight won't be able to tell you as much as someone who is still a troublemaker. Similarly, a first year teacher has a better sense of what that experience is like than a veteran teacher trying to remember his/her first year of teaching.
3. They belong to a culture that is fairly different from the researcher's. It will be harder to see differences if the group being studied is fairly similar to the researcher's, especially for adolescents, who may have a hard time taking on the perspective of another person. The ways in which the researcher and group being studied differ could relate to culture, age, occupation, religious beliefs, position in society, etc.
4. They have enough time to talk with the researcher. Qualitative research relies on a somewhat lengthy interview and may involve more than one interview with the same person. If the informant is very busy, it might be hard to schedule the time needed for interviews.

Once students have identified a group, event, or institution they want to study, have them make a list of possible informants. If they do not know specific names of people, help them identify positions or roles in the group. Students may need to talk with someone who knows the group or institution to get the names of appropriate informants. Identify several possible informants using the criteria listed above.

Planning the Interview

It is important that students think about the kinds of questions they want to ask before meeting with the informant. Remind students that their purpose is to understand the group/culture/institution the way the participants in it see it. For this reason, all questions should be open-ended ones. Closed-ended questions might lead to incomplete or misleading data due to students' inadvertent ignorance about the group or institution. It can be helpful to identify the elements of the group, culture, or institution in order to design questions that might elicit data about those elements. If students study a culture, elements might include:

- Food
- Marriage
- Religion
- Jobs
- Clothing
- Child-raising
- Education
- Music, Dance, Arts
- Shelter/Housing
- Government
- Ethics/Values
- Transportation
- Language
- Recreation

These elements are called cultural universals because they are present in all cultures in some form or another. While the ways in which they are expressed will differ across cultural groups, each culture will have its own approach to most of these categories, making them useful when structuring interview and observation instruments.

In addition to cultures, case and field researchers might study an institution such as a school, community agency, or religious group. Those studying a school might look at the following elements of each category listed:

- Purpose (educating students)
- Structure (teams, grade levels)
- Clients (students, employers)
- Customs (tap new club members)
- Challenges (reform, diversity)
- Sources of Support (community, newspaper, central office)
- Roles (teacher, administrator, counselor, etc.)
- Physical Setting (building, campus, etc.)
- Rituals (pep rallies, graduation ceremony)
- Typical Activities (classes, lunch, assemblies)
- Issues (accountability, finances, absences)

While the specifics (in parentheses) will change from institution to institution, the categories will often be similar across institutions.

Students can use their list of elements to brainstorm possible questions to ask in interviews. There will probably be different kinds of questions your students would ask if they were studying an ethnic group or a subgroup of kids in your school. Listed are some examples of questions they could ask informants about Vietnamese culture.

- *Could you describe a typical work or school day?*
- *What kinds of things does your family do in the morning before people leave for work or school?*
- *Do you usually eat breakfast? If so, what kinds of food do you eat? Is that a typical Vietnamese breakfast?*
- *Are there particular kinds of work that many Vietnamese do? Could you tell me more about it? Why do you think many Vietnamese people do those kinds of jobs?*
- *How important is religion in your culture? Is there any one religion that most Vietnamese practice? Has that changed since your family came to the United States?*
- *Do you think education is important? Why or why not? Is that a common view among Vietnamese?*

If students have chosen a group because of their different values or activities rather than different ethnic group or religion, they will have to design slightly different questions. Even though the informants probably speak English, students could still ask about language, since members of this group may have a special way of talking with each other or special words for things. Students might want to put more emphasis on questions about values, attitudes, and activities since those are what caught their interest in the first place. Examples of questions students could ask "musician" informants might include:

- *Could you describe a typical school day? What do you do during the time when you leave home in the morning until you go to sleep?*
- *What do you do in your free time?*
- *What do you think about school? What do you like? What do you dislike?*
- *What kinds of things do you do during class?*
- *If you could do anything you wanted for a year, what would you do?*
- *When you think about the people in school, how do you describe them?*
- *Do you have special words for different kinds of people or activities? Would you tell me some of them and what they mean?*

Conducting the Interview

Now students may be wondering, "How in the world am I going to get a complete stranger to answer my questions?" That's where the real skills of interviewing start to work! It all comes down to an attitude the researcher brings to the interview and the key words are "ignorant" and "nonjudgmental." These attitudes are particularly important when trying to understand what a group, culture, or institution means to the people who are a part of it, and informants within the group are the only ones who know. The researcher probably has some information, but it's likely that this information is from the point of view of someone outside of the culture. Below are some techniques students might use to get people to share an insider's view with them.

- *I am very interested in (the group/culture/institution). Could you tell me about . . . ?*
- *This may sound like a silly question, but I really don't know much about the culture of . . . .*
- *School/work/life seems different to different people. I really want to understand what it seems like to you.*
- *During recess I usually play ball. I never really noticed what other people were doing. Could you tell me . . . ?*

It is important that students not just say these things, but really believe them, or they will sound phony and the person won't want to talk with them. Researchers are there to learn about a new world and informants really are the teachers.

One of the hardest things about being a qualitative researcher is being nonjudgmental. People in other groups, cultures, and institutions do things differently—that's part of why researchers chose to study them in the first place. It's easy for researchers to assume that their way is the best way, but that attitude will interfere with quality research. The researcher's job is to understand, not to approve or disapprove. Listed are some tips that you can share with your students.

1. Try to understand what things mean to your informant or what they mean in his/her group, culture, or institution. The behavior may not seem quite so strange once you understand the reasons behind it. If you knew that in the past people often got trichinosis after eating pork, the current Kosher ban on eating pork may make more sense.

2. Think of customs you practice that may seem bizarre to others. Pierced earrings and nail polish are two examples. Thinking about these customs should help you develop a less judgmental attitude about the customs of others.
3. Think about the crew members of Star Trek and how they acted when meeting creatures far stranger than the people you will ever interview. The crew always tried to understand and respect the culture of whatever place they visited or beings they encountered. In their case, it was often a matter of survival. For you, it will be a matter of learning and professionalism.

Qualitative researchers might conduct several interviews with the same person so that they can confirm earlier answers, ask new questions that may have been suggested by earlier interviews, and give the informant time to remember more information. Researchers may also want to interview several people from the same group to see how similar their answers are. These comparisons will help the researcher distinguish between what is common to the culture and what is only true for particular individuals.

As in other interview situations, it is best if students can tape record the interview. (See Chapter 4 for specific suggestions about interview procedures.) Remind students to take notes, since this written record is what they will be analyzing. If the informant would rather not be taped, students need to graciously set the recorder aside and get out extra paper.

Professional qualitative researchers have transcripts (exact written copies) made of their recorded interviews so they can look over the written copies more carefully. Transcripts may not be possible for your students, especially if interviews are long or numerous. Qualitative researchers often rewrite their field notes within a few hours (no more than 24) of the interview so they can add information while their memories are fresh. Students should make a habit of doing this procedure also. If they were able to record the interview, they should replay the tape and add to their notes as they listen. Have them do this several times until they are sure they have notes on everything that seemed important to the informant. They can continue this process until they have a verbatim transcript, but you will have to weigh the time and tediousness of the transcription process against the value of a complete transcript.

Once students have completed their initial data gathering, they should do a preliminary analysis. The qualitative data section of Chapter 6 explains how to do this. The data analysis process should leave students with some tentative hypotheses and perhaps additional questions. It is perfectly normal in case studies and field research to loop through the cycle of hypothesis, data gathering, and data analysis more than once. Remind students to keep an open mind to new hypotheses which the data might suggest.

It also can be beneficial to share the results of the case study or field research with the subjects, asking if there are inaccuracies, anything they felt was left out, or anything they are not comfortable having published or shared with your intended audience. Researchers are not obligated to make the changes suggested, but should consider them carefully in light of the other data that have been gathered. Not only is this consultation courteous to the subjects of your case and field research, but their input can increase the richness and accuracy of the study.

CASE AND FIELD RESEARCH EXAMPLES

General

1. *How did (school athlete) achieve success?*
2. *Why is (popular student) popular?*
3. *Why is (teacher) considered a good teacher?*
4. *How would someone new to our school describe it?*
5. *How does a student who uses a wheelchair experience our school?*
6. *What factors make (youth-serving community group) successful?*

Science

1. *How healthy is my current life-style?*
2. *How environmentally "friendly" is my school?*
3. *What does (a vegetarian) eat and why?*
4. *Why does (a cigarette smoker) smoke?*

5. *What is it like to be an animal rights activist?*
6. *What kinds of trees/plants grow in our school/neighborhood?*

Social Studies

1. *What sociologically distinct groups exist among my student body? How does one of those groups experience the school or town?*
2. *How do kids who are often sent to the office for discipline perceive my school?*
3. *How prepared is my community for a natural disaster?*
4. *What is it like to be the mayor of my town?*
5. *What is life like for a person receiving public assistance?*
6. *What are the traditions of our school? How did they originate?*

Language Arts

1. *What kind of a life did (local author) live and how did that affect his/her writing?*
2. *What is a day in the life of a local newspaper reporter or TV newscaster like?*
3. *What made Martin Luther King, Jr. such an effective communicator?*
4. *What makes "The Simpsons" so appealing to people?*
5. *What is the experience of students in a reading/writing workshop class?*
6. *How does (local theater group) prepare and produce a play from start to finish?*

Mathematics

1. *How does cooperative learning affect a mathematics class?*
2. *How are homogeneously grouped and heterogeneously grouped mathematics classes different and alike?*
3. *How does (an excellent math student) learn mathematics?*
4. *How does (person in a career in which I am interested) use mathematics in everyday life?*
5. *What do mathematicians do?*
6. *How do young children learn what numbers mean?*

Art and Music

1. *How does (local composer) create a piece of music from start to finish?*
2. *How does (local artist) create a work of art from start to finish?*
3. *How did (famous composer's, musician's or artist's) life affect his/her work?*
4. *What is it like to go to a postgraduate art school?*
5. *What is the life of a working artist/musician like?*
6. *How is the high school band halftime show created and produced?*

Foreign Language

1. *How do students who speak English as a second language go about learning it?*
2. *Why is/was (famous person who speaks the language I am learning) so influential in his/her country?*
3. *What is it like to learn a foreign language through immersion?*
4. *What is/was it like to live in a country where they speak the language I am learning?*
5. *How does my class help and/or hinder the learning of a foreign language?*
6. *How do (classmates who speak fluently) go about learning to speak a foreign language?*

Case and Field Research Activity 1

Teacher of the Year

If the choice were yours, who would you name "teacher of the year" in your school?

Why that person?

Do you think others would agree?

Try to identify one or two teachers many would agree are excellent. Talk with administrators, counselors, and other teachers in your school, as well as students from a variety of subgroups in the school. As you talk with them, be sure to find out the criteria they are using when making their recommendations. Why do they think particular people are effective teachers?

You may or may not agree with their nominations or their reasons, but it's important to get a broad range of opinions before selecting the person you want to study.

Once you have identified your "teacher of the year" nominee, think about your research question. A general research question could be "Why is (teacher) considered such an excellent teacher?" You might have a more specific question, depending on the person you are studying and the reasons you chose him/her. Examples could be "How does Ms. Jones maintain such high standards while still having students adore her?" or "How does Mr. Martin develop and maintain such a positive relationship with so many different kinds of people?"

You also need to think about the data you would like to gather. You should identify people to interview who could provide data that would answer your research question. These people could include a variety of students, former students, other teachers (particularly those in the same team or department), school administrators, counselors, and the teacher him/herself. Develop interview questions and carry out your interviews using the suggestions in Chapter 4.

Another rich source of data is observation. Try to arrange to observe this teacher in settings where he/she displays the kinds of behavior in which you are interested—teaching a class, before/after school, in the halls between classes, coaching an academic or athletic team, in homeroom, etc. Check Chapter 4 for important suggestions about observing accurately and unobtrusively.

Depending on your research question, there may or may not be relevant documents to study. If the teacher's strength is instruction, you might want to look at lesson plans (if they exist). If the teacher is known for creativity, you might want to look for examples in items in the classroom, props used in teaching, etc.

(continued on next page)

Case and Field Research Activity 1

Once you have tentative ideas about your research question and data gathering plan, make an appointment to talk with the teacher you wish to study. When you have a few minutes to talk, tell the teacher that you want to do a case study of an excellent teacher and the reasons you chose him/her. After explaining the data you'd like to gather and how you would like to go about obtaining it, ask permission to conduct the case study. Consider having him/her sign a permission form based on the one for interviews in Chapter 4.

If the teacher is not willing to be the subject of your case study, accept the decision, thank him/her for taking the time to talk with you, and express your appreciation that they are the kind of teacher you admire. Consider the reasons he/she might not have wanted to be the subject of this case study. Are there some ways you could change your data gathering or sharing of results that might reduce those objections?

Revise your plan, if necessary, and make an appointment to talk with your next candidate for "teacher of the year."

Once you have identified a subject for your case study and secured permission, finalize your research question(s) and data gathering plan. Make appointments for interviews and observations, gather together your interview questions, tape recorder, and lots of paper for observations and notes, and begin! See the end of the "Case and Field Research" section for ideas about analyzing your data and drawing conclusions.

Case and Field Research Activity 2

Researching Role Models

There's a lot of talk these days about role models for young people, much of it about the negative role models evident in the media. We'd like to encourage you to do a case study of someone close to home that you feel is a good role model for people your age.

Alone, with two or three peers, or as a class brainstorm a list of adults in your community that you think might be good role models. Think about adults in your family, neighborhood, school, community, local government, local businesses and professions, volunteer organizations, religious groups, etc. Discuss the qualities that make these adults good candidates for role models. You might want to talk with administrators, counselors, and other teachers in your school, as well as students from a variety of subgroups in the school. As you talk with them, be sure to find out the criteria they are using. Why do they think particular people are good role models?

You may or may not agree with their nominations or their reasons, but it's important to get a broad range of opinions before selecting the person you want to study.

Once you have identified your "role model," think about your research question and the data you would like to gather. A general research question could be "Why is (person) considered such an excellent role model?" Others might concern how that person became the kind of person he/she did, why he/she is so effective at what he/she does, and what keeps him/her going when the going gets tough. You might have more specific questions, depending on the person you are studying and the reasons you chose him/her. Examples could be "How did Ms. Gomez know she could be more than people around her kept telling her?" or "How does Mr. Smith maintain such a positive attitude when so much has gone wrong in his life?"

Next consider your potential data sources. You should identify people you could interview who could provide data that would help answer your research question. These people could include the person's family, co-workers, friends, people who have been helped by the person, and the person him/herself. Develop interview questions and carry out your interviews, following the suggestions in Chapter 4.

Another rich source of data is observation. Try to arrange to observe this person in action, where you'll be able to observe the kinds of behavior in which you are interested. These observations could include the person at work, with family, during leisure pursuits, coaching a team, tutoring a student, or doing whatever it is that you admire. Check Chapter 4 for important suggestions about observing accurately and unobtrusively.

Depending on your research question, there may or may not be relevant documents or artifacts to study. Look at trophies, plaques, and citations on the wall to see the kinds of groups that have recognized the person. If the person is likely to have been discussed in the media, check for newspaper articles. The person may keep a diary and you may be lucky if he/she decides to share excerpts of it with you.

(continued on next page)

Case and Field Research Activity 2

Once you have tentatively decided on research question(s) and a data gathering plan, make an appointment to talk with the person you wish to study. When you have a few minutes to talk, tell the person that you want to do a case study of an excellent role model and the reasons you chose him/her. After explaining the data you'd like to gather and how you would like to do that, ask permission to conduct the case study. Consider having him/her sign a permission form based on the one for interviews used in Chapter 4.

If the person is not willing to be the subject of your case study, accept the decision, thank him/her for taking the time to talk with you, and express your appreciation for being the kind of role model he/she is. Consider the reasons he/she might not have wanted to be the subject of this case study. Are there some ways you could change your data gathering or sharing of results that might reduce those objections? Revise your plan, if necessary, and make an appointment to talk with your next candidate for outstanding role model.

Once you have identified a subject for your case study and secured permission, finalize your research question and data gathering plan. Make appointments for interviews and observations, gather together your interview questions, tape recorder, and lots of paper for observations and notes, and begin! See the end of the "Case and Field Research" section for ideas about analyzing your data and drawing conclusions.

Case and Field Research Activity 3

Do Birds of a Feather Flock Together?

Since it may be difficult to visit faraway islands to learn first-hand about other cultures, you might want to start by studying a group or culture closer to home. Within your school there are different cultures—adolescents, teachers, administrators—and each of these probably includes subgroups with different customs and beliefs. For adolescents the groups might center around skills or activities, music, academics, athletics, skateboarding, or school clubs. For example, varsity athletes may share a culture, one that might center around games, practice, working out in the off season, hair styles, parties, etc. Because it is unlikely that the particular cultures in your school have been studied, this may be your opportunity to learn the skills of case and field researchers, create new knowledge, and gain a different perspective on your school.

First thing you'll need to do is choose a subgroup within the school to study. Brainstorming with two or three fellow students, see if you can list at least ten possible groups (twenty if you're in a large or diverse school). Remember that in brainstorming, your goal is to list as many groups as you can. At this stage, don't worry if they'll be good ones to study or if you are interested in them. Later you'll decide which ones might work. If you get stuck, try to think in categories, including some from each of the following:

1. *Roles Within the School*—These include teachers, teacher aides, counselors, administrators, janitorial staff, cafeteria workers, office aides, parent volunteers, etc.
2. *Clubs*—What organized activities exist at your school? Think about athletics (varsity and intramural—male, female, and coed), service clubs (Junior Beta, Key Club), academic groups (Spanish Club, National Honor Society), musical groups (band, chorus, orchestra, pep band), drama (theater club or class, musicals), governance groups (Student Council, Student Court, peer mediators), publications (yearbook, newspaper, literary magazine), etc.
3. *Social Groups*—Think about the ways you and other students talk about the student body. Are there certain groups that might even have distinct names such as Jocks or Preps? When kids gather before or after school, are there certain groups that hang around together?
4. *Ethnic Groups*—Does membership in an ethnic group (Anglo American, African American, Asian American, Hispanic American, etc.) seem to define subgroups of students in your school?

Now that you have a list of possible groups to study, how will you decide which one to pick? One way is to use criteria. Think about the groups you have brainstormed in terms of the following four criteria:

1. Is there a *distinct culture* that is different from that of the majority culture? Consider clothing, symbols, language, life-styles, beliefs, activities, and other customs. If the group shares most of the customs of the majority culture, it may not be different enough to make an interesting study. Even within groups, some may have adopted more of the majority culture than others.
2. Are there *enough people* from this group in the school to study? A group that has only a few members will be hard to investigate.
3. Am I *interested* in this group? Do I have a strong enough interest to keep me going on a somewhat long term study?
4. Will I have enough *access* to members of this group to do my study? Don't give up too soon on this one, just because the people seem different from you. Part of what you'll learn as a field researcher is how to relate to people who seem different. But if hardly any of the people speak English, and you don't speak their language or it would be difficult to spend time with them at school, this may make your study too difficult.

(continued on next page)

Case and Field Research Activity 3

Follow the guidelines in the "Case and Field Research" section above and in Chapter 4 to design appropriate observations and interview questions, gather data, and make notes as complete as possible. Then consult the "Qualitative Research" section of Chapter 6 to see how to analyze your data.

In making conclusions, you can only speak authoritatively about the particular subgroup you studied. Do you wonder if what you found out about your group might be true for others? For example, in what ways do you think the experiences, life-styles, and values of African American students at your school might be similar to and different from those at another school? How would working as a teacher at your school be similar to and different from teaching at a different school in your district? A private or parochial school? While your field research can't answer these questions, it might suggest other avenues of research you can pursue using other research designs. Talk with your peers about hypotheses raised by your field study and make an appointment with your teacher if you think you might like to pursue further research.

Case and Field Research Activity 4

What Does It Take to Have a Culture?

One step further from your culture than a subgroup in your school is a cultural or ethnic group in your community. There are many groups that have customs and beliefs that may differ from some of those of the larger American culture. These people may have in common their

Nationality or Ethnic Group: Mexican, Vietnamese, Bosnian, Jordanian, Scandinavian, Japanese, Nigerian, French, Cuban, etc.

Religion: Jewish, Catholic, Protestant, Baptist, Pentecostal, Mormon, Hari Krishna, Greek Orthodox, Buddhist, Muslim, etc.

Occupation: farmers, actors, scientists, musicians, police officers, auto mechanics, doctors, journalists, teachers, insurance agents, photographers, etc.

Think about the community in which you live. Does it include some of the cultures listed above? Which ones?

Some others?

How are these cultures similar to yours?

How are they different?

(continued on next page)

Case and Field Research Activity 4

The first thing you'll want to do is choose a culture to study. Brainstorming with two or three fellow students, see if you can list at least ten possible cultures (twenty if you're in a large or diverse community). Remember that in brainstorming, your goal is to list as many cultures as you can. At this stage, don't worry if they'll be good ones to study or if you are interested in them. Later you'll decide which ones might work. If you get stuck, try to think in categories, including some from each of the following:

1. *Ethnic Groups in Your Community*—Think of different kinds of ethnic restaurants, try to identify special celebrations (Greek Festival, Chinese New Year), look through the phone book for last names from a particular culture, or ask the principal or local religious leaders about ethnic groups in the community.
2. *Religious Groups* (particularly those whose customs may differ from the culture of the majority in ways other than religion)—Look in the yellow pages of the phone book for churches and religious organizations.
3. *Jobs or Careers*—The culture of work differs across types of jobs (law enforcement, health, education, food service, etc.) as well as occupational groups (professional, skilled labor, unskilled labor, etc.). Talk with your school counselor to identify a variety of job types and categories.

Now that you have a list of possible cultures to study, how will you decide which one to pick? Think about the groups and cultures you have brainstormed in terms of the following four criteria:

1. Is there a *distinct culture* that is different from that of the majority culture? Consider clothing, language, religion, food, music, dance, life-styles, beliefs, and other customs. If the group shares most of the customs of the majority culture, it may not be different enough to make an interesting study. Within cultures, some people may have adopted more of the majority culture than others.
2. Are there *enough people* from this culture to study? A group that has only a few members will be hard to investigate.
3. Am I *interested* in this culture? Do I have a strong enough interest to keep me going on a long term study?
4. Will I have enough *access* to members of this culture to do my study? Don't give up too soon on this one just because the people seem different from you. Part of what you'll learn as a field researcher is how to relate to people who seem different. However, if hardly any of the people speak English and you don't speak their language or if they live and work 20 to 30 miles away, your study may be too difficult for you.

If you are truly fascinated by a particular culture and it didn't rate well in your analysis, look again at the criterion on which it received a low score. Is there something you could do? For example, there may be a low score for "access" to a group of Vietnamese because many recent immigrants don't speak English. If you could find an interpreter or limit your study to Vietnamese children (who are more likely to speak English), you might improve the "access" rating.

Follow the guidelines in the "Case and Field Research" section above and in Chapter 4 to design appropriate observations and interview questions, gather data, and make notes as complete as possible. Then consult the "Qualitative Research" section of Chapter 6 to see how to analyze your data.

In making conclusions, you can only speak authoritatively about the particular culture you studied. Do you wonder if what you found out about your group might be true for others? For example, in what ways do you think the experiences, life-styles, and values of Vietnamese immigrants might be similar to those of other immigrants? How would working at one national insurance company be similar to and different from working at other insurance companies? Other white-collar jobs? While your field research can't answer these questions, it might suggest other avenues of research that you can pursue using other research designs. Talk with your peers about hypotheses raised by your field study and make an appointment with your teacher if you think you might like to pursue further research.

Developmental Research

Developmental research is another subcategory of descriptive research. It examines changes and patterns of growth across time. You might think of it as an elongated descriptive study. In essence, developmental research asks, "How has _______________ changed over time?"

There are two large categories of developmental research: longitudinal and cross-sectional. Longitudinal studies follow the same subjects over an extended period of time. Studies that follow children born to mothers who use crack cocaine through their childhood or children who participated in Montessori preschools through elementary school, or pre-service teachers through school, student teaching, internship, and their first few years teaching are all considered longitudinal studies because they follow the same people for several years. You may wonder if you can do a longitudinal study on a nonliving thing, for example an institution or city. The term developmental research is usually reserved for studies dealing with the growth and development of humans or animals. (Sometimes the term "trend studies" is used to describe studies that examine changes in nonliving things in order to predict future development. A researcher might, for example, undertake a trend study on the growth in new construction in a particular city in order to predict future transportation needs.) Because true longitudinal studies require years, few middle and high school students are in a position to pursue them. They could, however, conduct longitudinal studies that extend throughout the school year. Because adolescence is a time of many physical and psychological changes, there may be measurable changes in certain variables across the nine months of the school year.

Cross-sectional studies offer an alternative when it is not possible to gather data about the same group of subjects over time. This approach to developmental research gathers data from groups of subjects at different developmental levels, in order to approximate data from the same individuals over time. Someone interested in researching changes in adolescents' sleeping patterns from age eleven to nineteen might not want to wait nine years for results. Instead, he/she could identify groups of eleven, thirteen, fifteen, seventeen, and nineteen-year-olds. The researcher could then compare the average number of hours of sleep adolescents get at each age and make inferences about patterns of change.

As you can imagine, this type of research presents numerous difficulties, particularly in determining whether or not the groups are equivalent. The biggest threat to the validity of cross-sectional studies is that groups of people have lived through different times in history and may be affected by historical events or trends. While generational differences may not matter when researching changes in height over a short period of time, it could affect your data about the number of hours adolescents sleep. If there is a popular television show on late at night during your data gathering period, younger adolescents may stay up later than they usually do, distorting your data. People who lived through the Depression are likely to have different attitudes about saving money, just as people who came of age in the Sixties may have different attitudes about politics. Nonetheless, adolescents who wish to examine changes across grade levels by studying several samples at different grade levels could easily undertake cross-sectional research, as long as they remain aware of possible challenges to the validity of their study. Following the research examples, we have included four cross-sectional developmental research activities your students might want to pursue. We hope you will add more ideas to the developmental research examples.

DEVELOPMENTAL RESEARCH EXAMPLES

General

1. *Do children's perceptions about the effects of divorce on their friends change from 6th to 12th grade?*
2. *How do students' preferences in music change between the ages of 10 and 18?*
3. *How do students' friendship patterns change from 6th to 8th (or 9th to 12th) grade?*
4. *How do students' likes and dislikes of school subjects change from 1st to 12th grade?*
5. *How do students' identification of the most critical problems facing the world (our country) change between the ages of 10 and 18?*
6. *How do students' intended careers change from 1st to 12th grade?*

Science

1. *How does the baby gerbil (or other animal) in our class change over the span of six months?*

2. *How does the number of sit-ups completed in two minutes change from 6th to 8th grade?*
3. *How do changes in height vary for boys and girls between the ages of 10 and 15?*
4. *How do students' eating habits change from 6th to 12th grade?*
5. *How do students' capacity for formal operations change from 6th to 12th grade?*

Social Studies

1. *How do students' attitudes about cheating change from 9th to 12th grade?*
2. *How do people's attitudes about saving and spending money change from age 5 to age 60?*
3. *How do children change in their ability to understand the concepts of past, present, and future between the ages of 4 and 18?*
4. *How do children's friendships with the opposite sex change from ages 2 to 18?*
5. *How do children's extracurricular activities change from ages 6 to 18?*

Language Arts

1. *How do the topics about which children write change from 6th to 12th grade?*
2. *How did (particular author's) writing change from his/her first to last work?*
3. *How do students' attitudes about writing change from 6th to 12th grade?*
4. *How do students' preferences in reading material change from 6th to 8th (or 9th to 12th) grade?*
5. *How does students' comfort in speaking in front of a group of peers change from 6th to 8th (or 9th to 12th) grade?*

Mathematics

1. *How does students' understanding of fractions change from 6th to 8th grade?*
2. *How does students' understanding of algebra change from concrete to abstract when using manipulatives?*
3. *How does students' understanding of mathematics change from 6th to 8th (or 9th to 12th) grade?*
4. *How do boys' and girls' self-concepts with respect to mathematics change from 6th to 8th grade?*
5. *How do students' problem solving abilities change from 6th to 8th grade?*
6. *How do students' uses of mathematics in everyday life change from 6th to 12th grade?*

Art and Music

1. *What stages do students go through in learning to draw perspective?*
2. *How did a particular artist's art change throughout his/her lifetime?*
3. *How do children's abilities to accurately draw people change between the ages of 3 and 18?*
4. *How does the playing of instruments change from the beginner to proficient stage?*
5. *How did a particular composer's musical compositions change over his/her lifetime?*

Foreign Language

1. *How does the ability to speak a foreign language change across the first two years of study?*
2. *How does the ability to speak English change across the first two years in this country for students whose native language is not English?*
3. *How has students' interest in learning Spanish, French, and Japanese changed over the last 20 years?*
4. *How does a child's ability to learn a second language change between the ages of 2 and 18?*
5. *How has a dialect of English or a foreign language changed over the past 20 years?*

Developmental Research Activity 1

Getting Up in the World

How does student height change from 6th grade to 8th grade?

Of course, most students get taller, but are the changes constant?

Do students grow about the same number of inches each year or do they grow more some years than others?

Are there differences in the patterns of boys' and girls' growth?

To find out, you will need to find the average height of students at each grade level. Using sampling techniques from Chapter 5 or those suggested by your teacher, measure the height of a sample of students at each grade level. Be sure to record heights of girls and boys separately so you can see if there are gender differences. Your teacher can suggest ways to get permission to sample and measure students in other classes. If you feel students might be embarrassed to have their height measured, you might consider measuring in centimeters rather than feet and inches. You can always convert your measurements back once you have found the averages.

Once you have a list of heights for each grade level, you will need to find the mean (average) for boys and girls at each grade level, as well as for the grade as a whole. (You can't just average the mean of boys' and girls' height to find average height unless there are exactly the same number of boys as girls in each sample.) To find the mean, add up all the scores and divide by the total number of scores. If you have a large number of subjects, you will probably need to use a calculator. It will be easiest to round each height to the nearest centimeter or inch before beginning your calculations.

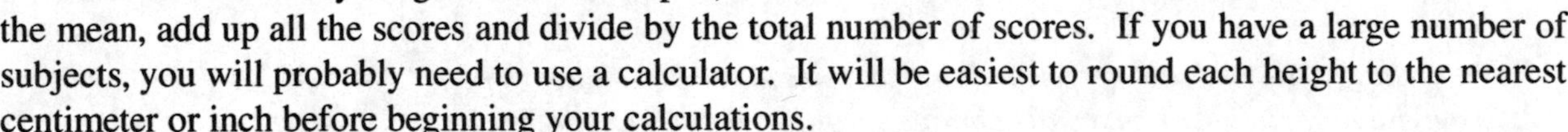

Make a line graph showing the average height for each grade level. You may want to use three different lines, one for girls, one for boys, and one for all students at a grade level. Look for patterns. At what level did students seem to grow the most?

Do you think this is always true?

How could you find out?

Are you interested in your future growth? See if you can find someone at a nearby high school to do this same research. While you probably will not be the exact same height as the average, the pattern might give you some idea of growth patterns for older adolescents.

Developmental Research Activity 2

Thinking Across the Ages

Do you think differently than a four-year-old? How about a 21-year-old? Many researchers believe that human beings' ways of thinking change as they grow up. One famous psychologist, Jean Piaget, believed that individuals go through a series of stages in which their ways of thinking change in important ways. In this study, you will examine the thinking of students aged four, seven, and ten to see if there are differences in the ways they understand changes in a ball of clay. This study could also be called a *cross-sectional* study because you are studying a developmental process by examining several children at different ages rather than waiting for a particular child to grow up. We could conduct a similar study using longitudinal research by watching the same child from age four to ten, but it would take a long time! In fact, Piaget developed many of his theories observing his own children over many years.

In this study you will observe students' ability to *conserve matter*. A person who can conserve matter will recognize that if you take a ball of clay and change its shape, the amount of clay has not changed. A person who cannot conserve might think there is more clay or less clay if the shape changes.

First, you will need to identify three children—one age four, one age seven, and one age ten. Be sure to ask parents' permission before asking the students to participate. You'll also need to prepare the materials needed for the activity. See if you or your teacher can borrow some plasticene clay. (You should be able to find some in most elementary school classrooms.) Divide it into two equal size balls of clay, about three to four inches in diameter. For the activity, you will need to meet with each child individually in a quiet place with few distractions. For each child, follow the procedure on the next page. Take careful notes on the children's responses, trying to record the child's exact words. Examine your results. Compare your findings with those of your classmates. You may want to read about Piaget's theories to find out if your results support his ideas.

(continued on next page)

Developmental Research Activity 2

Conservation Activity

Age of Subject ____

1. **Show the student two identical balls of clay. Ask the student if they are equal. If the student doesn't understand the word "equal," ask if there is the same amount of clay in each ball.**

   Student Response:

2. **Flatten one ball into a "pancake." Ask the student if they are still equal. If the student says they are not the same, ask which one has more clay. How can they tell?**

   Student Response:

3. **Roll the pancake back into a ball. Ask if they are the same now.**

   Student Response:

4. **Without changing the clay, ask, "If I made this ball into a pancake, would the pancake have more clay, less clay, or the same amount? Why?"**

   Student Response:

5. Thank the child.

Developmental Research Activity 3

Who Is on the Fast Track?

Do you have the same attitudes about the importance of doing well in school as you did in elementary school? Do you think most students show the same pattern of attitudes as you? This activity can help you find out. You'll need to find out how important school success is to students at each grade level you are studying, perhaps grades 6 to 12 or 1 to 12. First, develop a simple survey to find out students' attitudes. You will only need one or two questions. Be sure that your survey is easy enough that the youngest students in your sample can complete it. If you plan to look for differences based on gender, be sure to ask students to indicate if they are a boy or a girl. One possible question is
"How important is it for you to do well at school?" (Getting good grades is one way to think about doing well.)

1	2	3	4	5
Not important	Not too much	Don't know	Kind-of important	Very important

Next, select a sample of students at each grade level. If you do not know how to select a sample, see Chapter 4 or ask your teacher for suggestions. You will also need your teacher's help in getting permission to select and survey students.

After you have surveyed students at all grade levels, examine your results. If you will be looking for differences based on gender, separate your surveys into piles for girls and boys at each grade level before finding the average score. You will need to find the average for boys, girls, and all students at each grade level. Do you see any trends?

Does the importance of doing well stay the same across grade levels? Or does it rise and fall in patterns?

Is it the same for boys and girls?

You may want to create a graph illustrating the change in importance of doing well in school across grade levels. One method for showing such changes is a line graph with a different color for boys, girls, and a combined average. You could put the grade levels across the bottom of the graph and the average importance rating on the side. Do you think your results would be true for another group of students in another school?

While developmental research only tells you about changes and not the reason for the changes, how might you account for the results? If there were changes in how important school success is for students, why do you think that might be?

How do you explain gender differences, if you found such differences?

If you are interested in seeing if your hunches (hypotheses) are supported by data, you could develop a survey or set of interview questions to ask a sample of students at each grade level.

Developmental Research Activity 4

From YUCCH to YES!!

This developmental research study will examine two questions that may be important in your school: "What do boys think about girls?" and "What do girls think about boys?" Think about how you feel about the opposite sex today. Have you always felt that way? This study will try to determine how the ways boys feel about girls and girls feel about boys change as individuals mature.

For this cross-sectional study, you will develop a survey to be given to samples of students in grades one, four, seven, and ten. By examining differences in the responses, you can make hypotheses about how boys' and girls' attitudes change—or don't change—as they grow older.

First, you will need to construct your survey. Because some of your subjects will be very young, you will need to word your questions carefully so that even first grade students can understand them. It will be easiest if subjects can respond by circling or checking an answer rather than having to write a response. It also may be easier to write two separate surveys, one for boys and one for girls, since young children may have trouble with the term "the opposite sex." For the girls' survey you might consider questions such as

I like to have friends who are . . . boys _____ girls _____ both _____ .

I have a boyfriend. Yes _____ No _____

I would like to have a boyfriend. Yes _____ No _____

A lot of my friends are boys. Yes _____ No _____

Most of the time, being with boys is . . . fun _____ not fun _____ .

I would rather spend my fun time with . . . boys _____ girls _____ .

Be sure to field test your survey with students (who will not be part of the study) at each grade level (one, four, seven, and ten) to make sure the questions are clear and easy to understand.

Next, you will need to identify at least ten students at each grade level to complete your survey. Your teacher may need to help you make contact with teachers in other buildings in order to get permission to do your study. Also, be sure to get permission from the principal of any building in which your survey will be distributed.

Examine your data. Do you see trends across grade levels?

You may want to do follow-up interviews with a small number of students to find out what factors affect students' attitudes at varying ages.

Correlational Research

Our next subcategory of descriptive research is correlational research, which investigates the relationships among variables. Students may conduct correlational research that is either descriptive or historical. Studies that investigate the relationships between time of day and amount of crime, attitudes about immigration and sense of economic well-being, or arm span and length of football pass in the NFL can be described as correlational. Closer to home, students might investigate the relationships between age and bedtimes/curfew, number of hours worked after school and grade point average, or height and shoe size. Correlational research, with variations in how the data are analyzed, is appropriate for middle and high school students.

A correlation expresses the strength of the relationship between two variables and can be either positive or negative. If two variables correlate positively, the value of one goes up as the value of the other goes up. For example, age and height are usually positively correlated in elementary, middle, and high school—as children get older, they usually get taller. Two variables can correlate negatively and still be strongly related, but in that case, the value of one goes up as the value of the other goes down. In theory, the more hours spent practicing a musical instrument, the less mistakes a player should make. That relationship would illustrate a negative correlation as the two variables are related, but move in opposite directions. Whether positive or negative in direction, correlations can vary in magnitude. The stronger the correlation, the more likely it is that individuals can predict change in one variable by knowing the change in the other. If a perfect correlation existed, they could make exact predictions. For example, if there were a perfect correlation between years of teaching experience and teaching ability, you could know a person's teaching ability simply by asking how many years he/she had taught. Unfortunately, few variables are perfectly correlated. In most cases, correlations can provide an idea of what is likely to occur. Graduate schools use the Graduate Record Exam (GRE) or Miller Analogies Test (MAT) along with undergraduate grade point average as admissions criteria because they believe students with higher GRE or MAT scores will be more successful in graduate school. They came to this belief as a result of research on thousands of students that indicated a statistically significant correlation between test scores and first year grade point average. Because of these correlations, graduate schools continue to use scores from standardized tests as one of several criteria when admitting students.

There is one really important thing you and your students need to remember about correlational research—correlation does not mean causation! Unlike experimental research, correlational research designs cannot investigate cause and effect relationships. They can tell a person there is a relationship between two variables, but cannot say that one causes the other. If student researchers found a high negative correlation in their high school between cigarette smoking and grades received—the more cigarettes students smoked, the lower their grades—they could not assume that smoking caused low grades. It is possible that smoking causes low grades through some physiological interaction, low grades cause students to smoke (because of stress or some other cause), or some other variable (peers, self-concept, parental role modeling, etc.) causes both smoking and low grades. Regardless of the strength or direction of a statistically significant correlation, the only thing the researcher is justified in saying is, "The data revealed a strong positive (or negative) correlation between the variables," not that one caused the other. Methods for analyzing correlational research are discussed in Chapter 6. (Note: If students will be analyzing correlational data using one of the statistical formulas, 30 subjects is usually considered the minimum sample size.)

CORRELATIONAL RESEARCH EXAMPLES

<u>General</u>

1. *What is the relationship between hours of TV watched per week and grades?*
2. *What is the relationship between month of the year and number of days students in our school are absent?*
3. *What is the relationship between gender of student and type of pet?*
4. *What is the correlation between amount of exercise and body weight?*
5. *What is the correlation between hair style and social values?*
6. *What is the correlation between interest in an academic subject and level of achievement?*
7. *What is the correlation between amount of violence depicted and commercial success of movies?*

Science

1. *What is the relationship between age and calories consumed at lunch?*
2. *What is the relationship between the amount of orange juice consumed and the number of colds in a winter?*
3. *What is the correlation between barometric pressure changes and student misbehavior?*
4. *What is the correlation between amount of exercise and days of illness?*
5. *What is the correlation between days of sunshine and number of suicides?*

Social Studies

1. *What was the relationship between number of horses and number of automobiles in the county between 1900-1950?*
2. *What was the relationship between number of mill workers and total town population 1900-1940?*
3. *What is the relationship between mortgage interest rates and home sales?*
4. *What is the relationship between the unemployment rate and the crime rate?*
5. *What is the relationship between political party and socioeconomic status?*

Language Arts

1. *What is the correlation between how much students read at home and their grades in language arts class?*
2. *What is the correlation between parents' and their children's preferences in reading material?*
3. *What is the correlation between gender and preference in reading material?*
4. *What is the correlation between writing grades and amount of reading done?*
5. *What is the correlation between amount of time spent practicing and number of errors in public speaking?*

Mathematics

1. *What is the correlation between gender and attitude toward mathematics?*
2. *What is the correlation between achievement in mathematics and in language arts?*
3. *What is the correlation between achievement in mathematics and career preference?*
4. *What is the correlation between success in geometry and success in algebra?*
5. *What is the correlation between computational accuracy and problem solving ability?*
6. *What is the correlation between use of a calculator and rote memory of simple computational facts such as multiplication tables?*

Art and Music

1. *What is the relationship between minutes practiced and mistakes made in a music lesson?*
2. *What is the correlation between parents' and their children's preferences in music?*
3. *What is the correlation between age and music preference?*
4. *What is the correlation between years of formal art study and success in the commercial art world?*
5. *What is the correlation between grades in art/music classes and grades in academic classes?*
6. *What is the correlation between attitudes toward art classes as an elementary student and enrollment in high school art classes?*
7. *What is the correlation between amount of formal education and preferences in art medium?*

Foreign Language

1. *What is the relationship between student ethnicity and enrollment in foreign language classes?*
2. *What is the relationship between grades in language arts and in foreign language classes?*
3. *What is the relationship between enrollment in foreign language classes and travel to foreign countries?*
4. *What is the correlation between enrollment in foreign language classes and intention to go to college?*
5. *What is the correlation between grades in foreign language classes and conversational fluency in the language?*

Correlational Research Activity 1

What's Liking Got to Do With It?

Do you think there is a relationship between which subjects students like and the grades they get in those subjects? ___ Yes ___ No. If so, do you think it's a positive relationship, with higher grades in subjects students like most?

Or would you expect to find a negative correlation, with higher grades in least-liked subjects and lower grades in most-liked subjects?

Think about your hypothesis, considering what is true for you, what you've heard others say, and what seems logical. Then record your hypothesis below.

I do ___/do not ___ think there is a correlation between students' enjoyment of an academic subject and the grades received in that subject.
If you think there is a correlation, do you think it is a positive or negative one? __________
Why?

In order to gather data with which to answer your question, you'll need to get information from a random sample of students. You can use the questions on the next page or design your own, but you'll need some numerical measure of grades and level of liking for subjects.
After you have gathered the data, use either the graphing method or the correlation formula explained in Chapter 6 to see if your hypothesis has been supported by the data. How do you explain your results?

How might this information be useful to students?

Teachers?

School administrators?

(continued on next page)

Correlational Research Activity 1

Sample Questionnaire

We are doing research about students and academic subjects and would appreciate your answers to the following questions. Please do NOT put your name on this paper and please be honest.

1. In the space below, please write what grade you are in.
2. For each subject listed below, put the grade you usually get in that subject. If you have gotten different grades, put the average.
3. Based on how much you like the subject, please rate each subject on the following 1-5 scale. Rate your liking of *the subject itself,* not this year's teacher or class.

1	2	3	4	5
Hate it!	Dislike it.	It's OK.	Like it.	Love it!

For example, if you got two C's and a D in Greek this year and generally dislike Greek, you would fill in the form like this:

Subject	Grade	Liking
Greek	*C*	*2*

- -

Grade level you are in:________________________________

Subject	Grade	Liking
Language Arts	_______	_______
Science	_______	_______
Social Studies	_______	_______
Mathematics	_______	_______
Physical Education	_______	_______
Other (art, music, technology, etc.)	_______	_______
________________	_______	_______
________________	_______	_______
________________	_______	_______

Correlational Research Activity 2

Let's Settle the Television-Watching Argument

Do you ever get into discussions with your parents about watching television?
___ Yes ___ No
Do you argue about whether there is a relationship between the number of hours students watch television and their grade point average?
___ Yes ___ No

If there is a relationship, do you think it's positive, with higher grades going to students who watch more TV? Or do you think it's a negative correlation, with higher grades for those who watch less TV and lower grades for those who watch more TV? ___ Positive ___ Negative

Think about your hypothesis, considering what is true for you, what you've heard others say, and what seems logical. Then record your hypothesis here:

I do ___ /do not ___ think there is a correlation between students' grades and the number of hours per week that they watch television.
If you think there is a correlation, do you think it is a positive or negative one? __________
Why?

To gather data for this question, you'll need to get information from a random sample of students. You can use our questions or design your own, but you'll need some numerical measure of grades and the number of hours per week that students watch television. To be accurate, you might want to ask students a week ahead of time to record the number of hours they spend watching TV each day and total it for the week. It's easy to either overestimate or, more likely, underestimate the amount of time you spend watching TV. You can use the form on the next page or design one of your own. Perhaps your teacher will take two minutes at the start of each day for students to record their hours of TV watching from the previous day, while they can still accurately remember. On the next page, you will find one way to organize your questionnaire.
After you have gathered the data, use either the graphing method or the correlation formula explained in Chapter 6 to see if your hypothesis has been supported by the data. How do you explain your results?

How might this information be useful to students?

Teachers?

Parents?

(continued on next page)

Correlational Research Activity 2

Television Watching Recording Form

We are doing research about students and television and would appreciate your answers to the following questions. Please do NOT put your name on this paper and please be honest.

1. What grade are you in? _________
2. What is your grade point average? __________ If you're not sure, list the grades you got on your last report card in all of your subjects:
   English _____ Mathematics _____ Science _____
   Social Studies _____ Physical Education _____
   List other subjects and grades:
   _________________ _____
   _________________ _____
   _________________ _____
3. For each half-hour you watch TV, put a check on the line below the days of the week. Then add the checks and divide by two (because each check represents a half hour) and record the number of hours you watched TV that day on the second line. Add across to get the number of hours you watched TV in one week.

	Monday	Tuesday	Wednesday	Thursday
Checks	_______	_______	__________	________
Hours	_______	_______	__________	________

	Friday	Saturday	Sunday
Checks	______	________	_______
Hours	______	________	_______

TOTAL HOURS TV WATCHING FOR THE WEEK: _________

If the respondent provided grades instead of their average, here is how to compute the grade point average:

Multiply each A by 4 _____ Multiply each C by 2 _____
Multiply each B by 3 _____ Multiply each D by 1 _____

Add all the points and divide by the number of grades (subjects) he/she had. Round off to the tenths (one decimal place) and write this number in the space for GPA. (The number should be between 0 and 4.0, with 4.0 representing grades of all A's.)

Correlational Research Activity 3

The Higher You Get, the More There Is?

Do you have the feeling that every year you have more homework than the year before? Or are things getting easier as you move up in grade level? Or do you see no real difference? To put it more formally, "Is there a correlation between grade level and number of hours spent on homework?"

With this question, you need to define your terms more clearly because it could affect the outcome greatly. By hours of homework, do you mean the hours it would take to complete the homework that is assigned or the actual amount of time students spend doing homework?

Unfortunately, not all students do all of the homework that is assigned to them! So if they tell you how many hours they actually spend and you assume that number represents all the homework that was assigned, your conclusions could be faulty. One way around this dilemma is to ask students to record the actual number of minutes they spent doing homework, whether they did it all, and, if they did not complete their homework, have them estimate how many more minutes it would have taken to complete the work. With all this information, you would have the data to answer either question. Before you start data gathering, think about the following questions and write your hypotheses below.

Do you think there is a correlation between students' grade level and the number of hours per week that they actually spend doing homework? __________
If you think there is a correlation, do you think it is a positive or negative one? __________
Why?

Do you think there is a correlation between students' grade level and the amount of homework assigned by teachers? __________
If you think there is a correlation, do you think it is a positive or negative one? __________
Why?

To gather data for this question, you'll need to get information from a random sample of students in several different grade levels. You might see the biggest differences if you ask students in both middle and high school. It is especially important that your sample accurately represents the school population with respect to doing homework. You can use the questions on the next page or design your own, but you'll need some numerical measure of the number of minutes per week that students do homework, their estimate of how much time it would take to complete all that was assigned, and their grade level. (Be careful interpreting your data if many students use estimates instead of actual time. It's easy to either underestimate or, more likely, overestimate the amount of time you spend doing homework.) On the next page, we have outlined one way to design a questionnaire.

(continued on next page)

Correlational Research Activity 3

Homework Recording Form

We are doing research about homework and would appreciate your answers to the following questions. Please do NOT put your name on this paper and please be honest.

1. In the space below, write what grade you are in.
2. For each class you are taking, write down your homework assignment for each day before you leave school. Write in the names of other subjects you are taking on the blank lines.
3. Each night after you complete each assignment, record the number of minutes you actually spent doing it in the column labeled "Actual Time."
4. For any homework you did not do or did not finish, make your best guess about how many minutes it would have taken you to complete it and record that in the column for "Estimated Time."

Grade level you are in: __________

Monday Subject	**Assignment**	**Actual Time to Complete**	**Estimated Time to Complete**
Language Arts	______________	________	________
Science	______________	________	________
Social Studies	______________	________	________
Mathematics	______________	________	________
________	______________	________	________
________	______________	________	________
________	______________	________	________

Total for Monday, (date) ____________

Tuesday Subject	**Assignment**	**Actual Time to Complete**	**Estimated Time to Complete**
Language Arts	______________	________	________
Science	______________	________	________
Social Studies	______________	________	________
Mathematics	______________	________	________
________	______________	________	________
________	______________	________	________
________	______________	________	________

Total for Tuesday, (date) ____________

(continued on next page)

Correlational Research Activity 3

Wednesday Subject	**Assignment**	**Actual Time to Complete**	**Estimated Time to Complete**
Language Arts	______	______	______
Science	______	______	______
Social Studies	______	______	______
Mathematics	______	______	______
______	______	______	______
______	______	______	______
______	______	______	______

Total for Wednesday, (date) ______________

Thursday Subject	**Assignment**	**Actual Time to Complete**	**Estimated Time to Complete**
Language Arts	______	______	______
Science	______	______	______
Social Studies	______	______	______
Mathematics	______	______	______
______	______	______	______
______	______	______	______
______	______	______	______

Total for Thursday, (date) ______________

Friday Subject	**Assignment**	**Actual Time to Complete**	**Estimated Time to Complete**
Language Arts	______	______	______
Science	______	______	______
Social Studies	______	______	______
Mathematics	______	______	______
______	______	______	______
______	______	______	______
______	______	______	______

Total for Friday, (date) ______________

TOTAL FOR THE WEEK		______	______

(continued on next page)

Correlational Research Activity 3

After you have gathered the data, use either the graphing method or the correlation formula explained in Chapter 6 to see if your hypotheses have been supported by the data. One option is to look at the correlation between total minutes of actual homework done in one week and grade level. This correlation might tell you something about the relationship between grade level and doing homework. If you are curious about the relationship between grade level and amount of homework assigned (unfortunately not the same as homework done), use a combination of actual and estimated time to approximate the time it would have taken to do all assigned homework. Be aware that using estimates can decrease the reliability of your data. Depending on the data, consider converting your data from minutes to hours (divide minutes by 60; carry it out to two decimal places) if the numbers are large. How do you explain your results?

Correlational Research Activity 4

Can You Predict Shoe Size?

Do you think there is a linear relationship between how tall a person is and what size shoes he/she wears?

Ask each person in your class to write down his/her shoe size and height in feet and inches. Do this anonymously, as some people might be embarrassed by one or both of these measurements and you do want them to tell the truth! Be sure to have them indicate if they are male or female or collect sheets from boys and girls separately. Shoe sizes differ by gender and this could really mess up your data if they were combined. Someone (each subject or you, if you are not sure it will be done accurately) will then need to convert the height measurement into inches by multiplying the number of feet tall by 12 then add the additional inches (5'7" = [5 x 12] + 7 = 60 + 7 = 67"). Record these below:

	Female Subjects				Male Subjects		
	Height (ft. & in.)	Height (in inches)	Shoe Size		Height (ft. & in.)	Height (in inches)	Shoe Size
1)	________	________	___	1)	________	________	___
2)	________	________	___	2)	________	________	___
3)	________	________	___	3)	________	________	___
4)	________	________	___	4)	________	________	___
5)	________	________	___	5)	________	________	___
6)	________	________	___	6)	________	________	___
7)	________	________	___	7)	________	________	___
8)	________	________	___	8)	________	________	___
9)	________	________	___	9)	________	________	___
10)	________	________	___	10)	________	________	___
11)	________	________	___	11)	________	________	___
12)	________	________	___	12)	________	________	___
13)	________	________	___	13)	________	________	___
14)	________	________	___	14)	________	________	___
15)	________	________	___	15)	________	________	___
16)	________	________	___	16)	________	________	___

After you have gathered the data, use either the graphing method or the correlation formula for nonindependent samples explained in Chapter 6 to see if your hypothesis has been supported by the data. How do you explain your results?

Causal-Comparative Research

Causal-comparative research attempts to understand things that have already happened by looking back and comparing two groups of people, those for whom the outcome has happened and those for whom it has not. The researcher then attempts to see how the groups are different, based on a comparison of variables he/she believes relevant to the outcome. In the case of the lung cancer study done by the U.S. Surgeon General, variables included gender, race, economic status, type of employment, and smoking, among others. When the only significant difference between the groups with and without lung cancer was found to be smoking, the Surgeon General concluded that smoking was harmful to one's health. Some challenged this finding because there were those with cancer who had not smoked and there were smokers who did not have cancer. Like many other types of research, causal-comparative research deals with groups, not individuals. It is also a form of descriptive research, which means that it only describes what is, not *why* it is. Like correlational research, causal-comparative does not *prove* that one thing caused another.

Causal-comparative research attempts to understand which factors might account for something that has already happened. Because the outcome already exists, it is impossible to use experimental research to manipulate variables and see how they affect the outcome. For instance, many people are interested in reducing the number of school dropouts and would like to know which kids are most likely to drop out and why. But until a student actually drops out of school, the researcher doesn't know who to study. Also, by the time they have dropped out, the researcher can't really change things to see if he/she could have prevented it. Causal-comparative research is also useful if the outcome a person is studying is an undesirable one, such as lung cancer or sudden infant death syndrome (SIDS). In these cases researchers wouldn't want their study to progress to that outcome in order to study them and again don't necessarily know who will suffer from those diseases in advance. For these reasons, causal-comparative research is also called *ex post facto* research, Latin for "after the fact." Another use for causal-comparative research is identifying relationships that may lead to experimental studies. Because experimental studies are expensive and time-consuming, the use of causal-comparative research to identify likely causal relationships could provide greater efficiency in conducting research.

To conduct causal-comparative research, a researcher needs to first select two groups of subjects that differ in a way that interests him/her. They may differ in having or not having a particular characteristic (a job, being a dropout, smoking) or in having different amounts or levels of some quality (grade point average, popularity, athletic skill). It is important to clearly define the criteria for membership in each group. For example, a researcher might define the high grade point group as having a 3.5 average or higher, while the low grade point group might have a GPA of 1.5 or lower.

After a search of related research, the researcher can then identify one or more variables he/she thinks might explain the difference between the two groups. To continue the grade point average (GPA) example, possible hypotheses might include education level of the parent(s), having a job, self-concept, socioeconomic status, or others. These characteristics are called dependent variables, and a researcher needs to gather data for all subjects in both groups on any variables that he/she decides to include. Of those listed above, he/she could ask about parental education level and socioeconomic status (which could be offensive to some), inquire about a job, and give students a self-concept test. Once data are collected, he/she can analyze them using mean and standard deviation as well as the *t*-test, if applicable (see Chapter 6), in order to see if there are differences between the two groups on any of the dependent variables.

Interpretation of causal-comparative research is tricky. The cause-effect relationship may be what a researcher hypothesized, for example, that high self-concept leads to high GPA. It can also be the reverse, that high GPA leads to high self-concept. And it may be that some third cause—for instance, parental support—led to both high GPA and high self-concept. In some cases, it is clear which variable came first and which variable is more likely to be the cause of the other. In this example, parental education level generally came before the student's GPA. It is also unlikely that a student's GPA would affect the parents' level of education. So if the groups differed significantly in level of parents' educations, it is fair to assume that it might be a contributing factor to differences in GPA. In cases where it may not be clear which variable came first (for instance, if you are looking at a student's job status), you could look for changes in GPA before and after the student began his/her job to determine the direction of possible causation.

Students may confuse causal-comparative research with correlational or experimental designs. Causal-comparative research is like correlational in that no variables are manipulated and one must be cautious not to assume that the results *prove* causation by one or more of the variables. It is different in that causal-comparative research attempts to identify possible cause-effect relationships, while correlational research simply tells you which variables are related.

Causal-comparative research is like experimental design because both attempt to establish cause-effect relationships and both involve group comparisons. The key difference is that in experimental research, the researcher manipulates one or more variables to see what will happen as a result. In causal-comparative research, the result happened before the research began and the researcher is attempting to determine the cause after the fact. Also, significant findings in causal-comparative research only suggest a possible causal relationship, while significant findings in a well-conducted experimental design can prove a cause-effect relationship.

The kinds of questions appropriate for causal-comparative research include those about events that have already occurred. A researcher also needs to be able to identify groups for whom the outcome has and has not occurred and be able to gather data about those people. Below are some examples of causal-comparative research questions.

CAUSAL-COMPARATIVE RESEARCH EXAMPLES

General

1. *What is the difference between successful and less successful student athletes in my school?*
2. *How are school dropouts different from those who complete high school?*
3. *How are two schools, one with many behavior problems and the other with few, different?*
4. *How are students who drink alcohol regularly (once a week or more) different from those who do not drink?*
5. *What are the differences between students who apply for college and those who do not?*
6. *How are people who regularly read a newspaper different from those who do not?*
7. *How are students who have jobs outside of school different from those who do not?*

Science

1. *How are students with five or more cavities (tooth decay) different from students with two or fewer?*
2. *Why did some buildings survive an earthquake/hurricane while others were destroyed or severely damaged?*
3. *How are people who catch "what's going around" (cold, flu) different from those who do not get sick?*
4. *How are endangered species different from those that are not threatened or endangered?*
5. *How are families that recycle different from those that do not?*
6. *How are students who have smoked for at least one year different from those who do not smoke?*

Social Studies

1. *How are people who vote regularly different from those who don't vote?*
2. *How are people in my community who are economically successful different from those who are less so?*
3. *How are local heroes (those who rescued others, risked something for others) different from people who did not do those things?*
4. *How are students who like history different from those who do not like it?*
5. *How are politically stable countries different from those that are unstable?*
6. *How are countries/states with a high per-capita income different from those with a low per-capita income?*
7. *How are countries with a high rate of violent crime different from those with a low rate?*
8. *How are countries/states with a high incidence of infant mortality different from those with a low rate?*
9. *How are students who volunteer in the community different from those who do not?*

Language Arts

1. *How are students who enjoy reading different from those who do not?*
2. *How are writers who receive good grades for their writing different from those who do not?*

3. *How do popular movies and "box office bombs" differ?*
4. *How are poets different from novelists?*
5. *How are best-sellers different from less commercially successful books?*
6. *How are works written by authors who have committed suicide different from those who have not?*

<u>*Mathematics*</u>

1. *How are students who enjoy mathematics different from those who do not?*
2. *How are students who are successful in mathematics different from those who are not?*
3. *How are teachers who did well in math classes before college different from those who did not do as well?*
4. *How are people who chose math-related careers different from those who chose non-math related careers?*
5. *How are students who like using computers different from students who do not like using computers?*

<u>*Art and Music*</u>

1. *How are commercially successful artists different from those who have not been economically successful?*
2. *How are highly regarded artists different from those considered by critics to be minor?*
3. *How are good artists in our school different from those who are not as talented?*
4. *How are commercially successful musicians different from those who have not been economically successful?*
5. *How are highly regarded composers different from those considered by critics to be minor?*
6. *How are good singers different from good instrumentalists?*

<u>*Foreign Language*</u>

1. *How are students who take foreign language classes different from those who do not?*
2. *How are students who are fluent speakers of a foreign language different from those who are less fluent?*
3. *How are students who choose to study romance languages different from students who study non-romance languages? How are students who choose to study French different from students who study Spanish?*
4. *How are ESL (English as a Second Language) students who are fluent in English different from ESL students who are less fluent?*
5. *How are "living" languages different from those that are no longer used?*

Causal-Comparative Research Activity 1

The Difference Between Good and Great

You may admire other students you feel have succeeded in one area or another, even wondered what might have contributed to their success. These people might be successful in academic studies, music, athletics, art, or getting along with other people. Causal-comparative research might help you figure out how outstanding achievers differ from average achievers.

Your first task is to identify the area of achievement you are interested in researching. You'll need to distinguish outstanding achievers from average ones to know from which students to gather data. This task will be easier if there is a clear way to distinguish levels of achievement. For example, in sports the starting players are usually the best. In band, the better players compete for first and second chair in each instrument section. It might be harder to decide who is outstanding in getting along with others, but if this area of achievement is important to you, talk it over with your teacher and other interested students to decide how you could tell who is outstanding in this area.

Using your criteria, pick five students you consider outstanding in the area you want to research and five who are average in that area. The example using athletics illustrates the process, but you can follow these same steps for a different area. For athletics, choose a sport in which you are interested or the sport with the most accomplished athletes at your school. You might tell the coach what you are researching and ask him/her to identify six or seven students he/she considers outstanding. If the coach doesn't want to do this, you might need to choose them yourself, based on their performance (RBIs and batting average in baseball, average points and assists in basketball, etc.). You could then choose randomly from among the non-starting players to find the five students for your average achiever group.

You should explain your research to your subjects in general terms such as, "I'm trying to find out what factors contribute to students playing baseball for our school team." You don't want to embarrass anyone by letting them know you think they are outstanding or average. You should also make it clear to your subjects that their answers and identity will be kept confidential. Be sure you do keep it confidential! On a separate sheet of paper, list each student next to his/her code number. Put this information in a safe place. Any data you record should be identified by code number only. For example, be sure that only Pat's code number (and not her name) is on any survey she might complete or on your interview notes. It might help your analysis to code outstanding achievers with an "O" and a number and average achievers with an "A" and a number.

Now you'll have to identify factors you think might contribute to outstanding achievement in the area you have chosen to study. For athletics it might be age, size, practice time, or previous playing experience in community leagues or elementary school teams. For band, it might be private lessons, longer amounts of practice time, or parents who think it is important to play a musical instrument. You might want to ask a few students to sit with you and discuss possible factors before you make your final decision about what to include in your research. You might also want to interview an adult who knows about that area (coach, band director, teacher) to see what he/she thinks contributes to outstanding performance. You then need to construct a survey for your subjects to fill out or a list of questions you will ask them during an interview. This will help you find out whether each subject had each factor you think might be important. Write out your survey or interview questions now, then read the next two paragraphs and make sure you will get enough information to complete the chart.

(continued on next page)

Causal-Comparative Research Activity 1

When you are sure you have covered all the areas you want to explore, arrange to get your data, either by giving your subjects the survey and arranging when and how or by scheduling an interview in which you will write down the answers to your questions. Be sure to identify them only by code number on the survey or interview notes.

List each factor you hypothesized as important down the left side of the chart. Then, based on the data you collected, indicate whether each of your subjects has each factor. For example, if you identified playing in community leagues in elementary school as one factor that might make a difference, write yes or no under each subject, based on whether he/she played.

Students **Factors**	o1	o2	o3	o4	o5	a1	a2	a3	a4	a5

Look over your data. What patterns do you see?

In particular, look for factors that occur for most of one group of students (outstanding or average achievers) and not for most of the other group. This factor doesn't have to be present or absent in all five subjects in a category, but the difference between the number of occurrences in one group and the other should be at least three (for example, four outstanding athletes played Little League, while only one average player did: 4 - 1 = 3). If something is present for most of the subjects in both groups, it really doesn't explain the difference in their achievement.

What did you find?

In what ways are outstanding achievers different from average achievers?

(continued on next page)

Causal-Comparative Research Activity 1

Think about five more outstanding and average achievers in the same area of expertise. Do your results seem to apply to those students as well?

Do you think these same factors would explain differences in achievement in a different area of expertise? Why or why not?

Who in the real world might be interested in your results?

How do you think they could use them?

What would be the best way to communicate your findings and describe your research to this particular audience?

Check with your teacher to see if this project is something you can pursue.

Causal-Comparative Research Activity 2

Why Are Movies Popular?

Movie companies sure wish they could tell what elements would guarantee that a movie would be popular. Unfortunately, you can never know for sure until the movie is finished and out in theaters. While causal-comparative research won't guarantee that what you found out for the past will be true for the future, it might give you some clues.
Your first task is to identify five popular movies and five that were not considered popular. How could you do this?

While your personal preferences and those of your friends are important to you, how would movie studios be able to identify movies preferred by most people? Most likely, studios use the amount of money earned by the movie to gauge how well liked it is. Locate the five movies that have made the most money in the last ten years. You can find this information in movie reference books, and it is sometimes mentioned in the newspaper. Your local movie critic might know how to find the most recent figures. For comparison purposes, you'll also need the names of five movies that did not make much money, perhaps even lost money. You'll have more choices for this category! When you have selected your movies, list them in the spaces below.

Popular Movies	**Unpopular Movies**
P1________________	U1________________
P2________________	U2________________
P3________________	U3________________
P4________________	U4________________
P5________________	U5________________

Now it's time for some thinking and perhaps some research. You need to decide which factors you think might be the difference between a hit movie and one that is not a hit. Could it be the people involved—famous director, certain actors?

Perhaps it has to do with the type of movie—action adventure, science fiction, romance. Do you think level of violence is a factor?

Do technical factors such as special effects or makeup make a difference?

(continued on next page)

Causal-Comparative Research Activity 2

What about rating (G, PG, PG-13, R, NR-17, X)?

Does what the critics said and wrote about it make a difference?

Think about what you think popular movies have that unpopular ones don't have. When you have your hypotheses, list the factors below and put abbreviated descriptions of each down the left side of the data sheet.

For each factor, indicate whether each of the movies has that factor. For example, if you think having a famous director makes a difference, put yes or no under each movie, based on whether or not it had a famous director. You'll probably find that you have to look up some information about these movies in guides or other written and computer references.

Movies **Factors**	P1	P2	P3	P4	P5	U1	U2	U3	U4	U5

Look over your data. What patterns do you see?

In particular look for factors that occur for most of one group of movies and not for most of the other group. This factor doesn't have to be present or absent in all five movies in a category, but the difference between the number of occurrences in one group and the other should be at least three (for example, four popular movies have a famous director, while only one unpopular movie did: 4 - 1 = 3). If something is present for most of the movies in both groups, it really doesn't explain their difference in popularity. What did you find?

In what ways are popular movies as a group different from unpopular movies?

Think about five more popular and less popular movies. Do your results seem to apply to those movies as well?

If you think you are on to something, you might want to share your results with the heads of some of the major movie studios. They would certainly be interested in anything that could help them make a greater number of popular movies!

Causal-Comparative Research Activity 3

Have Jobs and Have-nots

In what ways do you think high school students who work are different than high school students who do not?

Could it be how rich or poor they are?

How much allowance they receive?

Whether or not they plan to attend college?

Would owning a car affect a student's decision to work?

Do you think a student's grade point average is a factor?

What about students' work ethic—how important they think it is to work?

Think about the students you know who work and those who do not work and the differences between these two groups. Also consider why people might work. When you have your hypotheses about what might distinguish workers from nonworkers, list the factors on the next page and write them in shortened form down the left side of the data sheet.

You will then need to identify ten students who currently work on a regular basis and ten who do not. Before you start, decide what your definition of work will be. Does baby-sitting count? How about doing chores around the house or neighborhood for pay? Or do you only want to consider it work if it is done for an employer the person didn't previously know, such as in a business or fast-food restaurant?

Because you will be asking your subjects some potentially personal questions, it is important that you ensure their confidentiality. You will need to make it clear to your subjects that both their answers and their identity will be kept confidential. Once you have identified students for both groups, assign each of them a code number and list both names and code numbers on a separate sheet of paper. Put this paper in a safe place. Any data you record should be identified by code number only. For example, be sure that only Jerry's code number (and not his name) is on any survey he might complete or on your interview notes. It might help your analysis to code workers with a "W" and a number and nonworkers with an "N" and a number.

Now you'll have to identify factors you think might distinguish between students who work and students who do not. It might be one of those listed above or something entirely different. You might want to ask a few students to sit with you and discuss possible factors before you make your final decision about what to include in your research. You also might want to interview a school counselor or the teacher in the cooperative work program, if your school has one. To gather information, you'll need to decide if you will have students complete a written survey or if you'd prefer to interview them. You'll then need to construct either a survey or list of interview questions. (See Chapter 4 for ideas.) Whichever form of data gathering you choose, be sure your questions help you find out whether each student had each factor you think might be important. Write out your survey or interview questions now, then read the next two

(continued on next page)

Causal-Comparative Research Activity 3

paragraphs and make sure you will get enough information to complete the chart.

When you are sure that you have covered everything in your questions, make plans for gathering your data. For surveys, decide the *who, where, when*, and *how* of distributing and getting surveys back. For interviews, schedule them at times convenient for both yourself and the subjects. Be sure to identify subjects only by code number on the surveys and interview notes.

List each factor you hypothesized as important down the left side of the chart. Then, based on the data you collected, indicate whether each of your subjects has each factor. For example, if you identified planning to go to college as one characteristic that might make a difference between workers and nonworkers, write yes or no under each subject, based on whether he/she planned to go to college. If your questions were not in a yes/no format, convert them now. For example, if you asked students their grade point average because you thought students with high grades were more likely to work, decide that all averages above a certain one (3.0, for example) indicate high grades and mark them yes.

Students Factors	w1	w2	w3	w4	w5	w6	w7	w8...	n1	n2	n3	n4	n5	n6	n7	n8...

(continued on next page)

Causal-Comparative Research Activity 3

Look over your data. What patterns do you see?

In particular, look for factors that occur for most of one group of students (workers or nonworkers) and not for most of the other group. This factor doesn't have to be present or absent in all ten subjects in a category, but the difference between the number of occurrences in one group and the other should be at least five (for example, eight workers come from divorced families, while only three nonworkers do: 8 - 3 = 5). If a factor is present for most of the subjects in both groups, it really doesn't explain the difference.

What did you find?

In what ways are students who work different from students who do not work?

Think about five more students who do and do not work. Do your results seem to apply to those students as well?

Remember that causal-comparative research can only describe relationships, not explain causes. For example, if you found that students who work have lower grades than those who do not, it could be that students with lower grades choose to work, that working leads to lower grades, or that both things are related to some other factor.

Who in the real world might be interested in your results?

How do you think they could use them?

What would be the best way to communicate your findings and describe your research to this particular audience?

Check with your teacher to see if this project is something you can pursue.

Historical Research

If descriptive research answers the question "How are things now?" historical research answers the question "How were things in the past?" Its purpose is to reconstruct the past as accurately and objectively as possible. You probably do not see historical research reported in popular publications as often as you do descriptive research, but it still surrounds us. An interview with Jimmy Carter about his presidency, a book of photographs of pioneer women, diaries from a great-grandparent, or even a magazine article about changes in evening wear over the last 50 years are reports of historical research. Students who interview alumni from their high school about school experiences in the 1950s, document the historical importance of a building in the town, or study how movies were used as propaganda early in this century are also conducting historical research.

Much historical research is appropriate and can be made interesting for adolescents. While students often seem uninterested when reading history textbooks about people who lived way back when, their interest increases as they begin to see the connection to their present lives. Middle school students asked to compare and contrast public sanitation practices of Colonial times and current times were quite interested in (and grossed out by) how people used to live.

One of the best ways to describe the role of a historian is to compare it to that of an investigative reporter. Reporters have to look for clues about things that have already happened, often from people who don't want to cooperate. Like reporters, the best sources of information for historians are original documents, actual participants, and eyewitnesses. While getting information from dead people is a bit more of a challenge for the historian than a reporter seeking information from uncooperative but living folks, the task of digging for and evaluating information is similar.

Some adolescents are familiar with investigative reporting, ranging from the **New York Times** to "Hard Copy." This familiarity should help them refine their conceptions of primary and secondary sources. For something to be a primary source, the author or creator of the document or artifact must have been a participant or direct observer of the recorded event. The astronauts and NASA personnel present at the time of the Apollo 13 flight were primary sources, while the director who made the movie about Apollo 13 was not.

The significance of primary resources does not mean that secondary sources are not worth studying. Though a secondary source is one or several times removed from the actual event, he/she still has information to share. The difference is that a secondary source reports the observations of others. In the Apollo 13 example, movie director Ron Howard has to interpret the information of others since he was not present at NASA or on the flight himself.

Much of the research students have done in school has used secondary sources from the school or community library, putting the student in the role of summarizing others' findings. In historical research, you want students to use critical thinking to evaluate primary sources themselves, then synthesize their findings to create an original thesis about their question. In a typical research report on life in the American colonies, a student would go to an encyclopedia, reference book, or other secondary source and take notes and summarize the information found. A student doing historical research on the same topic would instead seek out primary sources of information. He/she might look at paintings of the period, reproductions of catalogues, cookbooks, diaries, museum displays, or old magazines. The student would look for similarities and variations and draw conclusions from the data.

Good historical research starts with a question rather than a topic. The question gives structure to the research, constantly reminding the student about his/her purpose. Research questions vary in level of sophistication, with some more finely tuned than others. Most middle and high school students can draw conclusions about how life in the colonies differed from life today. A more able or experienced student researcher can choose a more focused research question, such as "How did life in the New England colonies differ from that of the middle Atlantic colonies?" or "How was the life of indentured servants different from that of slaves during the colonial period?" Regardless of the level of specificity or sophistication of the research question, the difference between historical research that uses primary sources and research reports based on secondary sources is that of transformation. Students conducting historical research make inferences, look for patterns, and draw conclusions from their data, rather than simply summarizing it. They also analyze the data for validity and reliability, are conscious of the difference between fact and inference, and are ever cognizant of the tentative nature of their conclusions.

In order to analyze primary sources, students must be able to discern possible motives, limitations, and biases inherent in primary sources and ascertain the degree to which they may limit the data. While an eyewitness is more likely to have an accurate perception of an event than someone once or twice removed from the event, all eyewitness accounts are not accurate, complete, or even truthful.

Is the clothing in the 1895 Bloomingdale's Catalog representative of the clothing worn by most people at that time? (Do most people wear clothing from Bloomingdale's today?) If there are differences between late 1800s catalogs from Bloomingdale's and Montgomery Ward, how might you explain those differences? The analysis involved in historical research is an outstanding opportunity to practice careful critical thinking.

Students conducting historical research can access a wide variety of sources. They can check with local and university libraries, archives, historical societies, museums, and other historical resources. Some museums have traveling boxes or suitcases with artifacts from a particular historical period that they loan or rent to schools. Several publishers also specialize in reproductions of original source documents (see item 9 below). Consider the following sources of historical information:

1. *Works of Art*—Look for reproductions, slides from museums, art books, or secondary sources that may reproduce original art works as illustrations.
2. *Magazines*—Many public libraries have periodicals dating into the nineteenth century, either in a back room or on microfilm. Don't hesitate to ask the librarian for assistance.
3. *Newspapers*—Microfilmed newspapers are even more common than other types of periodicals. Newspapers are valuable for more than their headlines. They are excellent sources of information about sports, weather, fashion, editorial cartoons, advertisements, or even the history of journalism.
4. *Books*—Don't hesitate to ask your librarian for assistance in locating originals or reproductions of books from the time period being studied. Reading about the changes in textbooks or school procedures is just not the same as reading the textbooks themselves. Museum stores, library sales, and used book stores can also serve as sources, frequently at minimal expense.
5. *Music*—Song lyrics from a particular period of history can provide valuable insights into the attitudes, activities, and concerns of the time. Along with song books from particular historical periods, music teachers or Arts in Education personnel may have recordings or sheet music or know where they can be found.
6. *Interviews and Surveys*—Few things students do in school can have as much long lasting value as preserving the written and oral history of their community. Older community members can provide information and insights unavailable through any other means. Added benefits include greater communication between generations and a validation of the knowledge and contributions of community members.
7. *Diaries and Journals*—Either family journals or reproductions available in libraries provide information on everyday life seldom found in history texts. Diarists comment both on the big events going on at the time (e.g., Civil War) and everyday life, allowing students to see a more personal view of big events, as well as their impact on people.
8. *Household Items and Other Artifacts*—Family collections, grandparents' attics, estate sales, or local museums can provide artifacts from which young historians can draw conclusions. **The Historical Supply Catalog** describes many items from earlier time periods that are being reproduced today, along with the companies from which you can order them and the prices.
9. *Historical Documents and Other Primary Source Materials*

   Teaching With Documents and other publications of the National Archives Trust Fund (NEDC Dept. 310, P.O. Box 100793, Atlanta, GA 30384; (800) 788-6282) include reproductions of historical documents, photographs, posters, political cartoons, letters, maps, interviews, diaries, federal population census, etc.

   Jackdaws are sets of reproductions of primary source materials (diaries, letters, telegrams, newspaper articles, maps, documents, etc.) related to various topics in U.S. and world history. Each portfolio includes historians' narratives about the topics and transcripts of hard-to-read material along with eight to eighteen primary source reproductions. These are available for purchase from Jackdaw Publications, P. O. Box 503, Amawalk, NY 10501-0503; (800) 789-0022; FAX (800) 962-9101.

Dover Publications, Inc. (31 East 2nd Street, Mineola, NY 11501) lists over 5,800 books in all fields, many of which are reproductions of historical materials such as old postcards of major cities, prints, posters, books of photographs, old catalogs, first-hand accounts of historical events, and thrift editions of classic fiction, nonfiction, plays, and poetry, etc., all at quite reasonable prices.

While it may seem overwhelming to locate primary source materials for individual investigations or class projects, the benefits to students of this kind of historical research are unique. Aside from the obvious benefits of exercising critical thinking, analysis, synthesis, evaluation and gaining familiarity with a variety of types of materials, this method of research brings history to life. Students who have been touched by the words, sounds, and images of real people from long ago, considered those peoples' lives and points of view, and drawn conclusions from those lives form links with the stories of history that are not forged in other ways. This power to touch the reality of history makes historical research a vital tool to consider, especially for teachers who are responsible for teaching world and U.S. history. Educators can collect materials from their local libraries, museums, historical societies, flea markets, estate sales, and used book stores. Even if they only buy a little bit each year, soon their personal or school collections will grow. Parents and community members are also great resources. They may be glad to donate historical items as they clean out their basements and attics.

Collections of historical materials can be quite flexible, serving as resources for a wide variety of research questions. A collection of maps, family photographs, first-hand accounts, reproductions of historical documents, songs, and a few family histories would allow students to investigate a variety of questions related to immigration.

- How were the experiences of Irish and Italian immigrants similar and different?
- Did any immigrants return to their native land soon after coming to America? If so, which ones and why?
- What was life like for immigrants after they arrived in the U.S.?
- How did U.S. citizens feel about the immigrants who arrived in the early 1900s?
- How does that compare to the feelings of current citizens about immigration today?

An 8th grade teacher of American history may want to acquire a few old **Life** magazines, copies of newspapers, and recordings of contemporary music (e.g., "Good-bye Mama, I'm Off to Yokohama") to add to a unit on World War II. These materials could lead to a class investigation of news coverage point of view or a study comparing music written about World War II and the Vietnam conflict. In each case, students are able to experience the thrill of wandering in the world of the past, investigating like bona-fide historians.

Be aware that historical research is not just for the history teacher. Each discipline deals with topics and concepts that have a history. The following section contains suggestions for historical research activities that may be carried out by individuals or groups in a variety of disciplines. Be sure to add your own ideas to our list of historical research questions.

HISTORICAL RESEARCH EXAMPLES

General

1. *How is 7th grade today different than when my parents were in school?*
2. *In what ways has this school changed since it was built?*
3. *What stores were on Main Street 25 years ago?*
4. *What have been the most popular girls' names over the last 50 years?*
5. *How have children's school clothes changed since my parents were in 8th grade?*
6. *What did my parents eat for lunch in 6th grade?*
7. *In what extracurricular activities did my parents participate in high school?*
8. *How is being a teenager now different than it was for my parents? My grandparents?*

Science

1. *How has the use of technology changed (a particular career) over the last 50 years?*
2. *How have diseases and medical care in our community changed over the last 100 years?*
3. *How has technology affected the development of weapons over the last century?*

4. *How have life-styles (eating patterns, jobs, exercise, recreation, etc.) changed over the last 50 years? How are these changes related to length of life and cause of death?*
5. *How has the power of scientists in American society (or governmental decisions) changed over the last 75 years?*
6. *What was the most common cause of death recorded in the local cemetery between 1850 and 1900?*

Social Studies

1. *What is the genealogy of my family for the last several generations? (Issues of privacy make it essential that this be an optional activity.)*
2. *How have jobs of members of my family changed in the last three generations?*
3. *How have race relations changed in this community over the last 50 years?*
4. *How have people's attitudes with respect to the Vietnam War changed over the last 25 years?*
5. *How has the power of the President changed in the last 100 years?*
6. *What happened in this town during WW II (or any other era)?*
7. *How have crime and law enforcement changed in this community in the last 100 years?*

Language Arts

1. *Was Francis Bacon the real author of the works of William Shakespeare?*
2. *How have the characteristics of heroes in movies changed over the last 40 years?*
3. *How has adolescent literature changed over the last 50 years?*
4. *How have portrayals of African Americans in literature changed since 1850?*
5. *What are the differences in the ways power is portrayed in 19th and 20th century literature?*
6. *What legends have been told about this community?*

Mathematics

1. *How has the population of this community changed over the last 50 years?*
2. *How have the prices of books changed over the last 50 years?*
3. *How have the salaries of professional baseball players changed over the last 75 years?*
4. *How has the power of computers and calculators changed over the last 50 years?*
5. *How has the percentage of the national budget devoted to defense changed over the last 100 years?*

Art and Music

1. *What role has music/art played in political movements since 1900?*
2. *What are the origins of heavy metal music?*
3. *How has classical music changed over the last 300 years?*
4. *How have changes in technology affected various art/music forms over the last 50 years?*
5. *How have standards for powerful art or musical works changed over the last 100 years?*
6. *What kind of music was popular when my grandparents were teenagers?*
7. *What crafts have been practiced in this area?*

Foreign Language

1. *What influence has the English language had on (foreign language) over the last 50 years?*
2. *How has the number of people speaking Spanish in the U.S. changed over the last 100 years?*
3. *How has Hispanic culture affected life in the United States over the last 50 years?*
4. *How has the rate of assimilation (characterized by learning to speak English) changed for U.S. immigrants over the last century?*
5. *How has the power of different cultures in the world changed over time and how have those changes affected the languages spoken by people?*

Historical Research Activity 1

Adolescence Across the Generations *

Have you ever wondered whether your grandparents spent their out-of-school time the same way you do when they were your age? This activity will give you the opportunity to find out and perhaps learn some more about how their lives were similar to and different from yours. You will need to write a letter to one of your grandparents or to someone who is about the same age as your grandparents. If you cannot write to your grandparents, your parents or teacher will help you find someone to write to. Write a letter asking them what kinds of things they did after school when they were your age. Be sure to tell them that this is a school project. You should enclose a self-addressed stamped envelope to help them write back quickly. When your class gets the letters back, you can compile your data by making a graph of all the things peoples' grandparents did after school.

The letter below is a model for such a letter, but don't feel that you have to copy it. Be yourself! Be sure to include these main parts:

1. Date
2. Greeting (Dear __________,)
3. Body of the letter (where you ask them to please tell you about their after school activities)
4. Closing (Love, or Sincerely,)
5. Your name

Sample Letter

January 15, 1998

Dear Grandma,

I am doing a research project for school to find out what kinds of things our grandparents did after school when they were in 9th grade. Could you please write back and tell me what activities you did? These might include chores, work, homework, reading, playing board games . . . whatever you and your friends did when you were my age. Thanks for helping me learn what life was like when you were my age.

Love,

Emily

If you have a chance to talk to your grandparents, you may want to ask them other questions about their activities. What else would you like to know?

**Adapted from a lesson by Clara Gerlach.*

(continued on next page)

Historical Research Activity 1

Use a line, bar, or circle graph to show the results of your class survey of grandparents' activities.

You might also want to check the generation between you and your grandparents by asking your parents about their school and after-school experiences. How is being in your grade today different than when your parents were in school?

Interview your parent or other adults their age to find out. What would you like to know about your parents' school?

About what they studied?

About extracurricular activities that were available?

About what happened to students who misbehaved?

About issues that concerned the students?

(continued on next page)

Historical Research Activity 1

Brainstorm (alone or with a partner) at least ten questions you could ask, then choose the three you are most interested in and write them on the lines below. You may want to ask the same questions as other students in your class so that you can get a broader picture of the times by gathering data from a larger number of subjects who probably attended different schools. Compare answers to find similarities and differences.

QUESTION: ____

ANSWER: ____

____

QUESTION: ____

ANSWER: ____

____

QUESTION: ____

ANSWER: ____

____

How else could you find out what it was like to be in your grade when your parents were in school?

You might look at old school photographs, yearbooks, or report cards. Maybe you could talk to their teachers. What else could you do to find out?

Historical Research Activity 2

Eyewitness to History

Have you ever wondered what it would have been like to have lived during the time of the American Revolution or crossed the plains in a covered wagon? If you want to know how it felt to be part of those events, you have to rely on diaries, letters, and other artifacts those people left behind. Fortunately, witnesses of many major historical events are still alive today and can provide important insights into recent history. In this study, you will pick one historical event and interview three to five individuals who remember that event. Using qualitative data analysis, you can examine themes in the interviews to help you understand the impact of the event.

Procedure:

1. Select a recent historical event that interests you. You may choose one from the following list or another event you'd like to study. Perhaps there was an event in your local area that was important to the community, for example, the flooding in the Midwest in 1993. It will be easiest to find subjects if you choose an event that happened no more than 50 years ago. You might want to study:
    - *The Assassination of John F. Kennedy or Martin Luther King, Jr.*
    - *The First Moon Landing*
    - *The End of World War II*
    - *The Gulf War*
    - *The Fall of the Berlin Wall*
    - *The March on Washington or the Civil Rights Movement*
    - *The Challenger Explosion*
    - *Protests of the Vietnam War*
    - *The Million Man March*
    - *A Particular Election*
2. Identify three to five individuals who can remember the event. If the event is recent enough, you will need to decide whether you want to interview individuals who were children at the time of the event or those who were adults. Your family, teachers, and neighbors may help you find subjects. If necessary, you may run an ad in the school paper explaining your project and asking for help.
3. Decide on questions for your interview. You might consider questions such as:
    - *Where were you during (the event)?*
    - *What were you doing?*
    - *How old were you?*
    - *How did (the event) affect you?*
    - *What did you think about it at the time?*
    - *How did (the event) affect the people around you?*
    - *What do you think about (the event) today?*
4. Make appointments to interview each subject. Be sure to be neat, prompt, and prepared for each interview. You probably will want to tape record the interviews. Be sure your recorder is operating properly before you set out and obtain the subject's permission before recording. (A sample permission form is found in Chapter 4.)

(continued on next page)

Historical Research Activity 2

5. Transcribe your interviews, if possible. Transcribing involves writing or word-processing exactly what the person said during the interview. You do this by listening to as much of the tape recording as you can remember, then typing exactly what is said. Start with a phrase or sentence. If a phrase is too long to remember accurately, choose a shorter amount. Once you have written or typed it exactly as the person said it, listen to another sentence or phrase and write it down verbatim (word for word). As you can imagine, this takes a lot of time, but it is important that you transcribe your interview accurately. It will be much easier to look for themes if the interviews are in written form. If the interview is not long, we encourage you to transcribe it. You don't have to transcribe the whole interview in one sitting.
6. Look for themes and trends in your interviews. How were the individuals' experiences similar?

How were they different?

Can you see any patterns in the similarities and differences?

If another student studies the same event, your data will be even richer. What can you learn from this data?

What questions does it raise?

Historical Research Activity 3

Teachers in the Late 1800s

Before reading the letter that is part of this activity, take a few minutes to think about what you think life is like for your teachers. What do you think they do when they aren't in school?

How much time do you think they spend doing work for school?

Where do you think they live?

What do you think their family lives are like?

In what community activities might they be involved?

You might want to ask a few of your teachers if they are willing to be interviewed. Be sure to let them know that it's fine with you if they don't want to answer some questions you ask.

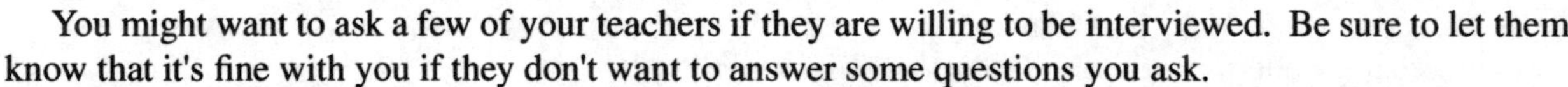

Think about what the teachers told you or your hypotheses about their lives outside of school. Now think about what you know about the late 1800s in America. What is different about life then and now?

Think particularly about what school was like back then, what kinds of people became teachers, and what you think their lives were like. List some of your hypotheses below about their lives outside the classroom, considering some of the same questions you considered for your current teachers.

On the next page is a transcription of a letter written by a teacher in 1889. The spelling and punctuation are transcribed as closely as possible from the original, which is faded and in some places hard to read. Use the Document Analysis Form (found in Chapter 4, Figure 4.3) to make observations about the document and hypotheses about the life of a teacher at that time. You may want to examine other primary source documents from the period to support your hypotheses. Possible sources might include letters or diaries written by teachers or textbooks written for teachers during the time period. After you've read the letter answer the following questions:

(continued on next page)

Historical Research Activity 3

Which of your hypotheses were confirmed by this letter?

What ideas did the letter suggest that you might want to add to your list about what life was like for teachers in the late 1800s?

How could you find out if this teacher's experiences were typical of most teachers at that time?

What other sources could you consult?

Feb.12.1889

Dear father & mother,

Thought I would make a change this week and write to you instead of Kitt. Everything is going on splendid and its the wonder of the nineteenth century that there could ever be a teacher who gave satisfaction to all everybody is talking about it, the Supervisor came up the other day to bring me some books; he came down to the agents and told him this was the best school in Jonesport, he praised it some to me and told me that Grace Crandon was having trouble in her school down to Kelleys Pt. Mr. Cummings said he wouldn't hesitate to give me any school in this town. Lots of the scholars from the other Dist. wanted to come down here but Mr. Cummings was afraid they might disturb the school that's what he told Mr. Dow but - I said he had nothing to say about it so they concluded to let them come but - they can't agree about the tuition thought it was to high but Eddie Farnsworth said he would come if he had to pay ten dollars so he is here. You remember Eddie don't you father; that red-haired, stout boy dressed in blue you used to meet last fall. The folks down here go nearly wild over my watch they never saw anything half as cunning and she keeps splendid time doesn't gain more than two minutes a week but - my ring I'm afraid is coming apart - when I come up home don't say anything about my buying it myself for I have lots of fun over it. We have had what you may call a snow storm today first one of the season about six inches has come. Mr. Down came and brought my leggings up to the school house and just as school was up Patten Down drove up with his sleds so we didn't get wet a bit I guess it has stopped snowing now. I go to every meeting and round to the houses and play Authors and other simple games and don't dare mention cards but wouldn't I like to have a good game of cards one night at the Circle some of the boys and girls had a pack of cards and played it almost drove me crazy but I didn't dare look towards them for all eyes are on me and that pack of cards has been the town talk ever since. Well this is the seventh week of school only five more and I shall be at home. If I mention going home now about three dozen will say I want to go with you if you will let me, they want to see where I live. I'm having full better times than I did last winter. Maria says where she boards there are three in the rooms and the vacant place is just for me and I ought to be there to fill it says she don't have as good times as we did in R.H. Mrs. Don's little boy looks like Wayne and keeps around me all the time Sunday morning she got up quite early and took him and came and got in bed with Lula and I we had fun for a while we have breakfast every morning at eight except Mon. morning when we get up at five.

Historical Research Activity 4

Commencement Programs

High school commencement is an important event in many people's lives. In this study, you will examine how commencements have changed or not changed from 1919 until today.

At the end of these directions, you will find a commencement program from Hampden Academy's Class of 1919 as well as the title page and table of contents from a guidebook entitled "What to Do Commencement Week." It was published in 1922.

Compare Hampden Academy's program with a recent commencement program from your high school. What similarities and differences do you notice?

Examine the table of contents of "What to Do Commencement Week." Make hypotheses about what might have occurred during a commencement week in 1922.

Using interviews and document analysis, try to find out how commencements at your high school have changed. It probably will be hard to find someone who graduated from your high school in 1919 or 1922, but you may be able to interview past graduates from 30, 40, or even 50 years ago. Perhaps your school district has copies of commencement programs. You might find old programs in the scrapbooks of relatives or neighbors. Using multiple sources of evidence such as interviews and documents is called triangulation. If you find the same thing in multiple sources, you can be more sure that it is accurate. For example, if you interview someone about a graduation held 30 years ago and you also find a commencement program from that year, you can check to see if they say the same things. If not, you will need to consider why they might differ.

You might even want to try to find a copy of "What to Do Commencement Week" or a similar guidebook from another time period. We found our copy at a used book store. Perhaps you can find something similar in your home town.

Information about past graduations might make an interesting display for commencement. You might even discover a past tradition you want to revive!

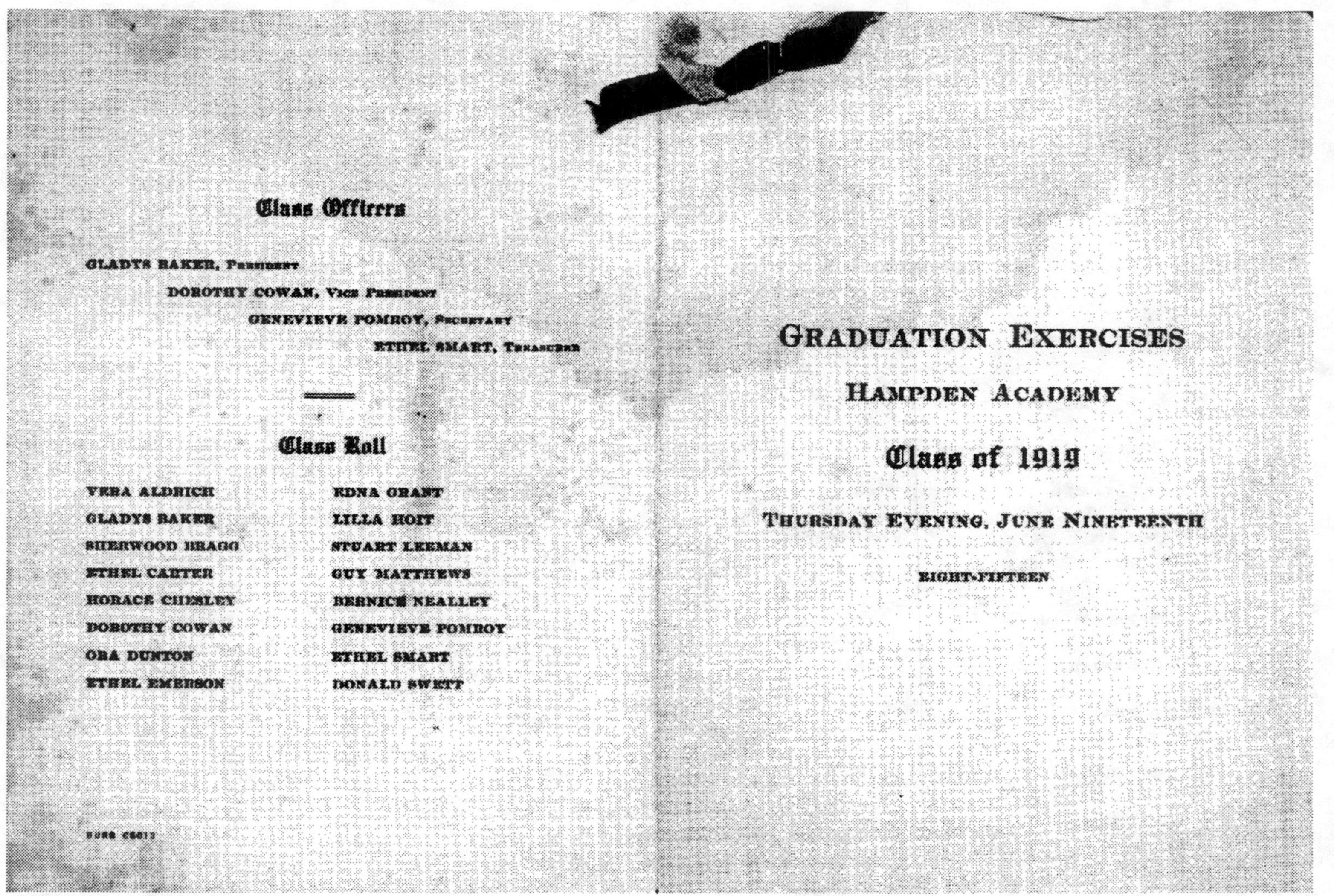

Class Officers

GLADYS BAKER, President
DOROTHY COWAN, Vice President
GENEVIEVE POMROY, Secretary
ETHEL SMART, Treasurer

Class Roll

VERA ALDRICH	EDNA GRANT
GLADYS BAKER	LILLA HOIT
SHERWOOD BRAGG	STUART LEEMAN
ETHEL CARTER	GUY MATTHEWS
HORACE CHESLEY	BERNICE NEALLEY
DOROTHY COWAN	GENEVIEVE POMROY
ORA DUNTON	ETHEL SMART
ETHEL EMERSON	DONALD SWETT

GRADUATION EXERCISES

HAMPDEN ACADEMY

Class of 1919

THURSDAY EVENING, JUNE NINETEENTH

EIGHT-FIFTEEN

(*figure continues*)

Figure 3.1. Commencement program from Hampden Academy's class of 1919.

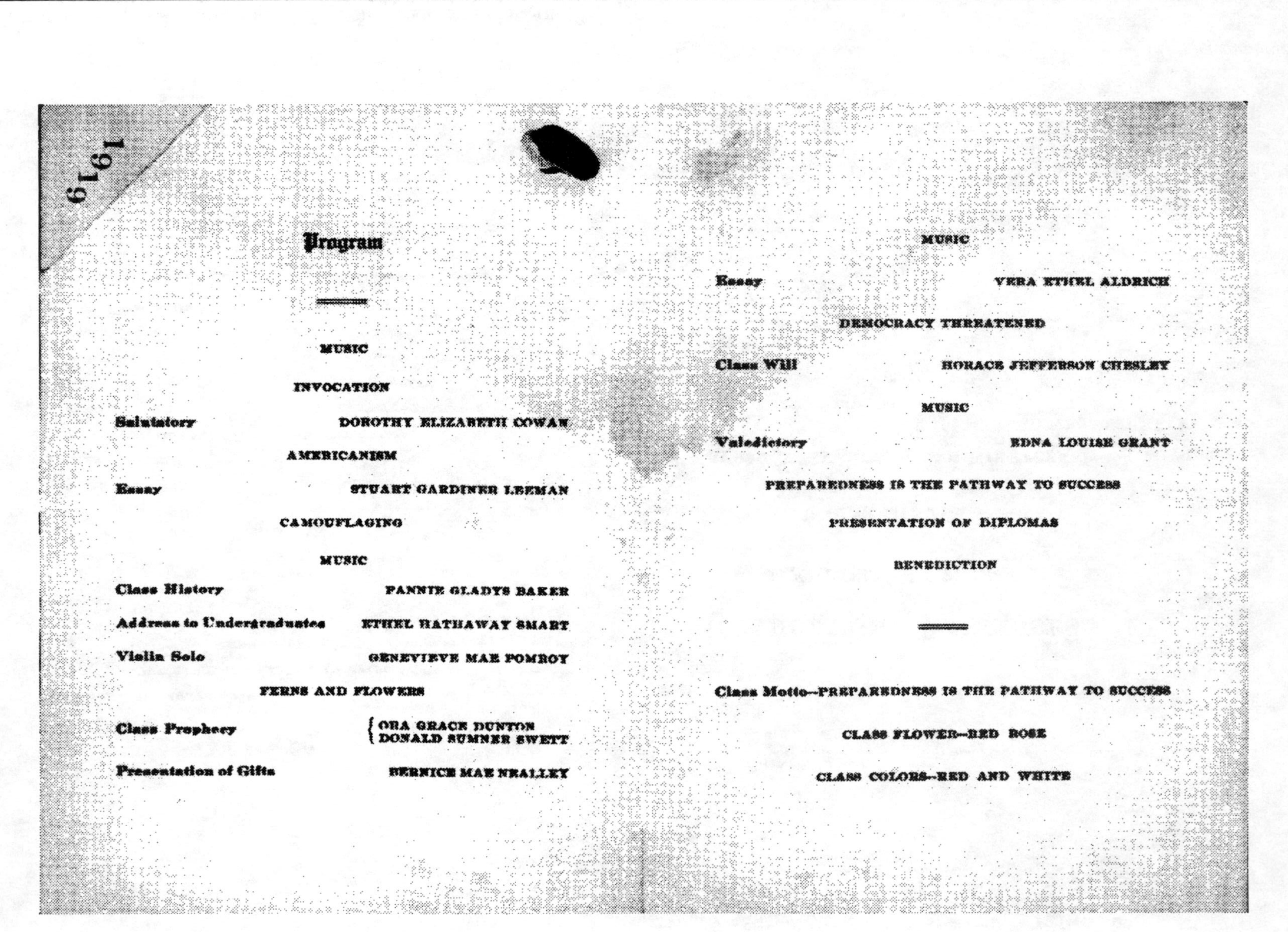

1919

Program

MUSIC

INVOCATION

Salutatory — DOROTHY ELIZABETH COWAN

AMERICANISM

Essay — STUART GARDINER LEEMAN

CAMOUFLAGING

MUSIC

Class History — FANNIE GLADYS BAKER

Address to Undergraduates — ETHEL HATHAWAY SMART

Violin Solo — GENEVIEVE MAE POMROY

FERNS AND FLOWERS

Class Prophecy — ORA GRACE DUNTON, DONALD SUMNER SWETT

Presentation of Gifts — BERNICE MAE NEALLEY

MUSIC

Essay — VERA ETHEL ALDRICH

DEMOCRACY THREATENED

Class Will — HORACE JEFFERSON CHESLEY

MUSIC

Valedictory — EDNA LOUISE GRANT

PREPAREDNESS IS THE PATHWAY TO SUCCESS

PRESENTATION OF DIPLOMAS

BENEDICTION

Class Motto--PREPAREDNESS IS THE PATHWAY TO SUCCESS

CLASS FLOWER--RED ROSE

CLASS COLORS--RED AND WHITE

Figure 3.1. Commencement program from Hampden Academy's class of 1919 (*continued*).

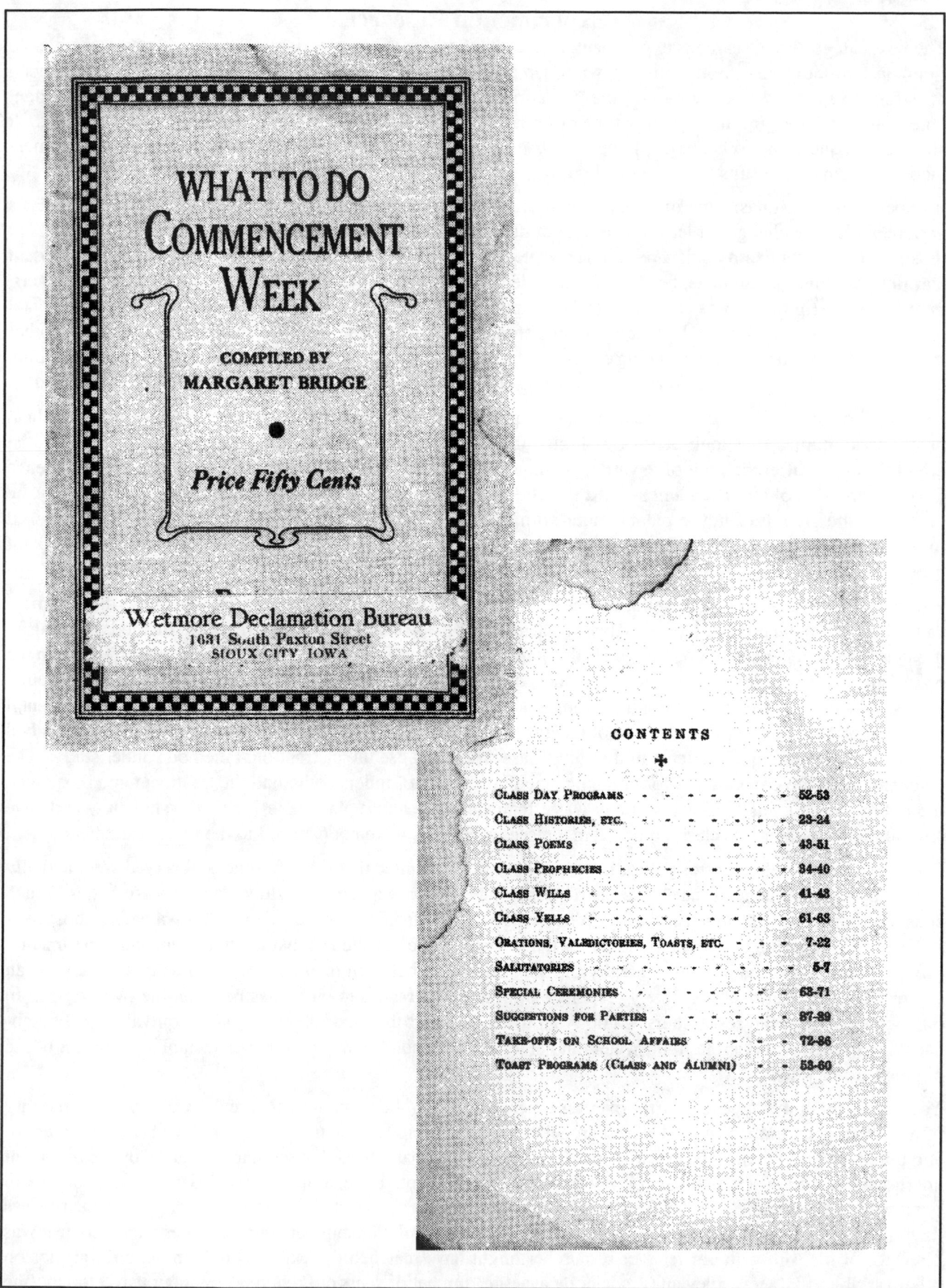

WHAT TO DO COMMENCEMENT WEEK

COMPILED BY MARGARET BRIDGE

Price Fifty Cents

Wetmore Declamation Bureau
1031 South Paxton Street
SIOUX CITY IOWA

CONTENTS

Figure 3.2. Sample pages from "What To Do Commencement Week."

Experimental Research

The next category of research is experimental research. Your image of experimental research may resemble old Frankenstein movies, with men in long white lab coats, surrounded by bubbling beakers and test tubes giving off strange vapors. While the movies may have made fun of it, true experimental research is a very important type of research design. It is the only type of research design that can investigate cause-effect relationships. It answers the question, "What would happen if . . . " by exposing experimental groups to some type of treatment then comparing the results with a control group.

In experimental and quasi-experimental research, unlike other types of research designs, the researcher manipulates variables. He/she changes at least one aspect of the situation being studied in order to determine the effects of those changes. For example, if a researcher wanted to know if a particular teaching strategy increased student learning of a foreign language, he/she must be able to use that strategy with some students and not with others, in order to determine if it was effective. This manipulation of variables is called the treatment. All experimental research involves a treatment, be that a teaching strategy, medicine, type of light, change in procedure, or other intervention. The key to understanding experimental research is to know that the researcher is not just describing a situation, but changing it in order to see what results from the intervention.

Examples of true experimental research include studies of drugs, new types of operations, or other medical procedures; studies that look at various kinds of lawn or plant fertilizer; and research that focuses on the effectiveness of different kinds of rewards for employees. You often see experimental research studies in science fairs. In one school fair, a student studied the effects of music on plant growth. In this experimental study, he compared the growth of house plants under normal classroom conditions with that of similar plants exposed to music several hours a day. The student was testing the treatment (music) to determine if it affected plant growth.

For experimental research to be valid, the researcher needs to be able to explain how he/she knows the treatment caused the particular effects. How can the French teacher be sure it was the new instructional methods that caused greater fluency in her students? How does the student know that it was the music that made the difference in the plants' growth? Experimental research is uniquely designed to answer these hard questions and it does this through the use of a control group. The control group is similar to the group receiving the treatment (the experimental group) in all ways except that it does not receive the treatment. In the foreign language experiment described above, a control group of students in the same class would not use the instructional methods under study. The teacher could then compare the foreign language fluency of the students who had the treatment and those who did not to see if the instructional strategy was effective. In the house plant experiment, the student would have similar plants in the same classroom, but in a place where they were not exposed to the music treatment.

Even the presence of a control group, however, does not guarantee that the differences observed were actually caused by the treatment. What if the instructional intervention was given to students who were better French speakers than those in the control group? What if the plants far from the music received less water than those near it? Effective experimental research demands that variables be controlled so that the treatment and experimental groups are as similar as possible. Ideally the only difference between the two is the treatment so that you can be sure that the treatment was likely responsible for any differences in outcomes between the two groups. In our two examples, the researchers would want to be sure that the student groups were equivalent in French-speaking ability, and that the light, water, and other growing conditions of the experimental and control house plants were identical.

You would think this type of control over an experiment would be enough to ensure the validity and reliability of an experiment, but it is not. The researcher can only consciously control those variables he/she is aware of and thinks might influence the experiment. It is still possible that effects that seem to be caused by the treatment are instead caused by a variable that is not part of the experiment. For example, what if extroverts respond more positively to the treatment in the French class and the experimental group has a much larger group of extroverts than the control group? No one hypothesized or noticed this relationship between variables, so no control was planned for it. Although our teacher-researcher might have matched the experimental and control groups on other variables that seem relevant (grade point average, number of years of French taken previously, etc.), he/she hasn't considered extroversion/introversion. It may appear that the instructional intervention was effective if the experimental group has higher fluency, when it really had to do with the number of extroverts in the group and not the treatment at all.

Because there is always the possibility of outside, unknown variables affecting the results of an experiment, it is necessary to find some way to control for them, i.e., random selection. When a researcher selects subjects for the treatment and control groups, each subject has an equal chance of being selected for either group. While it is still possible that many more extroverts will end up in one group when random selection is used, the laws of probability make that very unlikely. Random selection can be as simple as pulling names out of a hat or as sophisticated as computer generated randomization, as long as each subject has an equal chance of being selected for either group. Chapter 5 describes several ways to select subjects, but random selection is the only method that can be used in a true experiment. Indeed, random selection is a key part of what makes something a true experiment. There are many times when it is not possible to use random selection, especially for research in schools that would not appreciate classes being disrupted and rearranged to accommodate random selection of students for treatment and control groups. Where random selection is impossible, you can use other methods. If all other characteristics of the research are similar to the true experimental design besides random selection, the form of research is called quasi-experimental. As you can imagine, much educational research uses a quasi-experimental design.

It looks like experimental research is complex and difficult. However, middle and high school students should be able to conduct experiments of varying levels of sophistication with teacher guidance. One of the more interesting examples in our experience involved a 5th grader in a gifted program. As she entered the room, Amy commented that her mom was acting silly. When the teacher asked why, she replied that her mom had put gelatin and water on the house plants. When asked how the plants looked, she said fine. The teacher wondered aloud if maybe her mom had stumbled onto something and asked if Amy wanted to pursue it. With the teacher's assistance, Amy expressed her interest in the form of a research question, "Does gelatin improve the growth of plants?" They figured that as long as they were going to the trouble to set up an experiment, they might as well examine other additives. This particular experiment had three treatments (sugar, salt, gelatin) and two control conditions (plain water, no water).

In order to start, they first needed to operationalize the variables, which meant deciding what exactly the variables meant. In the research question "Do additives improve the growth of plants?" what terms needed to be defined?

Additives—Amy started with gelatin, what her mother was using, and decided to try sugar and salt as well. She could have chosen any other additives if she thought they might affect plant growth. Do you think the amount of additive in the water would matter? She tried it with three different strengths of solution to find out.

Growth—How could Amy measure growth? She looked at two measures of growth—how many seeds germinated and how tall the plants grew.

Plants—There are many different kinds of plants and the effect might be different depending on the kind Amy used. In this experiment Amy only had time to use one kind of plant, so the results only really applied to that plant. She chose rye seeds after a quite smelly pilot study trying to germinate lima beans.

What Amy did was operationalize the variables. Amy and her teacher agreed to let rye seeds equal *plant,* three different strengths of gelatin, sugar, and salt solutions equal *additive,* and height and number of seeds germinated equal *growth* for the purposes of this experiment. If they had chosen different additives, different kinds of plants, or number of leaves grown to stand for the variables, those representations of the variables would have been okay, too. It's just that when you do an experiment, you have to decide ahead of time what will represent or stand for the variables in your research question. You also have to remember that your results apply only to the specific variables in your experiment, though you can make qualified generalizations if you have operationalized your variables fairly.

The final research question was "Do more rye seeds germinate and do they grow taller with plain water, sugar water, salt water, gelatin and water, or no water?"

To control all other variables, the rye seeds were chosen randomly for treatment and control groups, all were planted in similar trays with the same growing medium and placed in the same location to control for type and amount of light. They also made sure that the percentage of additive for each treatment solution was the same (5, 10, and 20% for each treatment).

Amy carried out this experiment over the course of about three weeks with the assistance of another student who helped her count, measure, and graph the number of seeds that germinated in each tray and the plants' height twice a week. At the end of the experiment, Amy was forced to acknowledge that her mom wasn't crazy, but her mother wasn't totally vindicated, either. Both the sugar and gelatin additives resulted in the best growth, followed by plain water. As she hypothesized, salt water was not terribly effective, and the seeds that were not watered never germinated.

Amy's research was a true experiment. Three treatments (gelatin water, sugar water, salt water) were applied to experimental groups and were compared to two randomly selected control groups. One developmentally appropriate way to help students understand why the conditions for a true experiment are necessary is the idea of fairness. Adolescents can relate to the need for conditions to be fair in an experiment, which in Amy's case meant that all the plants needed to have an equal chance to grow. The research term for keeping a level playing field is "controlling variables," which is necessary so all groups are equal in every way except the treatment.

Experimental research can be planned using several different research designs. Here we will only deal with the two we feel are the most powerful and appropriate for middle and high school students, the post-test only control group design and the Pre-test/post-test control group design. These designs are diagrammed in Figure 3.3.

In the post-test only control group design, the researcher compares the results of a treatment on both an experimental and control group, both of which have been chosen using random selection. This design is most appropriate for studies in which a researcher cannot assess the groups before the treatment or when a pre-assessment might affect the treatment. For example, Amy's study, which described the effects of different solutions on the growth of rye seeds, used a post-test only control group design. Since all plants started as seeds, it would have been impossible to evaluate their growth before the experiment began.

In other cases, merely giving a pre-test might affect the way a treatment works. For example, if a researcher wanted to investigate the effects of a particular treatment on gender stereotyping, he or she might be concerned that any type of pre-test evaluating such stereotypes might affect the way the treatment worked. Perhaps merely taking the pre-test might cause subjects to start thinking about the issue of stereotyping and would make the treatment more effective than it would be for a group that had not taken the Pre-test. In such a case, it would be best to use a post-test only. If the experimental and control groups were randomly selected and are large enough, it can be assumed that they were equivalent before treatment.

The other design, the pre-test/post-test control group design, also uses randomly selected experimental and control groups, but assesses both groups before and after treatment. This design is frequently used in quasi-experimental designs, in which random assignment is impossible. If you want to know for sure that the treatment and control groups were not different, a pre-test will allow you to show this. You might also want to examine the degree of change that results from your treatment. In that case, you would need pre-test scores in order to compute the difference between those scores and post-test scores. Like many recent changes in assessment, Pre-tests and post-

Experimental Designs

Post-test Only Control Design

Experimental Group	Treatment - - - - - - - - - - - >	Post-test
Control Group		Post-test

Pre-test Post-test Control Design

Experimental Group	Pre-test - - - - - - - - > Treatment - - - - - - - >	Post-test
Control Group	Pre-test ->	Post-test

Figure 3.3. Experimental designs.

tests don't have to be written tests. For example, imagine that a 6th grade student wanted to investigate whether studying a unit on women in sports affected the number of girls playing extracurricular sports. The student might count the number of girls playing sports from the class that had the unit and compare that to girls from another class at the same grade level. In this study, it would be very important to have counted the number of girls from each class who went out for sports teams before the treatment began. Otherwise, it would be impossible to tell if any differences observed came from the treatment or a previously sports-minded class.

Before ending this section, it is important to discuss research ethics. In many other types of research designs the researcher merely records and/or analyzes events or data. In experimental research he/she manipulates variables, which introduces an ethical dimension. While middle and high school students won't face the dilemma of medical researchers deciding to give or withhold experimental drugs, they do need to be aware of the possible effects, both physical and psychological, on their research subjects. Obviously human subjects should never be involved in any school experiment in which there is the slightest possibility of physical or psychological harm. It is also essential that animal subjects be treated humanely and protected from danger or injury. If it is necessary to raise animals in less than optimal conditions, as in experiments on diet and nutrition, such studies should be brief and all animals returned to optimal conditions as quickly as possible.

If a study being considered might diminish the quality of life of any living thing, encourage the student to carefully consider whether primary data is truly necessary. If they are committed to knowing the answer to the question, it may be available in secondary sources. If their commitment is more toward conducting an experiment, perhaps they can be helped to find one that will not jeopardize living things. There has been more and more public pressure for commercial and medical researchers to limit animal research to essential investigations. Novice researchers should be encouraged to do the same. As important as we believe it is that students become real researchers, we would never want to see data gathering occurring at the expense of ethical considerations. Also, most adult researchers must have their research design approved by a committee that considers the ethical dimensions of the plan before they can begin. Having the teacher screen research designs for ethical implications does replicate the real-world conditions of research scientists.

Below you will find a list of activities and suggestions for experimental research.

EXPERIMENTAL RESEARCH EXAMPLES

General

1. *Which of three programs is most effective in changing students' attitudes toward substance abuse?*
2. *Does clothing worn affect the attitude and behavior of those with whom a person interacts?*
3. *Does listening to music while doing schoolwork affect the quality of the work done?*
4. *Do students who study a little each day do better on tests than students who cram the night before?*
5. *Which is more effective in increasing student performance—an academic honor roll or an "On A Roll" that recognizes students who have brought their grades up?*

Science

1. *What is the effect of studying nutrition on 8th graders' snacking habits?*
2. *Do batteries stored in the freezer last longer than those stored at room temperature?*
3. *Do athletes who drink Gatorade® perform better than athletes who drink water?*
4. *Can students lower their blood pressure by receiving informational feedback?*
5. *What is the effect of increasing the number of coils on the power of an electromagnet?*
6. *What type of hydroponic solution is most effective in growing tomatoes?*
7. *What is the effect of disinfectant on bacteria growth on cafeteria tables?*
8. *What is the effect of color on taste tests?*

Social Studies

1. *What is the effect of conflict resolution training on the number of physical conflicts among students?*
2. *What is the effect of a multicultural training program on students' attitudes toward different racial and ethnic groups in the school?*

3. *What is the effect of job training programs on the length of time people receive public assistance (welfare)?*
4. *What are the effects of negative versus positive campaigning on election results?*
5. *What is the effect of in-home parent education programs for preschool children on their later school success?*

Language Arts

1. *What is the effect of one week without watching television on the number of books read by students in our school/class?*
2. *What is the effect of visualization training on elaboration and description in students' writing?*
3. *What is the effect of practice on students' comfort and competence in public speaking?*
4. *What is the effect on comprehension of matched conditions regarding auditory or visual learning?*
5. *What is the effect of increased descriptive language on the perceived power of introductory paragraphs?*

Mathematics

1. *What is the effect of using calculators on student success in mathematics?*
2. *What is the effect of using manipulatives on student success in mathematics?*
3. *What is the effect of instruction that differentiates for learning style on students self-concept related to mathematics?*
4. *What is the effect of cooperative learning on achievement and liking mathematics?*
5. *What is the effect of using* **Hands-On Equations®** *on learning algebra?*

Mathematics is used to quantify outcome variables in order to compare treatment group outcomes to control group outcomes. Topics/concepts/skills relevant to experimental research might include:

1. *Theory behind inferential statistics.*
2. *Statistics such as chi square and the t-test.*
3. *Normal curve.*
4. *Standard deviation.*

Art and Music

1. *Which artistic medium (or musical style) is most effective for communicating a particular emotion?*
2. *What is the effect of different kinds of music on people's moods?*
3. *Which works of art most improve students' opinions of the attractiveness of a classroom?*
4. *What type of music is most powerful in stimulating plant growth?*
5. *Are visual images or written communication more powerful ways to convince students to recycle?*

Foreign Language

1. *Do students who study vocabulary with a partner learn better than students who study alone?*
2. *Is memorizing dialogue, learning vocabulary and grammatical rules, or whole language more effective in learning a foreign language?*
3. *Do students who know one romance language learn another romance language more easily than those who do not know a romance language?*
4. *What is the effect of immersion on learning a foreign language?*
5. *Does learning a foreign language increase expressive power (ability) in one's native language?*

Experimental Research Activity 1

Memory Strategies . . . What Did You Say?

This experimental study will help you determine if a memory strategy helps subjects remember items on a list. You will need a minimum of 20 subjects, randomly divided into experimental and control groups. It will be important to keep the groups separate. You do not want the treatment group to hear the task given to the control group or vice versa. Think about why it is important to keep the groups separate. Follow the listed procedures for each group.

CONTROL GROUP

Make sure your control group is seated comfortably and that each subject has a pencil and paper. You may want to provide prenumbered answer sheets. Give directions clearly and make sure each person understands the directions before beginning the task.

Control Group Directions:

In this experiment we want to see how well students can remember items on a shopping list. I will read you a list of fifteen items. Try to remember as many of the items as you can. You may not make notes while I am speaking. Just use your memory. When I have completed the list, I will ask you to write down the items you can remember. Are there any questions?

Read the list below at the rate of about one item every five seconds. When you have completed the list, ask the subjects to write down as many items as they can remember.

- eggs
- shoelaces
- shampoo
- bird seed
- socks
- hot dog rolls
- a flower pot
- a comb
- peaches
- a pen
- a hanger
- a notebook
- a kite
- a stapler
- an airplane

TREATMENT GROUP

Your treatment group should be seated and provided with materials in a manner identical to that of the control group. Again, be sure to give directions clearly and make sure all the subjects understand them before proceeding.

Treatment Group Directions:

Today we are going to learn a memory strategy that can be useful in remembering lists. You might use this strategy to remember items to buy, errands to run, or even ideas for a test. After I have taught you the memory strategy, I will ask you to use the strategy to remember items on a shopping list.

(continued on next page)

Experimental Research Activity 1

For this memory strategy, you need to visualize your home or another place you know very well. Picture the path you would take to enter. Think about where you would go first, where you would walk next, and so forth. Try to picture each area as clearly as possible. Picture yourself walking through your whole home in a path you can remember. Picture yourself doing that now. [Wait about 30 seconds.]

Now, we will use that path to help you remember a list. The trick is to picture the things on the list in your home, right along the path you are walking. For example, if I have to remember to buy chocolate chips, bananas, and a baseball, I might picture chocolate chips scattered on my front porch, bananas, hanging from the door knob, and a baseball right inside the front door. If I had a longer list to remember, I could picture things in several rooms of my house. Let's practice this technique with a short list. I will read the list and you imagine yourself walking through your home, picturing each item in a different spot along the path. Here is the list. Try to picture each item clearly.

- *grape jelly*
- *a spoon*
- *a basketball*
- *a candy bar*
- *Band-Aids*

How did you picture these in your home? (Call on several subjects to describe the process. Explain the process again if necessary.)

This time we will use a longer list. There will be fifteen items, so you will need to picture yourself walking through several areas. Try to make the picture very clear. When I have finished the whole list, I will ask you to write down the items on the list. Do not write anything until I ask you to. Are there any questions?

Again, read the list at the rate of about one item every five seconds. When you have completed the list, ask the subjects to write down as many items as they can remember.

- eggs
- shoelaces
- shampoo
- bird seed
- socks
- hot dog rolls
- a flower pot
- a comb
- peaches
- a pen
- a hanger
- a notebook
- a kite
- a stapler
- an airplane

Compare the results of the treatment and control groups. How many items did each group remember?

(continued on next page)

Experimental Research Activity 1

Does the memory strategy appear to be effective?

You may want to use a *t*-test to find out if any differences you found were statistically significant (see Chapter 6 for more information).

**A Quasi-Experimental Variation

You could do a similar study using intact groups (such as two different classes) instead of randomly selected treatment and control groups. With pre-existing groups, you cannot assume that the groups were equal before the treatment. Describe how you would have to alter the experiment to control for possible group differences.

Experimental Research Activity 2

Increasing Your Vocabulary

Do you think studying vocabulary words with a partner would raise your score? Try this experiment to find out. You will need your teacher's cooperation. Follow each step carefully.

1. Divide the class randomly into two equal groups. You might put everyone's name in a hat and take turns pulling out names for Group One and Group Two in order to create a random sample.
2. Students in Group Two need a partner. Put all the Group Two names back in the hat and pull them out two at a time to see who will be partners. People in Group One do not need a partner.
3. Every day for one week, both groups should study either vocabulary words they don't already know or words in a foreign language for ten minutes. Students in Group One should study by themselves. Students in Group Two should study with their partners. Partners may quiz each other, read the words together, or do anything they can think of to help each other learn the words as long as they work actively together. This process is your treatment.
4. On Friday, everyone should take the test on the words. Partners are not allowed to help each other during the test.
5. Which group do you think will do better? Why?

You can graph the total number of words correct for each group to see which group scored highest. (Be sure the number of students in each group is equal. If not, randomly remove enough scores from the larger group to make the groups the same size before graphing.) You can also find the average score for each group and compare the two. To find the average, add all scores within a group, then divide by the number of scores. Do the same for the other group. Are they different? Use the *t*-test statistic explained in Chapter 6 to see if the difference is big enough to be significant, that is, likely to be related to the treatment rather than due to chance alone.

Experimental Research Activity 3

Does Studying Pay Off?

In this activity you'll gather data that could answer the question, "Does studying for a test help performance on the test?" What do you think?

You'll have to decide to carry out this quasi-experiment *before* your teacher begins instruction about a particular skill or topic because some of you will not be able to study for the quiz as part of the experiment.

NOTE TO TEACHERS: Let students know ahead of time that you will either not count this quiz toward the class grade or will allow the control group to study and retake the quiz for credit after the experiment is over. That should make the control group more willing to stick to their treatment condition of "no studying."

Before the start of instruction, randomly choose half the students in the class for the treatment group; the other half will be the control group. (See Chapter 5 for ways to choose a random sample.) Make a list of students and their group designation and make sure all students know which group is theirs. The treatment group should study for the quiz at home and will be given class time the day of the quiz for some last minute studying. The control group will agree not to study at home and will just sit or read a book (non-quiz-related) while the treatment group studies the day of the quiz.

The teacher should make up a quiz that adequately tests whatever content or skill he/she will be teaching. Instructional time for the skill or topic should take from one to four class periods. During this time, the teacher should treat all students alike, but end each class with a reminder to the treatment group students to study and the control group not to study.

The day of the quiz, the teacher should allow treatment group students to study for 10-15 minutes in class. He/she should make sure students in the control group do not study. They can read, sit quietly, work on assignments from another class . . . whatever is acceptable behavior. The teacher should administer the same quiz to all students, allowing the same amount of time for completion. Ask students to write whether they are in the "treatment" or "control" group on the *back* of the quiz paper (so grading isn't influenced). If it is the kind of quiz students can easily assess, they can switch papers and grade them, indicating at the top the number correct or the number of points earned. If grading requires the teacher's judgment, he/she should collect and grade the papers.

To analyze the data, find the average score of both the treatment and control groups by adding all the scores in each group and dividing by the number of students in the group. You may be able to "eyeball" it if there is a large difference in the mean scores, but to be sure if the difference is significant, use the *t*-test for independent samples (explained in Chapter 6).

(continued on next page)

Experimental Research Activity 3

Did studying help, hurt, or make no difference?

How do you explain your results?

Is it important to know if or how much the treatment group students studied outside of class?

Do you think your results would be the same for different topics or skills? Why or why not?

In a different class of students? Why or why not?

Experimental Research Activity 4

Are Four Heads Better Than One?

You have probably used the strategy of brainstorming to help generate a large number of ideas. Researchers do not agree about the most effective way to use brainstorming. In this study, you will investigate whether groups generate more ideas if they brainstorm together or individually.

You will need at least 20 subjects divided into treatment and control groups. The treatment and control groups must be of equal size. Both the treatment and control groups should be divided into brainstorming groups of 3-5 members. It does not matter whether you form groups of 3, 4, or 5 members, as long as the groups are the same size. For example, if you have 15 people in your treatment and control groups, you could form groups of 3 or groups of 5. If the number of people in the group is not divisible by 3, 4, or 5 you will need to randomly eliminate students until you have a group that can be evenly divided. Do not let the treatment or control group hear the other group's task unless their task is already completed.

Control Group Procedures:

Review the rules for brainstorming. (Think of as many ideas as you can. Build on the ideas of other members of your group. Think of wild and crazy ideas. Do not criticize anyone's ideas during brainstorming.) Make sure each group has a person to serve as the recorder and that each recorder has a paper and pencil. Give the following directions.

In this experiment, we are trying to find out how many ideas students have when they brainstorm together in a group. I will give you a question and your group should work together to come up with as many ideas as you can. Be sure your recorder writes down all your ideas. Remember that your task is to come up with as many ideas as possible. Are there any questions? The question is "Imagine you just found out your great uncle Fred died and left you the contents of his pencil company's warehouse. You are now the proud owner of one million pencils. Your task is to think of all the many, varied and unusual things you could do with the pencils besides write with them." (Give the group 5 minutes to work.)

Treatment Group Procedures:

Review the rules for brainstorming. (Think of as many ideas as you can. Build on the ideas of other members of your group. Think of wild and crazy ideas. Do not criticize anyone's ideas during brainstorming.) Make sure each student has a paper and pencil. Give the following directions.

In this experiment, we are trying to find out how many ideas students have when they brainstorm by themselves and then combine their ideas in a group. I will give you a question and you should work by yourself to come up with as many ideas as you can. Be sure to write down all your ideas. After you have completed your list, we'll combine your ideas in groups. Remember that your task is to come up with as many ideas as possible. Are there any questions? The question is "Imagine you just found out your great uncle Fred died and left you the contents of his pencil company's warehouse. You are now the proud owner of one million pencils. Your task is to think of all the many, varied and unusual things you could do with the pencils besides write with them." (Give subjects 5 minutes to work.)

Now we will combine our ideas in groups and see how many we have. When you are in your group, you will need to count the total number of different ideas your group generated. If more than one person had the same idea, you may only count it once. One way to do this is to have each group member read his or her list aloud. If other members of the group had the same idea, they should cross it off their lists. After each member has read his or her list, count the total number of different ideas in the group.

(continued on next page)

Experimental Research Activity 4

Compare the number of ideas generated by the groups in the control situation with the number of ideas generated by treatment groups. Which group had more ideas?

How could you find out if the differences are statistically significant?

How could you explain reasons for your results?

Quasi-Experimental Research

Sometimes it is not possible to randomly assign subjects to treatment and control groups. This phenomenon is quite common in schools where few administrators or teachers would tolerate having their classes disrupted in order for a researcher to randomly assign students to new groupings for the duration of a research project. In those cases, researchers conduct quasi-experimental research in which they attempt to control for differences between groups as well as they can short of random assignment.

If teachers are using intact classrooms, they should think carefully about any systematic differences between groups that might affect their results. Obvious ones include ability grouped classes, elective classes that might draw students with particular interests or talents, and extracurricular groups. Less obvious, but still important, are differences resulting from the master schedule. In some middle schools, all band students or students in gifted programs are put on one team to facilitate scheduling of the special classes. Schools using special education collaboration models might concentrate students with disabilities on one team to allow the collaboration teacher to work with those students. These arrangements would make it less likely for students on that team to be similar to students on the other team(s). In high schools, teachers should beware of classes that are scheduled the same period as classes that draw students of a particular ability level (French 4, Calculus). If a school is small or several high level classes are scheduled the same period, it is likely that the remaining classes may not be typical of the average ability level in the school. If gender or ethnicity are relevant variables in the research, teachers should look carefully for classes that might disproportionately attract students of particular gender or ethnic groups: technology, home economics, English as a Second Language, Black History, etc.

Just because students in the classes are not representative of the entire student body is not reason to eliminate those classes as research subjects. It is critical, however, to consider how or if those differences affect the research question or treatment. Effects of exercise on alertness in class may have no relationship to gender or ethnic group, while competitive versus cooperative classroom conditions may well be related to differences in gender and ethnicity. After doing their best to find groups that are as alike as possible, researchers should evaluate carefully the potential effect of the differences that do exist. They can still carry out the research, though they should comment on the possible effects of the nonrandom selection of subjects in the discussion when they share their results.

Young researchers can increase the sophistication of quasi-experimental research by using a pre-test/post-test control group design. In this approach, they assess treatment and control groups both before and after treatment. They can account for any initial differences in the groups by comparing gain scores (post minus pre) instead of post-test scores. For example, a researcher comparing the effects of two reading programs might not be able to randomly assign students to programs, but might be able to assess their reading levels before the treatment to see if they are similar (or take pre-existing differences into account when analyzing the results). If students conduct experiments in which groups cannot be randomly assigned, it is best to use both pre- and post-tests. As we mentioned in the previous section, pre- and post-tests are not always written tests. If a sophomore wanted to find out if studying about nutrition affected students' snacking habits, she could ask students to keep a food diary for a few days before the nutrition unit, then again for a few days after the unit. Instead of just looking at what the kids ate after the unit was finished, she could then see if eating habits changed. Otherwise, it would be impossible to tell if any differences observed came from the treatment or a previously health-minded class.

QUASI-EXPERIMENTAL RESEARCH EXAMPLES

(Many of these will be similar to examples of Experimental Research. The difference is that subjects are not randomly assigned to treatment and control groups, e.g., using pre-existing class groupings in school settings.)

<u>General</u>

1. *Which of three programs is most effective in changing students' attitudes toward substance abuse?*
2. *Does clothing worn affect the attitude and behavior of those with whom a person interacts?*
3. *Does listening to music while doing schoolwork affect the quality of the work done?*
4. *Do students who study a little each day do better on tests than students who "cram" the night before?*
5. *Which is more effective in increasing student performance, an academic honor roll or an "On A Roll" that recognizes students who have brought their grades up?*

Science

1. *What is the effect of studying ecology and recycling on the recycling practices of middle school students?*
2. *What is the effect of participation in lab experiments on students' understanding of science concepts?*
3. *What is the effect of participation in a simulation of predators and prey on students' understanding of the food chain?*
4. *What is the effect of incorporating spatial and kinesthetic learning activities on students' understanding of the makeup (nucleus and electron shell) of molecules?*
5. *What is the effect of a semester-long health class on students' eating practices?*

Social Studies

1. *What is the effect of conflict resolution training on the number of fights in which middle school students engage?*
2. *What is the effect of studying cultural diversity on the interaction patterns of students in our school?*
3. *What is the effect of a consumer economics unit on students' purchasing practices?*
4. *What is the effect of using a curriculum based on Gardner's Multiple Intelligences (**History Alive!**) on students' understanding of the American Revolution?*
5. *What is the effect of the civics class on attitudes toward government and voting practices of high school seniors?*
6. *What is the effect of a U.S. government course (or working in a political campaign) on students' beliefs about their power as individual citizens?*

Language Arts

1. *What is the effect of a book reading contest on the number of books read by students?*
2. *What is the effect of using literature discussion groups on students' reading enjoyment?*
3. *What is the effect of role playing on students' public speaking ability?*
4. *What is the effect of participation in a debate unit on students' abilities to write persuasively?*
5. *What is the effect of training in speed reading on students' comprehension?*

Mathematics

1. *What is the effect of using manipulatives (algebra tiles) on students' understanding of multiplying polynomials?*
2. *What is the effect of using a problem solving approach to teaching mathematics on students' standardized test scores?*
3. *What is the effect of using kinesthetic learning activities on students' understanding of area and perimeter?*
4. *What is the effect of using learning style-differentiated activities on students' understanding of mathematics?*
5. *What is the effect of ability grouping on student learning of mathematics?*

Art and Music

1. *What is the effect of training in **Drawing on the Right Side of Your Brain** on students' accuracy in representing realistic figures using pencil sketches?*
2. *Does participation in an Artist-In-Residence program increase students' interest in art or music?*
3. *Does using current popular music to study music theory increase students' understanding?*
4. *Are inductive or deductive strategies more effective in teaching students to draw with accurate perspective?*
5. *Does training in visual imagery increase the quality of students' art projects or musical performance?*

Foreign Language

1. *Which is a more effective way to learn a foreign language: memorizing and practicing dialogues in the textbook or conversing with another student about topics of your choice?*

2. *Is memorizing dialogue, learning vocabulary and grammatical rules, or whole language more effective in learning a foreign language (using intact classrooms)?*
3. *What is the effect of watching foreign language movies on students' accuracy in pronunciation?*
4. *What is the effect of immersion on the learning of a foreign language?*
5. *Does learning a foreign language increase expressive power (ability) in one's native language?*

Quasi-Experimental Research Activity 1

Aw, Why Can't I Listen to Music?

Today you'll have a chance to experimentally investigate a question that often provokes conflict among teens and adults: Does listening to music while doing schoolwork distract students? (Interview Activity 2 also investigates this question by using interviews with students, teachers, and parents. You might want to compare your results from the two data gathering approaches.)

For this activity the experimenter will need to:

1. Make copies of the three quiz sheets for each student in the class.
2. Locate a rock music tape/CD and a tape/CD player that will play loudly.
3. Warn your neighbors that on the day of this activity you will be playing music at a rather loud volume for two minutes while you conduct a scientific experiment.
4. Test volume levels on the player so you'll know where to set the control for "background level" and "loud." Also note the location (CD track number or counter number on a tape player) where each song begins. You can use the same song twice or two different songs that have the same rhythm; one for the experimental condition of "background" and one for "loud."

Experimental Procedure:

1. Pass out "Sheet #1" face down to all students. Tell them that this will not count toward their class grade. Ask them to do their best and work quickly and quietly. Time them (with a stopwatch, if possible) and allow *exactly* two minutes. Remind them that they must start and stop exactly on time if the experiment is to work. In the meantime, have the tape/CD set at the beginning of the first song.
2. When you are ready to begin the timing, tell them to start. At the end of two minutes, say "Stop." Have students turn their papers face down and put them in their desks or somewhere else out of the way.
3. Pass out "Sheet #2" face down. Be ready to start the music at a volume you would describe as background music. (Check it ahead of time so you don't test it when your subjects are present.) Start the music and the timing at the same time and again give students exactly two minutes to work. When the time has expired, have students put the second sheet aside. Reset the tape or CD player to the beginning of the second song.
4. Pass out "Sheet #3" face down. Adjust the volume so it is too loud to carry on a normal conversation. Again, start the music and the timing at the same time and give students exactly two minutes to work.
5. Have students exchange papers to check their work. (Exchanging papers will prevent possible embarrassment later when they will call out scores for recording.) You can call out the correct answers, pass out an answer sheet, or have the correct answers written on an overhead or blackboard. Instruct students to record the number of correct answers at the top of each page.
6. On the board, make a chart with boxes for "Silence," "Soft," and "Loud." Focusing on one treatment condition at a time, have students call out the score of the paper they checked while you record them. Then ask students to figure out the average score for each of the three treatment conditions (by adding up all the scores and dividing by the number of scores reported). You may not be able to tell if the scores are significantly different or if the differences are due to chance alone unless you do a *t*-test, explained in Chapter 6.

(continued on next page)

Quasi-Experimental Research Activity 1

7. What conclusions can you draw from your results? What might account for the differences or lack of differences?

8. We said earlier that in an experiment, you have to keep all the variables the same, except the one you are manipulating/testing. In this case, what was the variable you were testing?

What variables did you change within the experiment?

What variables did you keep the same?

What other variables might have affected performance?

What would have happened if the problems on one sheet had been harder than the problems on another sheet?

(continued on next page)

Quasi-Experimental Research Activity 1

SHEET #1

1. 4596
   5287
   6442
   +1357

2. 692873
   -580939

3. 57046
   x 28

4. 87) 40455

5. 8 hrs. 27 min. = ____ min.

6. 473 min. = ____ hrs. ____ min.

7. Nine hours after 7:15 p.m., what time is it?

8. 7.03 x 3.4 =

9. 19.3 + 2.8 + .72 + 38 = ____

10. Mary bought 5 rulers at 59 cents each. If there was no tax, how much did they cost?

    How much change should she get from a $5 bill?

11. How many feet of tape would be needed to wrap once around a box 6 ft. long and 2 ft. wide, taping around the length of the box?

12. 9 7/16 = _____ 16ths

13. How many dimes would you get for eight $1 bills and twelve nickels?

Quasi-Experimental Research Activity 1

(continued on next page)

SHEET #2

1. 5942
   6257
   1359
   2497
   + 1875

2. 493851
   -282928

3. 40762
   x 47

4. 94) 26790

5. 212 inches = ____ ft. ____ in.

6. 9 ft. 5 in. = ____ inches

7. Eight hours after 6:20 a.m., what time is it?

8. 2.08 x 8.3 =

9. 27 + .18 + 1.7 + 22.4 =

10. How many 32 cent stamps can you buy with $5.00? (There is no tax on stamps.)

    How much change will you receive?

11. How many feet of fence would you need to go around a 60 ft. by 30 ft. pasture?

12. 7 13/14 = _____ 14ths

13. How many quarters would you get for seven $1 bills and five dimes?

(continued on next page)

Quasi-Experimental Research Activity 1

SHEET #3

1.
```
  2589
  3124
  9571
  5814
+ 6553
```

2.
```
  549762
 -238947
```

3.
```
  29075
  x  39
```

4. $67\overline{)38458}$

5. 82 ounces = ____ lbs. ____ oz.

6. 4 3/4 lbs. = ____ oz. (weight, not volume)

7. 10 hours after 8:45 a.m., what time would it be?

8. 5.06 x 4.8 =

9. 2.3 + 54 + .17 + 22.9 =

10. How many 75 cent subway tokens could you get for $5.00?

    How much change should you get back?

11. How many feet of lace would you need to put around the edge of a rectangular table cloth 7 ft. long and 4 ft. wide?

12. 8 7/12 = ____ 12ths

13. How many nickels equal two $1 bills and seven dimes?

(continued on next page)

Quasi-Experimental Research Activity 1

ANSWERS

SHEET #1	SHEET #2	SHEET #3
1. 17,682	1. 17,930	1. 27,651
2. 111,934	2. 210,923	2. 310,815
3. 1,597,288	3. 1,915,814	3. 1,133,925
4. 465	4. 285	4. 574
5. 507 min.	5. 17 ft. 8 in.	5. 5 lbs. 2 oz.
6. 7 hrs. 53 min.	6. 113 in.	6. 76 oz.
7. 4:15 a.m.	7. 2:20 p.m.	7. 6:45 p.m.
8. 23.902	8. 17.264	8. 24.288
9. 60.82	9. 51.28	9. 79.37
10. \$2.95, \$2.05	10. 15, \$0.20	10. 6, \$ 0.50
11. 16 ft.	11. 180 ft.	11. 22 ft.
12. 151 16ths	12. 111 14ths	12. 103 12ths
13. 86	13. 30	13. 54

Quasi-Experimental Research Activity 2

Are You Better Off With or Without?

Some adolescents prefer working in groups to learn and study, while others do not. Teachers and parents are naturally concerned about how much students learn. Here is your chance to investigate, in a small way, if there are learning differences depending on learning conditions. The question we will investigate is, "Are there differences in quiz scores of students who learn individually, learn in a group and test individually, and learn in a group and receive a grade based on the average score of the group?"

For this to be an accurate test of learning, it is important that what you learn is fairly new to most students. The teacher can choose a topic or skill in his/her academic discipline that is not normally taught in school or can choose a topic or skill related to a hobby or other area not usually taught in school such as entomology, linguistics, anthropology, tessellations, Latin, or first aid. The teacher should make sure that the topic or skill he/she selects is something students can help each other study/practice. (Speed reading might not work.)

Shorter Version of the Experiment:

Randomly select three groups in the class, using one of the methods explained in Chapter 5. Randomly assign each group to one of the three treatment conditions—learn alone, test alone (control group); learn together, test alone; learn together, group grade. (Directions that can be given to each group as a reminder of the guidelines for their group are located at the end of this activity.)

1. Students in the "learn alone" group should not interact with other students during instruction, practice activities, exercises, or any other part of the instruction. If students have questions, they should raise their hand and ask the teacher. Their grade will be the grade they get on the quiz, which they will complete without any help from others.
2. Students in the "learn together, test alone" group should subdivide into groups of three or four students each and turn their desks/chairs facing each other whenever the teacher is not directly instructing the class. They should help each other understand what is being taught, answer questions other members of the group have, help each other complete the practice activities, and make sure each person in the group learns as much as he/she can. When the time comes for the quiz, they will take it alone. Their grade will be the grade *each individual* gets on his/her quiz.
3. Students in the "learn together, group grade" group should also subdivide into groups of three or four students each and turn their desks/chairs facing each other whenever the teacher is not directly instructing the class. They should help each other understand what is being taught, answer questions other members of the group have, help each other complete the practice activities, and make sure each person in the group learns as much as he/she can. When the time comes for the quiz, they will take it alone. Their grade will be the *average* of the quiz grades of the group members. How well others in the group do *will* affect their grade!

The teacher should proceed to teach a skill or content for one to four class periods, allowing time during each class for the groups to work together. While the groups are working together, students in the "learn alone" group should work individually on the assignment. Students in the two "learn together" groups should be helping each other learn and complete the activities.

(continued on next page)

Quasi-Experimental Research Activity 2

On the last day, the teacher should give all groups about ten minutes to study, with "learn alone" students studying on their own and the "learn together" students helping each other. After this study time, the teacher should give the same quiz/assessment to all students, allowing all students the same amount of time to complete it. If the answers are clear-cut enough for students to grade, have groups switch papers, grade them, and put the number of correct answers or number of points at the top of the paper. (If the teacher needs to grade them, he/she should do so and proceed with the remaining directions the next day.)

The teacher should return the papers to the original subgroups and have students in each of the treatment conditions (learn alone, test alone; learn together, test alone; learn together, group grade) find the average grade within that group by adding all scores and dividing by the number of people in the subgroup. *For the "learn together, group grade" group, this mean score also becomes the individual grade for each student in the subgroup.*

To see if there are significant differences, first compare the average score of the control group (learn alone) with that of the learn together, test alone group using the *t*-test for independent samples (explained in Chapter 6). Then compare the control group's scores with those of the learn together, group grade group, using the same *t*-test. You could also compare the "learn together, test alone" group's average with that of the "learn together, group grade" group to see the effect of group grading. (Doing multiple *t*-tests (A-B, B-C, A-C) increases the chance of finding significant results when there are actually no significant differences among them. In such cases, more sophisticated researchers would use the ANOVA statistic, which is beyond the scope of this book.)

How do you explain your results?

What other factors might have accounted for what happened?

How could you control for those factors if you were to do this experiment again?

Written Directions for Each Group:

1. *Students in the "learn alone" group should not interact with other students during instruction, practice activities, exercises, or any other part of the instruction. If you have questions, raise your hand and ask the teacher. Your grade will be the grade you get on the quiz which you will complete without any help from others.*
2. *Students in the "learn together, test alone" group should subdivide into groups of three or four students each and turn your desks/chairs facing each other whenever the teacher is not directly instructing the class. You should help each other understand what is being taught, answer questions other members of your group have, help each other complete the practice activities, and make sure each person in your group learns as much as he/she can. When the time comes for the quiz, you will take it alone. Your grade will be the grade you get on your quiz.*
3. *Students in the "learn together, group grade" group should also subdivide into groups of three or four students each and turn your desks/chairs facing each other whenever the teacher is not directly instructing the class. You should help each other understand what is being taught, answer questions other members of your group have, help each other complete the practice activities, and make sure each person in your group learns as much as he/she can. When the time comes for the quiz, you will take it alone. Your grade will be the average of the quiz grades of your group members. How well others in your group do will affect your grade!*

(continued on next page)

Quasi-Experimental Research Activity 2

Extended Version of the Experiment:

In this version of the experiment, the whole class will experience all three treatment conditions. The teacher will need to prepare three sets of lesson plans and quizzes that will be used sequentially. The content of all three should be similar in both difficulty and novelty for the students. Because of the time involved, the teacher might want to create instructional "units" of only one or two class periods in length, with an additional class for studying and taking the quiz.

In the first portion of the experiment, all students will experience the "learn alone" condition. They should not interact with other students during instruction, practice activities, exercises, or any other part of the instruction. If students have questions, they should raise their hands and ask the teacher. Their grade will be the grade they each receive on the quiz which they will complete without any help from others.

The teacher should proceed to teach skill or content for one or two class periods. On the last day, he/she should give students about ten minutes to study alone. The teacher should then give the quiz/assessment to all students, allowing all to have the same amount of time to complete it. If the answers are clear-cut enough for students to grade, students should switch papers and grade each other's by putting the number of correct answers or number of points at the top of the paper. (If the teacher needs to grade them, he/she should do so and save all papers for the data analysis portion.)

The second treatment condition is "learn together, test alone." The teacher or experimenter should randomly divide the class into groups of three or four students each. The teacher should teach for part of each class period, making sure there is time during each class for the groups to work together and that the activity or assignment is appropriate for group work. Groups should turn their desks/chairs facing each other whenever the teacher is not directly instructing the class. They should help each other understand what is being taught, answer questions other members of the group have, help each other complete the practice activities, and make sure each person in the group learns as much as he/she can. When the time comes for the quiz, students will take it alone. Each student's grade will be the grade he/she receives on his/her own quiz. On the last day, the teacher should give students about ten minutes to study with their small group. He/she should then give the quiz/assessment to students, allowing all to have the same amount of time to complete it. If the answers are clear-cut enough for students to grade, students should switch papers with people in another group and grade each other's, putting the number of correct answers or number of points at the top of the paper. (If the teacher needs to grade them, he/she should do so and save all papers for the data analysis portion.)

The third treatment condition is "learn together, group grade." The only difference between this group and the previous one is that each student's grade will consist of the average grade of the students in his/her small group. It will be a "cleaner" experiment if you use the same subgroups as you did in the "learn together, test alone" condition, but if the teacher feels the need to reassign groups, he/she should do it randomly and reassign the whole class.

The teacher should teach for part of each class period, making sure there is time during each class for the groups to work together and that the activity or assignment is appropriate for group work. Groups should turn their desks/chairs facing each other whenever the teacher is not directly instructing the class. They should help each other understand what is being taught, answer questions other members of the group have, help each other complete the practice activities, and make sure each person in the group learns as much as he/she can.

When the time comes for the quiz, they will take it alone. Their grade will be the *average* of the quiz grades of the group members. How well others in the group do *will* affect each person's grade! On the last day, the teacher should give students about ten minutes to study with their small group. Give the quiz/assessment to students, allowing all to have the same amount of time to complete it. If the answers are clear-cut enough for students to grade, students should switch papers with people in another group and grade each other's by putting the number of correct answers or number of points at the top of the paper. (If the teacher needs to grade them, he/she should do so and save all papers for the data analysis portion.)

(continued on next page)

Quasi-Experimental Research Activity 2

Data Analysis

Have each subgroup from the "learn together, group grade" condition find the mean score of that group by adding all scores and dividing by the number of people in the subgroup. *This score now becomes the grade for each student in the "learn together, group grade" subgroup.* Give students a list of scores (without names) from the class for each treatment condition (learn alone; learn together, test alone; learn together, group grade) and have them find the class average for each group.

To see if there are significant differences, first compare the average score from the control condition (learn alone) with that of the learn together, test alone condition, using the *t*-test for nonindependent samples (explained in Chapter 6). Then, compare the control group condition with that of the learn together, group grade condition, using the same *t*-test. Students can also compare the "learn together, test alone" average with the "learn together, group grade" average to see the effect of group grading. (Doing multiple *t*-tests (A-B, B-C, A-C) increases the chance of finding significant results when there are actually no significant differences among them. In cases like this, more sophisticated researchers would use the ANOVA statistic, which is beyond the scope of this book.)

How do you explain your results?

What other factors might have accounted for what happened?

How could you control for those factors if you were to do this experiment again?

Quasi-Experimental Research Activity 3

Seeing, Hearing, Doing

Some students learn more by reading text themselves, while others get more information by listening. These represent two of three kinds of learning modalities: visual (seeing), auditory (hearing), and kinesthetic (doing). This experiment will give you a chance to experience visual and auditory learning modalities and analyze your data in two different ways.

Do you think students will learn more from listening to someone read to them or by reading it themselves? Why?

Before you begin, you will need to pick out two reading passages (one to two pages in length). The passage can come from a textbook, magazine, nonfiction book, or other written source. To minimize possible differences besides delivery mode, both sets of text should be about the same general topic and length. Make sure there is a copy of the second reading for each student. (You only need one copy of the first passage since you will be reading that passage to the group.) You will also need to construct a brief quiz about each reading passage ahead of time. Be sure to include both low level, literal questions (who, what, when, where) and higher level, inferential questions (how, why, implications, etc.). Students should be able to complete the quiz in less than ten minutes.

Explain to the students that you will first read a passage to them and that they must listen carefully because there will be a brief quiz immediately following. Read the passage slowly and clearly. Do not elaborate, explain, or answer questions. Just read what is on the page.

Now either pass out the quiz (if you have prepared enough copies ahead of time) or tell students to put their names on a piece of paper. Before beginning the quiz, ask students to indicate at the top of the quiz or paper whether they understand more clearly when they read to themselves or when they listen to someone else read to them (by writing "read" or "listen"). Then proceed with the quiz. If you have not run it off ahead of time, you can read the questions aloud or write them on an overhead projector transparency or blackboard and ask students to write their answers on a piece of paper.

Next, tell them that they will have X minutes (you decide, based on length and difficulty of the reading material and students' reading abilities) in which to read a passage on their own. At the end of the reading time, they will again take a short quiz about what they read.

When their reading time is over, students should skip a few lines on their quiz papers and head the second section "Read on my own." They should then answer the questions you have prepared about the second reading passage.

If the answers are clear-cut enough for students to grade, students should either grade their own papers or switch with a partner and grade each other's by putting the number correct or number of points at the top of the paper. (If the teacher needs to grade them, he/she should do so and save all papers for the data analysis portion.)

Invite students to first analyze whether students scored higher on the quiz during the "read" or "listen" conditions of the experiment by comparing the scores from each trial using the *t*-test for nonindependent samples (See Chapter 6). What did you find?

Were your results statistically significant?

(continued on next page)

Quasi-Experimental Research Activity 3

Did the results confirm or challenge your hypothesis?

How do you explain those results?

You may be wondering if some students do better reading while others do better listening. How can you find out?

Look once again at the quizzes and circle the score for the condition that matches the preference written at the top of the paper. (If a student said he/she preferred reading, circle the score from the trial when he/she read. If the student preferred listening, circle the score from the first trial, when someone else read the passage aloud.) Put a square around the score received during the non-preferred modality. Now make a list of scores received by students using their preferred modality (all the circled scores) and another list of scores from their non-preferred modality (squares). (Each student should have one score on each list.) Analyze these new groups of data (preferred modality versus non-preferred modality) using the *t*-test for nonindependent samples. What did you find?

Were your results statistically significant?

How do you explain those results?

What implications do your findings have for teachers?

Quasi-Experimental Research Activity 4

Smiles Versus M&M®'s

Psychologists and citizens have long debated the use of rewards to shape the behavior of children and adults. Two categories of rewards have been studied: (1) material rewards, which are physical things such as money, food, trophies, and grades; and (2) social rewards, which are non-tangible behaviors like praise, smiles, compliments, free time, etc. Do you think rewards would influence the behavior of students in your class? _______________ Why or why not?

Do you think students your age would respond more to material or social rewards? _______________ Why do you think that?

Do you have more specific hypotheses related to particular subgroups of students (gender, socioeconomic status, self-concept)?

In this experiment you'll have a chance to investigate some of these questions. You will first need to decide which material and social rewards to use. For material rewards, consider inexpensive materials such as M&M®'s, pencils, small cookies, pretzels, etc. For social rewards, consider verbal praise, affirming smiles and nods, free time, social time, computer time, being first to leave at the end of class, etc. *Remember that rewards are only rewards if they are seen as positive and desirable by the people who will be getting them.* Kids who do not like computers will not work hard for the "reward" of extra computer time. Students trying to eat a healthier diet will probably not appreciate M&M®'s as rewards. Consider having a choice of rewards (social the first time, material the second time) from which students can select using tokens they earn during the experiment.

Next, decide on the behavior you want to influence. It's easier to reward students for doing something (staying on task, answering questions, having original answers, having correct answers, raising their hands, smiling) than for *not* doing something (not talking, not chewing gum, not disturbing others, etc.). After considering the kinds of lessons that will be taught and the rules of your classroom, choose an appropriate behavior you wish to try to increase in students. (Based on human decency and the ethical guidelines of research, the behavior you try to influence should not be harmful or embarrassing to the subjects.)

Before you start the experiment, you'll need to establish a baseline, which is a count of how many times students performed the target behavior (the one you've chosen to try to increase) *before* you started your treatment (rewards). A few days before the start of the experiment, either devise a way to record the number of incidences of the behavior yourself or recruit a student or colleague to count for you. (Be sure the recorder has a clear understanding of what constitutes the behavior. For example, if you are counting number of students who contribute to a discussion, you need to decide whether to count a student who contributes without being called on or a student who repeats a previous comment.)

(continued on next page)

Quasi-Experimental Research Activity 4

For one or more class periods, use your chosen reward for the behavior you have targeted. Be sure you or an assistant records the number of incidents of the target behavior. (We suggest starting with social rather than material rewards.) You may want to skip a few days before trying the other reward condition, to give things a chance to get back to baseline levels. During the next experimental session, use the other type of reward for the same number of class periods to try to increase the same behavior you targeted earlier. Again, be sure you have an assistant accurately record incidents of the behavior.

Do you think students are more likely to respond to the rewards if they are told ahead of time that they will be rewarded? If you have time, try the experiment using both conditions: (1) Reward students in your chosen manner without explanation, and (2) Explain ahead of time that you will be rewarding or acknowledging (this particular behavior) by giving students (material or social reward you've chosen) each time they exhibit the behavior. Record instances of behavior separately by condition (explained, not explained) and type of reward (material, social).

You can analyze these data in several ways. Students can compare the number of times the behavior was shown under material versus social reward conditions. They can also compare conditions of being told ahead of time and not being told, within each reward type and across types (by combining data from both reward conditions). You'll use the *t*-test for nonindependent samples (see Chapter 6) to compare data from two conditions.

What did you find?

Was it statistically significant?

Why do you think those results occurred?

From just an effectiveness perspective, would you recommend that teachers use rewards to influence students' behavior?

Considering the ethical dimension, rather than the effectiveness one, how do you feel about the use of rewards in school?

Does it make a difference if they are material or social rewards?

Consider sharing your findings and opinions with administrators or teachers at your school.

Action Research

Action research occurs when an individual examines and attempts to understand and improve an aspect of his/her life (personal, professional, etc.). It is a more structured and organized approach to problem solving and involves the use of data to generate hypotheses and evaluate changes. Examples of action research include teachers who attempt to increase student participation in their classes, educators who increase a sense of community in the class through cooperative learning, or curriculum specialists who differentiate curriculum and instruction for gifted students. Unlike other approaches to research in which the research design cannot be changed once the study has begun, action research allows changes during the course of the study. The researcher does not start with a set hypothesis to test, but rather a dilemma to investigate. Often what is discovered during this process will suggest the next steps a researcher must take.

In action research, an individual investigates a particular dilemma in which he/she is directly or indirectly involved. Thus, the findings are not really generalizable, since they were generated in response to a particular dilemma in a particular setting. While they are quite useful to the person(s) involved, the results of action research can provide only general guidance to others outside that setting, much like case and field research.

To conduct action research, one must first identify a dilemma, which can be a goal, problem, or issue that warrants improvement. One teacher who used math manipulatives extensively in lessons noticed that the students rarely used the manipulatives when working on their own. He wondered why they did not use them in situations when it would have been quite appropriate.

The teacher took the time to document what students did when they worked independently on mathematics. He set up opportunities in which the use of manipulatives would have been appropriate and observed students at work and interviewed them about what they were doing and how they chose to do it. After a while, he directed the interviews a bit more, asking if there was another way the students could solve the math problems. Many students mentioned manipulatives, so the teacher then asked why they hadn't chosen to use them. After some hemming and hawing, and once he assured them that he really wanted to know, they answered, "The manipulatives were too high on the shelf to reach," "There was a group in front of the cabinet and you told us not to bother anyone else who was working," "We didn't know where they were and you were busy with other students," etc. The teacher was quite surprised, but quickly realized that all the things the students said were true. Students didn't use manipulatives during independent work because they were not easily accessible, given the way the classroom was structured. At this point, he had completed his action research. He found out the answer to his dilemma of why students were not using manipulatives independently and had some ideas about how he could remedy that situation.

After answering the dilemma and proposing action steps, the action researcher can choose to implement the action steps and study their effect. The teacher we have been discussing could have rearranged the room, making the manipulatives more accessible, and could have gathered more data to document whether that change affected students' use of them. Action research consists of a careful study of a dilemma or situation, finding answers to the dilemma, and proposing action steps.

In a different example, another teacher noticed that some of her students seemed uninvolved or uninterested in her subject. She observed them, noted times they were more and less involved, and interviewed them about their involvement. Her data suggested the hypothesis that modifying teaching styles to accommodate more variety in learning styles can lead to increased learning and enjoyment on the part of all students. She investigated various learning styles models, decided which one to use, and learned enough about it to implement it accurately. To decide if this strategy was successful, she examined achievement using grades on projects and tests and assessed student feelings about the class and subject, by using journal entries, surveys, interviews, and observations about participation and mood. She then taught a unit that used style differentiated instruction, gathered data about student achievement and feelings, and analyzed this data. This data helped her decide if instruction based around learning styles had been an effective change to incorporate into her teaching practices.

A person could also undertake action research in connection with a group or organization in which he/she operates. A decline in a club's membership is a dilemma someone might want to investigate. The interested member can interview people who have left the club about why they left and interview potential members who came once or twice, but did not return. He/she can also interview people who have never shown interest in the club about their perceptions of it. Document analysis can include analysis of any written or graphic material about the club including brochures, posters, descriptions in newspapers, etc. The action researcher should try to step outside his/her personal knowledge and feelings to see how the club appears to others. Finally, he/she might want to carefully observe what occurs when new members attend get-togethers of the group. Are they included? Involved in the activities and plans of the group? Once the researcher gets a sense of what the problem is, he/she can decide what steps might address the dilemma, then implement one or more while continuing observation, document analysis, and interviewing. If one strategy doesn't seem to be helping, he/she can try another for a while. By keeping track of which action steps were tried and what effects they had, the researcher is in a better position to understand which strategies were effective and possibly to share those ideas with others in similar situations.

Action research about personal issues operates in much the same way. The action researcher first identifies a dilemma (not enough time to get my work done, not feeling physically healthy, bored on weekends, etc.), documents existing behavior through self-observation (journals, time diaries, etc.) and conducts interviews with others who might provide insight into the dilemma. Once hypotheses about the cause of the dilemma become clear and seem validated by the data, the person should then propose action steps for making a change. Next, the researcher decides whether to implement the action steps and, if so, whether to collect data to document possible changes resulting from that action.

ACTION RESEARCH EXAMPLES

General

1. *How could I get along better with my teachers?*
2. *How could I get more involved with extracurricular activities in my school?*
3. *How could I increase the amount of time I spend doing things I want to do?*
4. *How could I make new friends?*
5. *How could I reduce the number of conflicts I get into with parents or siblings?*

Science

1. *Am I eating in healthy ways, that is, closer to the recommendations of the FDA Food Pyramid?*
2. *How could I be more efficient in my use of electrical energy?*
3. *Do I get enough exercise to maintain health and good feelings?*
4. *How could I do more to recycle?*
5. *How could I increase my enjoyment of and achievement in my science class?*

Social Studies

1. *How could I reduce the number of conflicts I get into with other students?*
2. *How could I make a difference about (a current community issue)?*
3. *How could I find out more about my personal and family history?*
4. *How could I earn money while not interfering with my school achievement?*
5. *How could I increase my understanding and appreciation of people different from me?*

Language Arts

1. *How could I increase my enjoyment of reading?*
2. *How could I increase my competence and comfort when speaking before groups?*
3. *How could I become a better listener?*
4. *How could I become a better writer?*
5. *How could I find books I will enjoy reading?*

Mathematics

1. *How could I win mathematics competitions?*
2. *How could I convince more girls to take higher level mathematics courses?*

3. *How could I increase my score on the math portion of the SAT?*
4. *How could I make math class a more enjoyable experience?*
5. *How could I use statistics and probability to make better decisions in my life?*

Art and Music

1. *How could I become more accurate in my representational drawings?*
2. *How could I reduce the number of mistakes my section makes when playing a musical piece?*
3. *How could I better convey the emotion or message in my artwork?*
4. *How could I become a better singer?*
5. *How could I sell my artwork or market my musical abilities?*

Foreign Language

1. *How could I learn more about the people and cultures where my foreign language is spoken?*
2. *How could I become a more fluent speaker of (foreign language)?*
3. *How could I get more of my friends to sign up for foreign language classes?*
4. *How could I make my study of a foreign language more interesting?*
5. *How could I increase the amount of time outside of class that I use my foreign language?*

Action Research Activity 1

Rethinking Friendships

Are you satisfied with the number and quality of your friendships? As children move into and through adolescence, they often seek different qualities in friendships. This might be a good time to evaluate whether you want to make any changes in this area of your life. Children in elementary school often choose friends on the basis of shared experiences, that is, kids with whom they can share activities and interests. If you enjoy sports, play-acting, or computer games, you probably were friends with people who also did those same things. As children get older, they start to want friends with whom they can share feelings and thoughts more so than activities. Moving into adolescence, they might start having more friends of the opposite sex. As they get into larger schools, they may also meet people outside of their neighborhood and may start to meet people different from them in several ways.

As a way to start looking at the whole range of friendships, make a list of the people you consider close friends and describe why you feel close to them. On another sheet of paper, list people you consider to be casual friends and describe what it is you share with each of them.

Analyze each list in several ways. Draw several columns down the right side of the page so you can indicate various aspects of each friendship. You might want to consider the following questions:

1. Do I feel good about this relationship?
2. Do I trust this person?
3. Do I respect this person?
4. Do I genuinely like spending time with this person?
5. Do my other friends like this person?
6. Do/would my parent(s) like this person?
7. Does he/she bring out my best or my worst?
8. Is he/she the same gender?
9. Is he/she the same race or ethnic group?
10. Is he/she about the same age?
11. Is he/she of a similar socioeconomic status?

What other questions or concerns do you have about your friendships?

Answer these questions honestly, first about your close friends, then about your more casual ones. Are you satisfied with your answers? (We hope the answers to the first six are "yes," to #7 "best," and to the last four at least some are "no." A variety of friends who are affirming of your best self provides a strong base for learning, growing, and having fun.)

If you are not entirely satisfied with your friendships, identify areas of concern. What do you wish was different?

(continued on next page)

Action Research Activity 1

Think about what you do and how it might affect your friendships. Do you always insist on having your way?

Never have an opinion?

Wait for others to invite you to join them?

Go along with behavior with which you disagree?

Put down other students?

Think about behaviors of yours that might contribute to some of the aspects of your friendships with which you are unhappy, and list them below.

How could you gather data about these behaviors?

Which people could you interview?

How could you get feedback about how you interact?

How could you get feedback about others seem to respond to you?

(continued on next page)

Action Research Activity 1

Maybe you could enlist a trusted friend to gather data, so you can get another perspective. Gather data for a week or so until you feel you have a clear understanding of what is going on. Do you have some hypotheses about what you might be doing to contribute to the situation with which you are dissatisfied? What are your ideas?

What action steps could you take that might move your friendships in a more positive direction? List everything you can think of, whether you think you would actually do these actions or not. Consider asking another person to help you think of additional possible action steps.

Now go through the list and put a check next to all ideas you feel would be effective in bringing about the desired changes. Go back through those with checks and circle those you are willing to try. By yourself or with a colleague, write an action plan for what you will do differently for the next two weeks. Create a way to record whether you actually carry out the steps, then implement your plan and record what you do. At the end of the time period, assess whether the action steps you took led to the changes you hoped for. If not, reflect on why they did not work. Did you implement your behavior changes consistently and positively?

Do you need to consider different action steps?

Was your analysis of the problem accurate?

You may need to start the action research cycle over again, something that is often the case.

Action Research Activity 2

How Healthy Are You?

How healthy are you? Do you feel energetic and fit? Do you wonder where you stand with respect to all the health factors that are important today? The first step in action research is to see where you stand right now. Consider the following categories of health. Choose one or more about which you have concerns.

Fitness: Can you walk long distances or up stairs without becoming winded? Can you keep up when playing physical sports?

Weight: Check your weight against one of the charts for recommended weight ranges for people of various ages and heights.

Body fat: See if your physical education teacher, school nurse, or health professional can check your percentage of body fat. It's a simple test using calipers to measure fat under your upper arm and near your midriff.

Diet habits: Does your eating pattern follow the FDA Food Pyramid? Is your diet low in fat and high in fiber? Are you getting the appropriate number of calories (not too many or too few) for your stage of development? Do you keep "junk food" to a minimum?

Eating disorders: Do you feel that you need to diet even though your weight is in the normal range on height/weight charts? Do you eat less than 1000 calories each day? Do you binge (eat a great deal of food in a short amount of time)? Do you make yourself throw up in order to lose weight?

Risky behavior: Do you use drugs or alcohol? If so, think about how, where, with whom, and why you do that. Do you always use seat belts when driving or riding in cars? Do you insist on not letting anyone drive if they are under the influence of drugs or alcohol? Do you engage in risky sexual behavior?

Exercise: Do you engage regularly (30 minutes, three times a week) in aerobic exercise? Are you limber and flexible?

Mental health: Are you depressed? Have you ever considered suicide? Do you have extreme mood swings—feeling manic some times and depressed other times? Do you have anxiety attacks?

Once you have identified one or more areas of interest, list observations (including measurements, time diaries, food diaries, etc.) you can make about your current activities or state of health. Talk with your teacher or other resource person (physical education teacher, school nurse, health teacher, school counselor, coach) about what kind of data you should record to better understand your present health status. Then, as objectively as possible, record that data for at least one week (two is probably better). Try not to change your behavior just because you are recording data. Changing your behavior at this point defeats the purpose of the action research.

Once your data collection is complete, analyze it. You'll probably have to compare your habits against some expert standard or recommendations such as the FDA Food Pyramid for diet, or height/weight charts for weight. Based on this comparison and consultation with a resource person, decide if you are satisfied with your current status in the health area(s) you explored.

If you would like to make some changes, list some possible action steps you could take. Check with print and human resources for additional ideas and decide which of the action steps are likely to be most effective. You also need to check with yourself to see which ones you are most likely to stick with. Implement one or more action steps, making notes about the changes you implemented (what you ate, how long you exercised, etc.). After an appropriate amount of time (probably at least two weeks, depending on which action steps you took), reassess your health status using similar measures to the ones you used at the start of your study. If your action steps are helping, continue to monitor what you do and what kind of changes result.

If your action steps have not been effective, you might start another cycle of action research to investigate why you did not implement them or why they don't seem to be resulting in changes. You need to decide whether you should try something new or stick with the original action steps for another few weeks.

Action Research Activity 3

Could You Make Studying a Better Experience?

How satisfied are you with your study habits? Are they effective? Enjoyable? Use action research to investigate this aspect of your life. Reflect on and evaluate the following aspects of your study habits:

Time:

- Amount of time spent studying on the average weekday
- Amount of time spent studying on the average weekend day
- Percent of time actually spent studying (as opposed to daydreaming, looking for materials, rearranging things, organizing, etc.)
- Wakefulness—are you too tired to concentrate well
- Other:

Place:

- Physical comfort
- Adequate light, space, etc.
- Noise/distractions
- Other:

Context:

- Alone or with friends
- Rushed/last minute
- Understand what needs to be done
- Have materials you need
- Other:

Psychological variables:

- Are you tense, stressed out?
- Are you distracted by other concerns?
- Do you feel confident about your ability to do what needs to be done?
- Are you a perfectionist to a degree that it gets in your way?
- Do you not care enough about what you are doing to do it well?
- Other:

What other factors seem to impact the success or failure of your study habits? List them below, then evaluate the role they play in your current study habits.

(continued on next page)

Action Research Activity 3

Look over your responses to see if you can come up with some hypotheses about why your study habits may not be as effective as they could be. Enlist someone else in this process, since they may bring a different perspective to the situation. What factors might need to be changed in order for you to study more efficiently and effectively?

Brainstorm possible solutions for each factor.

At this point, don't judge your possible solutions for effectiveness or likelihood of implementation, just list as many ideas as you can for each. It is helpful to invite others to brainstorm with you since they may have additional ideas that may trigger new ideas to add to the list.

When you have exhausted possible ideas for action steps, go back and rate each on several criteria. Listed are four that seem relevant (add others that are important to you).

- Which would have the greatest impact on the effectiveness of my studying?
- Which would have the greatest impact on the efficiency of my studying?
- Which am I most likely to implement and stick with?
- Which would have the least negative impact on others?

When you have identified action steps you'd like to take, make a plan for implementation, discuss it with others who might be affected, and devise a way to record how well you implement your plan. Try it for two weeks, then reflect on how well you implemented the steps, what kind of impact it had on your study habits, and whether you want to stick with those changes or try new ones. Good luck!

If you are successful, consider offering your services as a study consultant to other students. While the solutions that worked for you might not be right for them, you can help them use the action research process to identify solutions that will work for them.

Action Research Activity 4

Making the Most of 24 Hours

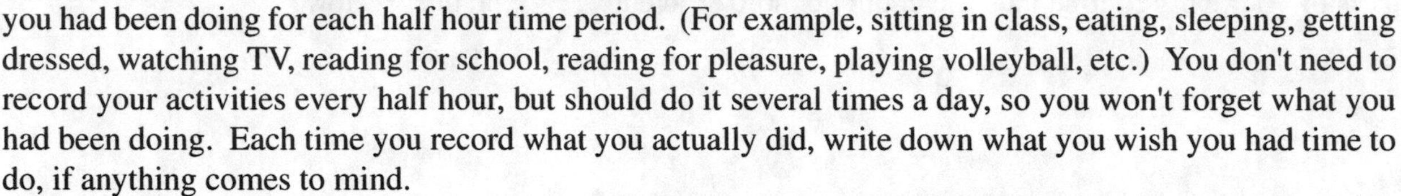

Do you feel you never have enough time to do what you need and want to do? Since it's unlikely anyone will create a day with more than 24 hours, take a look at how you use the time you have.

Start by creating and keeping a time diary for at least one week. Draw lines on a piece of paper dividing it into 48 half-hour intervals, with a section on the back or at the bottom labeled "What I wish I had time to do." Make copies for each day you will be recording your activities. At several times during the day, note the main activity you had been doing for each half hour time period. (For example, sitting in class, eating, sleeping, getting dressed, watching TV, reading for school, reading for pleasure, playing volleyball, etc.) You don't need to record your activities every half hour, but should do it several times a day, so you won't forget what you had been doing. Each time you record what you actually did, write down what you wish you had time to do, if anything comes to mind.

After you have recorded your activities for a week, look over your lists and decide on categories. You might include eating, sleeping, personal grooming, school-related activities, recreation, work, etc. Add up the number of hours you spend in each activity and find a daily average for weekdays and for weekends. What do you think about the way you spend your time?

Are you appalled at how much time you spend on grooming or watching television?

Do you think you don't get enough sleep?

Analyze your lists of "What I wish I had time to do." Are there activities you consistently feel you don't have time to do?

(continued on next page)

Action Research Activity 4

For which of these activities is it worth trying to find more time in your day?

Now comes the hard part—balancing wants and shoulds, short and long-term rewards. Are there some parts of your daily routine that you could do more efficiently? Which ones? How?

Are there activities that don't bring you much satisfaction and take time away from what you could be doing? Which one(s)? What would happen if you eliminated those?

How can you reduce the time you spend in unfulfilling activities, while still meeting responsibilities you have to your family, school work, and (possibly) employer?

Decide on some possible changes in how you spend your time. If these changes will impact others (parents, friends, employer, coach), discuss them with the people who will be affected. Tell them what you are trying to do and ask for their support and/or suggestions. Implement your action steps for a few weeks, then keep a time/wish diary for another week. Analyze it in the same way as before and see if you are more satisfied with how you spend your time. If so, check for unexpected negative consequences, then congratulate yourself! If you are still not satisfied, go through the action research cycle again, looking for other ways you could rearrange your activities to bring you greater satisfaction.

Data Gathering

Chapter 4

Once a researcher has defined a research question and selected a research design, the next step is to gather data. Data may be gathered in several different ways. In this section we will discuss four general techniques for data gathering: observation, survey, interview, and document analysis. In each case, the data gathered are raw data from primary sources. Students gathering this type of data are involved in first-hand interaction with knowledge interpretation and production, rather than consuming someone else's "preprocessed" information. Activities to practice each type of data gathering are included at the end of each section. As with the research design activities, the first two studies are probably most appropriate for middle school students and the second two for high school students, but you may find that students' needs and interests lead you to use the activities in other ways.

Observation

Observation may be described as "to see or sense through directed careful analytic attention" (**Merriam Webster, 1974**) or "to look like a scientist looks" (a young student). When a researcher observes, he or she carefully attends to events and then records and analyzes them. Although we most commonly associate observation with sight, we can also "observe" sounds, smells, or even tastes. Observation is an appropriate data gathering technique when the event(s) to be studied are currently occurring and accessible to the researcher.

There are two basic types of observations—frequency and descriptive. Frequency observations entail counting individuals, events, or objects. Descriptive observations are more open-ended and involve recording detailed notes on sights, sounds, and activities. Students who are learning to observe must practice attending carefully and objectively, focusing their attention, and recording their observations.

The easiest and most manageable type of observation for beginners is frequency observation. Consumer researchers who count the number of batteries necessary to run a toy for 12 hours are doing frequency observations. Likewise, the scientists who count the number of bacteria in petri dishes, statisticians who count hits, strike-outs, and errors at a baseball game, and market researchers who count the number of customers who stop at a particular display or the frequency with which customers order fries with their meals are doing frequency observation. Frequency observations are most often recorded using tallies. Students can tally the number of students coming to school late, the number of drivers who stop at the stop sign, or the number of times particular slang expressions are used in conversations.

Closely related to frequency observations are observations that measure or weigh designated items. Students who measure the growth of tomatoes in hydroponic solutions or weigh their growing guinea pigs are using observation skills. These same skills might be used to record the volume and weight of shoes collected at a second-hand shoe drive or to measure the average inches grown by males and females in various grades. Both frequency observations and related measurements demand a focused research question and clearly defined variables.

Descriptive observations are often used in situations where the variables or questions are less clear. If, for example, researchers want to know about differences in the ways boys and girls interacted in class, one possible approach would be to list interactions that might take place in class (asking questions, answering the teacher's questions, volunteering comments, etc.) and count the number of boys and girls participating in each activity. However, the researchers would only observe differences in the activities they had listed. Other variables would not be considered because no one had thought to count them. If, for example, three students refused to answer the teacher's questions, that activity might not be recorded because there was no place on the checklist for such a response. Not having a space for "refusing to respond" would be a problem since refusing to respond could be an important type of interaction between students and their teacher.

If the researchers are not sure which activities might show variation or are not sure what students do in the particular situation being observed, it might be best to take a less-structured approach. In a descriptive observation, the observer would not have a predetermined list of activities to check, but would sit in the classroom with a pad and pencil (or possibly a videotape recorder) and make detailed notes of everything observed. Later, the notes would be analyzed to determine the most important variables regarding student interactions.

Since it is extremely difficult to make notes on complex observations for an extended period of time, most descriptive observations use time sampling. In time sampling, the researcher chooses a time interval for observation and an interval between observations. For example, an observer who is interested in the relationship between airline safety and types of clothing worn by passengers might describe all the clothing worn by passengers boarding the plane during two minute intervals, two minutes apart. It is also possible to use time sampling with frequency observations. A researcher might decide to count the number of students in the hall for five minutes halfway through each class period.

It is essential that a descriptive observer take neat, accurate, and unbiased notes. In order for observations to be unbiased, the researcher must understand the distinction between an observation and an interpretation. "John didn't know the answer to the question and got mad at the teacher" is an interpretation of the situation, unless the observer is able to read John's mind. "John lowered his body in his seat and said, 'Who cares about that stupid stuff anyway?'" is an observation. Only observations should be recorded in research notes. Interpretation may come later during data analysis. Students who want to be descriptive observers must practice distinguishing observation from interpretation. They may practice observing peers in the cafeteria, waiting in line for fast food, or during extracurricular activities. It may also be helpful to examine advertisements or television news for evidence of observation or interpretation.

Descriptive observations demand much more complex observation and recording skills than frequency observations and thus are most appropriate for students with previous experience as observers. They are invaluable during situations with complicated variables or as a way to establish variables for a later frequency observation. After data have been gathered, descriptive observations also allow opportunities for complex analysis and interpretation that can provide appropriate challenges for students who have already completed simpler investigations.

Regardless of the type of observation pursued, researchers should follow several guidelines. First, especially for frequency observations, the observed behaviors must be clearly defined. The observer must be certain what, exactly, he or she is looking for. If, for example, a student wants to count the number of boys and girls who ask questions in class, should he/she count someone who asks to have something repeated? What about someone who makes a comment, but phrases it in the form of a question—should that question count? Even simple activities, such as asking questions, must be clearly defined. Clear operational definitions are of particular importance if more than one observer is contributing to a study. For example, if a team of five students wants to make descriptive observations of elementary students solving problems on the playground, it would be important that the team agree on how they will recognize "problems" or "problem solving." Otherwise, one observer might ignore behaviors that are observed by others because he or she didn't consider them to be part of the study.

Second, observers should be inconspicuous. People often behave differently if they know they are being watched. An observer with a clipboard sitting in front of class making marks each time a student responds is bound to have an effect on class discussion. Moving the observer to the back of the classroom can allow for more natural interactions to take place.

Consider the effects of location or time of day on the data. It may be important for students to observe in different places or at different times in order to get a more complete picture. If, for example, researchers want to observe the number of students carrying books home from school, they might consider whether observing students exiting the front door would give a representative sample of students. If students who drive to school exit through a side door, an important group of students might be missed. If students are observing homeroom behavior, there may be differences between the beginning and the end of the homeroom period or between 6th and 8th grade homerooms. Good observers are alert to the possible effects of time and location.

Finally, the observer should be aware of subjects' rights to privacy. In schools, it is always wise to get administrative permission before beginning any large scale observation activity. If the activity entails detailed observation of a particular teacher or student (for example, "a day in the life of a 9th grader"), written permission should be obtained from the individual or his/her parent.

Observation Activity 1

Paper or Plastic?

Do more people prefer paper or plastic bags for their groceries? Whether one is better than the other from an ecological standpoint really can't be answered by observation, but you can find out which is preferred by people in your town. You will first need to locate a grocery store that offers customers a choice of paper or plastic and look around for an inconspicuous place from which to watch the checkout lanes. Then make an appointment to talk with the store manager about the study you would like to do. Explain exactly what you will do, pointing out that you will not talk to anyone or disrupt the operation of the store as you observe. If he/she gives permission, make arrangements to observe on three different days, preferably at three different times of the day. Try to observe for at least 20 minutes each time, longer if possible. You will be looking at the type of bag used by the bagger. How will you know if some customers have no preference? Without bothering customers or interfering with the operation of the store, can you think of a way to tell if they express no preference between paper and plastic?

If not, you should ask the store manager which type of bag is used if the customer does not express a preference. Do you see why this is important? How might it affect your results?

Before you actually begin data collection, you might want to think of several activities you could be doing during your observations, so customers won't wonder why you are standing around. These activities should be things people might normally do in a grocery store, such as look at the ads, look at merchandise near the checkout lanes, wait for a ride, etc. You should also prepare a piece of paper, preferably folded small, on which to record the type of bag given each customer. Label the paper with the name and address of the store, the date, and beginning and ending times of your observation.

When you actually start, be sure to note which type of bag is used for each customer. Because it takes a while to ring up and bag groceries, you should be able to observe several checkout lanes by yourself. If you have a friend helping you, he/she can make independent observations and you can later compare your results for reliability.

For your second and third observations, choose the same store, but observe at different times of the day and on different days of the week. Do you think this will affect your results? Why or why not?

After your data collection is complete, tally your results and compare them. What conclusions can you make about people's preferences for paper or plastic grocery bags?

How will you account for the possibility that some people had no preference?

Do you think your results might have been different in another store? Why?

Observation Activity 2

And Now, a Word From Our Sponsor . . . .

With millions of dollars spent on ads each year, did you ever wonder how companies decide to advertise on television and during which shows they place their ads?

Do you have some hypotheses about the timing of television ads?

(One of ours is that ads occur more frequently toward the end of dramatic movies and less frequently before the tension mounts, though we've never gathered data to see if that hypothesis is true.) Here is your chance to investigate some research questions about television advertising through observation. Below are some questions about which you could gather data. Choose one that interests you or make up one of your own. Check with your teacher to make sure it is suitable for this type of data gathering.

1. Which products are advertised on particular types of television shows (college or professional sports, soap operas, network news shows, and children's cartoons)? For each commercial, write down the product being advertised, the show during which the ad appeared, the time of day, and the day of the week.
2. For how long and at what points in various shows do commercials appear? You'll need a stopwatch or a watch with a second hand to do the timing. Write down the name of the show and the date and time it begins. Once the show starts, keep track of how much time goes by before the first commercial. Time each commercial, writing down the name of the product and the amount of time the ad lasted. Do the same procedure separately for each commercial during each commercial break. Once the program starts again, time how long it runs before the next commercial break.
3. What types of people appear in television commercials? For each commercial, write down the product and the gender, race or ethnic group, approximate age, and general physical description (height, weight, attractiveness) of each person in the ad.
4. What have you wondered about television commercials? Write a question that could be answered by observation.

Observation Activity 3

Lunch Break

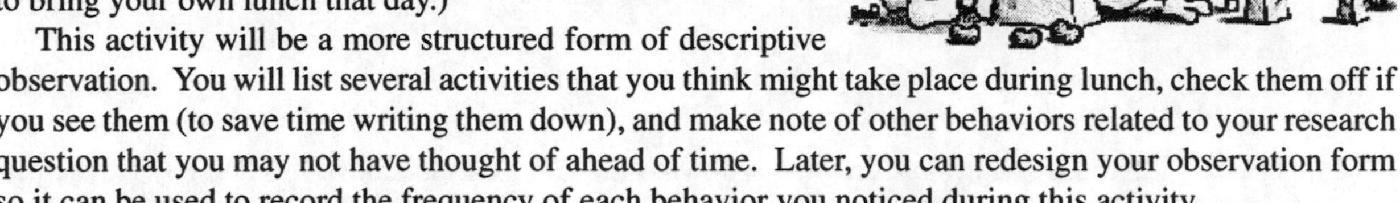

Lunch time is so short for most students that you probably don't spend much of your time observing others. However, it can be a fascinating time of day to observe your peers. Assuming your school has multiple lunch periods, see if you can observe during a period other than the one in which you eat. If this arrangement is not possible, try to reschedule when you eat so you can observe during lunch period. (You may need to bring your own lunch that day.)

This activity will be a more structured form of descriptive observation. You will list several activities that you think might take place during lunch, check them off if you see them (to save time writing them down), and make note of other behaviors related to your research question that you may not have thought of ahead of time. Later, you can redesign your observation form so it can be used to record the frequency of each behavior you noticed during this activity.

Several areas of investigation come to mind. We'll outline one for you and list suggestions for others at the end. We hope you will think of additional questions that you have about what students do during lunch and investigate those.

Select four students for your observation. Choose students you don't know well, as they are less likely to notice you watching them. Try to choose students one or two tables away from you, for the same reason, but be sure you have a clear view of their tray/plate. It might be easier if the four students you choose are all eating the same kind of lunch, so if possible, choose students who all bought a school lunch. Try to choose the students for observation randomly or make sure you have a diversity in gender, age, ethnic group, etc. so that you will have a chance to see if there are behavioral differences based on those factors.

For this observation, you will be observing eating patterns, that is, the order in which students eat their food. In descriptive observation, you write down all the different eating patterns as you observe them. It is sometimes easier to start with a list of things that you think are likely to occur. During your observation, check items on your list as you see them. You'll only have to write down behaviors you did not list, saving you time and extra writing. Afterward, be sure to draw a line through any listed behaviors that you did not check/observe. To begin this activity, brainstorm a list of all possible eating patterns. We've started the list for you.

- Finish all of one food before eating another food.
- Take one or two bites of one kind of food, then switch to another kind.
- Mix two foods together and eat them (example: mashed potatoes and peas).
- Drink milk/juice in between eating.
- Drink all milk/juice after finishing eating.
- (Add other possible eating patterns . . . .)

Once you have a list, copy it neatly in a format that will allow you to check each item as you see it. Discuss with your teacher and other students how you might go about choosing subjects, making notes, remaining unobtrusive, etc. Decide on what you think is the best procedure. It might be a good idea to visit the lunchroom at least once before your formal observation to decide where to sit, determine which students' trays you can observe from that position, practice picking out students to observe, etc. You may want to practice recording observations for a few minutes, just to be sure your form and procedures will work.

(continued on next page)

Observation Activity 3

When you are comfortable with your observation procedures, make arrangements to observe for one or two lunch periods. It should be possible to observe two people at a time if they are sitting relatively close together. Watch each pair for five minutes, recording their eating patterns by either checking options you have pre-written or jotting down brief descriptions. (If you're not sure whether something you see is the same as a listed item, write it down separately. You can always combine items later if you decide they are alike.) At the end of the first five minutes, identify a second pair of students to observe and repeat this procedure. If you find that you are unable to watch two people at the same time, watch one at a time for four minutes each. Try to watch people eat as soon as they sit down. When they get to the end of their meal and there is only one kind of food left, it will be hard to observe a pattern.

Immediately after your observations, look over your data. Rewrite any observations that are hard to read, draw a line through hypothesized behaviors that you did not actually observe, and jot down questions and hypotheses you have about what you just observed. Decide what the next step of your research will be. It might include doing a frequency observation in which you record the frequency that people use the eating patterns you discovered during your observations or it might include pursuing one of the other questions raised during your observation.

Some other questions that might be interesting to pursue through observations during lunch are:

- What visible patterns (race, ethnic group, age, etc.), if any, exist in seating arrangements of students? You can also observe to see if students sit together based on interests (sports, academics, etc.). To observe seating by interests, you'll have to know most of the students and their interests since you can't ask them during an observation.
- How many groups are made up of students of the same gender? Mixed gender?
- What proportion of students bring their lunch? Buy a school lunch? Buy from the a la cart line? Don't eat lunch?
- How many students eat everything on their trays? Leave some food on the tray? Eat additional food from other people's trays?
- How many students talk with food in their mouths? Gesture while they talk?
- How many students eat alone? In pairs? In groups of three or four? In larger groups?

(In selecting a question for investigation, you'll need to consider both your interests and the conditions under which you'll be gathering data. Depending on your school's lunchroom policies, it may not be useful to pursue some of these questions. Some schools' lunchroom policies will make it impossible to use observation to answer particular questions. For example, if students must sit at assigned tables or seats, the questions of who sits with whom will not reflect actual student choice. Be sure to choose a question that can be investigated within your school's policies.)

Observation Activity 4

Fantastic Fans

What do people do when they are spectators at an athletic event? If you are a careful observer, you can find out. You'll first have to choose an athletic event with lots of people attending. It could be a high school football game, a pro basketball game, a recreation league softball game, or any other sporting event where people are watching. First, you'll have to think about what types of behaviors to observe.

What do you think spectators at the event you will be observing might do? Do they watch the event? Cheer for the team? Talk to their friends? Think about the possibilities and list them below.

1. ____

2. ____

3. ____

4. ____

5. ____

6. ____

7. ____

8. ____

You might want to do a descriptive observation first in order to see all the possible behaviors students might exhibit. If so, take some blank paper to the next game and describe each type of behavior you see spectators doing. Examples might include talking to friends, eating, walking to another spot in the stands, cheering for the team, watching the game, watching the cheerleaders, etc. You only need to record each type of behavior once because you aren't counting behaviors this time. When in doubt, write it down. You can always combine categories later.

When you think you have noted all the spectators' behaviors, look over the list and see if there are some activities that seem alike and could be combined. For example, "eating a hot dog" and "drinking a cola" could be combined as "eating."

Once you're pretty sure that you have all the possible activities listed, create a tally sheet so you can easily record the number of times you observe each behavior. (If there are more than seven or eight activities, you might want to narrow your list down to make it possible to record accurately. Choose the activities you think are most likely to occur. If you have no idea, think about what you saw during your descriptive observations or do a "pilot" observation by attending a similar athletic event and seeing which 7-8 activities seem to occur most often.) Once you have created your observation instrument, you will be ready for your actual data gathering.

(continued on next page)

Observation Activity 4

Choose the event at which you want to observe. Be sure to consider whether that is a typical event, so you'll know how representative your data will be. For example, if it is "Kids' Cap Day" at your town's Class A baseball game, it is unlikely that the spectators or their activities will be typical of all baseball games. Once you have chosen your athletic event and organized your observation instrument, find a place where you'll have a clear view of the spectators without being easily noticed by the people you are observing. You'll be using a time sample approach in which you'll record behaviors every ten minutes. (This approach will allow you time to check your observation sheet for readability and completeness or time to enjoy watching the game! Keep track of time with a watch or stop watch.) If the event you attend has a lot of people, you might need to decide to observe a given group of people, perhaps those in one or more rows or sections.

To increase reliability, see if you can recruit a friend or two who will agree to observe spectators in different parts of the stadium or arena. Be sure they understand the categories you are using, the types of behavior they should record for each, and the time sampling plan you have chosen. Once the game is over, collect the sheets and compare them. If there are differences, how might you account for them?

Were your results what you expected? Why or why not?

Do you think your results might differ across sports? Why or why not?

Do you think spectators would do different things at a professional game versus a high school event of the same sport?

Would spectators do different things if the team was winning versus losing?

These are questions you could investigate with further observations.

Surveys

A second way to gather data is through surveys. In a survey, a series of questions is presented to a sample of subjects, either orally or in writing. Oral surveys may be conducted in person or by phone. Surveys have several advantages over observations or interviews. Unlike observations, a survey may concern events that are not currently occurring or that occur in other locations. For example, it would be impossible to gather observational data on community events in 1950 or future plans of students in another state. However, researchers could obtain this information through surveys. Surveys are similar to interviews in many ways, but they are less time-consuming, can be used with large samples, and allow the subjects to remain anonymous.

Like any type of data, surveys have limitations. A survey does not allow for the flexibility of an interview, can only gather information on predetermined questions, and may be misunderstood (or ignored) by the subjects. In any research study, the research question determines the choice of data gathering techniques. For clearly defined questions in which a large sample is desirable, a survey may be the best method for gathering data.

Guidelines for writing questions are the same for written and oral surveys. First and foremost, the survey should focus on the research question. Every item in a survey should be directed toward answering the basic question. Asking questions that are irrelevant to the research question wastes respondents' time and unnecessarily intrudes on privacy. Second, the questions should be clear. If all respondents do not understand questions in the same way, data may be confusing or even meaningless. Finally, researchers should remember that subjects answering a survey are doing them a favor. Not only should researchers scrupulously follow rules of common courtesy, but they should take every possible consideration to make the subjects feel comfortable and appreciated. While students do not often conduct surveys on personal or highly controversial topics (though they may want to), they should learn how to allow subjects anonymity and express appreciation for subjects' cooperation. They should also know that subjects should never have to pay for postage!

There are two basic types of survey questions, open and fixed (or closed) response. Open-ended questions such as "What is your favorite movie?" or "What strategies do you think would be most effective in reducing school violence?" allow subjects to respond as they choose. This format is similar to essay or short answer test questions. Fixed-response questions ask subjects to choose from a set of responses, somewhat like multiple-choice test questions. The differences between open-ended and fixed-response questions parallel the differences between frequency and descriptive observations in several ways. Like frequency observations, fixed-choice responses are easier to tally and organize, but gather more limited information. Like descriptive observations, open-ended questions are a rich source of data, but are more difficult to record and analyze than fixed-response questions. Common types of fixed-response questions include the following:

(1) Yes/no or true/false questions ask subjects to choose a positive or negative response. Two examples are

Do you favor the building of a fire station?	Yes	No
I play at least one varsity sport.	True	False

(2) Multiple-choice questions ask subjects to choose from a set of responses. Two examples are

I prefer snack foods that are:	a. sweet (like cookies)	b. salty (like chips)	c. neither
On school days I watch TV:	a. 0-2 hrs.	b. 2-4 hrs.	c. 4+ hours

Rating scales ask subjects to rate items on a designated scale. Scales should be clearly labeled and subjects should be told whether they can choose any point on the scale or must select a designated point. Researchers disagree about whether an odd or even number of points is best. An even number of points forces subjects to choose one side or another, while an odd number of points allows for a "neutral" middle point. It is important to decide which kind of scale best fits the research question. Rating scales include questions like the following:

Rate the following menu items from 1 to 5:

Tacos	1	2	3	4	5
Burritos	1	2	3	4	5
	Dislike A Lot		Don't Care		Like A Lot

How important do you think it is for teachers to enforce rules against wearing gang colors in school?

1	2	3	4
Not at all important	Not very important	Slightly important	Very important

Ranking questions ask subjects to rank responses in terms of importance or some other variable. Rankings are more difficult to analyze than other fixed-response items, but may be most appropriate for some research questions. One example is

Which factors are most important to you when choosing a movie?

Rank the following items in order of importance from 1-5 (with 1 being your most important reason).

Movie rating (PG, PG-13 etc.) _____
Movie reviews _____
Advertisements in newspapers _____
Promotions at the beginnings of other movies _____
Recommendations from friends or relatives _____
Friends who want to see the movie _____

Depending on the research question, different types of questions can be mixed within the same survey. If, for example, a student is researching the question "How much time do high school students spend on homework?" she might use only two multiple-choice questions, one asking for grade level and the second asking for the number of hours spent per night on homework. If her research question is more complex, such as "How do the amount, type, and difficulty of homework differ in 10th, 11th, and 12th grade?" her survey would also need to be more complex. She might include multiple-choice questions about the amount of time spent on each subject and rating scales regarding the difficulty of homework in each subject. She might even include an open-ended question asking students to describe their favorite (or least favorite) homework assignment.

Whichever type of questions researchers select, it is important for them to use clear and unbiased wording and make inclusive responses available. They should try to avoid the following pitfalls:

1. *Beware of jargon.* A student who has been researching a particular topic may use vocabulary that is unfamiliar to the subjects. It is unreasonable to assume, for example, that subjects will be familiar with terminology such as URL, polystyrene, World Wide Web, or even greenhouse effect.
2. *Watch out for "fuzzy" words* like "often," "regularly," or "middle-aged," which may have very different meanings for different subjects. If a question asks, "Do you exercise regularly?" some subjects might interpret "regularly" to mean daily and others may believe it means once a week or once a month.
3. *Don't ask more than one question at a time.* If a question asks, "Do you recycle glass and paper?" an individual has no opportunity to respond yes to one question and no to the other.
4. *Avoid loaded or leading questions.* You may have seen questionnaires distributed by politicians that ask questions clearly slanted toward a particular position. For example, one of us received a survey that said, "The latest FBI statistics reveal a staggering 14% increase in the number of handgun killings between 1990 and 1996. How concerned are you about the escalating gun violence in this country?"
   ___ I am extremely concerned and want to help end it.
   ___ I am concerned, but feel I can't do anything about it.
   ___ I'm not concerned.
   Using words like "staggering" makes it difficult for a respondent to say he or she is not concerned. If a survey is to represent the true ideas and opinions of the subjects, every alternative must look equally acceptable.
5. *Make sure that fixed response questions have a place for every possible answer.* Imagine, for example, a question that asks "What color is your hair? (a) Brown (b) Black (c) Blond." How would a redhead or a rock musician with blue hair respond? It is also important to make sure that the responses given are true alternatives. The question "Are you in (a) band or (b) chorus?" assumes that all students are in either band or chorus and that no students are in both organizations or in neither. Such assumptions can keep important information from being gathered.

6. *Use filter questions to guide subjects if all questions do not need to be answered by all subjects.* A filter question might ask, "Do you belong to any after-school clubs? Yes ___ No ___ If no, skip to question 6." Such questions avoid frustrating people who just responded that they do not belong to any clubs and then are asked to select their favorite club.
7. *Minimize the amount of writing subjects have to do.* Fixed-choice responses are not only easier to analyze, they are easier to complete. If you will be surveying people who do not read or write well or are less motivated to answer your survey, you will probably get more complete answers by having the researcher ask the questions orally and record the answers. Subjects will be more willing to answer questions, less likely to misunderstand the questions, and more likely to give more complete answers to open-ended questions if they do not have to write it themselves. Oral surveys, of course, demand more researcher time and cannot provide anonymity. However, they do allow researchers to involve nonreaders, poor readers, or individuals with limited written English as subjects.
8. *Put questions in a logical order.* Difficult or personal questions are best placed near the end of a survey. Doing so makes it easier for individuals to respond to the survey and more likely that they will complete it.
9. *At the beginning, include clear directions explaining the purpose of the survey and the way subjects should respond.* Should they circle or check either response? Is more than one response permitted? Be sure to include a thank you at the end.
10. *Field test the survey with subjects of an appropriate age before conducting the actual survey.* Field testing entails trying the survey out on a group of individuals similar to your research sample *before* conducting the actual research. Field testing allows researchers to identify questions that are unclear or places in which data may be incomplete or difficult to analyze. People who participate in the field test should not be included in the final study. After the field test subjects have completed the survey, ask them to describe areas of difficulty or questions that are unclear. Try tallying the results of the field test to see if responses are easy to analyze. The extent of field testing will depend on the sophistication of the research being conducted. Sixth graders conducting a district-wide survey on computer use by elementary students should probably try out the survey on five students in each elementary grade. High school juniors surveying the community might field test their survey on a random selection of parents or shoppers in a local mall.

Survey Activity 1

The Subject Is Subjects

What school subjects are the favorites of students in your class?

Do you think girls and boys differ in which subjects they like?

Use the survey below to find out. You may want to survey students in another grade to see if they like the same subjects.

School Subject Preferences Survey

We are interested in finding out which school subjects students like best and if boys and girls have different preferences. Please don't put your name on this survey, but do let us know a little about you by answering these two questions:
Are you a Boy _____ or a Girl _____? What grade are you in? _____

Below we have listed most of the subjects taught in our school. Please rate them by circling the number that indicates how much you like each one. Don't worry about whether you get good grades in the class or whether you like the particular teacher you have now. Just think about the subject itself and how much you like it.

English/Language Arts/Literature/Writing — 0 Never took it

1	2	3	4	5
Can't stand it	Dislike it	It's okay	Like it	Love it

Science — 0 Never took it

1	2	3	4	5
Can't stand it	Dislike it	It's okay	Like it	Love it

Social Studies/History/Civics — 0 Never took it

1	2	3	4	5
Can't stand it	Dislike it	It's okay	Like it	Love it

Mathematics/Algebra/Geometry/Calculus — 0 Never took it

1	2	3	4	5
Can't stand it	Dislike it	It's okay	Like it	Love it

Physical Education/Gym — 0 Never took it

1	2	3	4	5
Can't stand it	Dislike it	It's okay	Like it	Love it

(continued on next page)

Survey Activity 1

Foreign Language (Spanish, French, German, etc.) — 0 Never took it

1	2	3	4	5
Can't stand it	Dislike it	It's okay	Like it	Love it

Art — 0 Never took it

1	2	3	4	5
Can't stand it	Dislike it	It's okay	Like it	Love it

Music/Band/Chorus/Orchestra — 0 Never took it

1	2	3	4	5
Can't stand it	Dislike it	It's okay	Like it	Love it

Health — 0 Never took it

1	2	3	4	5
Can't stand it	Dislike it	It's okay	Like it	Love it

Home Economics/Cooking/Sewing — 0 Never took it

1	2	3	4	5
Can't stand it	Dislike it	It's okay	Like it	Love it

Computers/Typing/Keyboarding/Business Education — 0 Never took it

1	2	3	4	5
Can't stand it	Dislike it	It's okay	Like it	Love it

Technology/Shop — 0 Never took it

1	2	3	4	5
Can't stand it	Dislike it	It's okay	Like it	Love it

Other: ________________________________

1	2	3	4	5
Can't stand it	Dislike it	It's okay	Like it	Love it

Other: ________________________________

1	2	3	4	5
Can't stand it	Dislike it	It's okay	Like it	Love it

Survey Activity 2

What Do You Like?

What do you know about the talents and interests of students at your school? You probably know about your friends and about others who are active in prominent school activities such as athletics and student government. This survey is designed to help you learn about some of the less visible hobbies, talents, and interests of your classmates—those they pursue outside of school or those done by students with whom you might not normally associate. Learning the interests of students could help the school design more activities and clubs of interest to students, so consider sharing your results with school administrators or the student council.

Because you probably can't list every possible hobby or interest, this survey will use an open-ended format that allows students to name their hobbies and interests. Once you get an idea of the kinds of interests students have, you can go back with a closed-format survey if it is important to know how many students participate in particular activities. You can ask students these questions in person and record their answers. To get a larger number of replies, you can duplicate the survey and hand it out for students to complete themselves.

Survey of Hobbies, Interests, and Activities of Students

We are interested in the kinds of hobbies, interests, and activities of students our age. Please list below any that you have done on a regular basis while you were in this school. To help you, we've listed categories and examples, but please list any hobbies that you do that aren't already included. Do not put your name on the survey. When we have tallied the survey, we will report back to you about all the interests of students and possibly try to get some of them started as school activities. Thanks in advance for your help with this survey.

Sports (school teams, community leagues, Little League, or informal games in the neighborhood)—Examples: softball, volleyball, golf, swimming, tae kwon do, track, etc.

Collecting—Examples: stamps, coins, baseball cards, stuffed animals, etc.

(continued on next page)

Survey Activity 2

Arts/Crafts—Examples: painting, drawing, sculpture, stained glass, tie dye, painted sweatshirts, pottery, etc.

Hobbies—Examples: reading, cooking, sewing, crossword puzzles, writing, etc.

Games—Examples: card games, Nintendo, fantasy games, computer games, etc.

Music—Examples: playing an instrument, singing, composing music, listening to music, etc.

Other—Any other activity, hobby, interest, or talent you have that didn't seem to fit into one of the categories above.

Thanks for your help. We look forward to sharing the results of this survey with you!

Survey Activity 3

School Improvement

Everyone is interested in making the school a better place. We thought we'd give the students a chance to comment on their school and tell us what's going well and what needs improvement. Don't put your name on the survey and please take it seriously and be honest. We want to share the results with the school administrators and possibly the student council in the hope that they will work on areas students feel need improvement.

Complete the following survey by indicating your agreement or disagreement with each statement. Do this by circling the letters to the left, using the following key:

SA — Strongly Agree
A — Agree
N — Neutral - neither agree nor disagree
D — Disagree
SD — Strongly Disagree

SA A N D SD 1. What I learn in school seems important for real life.

SA A N D SD 2. Teachers help me learn and be successful at school.

SA A N D SD 3. Teachers care about me as a person.

SA A N D SD 4. I feel safe at school.

SA A N D SD 5. School is a friendly and supportive place.

SA A N D SD 6. The atmosphere at school is too competitive.

SA A N D SD 7. Schoolwork is not challenging.

SA A N D SD 8. There are extracurricular activities that appeal to me.

SA A N D SD 9. The work I am asked to do seems reasonable in order to learn.

SA A N D SD 10. I find my classes intellectually challenging.

SA A N D SD 11. My classes are interesting.

SA A N D SD 12. Other students' misbehavior interferes with my learning.

SA A N D SD 13. This school helps me grow as a person, not just academically.

SA A N D SD 14. The school is clean and attractive.

SA A N D SD 15. Principals and counselors do a good job here.

(continued on next page)

Survey Activity 3

Are there any other comments you'd like to make about specific things that are particularly good at school?

Areas that need improvement?

Survey Activity 4

What's the Scoop?

What's in the news in your school?

Your community?

What questions, problems, or issues are being discussed?

In this activity, you'll create a survey to find out what people think about a school or community issue. Consider a topic that is controversial or one on which a decision will soon be made so that your survey results might make an important contribution to the discussion or decision-making about that issue.

You might look in the newspaper to find an issue of concern or listen to what people are discussing at meals or in informal gatherings. Letters to the editor and editorials are good places to find out what is of interest to people in your community. A good issue for a survey is one that has more than one point of view. When you find an issue that looks interesting to you, write it below. Be sure you can describe at least two points of view or different positions on your issue. If you cannot, you will need to learn more about the issue or choose a topic on which you can find more differences of opinion.

My issue is . . .

Some people think . . .

Other people think . . .

(continued on next page)

Survey Activity 4

Now, write 3-5 open-ended questions about the topic. Check to make sure your questions are clear and unbiased and that they are understandable to the individuals you will be surveying. No one reading your survey should be able to tell what your opinion is. Write your questions below, then number them in a logical order, putting the hardest questions last.

Copy your questions on a clean sheet of paper and field test them on two or three people who are similar to those you plan to survey (similar in age, socioeconomic status, gender, race, etc.). If you want your survey to reflect the views of the entire community, your sample needs to be representative of the entire community. See Chapter 5 for information about choosing representative samples.

You can either ask the questions orally, recording the answers yourself, or give a written survey and ask individuals to write the answers. You might want to try it both ways to see if/how the format affects the answers.

Interviews

Interviews are the third type of data we will discuss. Like other kinds of data gathering, interviews have advantages and disadvantages and are best suited for certain types of research questions. Interviews can be more flexible than surveys, allowing for new questions as information is gathered. While the subject must be available (either in person or by phone), it is possible to collect data about past, present, or even future events. Interviews are ideal for complex issues or times when it is impossible to determine in advance exactly which questions will be important. Interviews allow researchers to probe for further information when a response is unclear and to follow up on leads or comments that would be ignored in a survey. However, interviews are very time-consuming, can be affected by the biases of the interviewer, cannot allow for anonymity, and usually allow a limited number of subjects.

Interviews can be structured, semi-structured, or unstructured. A structured interview is essentially the same as an oral survey. Researchers prepare questions in advance and ask them in precisely the same way of all subjects. Structured interviews often use fixed-response questions. Semi-structured interviews also have prepared questions, but the interviewer is free to probe, ask follow-up questions, and devise additional questions as the interview evolves. Semi-structured interviews are likely to contain a mixture of open-ended and fixed-response questions. Unstructured interviews are free flowing and have no preplanned questions. In some senses, a conversation with a new acquaintance may be categorized as an unstructured interview. Students new to the interview process will be most successful with structured or semi-structured interviews. It is essential that students receive instruction in interviewing and practice their interview skills in a familiar setting with people they know before attempting to gather research data.

The following guidelines can be helpful in preparing students for interviews:

Before the Interview. As is evident on good TV interviews, professional interviewers must do considerable background research. Student interviewers should not only review the general topic, but they should also find out as much as possible about the person they will be interviewing. For example, a student who plans to interview a former mayor about important events during the mayor's term should do substantial library research on the time period during which the mayor served and find out as much as possible about the mayors' accomplishments and challenges before writing interview questions. A good rule of thumb is that an interviewer should spend ten minutes of preparation for every one minute he/she spends interviewing. This type of preparation allows students to write clear, effective interview questions.

Before preparing interview questions, it is important that researchers decide exactly what it is they want to know. All prepared questions should directly concern or lead toward the major research question. For most interviews, it is best to avoid questions that can be answered "yes" or "no." In interviewing pet owners, for example, the question "Do you like your pet?" will probably yield brief, uninteresting answers. However, a question such as "What do you like about your pet?" will allow for richer, more descriptive answers.

Once the interviewer determines the questions, he/she should record them on an interview guide. Some students like to write each interview question on a separate note card so that they can write notes on the cards and reorder or eliminate cards as the interview progresses. Others may have trouble manipulating cards and may prefer to have questions written on lined paper with room for notes after each question.

Most students (as well as adult interviewers) benefit from a tape recording of the interview. An auditory recording provides an accurate record of both the questions and the responses that the researcher can review and analyze at will. It allows researchers the opportunity to preserve exact quotes and review ideas that they might have missed in the excitement of the moment. Students should practice operating the recorder, setting up the microphone, and changing the tape before the interview. Of course, it is essential to get the interviewee's permission before making any recordings. It is also wise (and professional) to have subjects sign a release form giving permission to use interview results in educational publications. Figure 4.1 shows a sample release form.

Whenever possible, the student should call and make the appointment for the interview. Not only is it good experience, but it is difficult for even the busiest adult to turn down a polite request from a young person. It is helpful for the student to have note cards which remind him/her of major questions he/she will ask and to rehearse the conversation prior to the actual phone call. Even with advance preparation, it is wise to have an adult present during the phone conversation in case unexpected questions arise. It is easier for students to have ready access to a responsible adult than to make an additional phone call later for more information.

During the Interview. Both students' appearance and demeanor should convey a professional image. While "Sunday best" clothing is not essential, students should realize that dressing neatly lets the respondent know that this interview is important and that the student takes his/her responsibility seriously. It is important that students choose quiet locations free from distractions, especially if they are tape recording the interviews. Recorders do not discriminate between relevant and irrelevant sounds as the human ear does and many recordings have been ruined by the hum of machinery, hall noises, or outside traffic that went unnoticed during the actual interview. It is usually best to begin an interview with an explanation of the purpose of the exchange and a short period of "small talk" to allow both the interviewer and respondent to feel comfortable. Once the interview has started, the following suggestions may be helpful:

1. *Listen carefully.* In most interviews, the answer to one question may prompt an idea for a new, interesting question.
2. *Ask for examples, details, or elaborations.* If anything is not clear, ask for further explanation.
3. *Use silence and accepting responses (uh-huh or a nod) to prompt subjects to continue.* Do not be too quick to jump in with a new question, especially with older subjects.
4. *Don't interrupt unless it is absolutely essential.*
5. *Try to maintain eye contact.* Even if you are taking notes, it is important to look at the interviewee periodically to indicate your interest.
6. *Take as many notes as possible without impeding the flow of conversation.* Writing down key words or phrases is sufficient if you have an audio recording to preserve exact quotations. You may want to invent your own abbreviations, for example, educ. for education, gd. for good, diff. for different, etc. As long as you know what they mean, abbreviation will save time and writing. After the interview, you can go back and clarify the notations.
7. *Write on every other line of the cards or notebook paper so that it is possible to add information or clarify notes.*
8. *Near the end of the interview, consider asking, "Is there anything important I haven't asked?"* The responses can be very enlightening.
9. *Bring the interview to a close by saying something like "One final question..."*
10. *Be sure to thank the person interviewed and follow up by sending a thank you note.*

After the Interview. Soon after the interview, it is wise to review, edit, and possibly recopy the interview notes. Students can expand abbreviated notes into complete words and sentences and add explanatory notes about tone or other nonverbal responses. Even the most seasoned interviewers occasionally make notes that seem perfectly reasonable at the time, but are incoherent a few days later. These difficulties are even more common with students, whose handwriting and spelling may become increasingly difficult to decipher as time goes by. A few minutes of review, while the memories are fresh, can be time well spent.

I hereby give permission to ______________________________ to use the tape, transcription, and contents of this interview for scholarly or educational purposes.

Signature ______________________________

Address ______________________________

____

Phone ______________________________

Figure 4.1. Interview release.

We recommend having students practice with classmates before they interview "real" subjects. In one possible activity, you can have each student write three or four questions regarding a topic of interest, e.g., what students enjoy doing in their free time. Next, divide students into groups of three to play the following roles:

(1) *Interviewer:* Introduce self, explain the purpose of the interview, ask questions, record answers, maintain eye contact as much as possible, and thank subject.

(2) *Interviewee:* Answer questions, let interviewer know if questions are unclear, and after the interview, tell the interviewer aspects that went well and aspects that might need improvement.

(3) *Coach:* Listen and watch carefully (no talking allowed during the interview!), ask interviewer and interviewee for feedback after the interview, and offer your own feedback (what was done well and what might need improvement).

Change roles until everyone has played each part at least once. A sample feedback form for the coach is found in Figure 4.2.

Interview Feedback Form

Coach: ____________________ Interviewer: ____________________

Introduction

Clear Questions

Follow-up Questions When Necessary

Answers Recorded Accurately

Eye Contact

Manners

Other

Thanks

Figure 4.2. Interview feedback form.

Interview Activity 1

Susan and the Sea Lions

Below is the first draft of Susan's questions for an interview with a researcher who studies the language and cognitive behavior of sea lions. Susan wants to find out what marine researchers do because she may be interested in pursuing this field as a career. Susan wants to make a good impression on the researcher so she wants her questions to be as professional as possible. Consider each question carefully. Decide if the question is: (a) appropriate for this interview, (b) totally inappropriate and should be dropped, or (c) poorly worded and should be rewritten.

If you choose (b), explain what is inappropriate about the question. If you choose (c), rewrite the question in a form that is more appropriate. For example, "How much money do you make?" is inappropriate because it is too personal and not essential to know. You should either drop it or, if the question of salary or life-style is important, reword it so that it is less personal: "Does a career in marine science research require economic sacrifices?"

Save Susan from major embarrassment by giving feedback on these questions before she meets with the marine researcher.

(a) appropriate for this interview
(b) totally inappropriate and should be dropped
(c) poorly worded and should be rewritten

1. Do you like your job? (a) (b) (c)

2. Do you smell like fish when you get home? (a) (b) (c)

3. What don't you like about your work? (a) (b) (c)

4. What did you have to do to prepare for this kind of job? (a) (b) (c)

5. Is it pretty easy to get a job like this? (a) (b) (c)

6. Are you married? (a) (b) (c)

(continued on next page)

Interview Activity 1

7. What do you think you might be doing in five years? (a) (b) (c)

8. Do you like sea lions? (a) (b) (c)

9. What do you think is the most interesting thing about your work? (a) (b) (c)

10. What do you say when people say this kind of research is a waste of taxpayer's money? (a) (b) (c)

11. Is it hard to train sea lions? (a) (b) (c)

12. Don't you just hate getting up early in the morning? (a) (b) (c)

13. Would you describe your job as exciting? (a) (b) (c)

14. Do you have to work hard to do this job? (a) (b) (c)

15. Do you have to be smart to do your job? (a) (b) (c)

Interview Activity 2

Schoolwork and Listening to Music: The Investigation Continues

A perennial argument between teenagers and their parents and teachers is whether listening to music while doing schoolwork is distracting. This activity will allow you to use a structured interview format with both students and adults to compare their opinions about this controversial topic. You might also want to compare your interview data with the results you obtain from Quasi-Experimental Activity 1 which deals with the same question using a different research approach. For today, you'll need enough student and adult interview questionnaire forms and interview feedback forms (Figure 4.2) for each student.

In this activity, you'll practice interviewing your classmates first and get feedback that will prepare you for interviewing others later. Interviewing is something that requires practice, patience, and skill to keep people on the topic. Today you'll get into groups of three and practice using the interview questions (called the interview schedule) with your classmates. Within each group of three you'll have a turn as the interviewer, the person being interviewed (called the interviewee), and an observer. You'll be using the same interview schedules that you'll be using to ask other adults and students about their attitudes about listening to music while doing school work.

Practice Interviews

Interviewer: Ask the questions on the interview schedule (questionnaire) and record the answers as quickly and carefully as you can. In most cases you'll just have to check the answer they give, but for the open-ended questions try to write down what the person says. (Do not take so long that they have to sit and wait for you to finish writing.) If the person adds something important related to an answer, try to write it down, even if you can't get every word. Be sure not to influence him/her in any way. If the interviewee doesn't answer the question completely, encourage him/her to give a more complete answer by asking questions such as "Could you tell me more?" or "Is there anything else you want to add?" If the interviewee tries to change topics, politely bring him/her back by saying, "We can talk about that later, after the interview" or something similar.

Interviewee: Answer the questions in a truthful manner. If you are asked questions from the adult interview schedule, try to answer them as you think you would if you were a teacher or parent. Don't try to give the interviewer a hard time.

Observer: Watch to see if the interviewer reads the questions clearly. Does he/she read the questions in an unbiased manner so the interviewee doesn't feel led to answer them a certain way? Does the interviewee seem to understand the questions? Do you think the answers represent the real feelings of the interviewee? What did the interviewer do well? What could he/she do differently next time to make for an even better interview? You might want to make a few notes on the Interview Feedback Form (Figure 4.2) while the interview is going on.

Allow about three minutes for each interview. (Have the teacher or observer keep time.) At the end of each interview, the observer should share his/her observations and all three people should discuss the interview for about four minutes. When they are done, they should change roles: the interviewer becomes the interviewee, the interviewee becomes the observer, and the observer becomes the interviewer. Repeat the process, then switch roles again so each person has experience with each role.

After all students have had a chance to experience each role and get feedback, discuss the experience as a large group. Did you have any challenges you would like to discuss? Any concerns about things that might arise in real interviews that didn't necessarily happen today? Discuss possible solutions to any problems or questions. Interviewers must also respect people's privacy by not telling others what particular people said. It's okay to say, "Someone I talked to said . . ." but you should not use people's names.

(continued on next page)

Interview Activity 2

If there is extra time, you may want to role play more difficult interviews: someone who talks on and on, someone who asks the interviewer's opinion, or someone who says "I don't know" to everything.

Actual Interviews

Once you feel comfortable in your role and have mastered the basics of interviewing skills, work as a group to identify adults and other students to interview. It would be good if each student could interview two adults (preferably one parent and one teacher) and two students. Remember the need for a representative sample (see Chapter 5 for ways to select samples). To improve your interview skills, try to interview two people you know only slightly and two people you hardly know at all. Decide among yourselves who will interview which teacher so that no one gets swamped with requests and students don't get duplicate data.

Each student will need two student questionnaires and two adult questionnaires. Once someone has agreed to be interviewed, you should ask for any information that is missing from the top of the page and then proceed with the interview. Tell him/her about how long the interview will take (based on how long your practice interviews went). The interviewer should fill in the rest of the information (date, place, interviewer name) later, so the interviewee doesn't have to wait. Be sure to thank him/her for his/her time and thoughtfulness at the end of the interview. Decide on a date by which all interviews will be completed and help others make the deadline.

When all the data are gathered, group adult and student interviews in separate piles and decide which students will work with which data. You will get more information if you divide the adult pile further into teachers and parents. You can see if there are differences among the adult role groups, and you can still add the two groups together to get data for "adults." Compile data from all the questionnaires in each category (parent, teacher, student) on one sheet. It may be more efficient for each person to compile a subset of the data, then combine those subtotals.

For closed-ended questions, just count the number of responses to each answer. Be sure to write down any additional answers people provided. For open-ended questions, record answers in phrase form. Later, work with a partner to see if some of the responses can be grouped into categories.

You can analyze your data in several ways. One is to compare the responses of teachers and parents. Another is to combine the two sets of adult responses and compare them to student responses. You can make bar, line, or circle graphs representing your results or report the results using percentages. If you are comparing two groups, consider using the chi-square statistic to see if differences are significant for particular questions (see Chapter 6).

(continued on next page)

Interview Activity 2

INTERVIEW QUESTIONNAIRE - STUDENTS

Interviewer: ____

Student being interviewed: ___________________________________

Grade level: ____ Date of interview: ______ Place: _______________

"Hello, I'm ______________. Our class is trying to find out people's ideas about listening to music while doing school work. I'd like to ask you a few questions about this topic. Please be honest in your answers. All the answers will be grouped together and no one else will know what you said."

1. How many days a week do you usually do homework? _____

2. Do you listen to music while you do your work?
____ all the time ____ usually ____ sometimes ____ never (if "never", skip to #5)

3. What kind of music do you usually listen to?
____ rock ____ classical ____ jazz ____ rap ____ other: ____________________

4. How loud is the music while you do homework?
____ very loud ____ loud ____ average ____ soft ____ very soft

5. Do you think listening to music while working makes doing work
____ easier, ____ harder, or ____ makes no difference?

6. Compared to doing school work when things are quiet, do you think listening to music makes doing your work take ____ more time, ____ less time, or ____ about the same amount of time?

7. When you listen to music, is the quality of your work (how well you do it)
____ better, ____ worse, or ____ the same as if you did it when it was quiet?

8. How are your grades in school?
Mostly ____ A's ____ B's ____ C's ____ D's ____ F's

9. Is there anything else you'd like to say about the whole idea of listening to music while doing school work?

Thank you very much for your time.

(continued on next page)

Interview Activity 2

INTERVIEW QUESTIONNAIRE - ADULTS

Interviewer: ____

Adult being interviewed: ______________________________________

Role (teacher, parent, etc.): _______________________ Date: ________________

"Hello, I'm ____________. Our class is trying to find out people's ideas about listening to music while doing school work. I'd like to ask you a few questions about this topic. All answers will be grouped together and no one else will know what you said, so please be honest. When you answer these questions, think about kids in the ____ th grade."

1. Do you think that listening to music would make doing school work
   ____ easier, ____ harder, or ____ have no effect?

2. Do you think listening to music while doing school work would make the quality of the work
   ____ better, ____ worse, or ____ have no effect?

3. Compared to doing work when things are quiet, do you think listening to music makes doing the work
   ____ take more time, ____ take less time, or ____ take the same amount of time?

4. If you had children in the ___th grade, would you let them listen to music while they did their homework?
   ____ yes ____ no (if no, skip to #7)

   would depend on ____

5. Which of the following kinds of music would you let your adolescent children listen to while they did homework? (mark all that apply)
   ____ none ____ rock ____ classical ____ jazz ____ rap

   ____ other: ____

6. Would you let them play it softly? ____ yes ____ no
   average volume? ____ yes ____ no loudly? ____ yes ____ no

7. Is there anything else you'd like to say about the whole idea of listening to music while doing school work?

Thank you very much for your time.

Interview Activity 3

Considering Careers

Many students your age are beginning to think about the kinds of careers that might interest them. Here's your chance to find out about a job or career from an insider. You will need to identify one or two jobs or careers about which you would like to know more. What might those be?

Interview Schedule

What would you like to know about these jobs? On a piece of paper, brainstorm (alone or with a small group of peers) a list of all the possible questions you might want to ask.

Did you consider asking about . . .

- What a typical day is like
- Chance for advancement
- Physical demands
- Favorite parts of the job
- General salary range
- Education/training needed
- Job security
- Co-workers
- Least favorite parts of the job
- Benefits (insurance, retirement, etc.)
- Working conditions:
  - indoors/outdoors
  - intense/casual
  - regular hours/changing hours
  - physical safety
  - work is varied/same
  - work with people, things, or ideas
  - amount of travel required
  - day/evening/night work
  - work alone or in groups
  - amount of supervision

Choose six or eight areas that are most important to you and write them in question form. Remember what you learned about making questions open-ended and neutral (not biased toward a particular answer). When you have finished a first draft of your interview questions, show them to a peer or your teacher for feedback. Make any needed revisions and put the questions in an appropriate order (more personal ones such as salary and likes/dislikes toward the end). Now type, word-process, or neatly write your final draft, being sure to leave plenty of room under each question for recording answers. Make at least one copy of your interview schedule for each person you wish to interview plus a few extra in case you need them.

Choosing People to Interview

If you are very focused on one job or profession, you might want to interview several different people who hold that job in order to get a broader picture. Try to find people who work for different companies or groups, as working conditions may vary. If you're not strongly drawn to one particular job, try to interview people in several jobs in which you have some interest.

(continued on next page)

Interview Activity 3

Ask your parents, teachers, neighbors, and friends' parents if they know people working in the jobs of interest to you who might be willing to be interviewed. If you come up blank, ask your teacher to devote a section of the classroom chalkboard to listing people you are interested in interviewing. Other students who use that classroom might see the list and have suggestions. The teacher may also be willing to circulate a list to faculty members to see if they have any suggestions. If all else fails, call an agency or group that employs people in your field and ask if there is someone who will talk with you.

Once you've gathered a list of people and their phone numbers, review procedures for asking for an interview. Know ahead of time where and when you would be able to meet the person or if you will need to conduct your interview over the phone. Try contacting the person long before you need to have the interview completed because it is sometimes hard to reach people by phone.

Immediately after your interview, review your notes and fill in any blanks. Rewrite any notes you can't easily read. Within 24 hours write and mail a note thanking the person for taking the time to talk with you and letting him/her know how it was helpful for you.

Compare what you discovered, both within and across job types. See if other students interviewed people who have jobs in which you are interested. Work together to find a way to record everyone's information to make it accessible and useful to each other. Before sharing your results, remember to remove all references to the person you interviewed (name, company/group). Use general descriptions such as "an area fire fighter" or "a large insurance company" in order to protect the anonymity of the people you interviewed.

Interview Activity 4

Back in the Good Old Days . . .

Everyone says that times have changed. Many say it is harder being a teenager these days than ever before. Was it easier for your parents or just different? Here's your chance to find out what kinds of things people your parents' and teachers' age worried about as teenagers.

Determine the approximate age of the people you wish to interview. Figure out how much older they are than you and subtract that from the current year to find the years when they were about your age. For example, if you are doing this activity in 1998 and are interested in people your parents' age, consider the decade from 1968-1978. (Assuming your parents are 20-30 years older than you, subtract that amount from the current year. Therefore, they were about your age between 1968 and 1978.) For grandparents, you should probably subtract 40-50 years from the current year.

You should do some background research to find out what was going on and the prevailing social problems that occurred during that time in the world, country, state, and community. This research will give you an idea of possible concerns of teenagers around that time. Also list concerns of people your age today so you can ask if these were also concerns of the adults when they were teens. Listed are some possibilities.

Concerns of Current Teens

- AIDS
- getting killed
- being popular
- getting a good job
- racism
- grades
- having friends

Possible Concerns Adults Had as Teens

- getting polio
- nuclear war
- being popular
- getting a good job
- racism
- war with Cuba, Russia, China
- being drafted into the military

Brainstorm lots of questions, then choose the ones that seem most interesting and relevant. Put them in order, starting with the least personal/controversial. Check them against the criteria for good questions earlier in this chapter. It would also be a good idea to try your questions out on one or two adults as a pilot study. Ask the interview questions as written, noting any times the interviewee seems confused or hesitant to talk. Afterward, ask the interviewee to give you feedback about the questions themselves and how you conducted the interview. Ask if any questions seemed confusing, embarrassing, or inappropriate. Use this feedback to revise your questions, if needed, before interviewing your subjects.

After your interviews have been completed, compare what you found out about the concerns of adults as teens and those of current teens. If other students interviewed adults on this same subject, find a way to record and share information so you have a larger data base from which to work. Before sharing your results, remember to remove all references to the person you interviewed (name, role in the community, etc.). Use general descriptions such as "a parent" or "someone my grandparent's age" in order to protect the anonymity of the people you interviewed.

Document Analysis

The final type of data gathering is document or artifact analysis. Document analysis involves observing and analyzing print or non-print primary resources. These resources may be photographs, government materials, diaries, archives, business records, periodicals, or other documents. Other types of artifacts that may be analyzed include works of art, clothing, furniture, jewelry, household objects, or any other source of data relevant to the research question. Because the documents or artifacts to be analyzed should be primary sources, it is most likely that students will work largely with printed documents, which are usually more accessible and easier to duplicate. However, museums and private collections may provide sources of other types of information.

Just as in descriptive observation, it is important in document analysis to distinguish between observations and interpretations. In many cases, the goal of document analysis is to make interpretations. However, the researcher must be clear about that intent and distinguish his/her opinions from the facts. If, for example, a young researcher examines three history textbooks from Kentucky in 1960 and finds that none of them contain information on any African Americans except Frederick Douglas and George Washington Carver, he/she might infer that little was taught about African Americans in U.S. history at that time. That inference, however, would be an interpretation or hypothesis. The only information the student knows for sure is that these three textbooks from 1960 do not contain any information about African Americans except for Frederick Douglas and George Washington Carver. It is possible that other books contain different information or that teachers taught material that was not in the textbooks. Additional information would be necessary to see which possibility seemed most likely.

It is also vital to be alert to the possibility of interpretation, inference, or bias on the part of the creator of the document or artifact being examined. Even primary source documents are not necessarily "true." Imagine the same event—for example, the election of the first female president of the United States—as it might be reported in **New Republic**, **Ms. Magazine**, and **The National Enquirer**. Each might have had an eyewitness at the president-elect's acceptance speech, but it is likely that the event would be portrayed very differently. Consider an 1887 household handbook published by a producer of patent medicine. Would it be a good source of information on home remedies? Looking at the book, it can easily give the impression that most people used that brand of medicine for all possible ailments—not necessarily an accurate representation of fact. Portraits and other works of art are often used as sources of information on clothing of various periods. However, if a portrait was painted for an individual who wanted to be remembered for his or her wealth, it may not be a good source of information on daily dress. Town Council minutes may not present a true representation of the work of the council if they do not include executive sessions. Each of these sources can provide valuable information, but only if the investigator carefully considers the intention of the source. Adolescents preparing for document analysis may benefit from practice in identifying and interpreting point of view in a variety of sources.

Other factors to consider when evaluating sources are timeliness and completeness. Timeliness refers to how contemporary a source is (i.e., it was created during the time it represents). A painting about the 1850s created in 1860 is more contemporary than one painted in 1960. All other things being equal, contemporary artifacts or primary documents are more likely to be accurate representations. Completeness refers to the thoroughness with which a topic is illustrated. Generally, several sources will prove to be more complete than any one source alone. Several magazines depicting women's fashions in the 1940s can show a greater range than any one magazine, which might be geared toward women of a particular region or economic status.

Some questions students can use when evaluating sources include:

1. What do I observe in/about this document or artifact? What can be objectively described and agreed upon by most people?
2. What suggests that this is a reliable depiction of the event? Which things correlate with other sources I have examined?
3. What suggests that this source might be biased, incomplete, or inaccurate? What do I know about its creator or author or the circumstances under which it was created? What, if anything, contradicts information about this topic in other sources?
4. Given all of the above, do I believe this source is reliable? Why or why not?

Once students have evaluated the source, they should analyze the document/artifact itself. A document/artifact analysis form can facilitate this process (see Figure 4.3).

Document/Artifact Analysis Form

Document/Artifact: ______________________________

Source: ______________________________

Date (if available): ______________________________

What can you observe from looking at this document/artifact?

What inferences or hypotheses can you make regarding this document or artifact?

What questions do you have about his document/artifact? How might you find answers?

Figure 4.3. Document/artifact analysis form.

In the first section, the investigator should record factual observations about the document or artifact. These comments should be objective descriptions with which any observer would agree. In the next section, he or she should record speculations, hypotheses, and other ideas he/she has about that particular observation. Later, the student can examine these speculations for patterns, check them against other evidence, and try to confirm or refute hypotheses about the document/artifact. A thoughtful researcher will also record any questions that come to mind while examining the document/artifact.

Figure 4.4 presents an example of a document recording form completed for an old photograph. Are there any observations, hypotheses, or questions you'd like to add to the form?

Document/Artifact Analysis Form

Document/Artifact: *Photograph from WWII Era*

Source: *Pictorial History of Camp Zachary Taylor*

Date (if available): ____________________

What can you observe from looking at this document/artifact?

Two people, each holding what looks like a stock of a long rifle.
They are wearing protective head gear and padded jackets.
Three men, possibly in uniform, are standing nearby watching them.
There are no leaves on the trees.
The men are wearing jackets.

What inferences or hypotheses can you make regarding this document or artifact?

Maybe they're just practicing and the protective clothing is so they don't get hurt.
Maybe the people watching are teachers or supervisors.
Maybe it's winter in the middle of the U.S. or fall/spring father north.

What questions do you have about this document/artifact? How might you find answers?

What are they holding? They don't look like real guns.
Are they fighting?
Have they bet on a contest between the people?

Figure 4.4. Document/artifact analysis form (competed).

Document Analysis Activity 1

Advertising Postcards

Think of the ways companies today try to convince the public to buy their products. There are advertisements on television, on radio, on videos, in newspapers and magazines, and on billboards. In the early 1900s, one form of advertising was the advertising postcard. In Figure 4.5 you can see reproductions of two advertising postcards. After examining the postcards, consider carefully the following questions: What can you observe about these documents?

What can you infer or hypothesize about these documents?

What questions do you have about the documents?

You may want to use a Document Analysis Form (Figure 4.3) to organize your thoughts.
Compare the strategies used on these postcards with examples of advertising today. In what ways are the strategies similar?

In what ways are they different?

You could investigate local antique stores for other examples of advertising postcards. You may also be able to find reproductions in books about advertising or in Dover Press' **Antique Advertising Postcards,** a book of reproductions. See if the inferences you made from viewing two postcards hold true when you have examined more examples.

POST CARD

PLACE
POSTAGE
STAMP
HERE

This space may be used for correspondence.

The Address to be written here.

Swift's "Premium Oleomargarine is packed under the supervision of United States Government Inspectors. You are assured of a pure, wholesome and appetizing spread for bread every time you buy "Swift's Premium." It is always uniform.

(figure continues)

Figure 4.5. Advertising postcards.

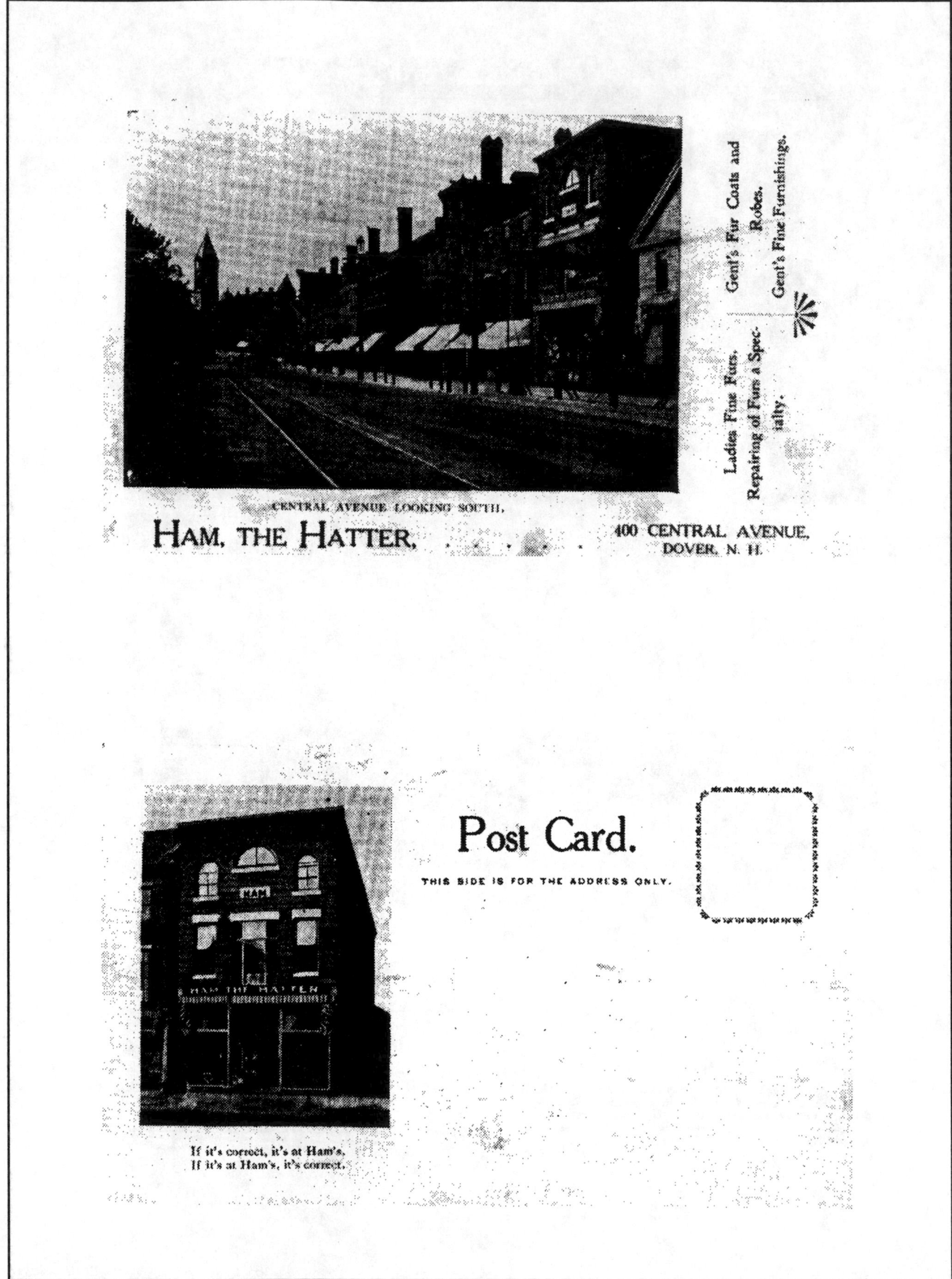

Figure 4.5. Advertising postcards (*continued*).

Document Analysis Activity 2

Old Periodical: The Youth's Companion

You may enjoy reading magazines or other publications written especially for young people. Libraries and newsstands have many examples of publications designed for students your age. In this activity, you will examine excerpts from **The Youth's Companion** (Figure 4.6), a periodical published in the early 20th century. This particular issue was published February 13, 1919. The first excerpt is called the masthead. The masthead gives the title of the periodical and other general information. The second excerpt includes sections from page 82, the "Boys' Page," and the third excerpt contains sections from page 86, the "Girls' Page."

Examine the excerpts carefully. You may wish to use a Document Analysis Form to record your observations, inferences, and questions. Compare the excerpts from the Boys' and Girls' pages to current periodicals designed for boys and girls. What similarities and differences do you observe?

You may want to examine other periodicals from different time periods to see if you find similar trends. You may find interesting periodicals in your local library, possibly on microfilm or microfiche or in flea markets and antique or used book stores.

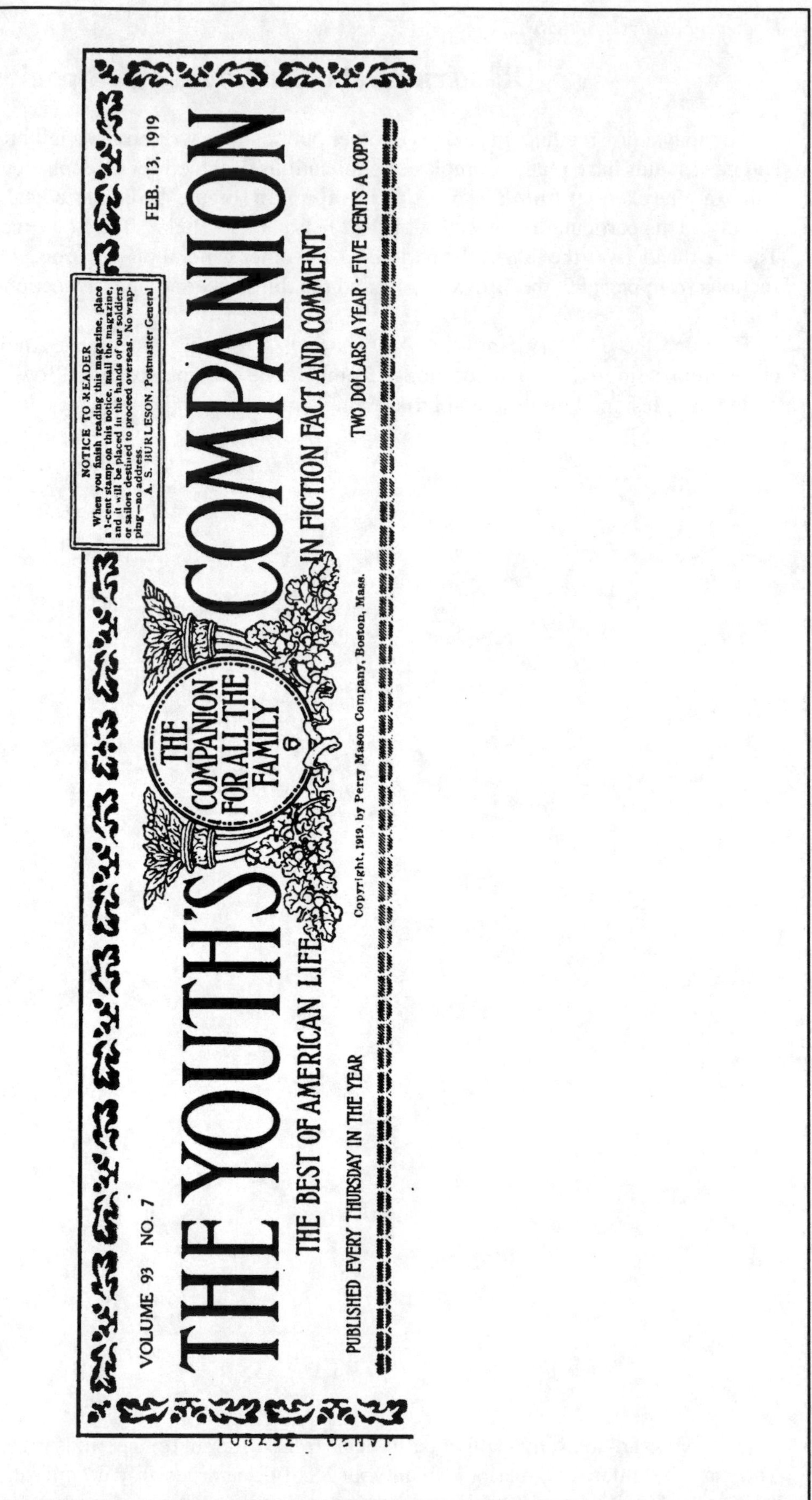

Figure 4.6a. Old periodical—The Youth's Companion: Masthead.

82 THE COMPANION FOR ALL THE FAMILY February 13, 1919

Ask any questions you wish about the contents of this page. They will be gladly answered.

BOYS' PAGE *for* FEBRUARY

Address your letters to THE EDITOR OF THE BOYS' PAGE, THE YOUTH'S COMPANION, BOSTON, MASS.

MEASURING WIND VELOCITY

HOW fast is the wind blowing today? The question has doubtless been in your mind many times. It is not difficult to make a contrivance that will answer it for you.

Before the invention of the revolving-cup gauge, or anemometer, gauges similar to the one shown in the figure were much in use and were recommended by some of the European meteorological societies. His gauge is not quite so accurate as the instruments now used by the Weather Bureau, but, except in vary light winds, it gives sufficiently correct result for ordinary purposes. The principle of it is that wind blowing at a certain velocity exerts a definite pressure on a plane surface placed at right angles to its course.

In the middle of a smooth board nine inches wide by about twelve inches long place another smooth board nine inches square in a vertical position. Screw them together, and brace them in the position with an iron bracket. On the upright board on the other side from the bracket attach with screws a weighting machine of the box type, with a metal platform at the top, and a clock-faced indicator graduated to read by ounces up at least fifteen pounds. Such machines are usually called "family" scales, and cost about one dollar and fifty cents.

The next step is to get a well-seasoned piece of white pine or whitewood planed on both sides, twelve inches square

and not more that one quarter of inch thick. Give it two or three coats of varnish; then drill four small holes through the scale platform and, centering the board on the scales, screw the platform to it by small screws through the four holes. To screw the base of the scales to the vertical board in the position shown in the figure, it is well to make four small holes through the flanges at the base.

The final step is to attach two small cords, one on each side, to the middle line of the twelve-inch piece, and to run them back horizontally through holes in the nine-inch vertical piece, and over small pulleys to weights that are just sufficient to pull the platform back so that the dial hand stands at zero. If you wish, you can add a small vane to the equipment to give the direction of the wind. When you place the gauge at right angles to the wind, the indicator will

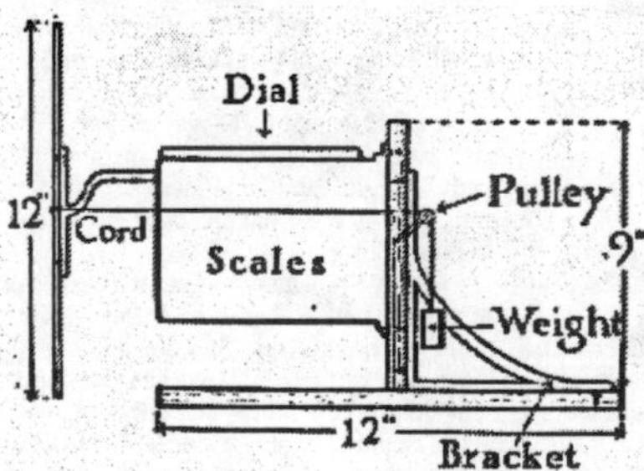

register the amount of pressure. From the following table you can then find the velocity in miles an hour:

Pressures on the scales	*Velocity of the wind*
12 oz.	12 miles an hour.
1 lbs. 2 oz.	15 miles an hour.
2 lbs.	20 miles an hour.
3 lbs. 2 oz.	25 miles an hour.
4 lbs. 8 oz.	30 miles an hour.
6 lbs. 2 oz.	35 miles an hour.
8 lbs.	40 miles an hour.
12 lbs. 8 oz.	50 miles an hour.
18 lbs.	60 miles an hour.

Small wind velocities cannot be measured by a gauge of this kind because the pressure to the square foot is too small. For example, the pressure at a velocity of five miles an hour is only twelve one hundredths of a pound, and at three miles it is only a little more than four one hundredth of a pound. Wind at those velocities is scarcely more than perceptible to a person standing in it; and at ten to twelve miles it is only a pleasant breeze. A common designation is :

121/2	miles an hour	fresh breeze.
15	miles an hour	moderate breeze.
20	miles an hour	strong breeze.
25	miles an hour	brisk wind.
30	miles an hour	strong wind.
40	miles an hour	high wind.
50	miles an hour	storm.
60	miles an hour	violent storm.
80	miles an hour	hurricane.

KNIGHTS OF THE CROSS

IT will take only a few minutes to make the board and the men for an interesting, new, two-player game called knights of the cross.

Draw on a piece of light-colored cardboard a diagram similar to the one shown in the illustration, and place the numbers on the proper squares. Then cut out of white pasteboard ten square small enough to fir comfortably into those of the diagram. Draw a circle in the center of five of the squares, which are to be the squires, and make crosses on the other five, which are the knights. After that, cut out three plain squares the exact size of the squares of the figure. Those are to be used as markers. Do the same with a strip of colored pasteboard, until you have made ten more squares—half of them squires, the others knights—and three larger sized plain squares.

To start the game arrange the knights and squires on the diagram in the manner indicated in the illustration. Place the plain squares at one side.

The knights—the pieces marked with crosses—may move only diagonally forward or diagonally backward to a vacant adjacent square. They must jump forward diagonally over an opponent's piece, or pieces, to a vacant square, one, two, three or four times, as the case may be. The squires—the pieces marked with circles—may move only directly forward, backward, or sideways, never diagonally, to a vacant adjacent square. They must jump directly forward over an opponent's piece, or pieces, to a vacant square, one, two, three or four times, as the case may be.

The five squares of the cross are exclusively for tallying and must not be used at any tine for play.

The object of the contest is for a player to maneuver his men so that he has a man on each of the five numbers—1, 2, 3, 4 and 5. For example, if he has one man on a square numbered 1, another on a square numbered 2, another on the square numbered 3, another on a square numbered 4, and another on a square numbered 5 before his opponent accomplishes the same task, he wins the game—no matter where his other five men are. The squares need not be adjacent. When he has completed the sequence, the player stops. The successful contestant, puts one of his three plain pasteboard squares, reserved at one side, on any of the five squares of the cross.

Each player them arranges his knights and squires on the proper square, and a new game begins. The successful player on the new game places one of his plain squares on one of the four remaining vacant squares of the cross.

The game continues in that way until one of the players covers three of the five sections of the cross with his three plain squares.

A SKIRT GAUGE

IF you like to work with tools, you will find good fun as well as profit in making skirt gauges out of odds and ends of lumber. You should be able to sell them to many women who do their own dressmaking. One boy, who used lumber thrown away by carpenters, sold his gauges for twenty-five cents each. If you use new lumber, and finish your product neatly with paint, shellac or varnish, thirty-five or even fifty cents would not be too much to ask.

Select a pine stick 16 inches long and about an inch square and plane it smooth. Every half inch along its length bore a hole with a No. 2 gimlet bit, as shown in the figure. For the base, use a block of wood 2 inches thick and about 6 inches square. Mark diagonal lines from the corners of the block to find the centre, then, holding the upright in place on the centre of the block, mark the size of its end. Now bore a hole in the square, chisel it out to the proper size and drive the upright into place. Provide a long knitting needle or piece of stiff wire to insert in the hole. Of course it must fit loosely, so that it can be adjusted to any height desired.

In using the gauge the dressmaker will set it under the skirt and turn the hem over the wire and pin it. She will then move the gauge along and continue to put in pins until she completes the circle.

THE ADDING MACHINE IMPROVED

IN the Boys' Page for January, 1915, The Companion printed directions for making a calculating machine that can be used to add single-digit figures of a total not over one hundred. A contributor sends a description of a simple way to enlarge the capacity of the machine to one thousand.

All that is necessary is to add another wheel that, like the others, is two inches in diameter and is divided round the circumference into then equal parts numbered form 0 to 9. On the outside of each of the numbers is a small brad, and attached to the middle wheel, over the figure 4, a metal or pasteboard pointer, as shown in the illustration. Between the upper and the middle wheel is a guide line. The upper wheel records the hundreds, the middle wheel the tens and the lower wheel the units.

When you begin to add, place the pointer attached to the toothed wheel between the brads at 0 and 9 on the upper wheel, and see that the arrows on the lower and the middle wheel are exactly opposite each other.

Suppose that the first two numbers in the column that you wish to add are 6 and 9. In the indentation opposite the number 6 of the board place the nail that serves as a movable handle, and turn the wheel counter clockwise until the nail is opposite the guide line, which in the illustration appears through the triangular opening in the point of the lower wheel. Then lift the nail and place it in the indentation opposite he number 9 of the board and turn the wheel until the nail is again opposite the guide line.

Continue in the same way until you have added the last digit. The figure on the upper wheel nearest the guide line will then be the first digit of the total; the figure in the middle wheel nearest the guide line will be the second digit; and the figure of the lower wheel nearest the guide line will be the third digit.

This model is about three inches wide by seven inches long, and is made from wood one quarter of an inch thick. The central guide line, a part of which appears through the triangular opening of the units wheel, is concealed above by the tens wheel and its metal lever.

In making the machine take care to construct the wheel accurately, and attach them to the board so that they will not revolve too easily. If the two upper wheels should move more than one space under each impetus of the units wheel, the accuracy of the adding machine would, of course, be destroyed.

Figure 4.6b. Old periodical—The Youth's Companion: Boys' page.

36 THE COMPANION FOR ALL THE FAMILY February 13, 1919

Ask any questions you wish about the contents of this page. They will be gladly answered.

GIRLS' PAGE for FEBRUARY

Address your letters to THE EDITOR OF THE GIRLS' PAGE, THE YOUTH'S COMPANION, BOSTON, MASS.

GARDENING FOR GIRLS

BEFORE the war few girls were really interested in cultivating a garden of their own or in helping to increase the crops on the family acres. All girls admired pretty garden clothes and, for the sake of wearing them, sometimes consented to lend a hand in weeding grandmother's flower beds; but few ever thought of cultivating the soil either as a means of keeping themselves in a good physical condition or as a way of earning pin money.

But the war changes all that. To-day finds the American girl not only helping in the field, in ploughing and harvesting, but also planning vegetable and flower gardens as a means of increasing our production of food as well as her own pocket money or the family income.

If the girl who is growing too fast will cultivate a small garden, give it a few months of faithful care, not only will she reap satisfactory harvests of fruit and flowers, but she herself will flourish and bloom. Fresh air and the intimate association with earth and nature work miracles in building health—and in building character, too, for a definite purpose diligently pursued is good for the soul.

One mother gave her daughter—who at the age of fifteen was pale, thin and anaemic—the entire charge of their yard, which measured forty by seventy feet. Since there was no man to keep it in order, for all the man power of the town had been called to military service or placed in essential industries, the yard had received only enough attention to keep it looking respectable. The girl undertook the work with indifference, but she conscientiously applied herself to it for the stipulated half hour every morning and every evening.

As the few trees were soon trimmed and everything was in good order, she found it necessary to plan work to keep herself busy. She began to read books about gardening and soon began to send regularly for the pamphlets that are to be had free of the Department of Agriculture. The subtle attraction of seed and plant catalogues began to take hold of her, and in a little while she was laying out beds and sowing seeds. The perfunctoriness of her work lessened as her enthusiasm awakened. As the spring days went on, she spent more and more time in the yard, digging, hoeing, raking with ever-increasing energy. She was often tired and stiff after her work, but she soon began to notice how good her simple meals tasted and how well she slept.

FIG. 2

She planned a small "picture" garden in the back part of the yard, in which she planted wild ferns and wild flowers gathered from the woods and fields. She learned how to hoard leaf mould, and how to transplant fir trees and small pines. Soon she began to take real delight in getting down to the good brown earth with her bare hands. As summer approached, she bought a small lawn mower and trimmed the grass herself, so that her family would not have to hire a boy to do it.

By that time the front lawn had become a stretch of green velvet, bordered with fringed wood fern and ageratum, and the picture garden in the rear of her yard taken on the colors of an Italian sunset; the girl had almost forgotten that she had ever been tired or cross; headaches and sleepless nights were also things of the past. Since then she has grown to be a strong, vigorous girl, and is now engaged in hard mental work for nine or ten months of the year. When she feels that she is in danger of being overtired, or when toward vacation time she begins to be conscious of "nerves," she seeks a spot where she can work outdoors and dig and plant to her heart's content; and when it is at all practicable she sleeps in the open.

ANOTHER GAME WITH NAMES FOR ST. VALENTINE'S DAY

A CORRESPONDENT writes that the hotel-register game published in the department pages some time ago was played with marked success at a church "sociable," and that it suggested another use of names in connection with an entertainment.

The new plan was carried out at a valentine party. Red cardboard hearts, two inches in diameter with loops of string attached were provided for the gusts to wear. Each heart was inscribed with a word and a figure. The word revealed the wearer's family name for the occasion and at the same time the particular part that he or she would be expected to play in the plans of the evening; the figure indicated the number of persons who would fall under particular classification.

Thus, if a heart was inscribed Speech, 3, the bearer understood that she belong to Speech family and was expected to search until she found two other members of it. If a second player's heart was marked Charade, 5, she must not stop until she had found the other four guests who were to act charades for the enjoyment of the gathering. Other family names were Stunt, Trick, Riddle and Gymnastics. One girl found herself labeled Solo, 1.

When the guests were at length correctly grouped, the members of each group consulted together and made plans how they should perform their particular part. No one was allowed to refuse.

Should the entertainment be held on All Fools' Day, the guests should wear fools' caps. Counterfeit refreshments should be served from a grab bag in true grab-bag style. After that, real refreshment should be served. Further adaptations of the game will suggest themselves for other special occasions.

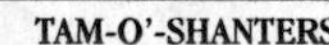

TAM-O'-SHANTERS

TAM-O'-SHANTERS are always popular with schoolgirls. They are not only comfortable but also economical and simple to make. A band of buckram or of pliable cardboard is all that is needed for a frame.

The tam-o'-shanter shown in Fig. 1 is made of Scotch plaid. It requires half a yard of material thirty-six inches wide. Cut two circular pieces, each eleven inches in diameter. Cut a paper pattern of the head size of a hat that fits well and, following that, cut an ellipse in the centre of one piece of the material: that piece is for the under side of the tam-o'-shanter. In cutting be sure to make a notch indicating the proper head size; and be sure to allow for seams—otherwise the tam-o'-shanter will be too large when finished. Seam the outer edges of the wrong sides of both pieces together, and turn the hat right side out. Cut a band of buckram about one and one half inches wide long enough to fit round the elliptical opening. Sew the ends of the band together, cover it with plaid material, and sew it into place, following the illustration here given. Line the hat with sateen or silk, trim it with a band of plaid or black ribbon, and finish it at the side with a flat, tailored bow.

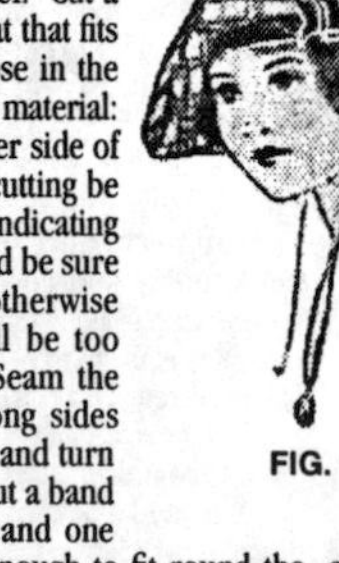

FIG. 1

THE COLLEGE TAM-O'-SHANTER

The college tam-o'-shanter shown in Fig. 2 is made of black or of any other colored velvet. It requires half a yard of material thirty-six inches wide. Cut two pieces of velvet, each eleven inches square. Cut an elliptical opening in one piece, fit it to your head, and allow for the seams and the head size, according to the directions given for Fig. 1. Make four false seams in the under-side piece, one at each point of that piece, and all running toward the centre. Seam the two squares of material together along the outer edges as you did in Fig. 1. Make a band of buckram one and one half inches wide, as in Fig. 1, to fit the size of the head and cover it by sewing on a piece of velvet or satin in soft folds. Line the hat with sateen or silk, and finish it with a tassel of silk or wool.

For novel trimmings for either of the tam-o'-shanters draw conventional "repeat" patterns round the velvet- or satin-covered band of buckram (see Fig. 2) and outline or embroider the design with a darning stitch in different colored silk or wool.

A SNAPSHOT HOLDER

SEND some of your most cheerful snapshots in this little holder to your friends—to soldier boys still in camp at home and across the water.

THE HOLDER WITH A SNAPSHOT IN PLACE

Take a strip of any stiff paper three and seven eighths inches by six and three eighths inches. Along the right and the lower side, draw lines AB and BCD (see the diagram), each five sixteenths of an inch from the edge. Crease the paper along those lines, and fold the left leaf, F, under, so that the edge is even with the creased edge, AB. Cut away the part DEC. Make an opening, G, in the right leaf one and three quarters inches by two and five eighths inches, with margins on each side five eighths of an inch wide.

Fold the paper again along the centre fold, EK, turn the narrow flaps, H and J, under, and after their corners have been mitred, as indicated in the diagram by dotted lines, paste and press the holder firmly into shape.

MORE NUT RECEIPTS

Cinnamon Nut Balls.—Beat two eggs until they are light and foamy. Add one half cupful of brown sugar, the same amount of molasses, one quarter cupful of milk, one teaspoonful of cinnamon ground fine, and one level teaspoonful of soda. Stir in enough rolled oaks or barley to make a stiff dough (a little flour may be added), and with your hands well floured roll the mixture into balls about the size of marbles. Place half nut meat in the centre of each ball; place the balls on a greased pan without crowding, and bake them in a moderate oven.

Baked Prunes With Nut Filling.—Soak some large prunes overnight. When they are ready to bake, remove the stones and wipe the fruit dry. Chop some nut meats rather fine and mix with them an equal quantity of maple or brown sugar. Beat the white of an egg very stiff, and into that fold the nut-and-sugar mixture. Fill the cavities in the prunes with the mixture, place them on a pan, and bake them in a moderate oven until they are plump. Serve them either hot or cold.

Ginger Nut Wafers.—Cream together one quarter cupful of butter or butter substitute and one half cupful of brown sugar. Add one half cupful of molasses and the yolks of two eggs that have been well beaten. Add one cupful of chopped nut meats, one quarter cupful of water, one scant tablespoonful of ginger, one level teaspoonful of soda dissolved in water, and enough rice flour to make a thin batter. Spread the mixture thin on the bottom of a well-greased pan, and bake until it is golden brown. Cut it into strips and serve it. You can also fashion figures or animals out of this mixture for favors. Use the cooky cutters that may be bought in the stores for that purpose and cut your mixture before you put it in the oven.

Figure 4.6c. Old periodical—The Youth's Companion: Girls' page.

Document Analysis Activity 3

Report Cards

If you were a student in 1896, what do you think your report card might have looked like? Look at the reproduction of a 7th grade report card from 1896-1897 in Figure 4.7. Use the Document Analysis Form to list your observations, speculations, and questions about it. Next, look carefully at a current report card from your school. Compare it to the one here from 1896-1897, looking for similarities and differences. Add these observations to your document analysis form and see if they lead to additional questions or hypotheses about report cards and what 7th grade was like in 1896.

What other sources could confirm or contradict your hypotheses about what 7th grade was like in 1896? See if you can find some of these sources and check your hypotheses.

A signifies . . . . Excellent.
B " . . . . Good.
C " . . . . Passable.
D " . . . . Deficient.

If in either Scholarship or Deportment a pupil fails to receive a mark as high as C he is in danger of losing his place in school.

PARENTS WILL PLEASE SIGN BELOW.

Sept. [illegible]
Oct. [illegible]
Nov.
Dec.
Jan.
Feb.
Mar.
Apr.
May
June

81-'96.

NEW HAVEN CITY SCHOOL DISTRICT.

Strong School.

REPORT OF

[illegible]

Room 12 VII Grade.

FOR THE YEAR

1896-97

	Sept.	Oct.	Nov.	Dec.	Jan.
Times Absent	0	2			
Times Tardy	0	0			
Conduct	a	a			
Reading	a	a			
Spelling	a	a			
Language	a	a			
Arithmetic	a	a			
Geography and History	a a	a a			
Composition					
Writing	a	a			
Drawing	a	a			
Music	a	a			
Sewing					
Cooking					
Woodwork					
General Standing	a	a			

	Feb.	Mar.	Apr.	May.	June.
Times Absent					
Times Tardy					
Conduct					
Reading					
Spelling					
Language					
Arithmetic					
Geography and History					
Composition					
Writing					
Drawing					
Music					
Sewing					
Cooking					
Woodwork					
General Standing					

Figure 4.7. Seventh grade report card from 1896-1897.

Document Analysis Activity 4

Yearbooks

You are probably familiar with your school's yearbook. (If not, try to examine a copy first.) Figure 4.8 shows yearbook pages from another time and place. Use the Document Analysis Form to record observations, then your hypotheses and questions about them.

Here are some questions you may or may not have considered:

1. Where and in what year do you think this yearbook was published? What clues did you use to guess that?

2. Is it a high school or junior high school yearbook? Why do you think that?

3. Look at the various racial and ethnic groups represented (and not represented) on the pages. What hypotheses do you have about the school based on that?

4. Can you estimate how many students graduated from this school this year? (These pages picture only the highest grade in the school.)

5. Do you see any patterns with respect to who is involved in various kinds of activities? Are there patterns within individuals' activities or patterns of involvement across individuals (certain kinds of people who tend to participate in the same activities)?

6. How do the activities in which students are involved compare to your school?

7. What else did you notice? What do you wonder about? On what evidence was that based?

Christmas Vacation Was a Welcome Respite from Work

JUDY ANN GARRETT—Diversified Cooperative Training 3, 4.
JANICE GARWOOD
ELLEN GAVENS
RAMIRO GAZO—Varsity Track 2, 3, 4; Varsity Volleyball 4.

~

DOUGLAS GEGEN—H.R. Treas. 4, Board Rep. 4; Chess Club 2, 3, 4; Science Club 2, Vice-Pres. 3, Pres. 4; Crescent Club 2, Chap. 3, 4; Concert Band 4.
CAROL ANNE GELPI—TIMES Staff 3, 4.
HARRIET GENANDES—H.R. Pres. 2, Vice-Pres. 3, Treas. 4, Board Alt. 4, P.T.S.A. Rep. 4; Concert Band 2, 3, 4; Marching Band 2, 3, 4.
BARBARA GEORGE—H.R. Chap. 3, Board Rep. 2, Health Council Alt. 3; Junior Classical League 3.

~

EVANGELINE GEORGE—H.R. Treas. 2, Student Council Rep. 2, 3, 4; Honoria 3, Treas. 4; National Honor Society 3, Sgt.-at-Arms 4; Mu Alpha Theta 3, 4; Junior Classical League 2, Vice-Pres. 3; Para-Medical 2, 4, Treas. 3; Health Council Hist. 3, 4; Orchestra 2, Vice-Pres. 3, Pres. 4; Big Sister 3, 4; Inter-Club Council 3.
ELIZABETH GIASI—H.R. Secy. 2, 3, TIMES Rep. 2, Student Council Rep. 2, 3, 4.
SILVIA GIL
SANDRA GILES—H.R. Student Council Rep. 2, 3; Thespians 3, 4; National Forensic League 3; Varsity Basketball 2.

Richard Chan, Senior Class treasurer and publicity chairman, puts up a bulletin board to promote spirit during the Christmas holidays.

(*figure continues*)

Figure 4.8. Yearbook pages.

Adolfo Garcia Was the President for Three Years

The Senior Class undertook to clean up the student parking lot. Nancy Massel, Adolfo Garcia, and Nancy Berk, with paintbrushes in hand, begin the task.

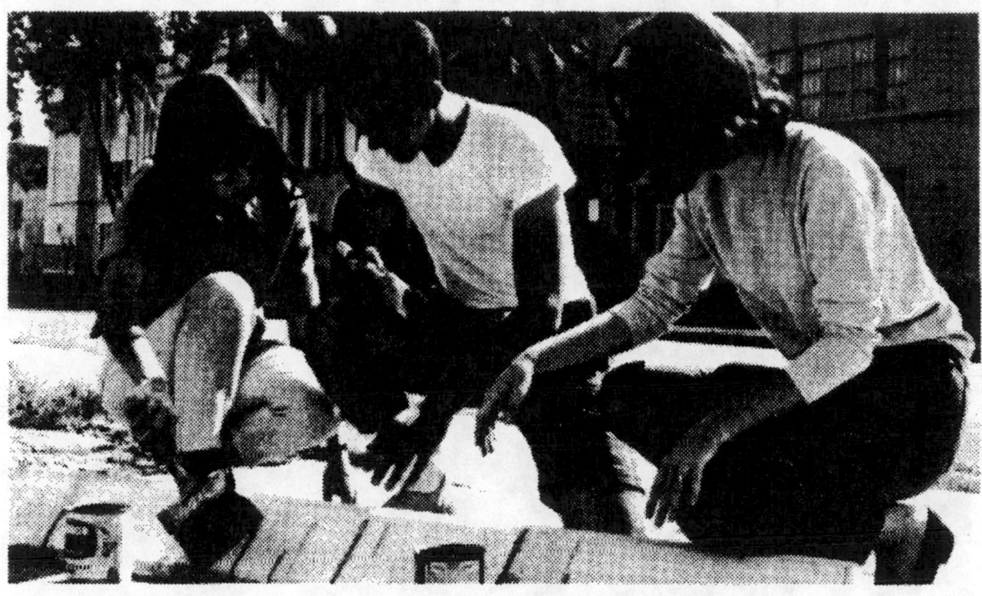

BETTY-JO GILMAN—H.R. Pres. 2, 3, 4; Honoria 3, Sgt.-at-Arms 4.
BRENDA GLENN—Majorettes 2, 3, 4.
STANLEY GLIKSMAN—H.R. TIMES Rep. 3, 4, Student Council Rep. 4, Health Council Rep. 4; Spanish National Honor Society 3, 4; Baseball Mgr. 2, 3, 4.
SAM GLOGGER—Hydronauts 3, 4.

~

AGUSTIN GOIRIGOLZARRI—Intramural Basketball 2; Intramural Softball 2.
SUSAN GOLDBERG—H.R. Secy. 2, Chap. 3, Student Council Rep. 2, 3, Board Rep. 4, Health Council Rep. 4.
MICHAEL GOLDFARB—H.R. Vice-Pres. 4; Interact 3, Board of Directors 4; Varsity Football 3, 4.
HUGH GOLDMAN

~

NANCY GOLDMAN—H.R. Student Council Rep. 2, Alt. 3, Board Rep. 2, 4; Student Council Treas. 3, 2nd Vice-Pres. 4; Interact Sponsor 4; Inter-Club Council Pres. 4; Honoria 3, 4; Hall of Fame 4.
EDWARD GOMEZ—H.R. Pres. 2, Vice-Pres. 3; Tri-M 2, Sgt.-at-Arms 3, Vice-Pres. 4; B-Squad Football 2; Concert Chorus 2, 3, 4; Boys' Chorus 3.
VICTOR GOMEZ—H.R. Student Council Rep. 2; Intramural Softball 2, 3; Intramural Basketball 2, 3.
WILLIAM GOMPERS—B-Squad Football 2; Varsity Golf 3.

(*figure continues*)

Figure 4.8. Yearbook pages (*continued*).

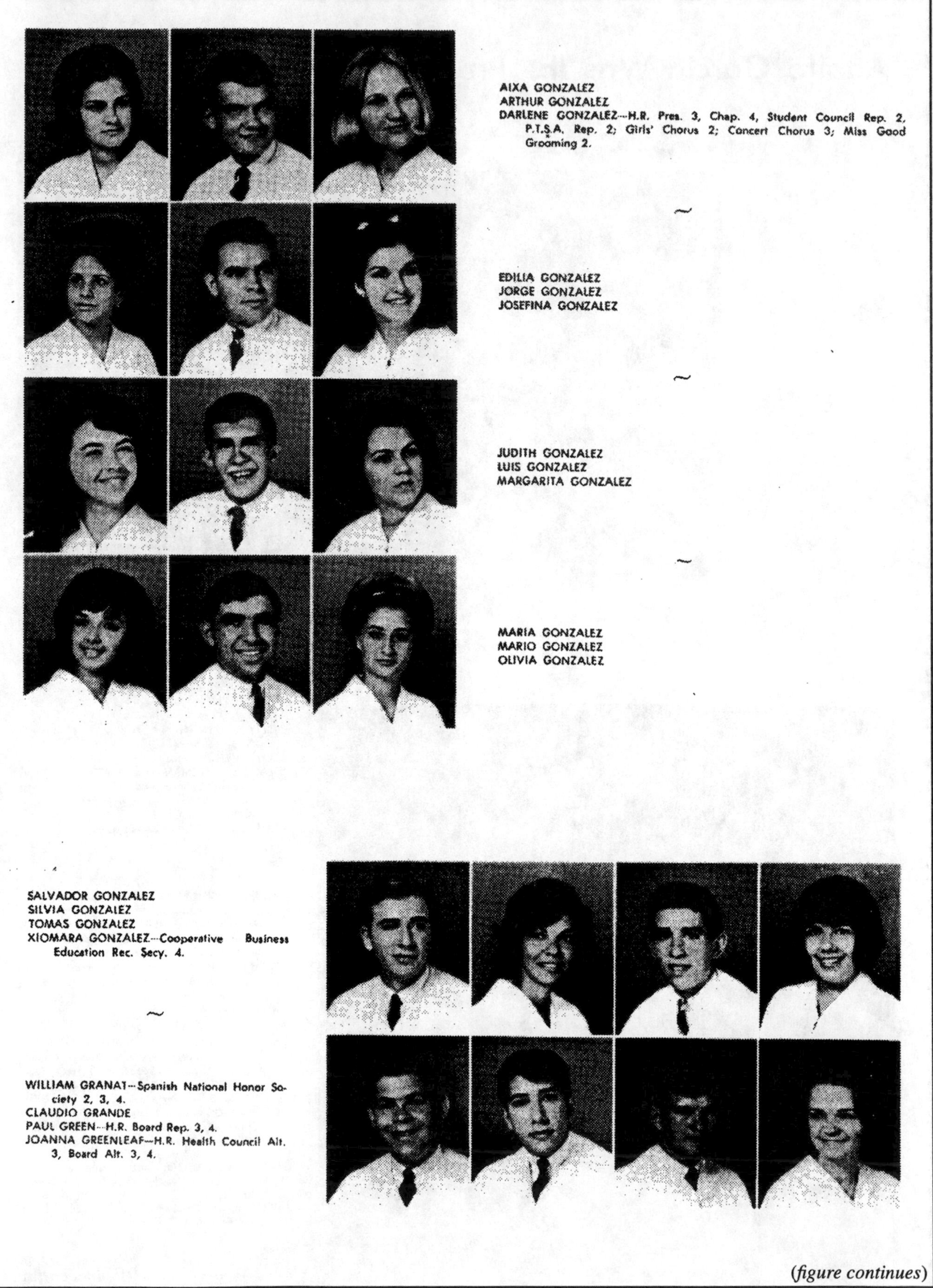
AIXA GONZALEZ
ARTHUR GONZALEZ
DARLENE GONZALEZ—H.R. Pres. 3, Chap. 4, Student Council Rep. 2, P.T.S.A. Rep. 2; Girls' Chorus 2; Concert Chorus 3; Miss Good Grooming 2.

EDILIA GONZALEZ
JORGE GONZALEZ
JOSEFINA GONZALEZ

JUDITH GONZALEZ
LUIS GONZALEZ
MARGARITA GONZALEZ

MARIA GONZALEZ
MARIO GONZALEZ
OLIVIA GONZALEZ

SALVADOR GONZALEZ
SILVIA GONZALEZ
TOMAS GONZALEZ
XIOMARA GONZALEZ—Cooperative Business Education Rec. Secy. 4.

WILLIAM GRANAT—Spanish National Honor Society 2, 3, 4.
CLAUDIO GRANDE
PAUL GREEN—H.R. Board Rep. 3, 4.
JOANNA GREENLEAF—H.R. Health Council Alt. 3, Board Alt. 3, 4.

(*figure continues*)

Figure 4.8. Yearbook pages (*continued*).

IRA GRIFFITH—H.R. Pres. 3, 4, Student Council Alt. 2; Key Club 2, Chap. 3, Jr. Director 3, Vice-Pres. 4; Tri-M 3, Chap. 4; Inter-Club Council Chap. 4; Class Sgt.-at-Arms 3, 4; Varsity Volleyball 2; B-Squad Football 2; Varsity Track 2, 3, 4; Concert Chorus 2, 3, Pres. 4; Pep Doll 4; Calendar Boy 3, 4; Big Brother 4; Jr. Joe 3; Mr. Hey Day 3; Homecoming King 4; Boys' State 3; Hall of Fame 4.
SALLY GRIFFITH—H.R. Secy. 2, 3.
JANIS GROH—H.R. Vice-Pres. 2, Board Rep. 2, 3; Little Women 2, Parl. 3, Treas. 4; Pep Club 3, Honorary 4; Girls' Council 2, 3, 4; Quill and Scroll 3, 4; MIAHI Managing Editor 2, Business Mgr. 3, Editor-in-Chief 4, Cheerleading Mgr. 4; Miss Good Grooming 2; Miss School Spirit 4; Homecoming Court 4, Interact Sponsor 4; Calendar Girl 4; Big Sister 3, 4; Hall of Fame 4.

RANDI GROSSMAN—H.R. Pres. 2, TIMES Rep. 2; Honoria 2, 3, Rec. Secy. 4; Pep Club 2, Honorary 3, 4; Cheerleader 3, 4; National Honor Society 3, 4; Class Treasurer 2; Girls' Council 3, 4; Hall of Fame 4.
NORMA GUERRA—Girls' Sports Club 2, Pres. 3, 4; Tri-Hi-Y Vice-Pres. 3; Varsity Volleyball 2, 3, 4; B-Squad Basketball 2, 3, 4; Varsity Track 2; Varsity Badminton 2, 3, 4, Varsity Softball 2.
SHARON GUEST—Future Secretaries of America 2, 3.

LINDA GUNTER—Thespians 2; Diversified Cooperative Training 3, Pres. 4, Majorettes 2.
DELLANIRA GUTIERREZ
JOSE GUTIERREZ

PEDRO GUTIERREZ—EL PANAMERICANO Staff 4; Varsity Football 3, 4.
REBECCA GUTIERREZ
STEPHEN HAMILTON—H.R. Secy. 4.

LOUIS HAMMOND
LYNN HANTZ
DAVID HARDY—B-Squad Football 2; Varsity Baseball 2; Varsity Football 3, 4; Varsity Volleyball 2.
BRYAN HARMS—National Forensic League 2, 3, 4; Thespians 2; Spanish National Honor Society 2.

JOSE HARO—H.R. Vice-Pres. 2, 3; Intramural Basketball 2, 3, 4; Intramural Volleyball 2; Intramural Softball 2; Track 2.
RANDALL HARRISON
JASON HARTMAN
SHIRLEY HAWKES—H.R. Secy. 2; Future Secretaries of America 2, 3; Junior Debs 2, 3, Parl. 4.

Figure 4.8. Yearbook pages (*continued*).

Sample Selection

Chapter 5

Though we gather data in order to answer a research question and generalize our results, it is not possible to gather data from everyone in the population we wish to study. For example, if our research question asks whether 9th graders prefer different sports than 12th graders, it would be impossible to survey or interview all 9th and 12th grade students in the world, the population in which we are interested. Even if our question only concerns 9th and 12th graders in our school, surveying every student could be a formidable task. The solution is to choose a sample, which is a smaller group that is representative of a larger population.

How Big Is Big Enough?

Believe it or not, the way the sample is chosen can be more important than the number of people in the sample. If our sample is biased in some way, our results will be less reliable, no matter how many subjects we have. There are statistical guidelines for choosing an appropriate sample size, but at this point it is probably more important to choose a number that is manageable in your situation and do everything you can to make sure it is representative of the population as a whole. It would be difficult for most adolescents to gather data from a sample large enough to make the statisticians happy (Isaac & Michael, 1981). For example, if students were surveying their senior class of 100 students, they'd need data from 80 students to convince the statisticians that their sample was large enough. Therefore, students should learn the importance of a representative sample, focus on how to create an unbiased sample, and choose a sample size that is practical for all involved. Students can still practice professional sample selection, data gathering, and data analysis techniques with smaller sample sizes.

Teaching Students About Sampling

Conducting a study with M&M®'s (or strips of paper or marbles) provides students with a concrete study in sampling. Most students have their favorite color and believe that there are less of that color than others. Invite them to investigate the question "Are there equal numbers of each color of M&M®'s?" While there will be a few students who would like to try, it usually only takes a few moments of reflection to determine that we could not possibly count all the M&M®'s in the world. They can, however, find a sample of M&M®'s to count and discuss whether the sample is representative of all M&M®'s that exist.

Ask students to imagine that a large bag of M&M®'s you show them represents all the M&M®'s in the world. Divide students into pairs or groups of three and give each 1/4 cup of M&M®'s on a piece of paper towel or a napkin. Have them count the number of each color in their sample, then list on the board or overhead the count from each group. Invite students to compare the counts from various samples and compare them to the bag as a whole. (You can find the total by adding up all the samples and comparing them to the whole using ratio or percent.) There is usually enough variation across samples for students to see that samples do give us clues about the population as a whole but that no one sample can guarantee the characteristics of the whole population. If you have time, you can give each group an additional 1/4 cup and have them recount and re-compare. Was a larger sample more representative of the population? Saving the data from several classes will allow your students to compare across classes, as well as determine how consistent the color distribution was across large bags of M&M®'s used in each class. Sampling Activity 1 "MMMMMM Good!" explains this activity in further detail and includes a form for recording data.

Choosing a Sample

If choosing a sample appropriately is more important than the actual number in the sample, how do you choose a representative sample? There are several ways, each with its own advantages and disadvantages. The easiest for teachers, of course, is to send students to the classroom of a supportive colleague to survey the students in his/her room. This method could, however, result in one of the most unrepresentative samples. Unfortunately, the research corollary of Murphy's Law applies: Generally, the more accurate a method is, the more challenging it is as well. The good news is that if teachers and students understand the strengths and weaknesses of the major types of sample selection, they can balance the need for accuracy and convenience according to the experience level of the students and the size, complexity, and sophistication of their research.

Random Sample

The sampling procedure that will give students a sample that best represents the population they are studying is random sampling. It is reliable because each subject in the population has an equal chance of being selected for the sample. There are two ways to choose a random sample—one is more useful with small populations and the other works best with large populations. With smaller populations, write the names of all people in the population (everyone in the 7th grade or all doctors in town) on small pieces of paper. Student can put all the names in a box, bag, or hat and draw out the number they need for their sample without looking. This method ensures that every person in the population has an equal chance of being selected for the sample. An honestly-run lottery or raffle is a good example in the real world of a random sample.

If the research question involves a large number of people from which to select a sample, it may not be practical to write all their names on little slips of paper. In that case, students can use a table of random numbers to help them choose a random sample. They'll also need a list with all the names on it. If the list is not already numbered, they can go through and number the names sequentially. Appendix A contains the table of random numbers. To use the table, they should first determine how many digits there are in the largest number on their list of subjects. For example, if they have a list of 950 subjects, they will be concerned with only the last three digits of the numbers in the table. They should then look at the last three digits of the first number in the table. If the first number was 65208, they would look for subject number 208 and select him/her for their sample. If the number was too large, they should simply skip it and go on to the next number. Imagine that a hypothetical row of the table was:

65208 39542 44009 44528 99967 18399

They would choose subjects 208, 542, 9, and 528. They couldn't use the 5th number, 967, because they only have 950 subjects in their population. They would go on to the next number and add subject 399 to the sample. They would continue in this way until they had identified the number of subjects needed.

Stratified Sample

One variation on a random sample is the stratified sample. Researchers use it when they want to know about the group as a whole and when they want to be able to analyze data about subgroups within the whole group. Therefore, they would use this sampling method if they thought some subgroups would have different opinions or answers about the question they are researching. For example, in presidential elections, campaign workers may suspect that older and younger voters might have different opinions about the candidates or that people of different economic status would find certain election issues more important than others. Campaign advisors would want to be sure that their public opinion samples included a representative number from each group (rather than leaving that up to chance) and that they could identify the views of the various subgroups.

On questions related to school or adolescents, what factors do you think might affect students' responses? Gender? Age? Grade level? Degree of academic success? Participation in sports? The question(s) students are researching will help determine if a stratified sample would be useful. For example, if they want to know if the school should spend more on athletic facilities, those active in sports are likely to have different answers than those who are not. It's less likely that students of different ages will respond differently, so it probably wouldn't make sense to stratify by age for that particular question. However, opinions about which social activities the student council should sponsor in a middle school might indeed differ by the age/grade of the student.

After they decide which factors about their subjects might lead to different answers to their research question, they can divide their population into groups based on these factors. Again, these factors could be gender, race, age, participation in some activity, etc. They will then conduct random sampling within each group. If their population subgroups are equal in size—equal numbers of boys and girls—their job is easy. They would also want 50% of their sample to be male and 50% to be female, the same proportion as in the population. They need to determine how many students are to be sampled, choose half randomly from among the boys' names and half their sample from the girls' names, and they are all set.

Unfortunately, numbers don't always work out that simply. Imagine that a teacher needs to make sure all grade levels in his/her four-grade high school are represented in his/her sample in the same proportion as they exist in the school. If there are 1000 students in a four-grade high school, he/she might select 25% of the students from each grade to make a sample of 100 students. However, it is likely that there are not equal numbers of students in each grade of a high school. If one grade has more students than another, it would need to have more representatives in the sample. For example, if seniors make up only 20% of the school population, they would need to comprise 20% of the sample as well. Likewise, if 35% of the high school consists of freshmen, the teacher would need 35 freshmen in his/her sample, along with the 20 seniors. Using a stratified sample, the teacher not only makes sure important subgroups are represented accurately, but he/she also make sure that he/she is able to analyze the data by subgroups to see if there are actual differences. The teacher could accurately represent the views of the school and also see if seniors differed in their responses from freshmen. Once he/she determined the number needed from each grade, he/she could select them using either the name-in-the-hat method or a table of random numbers. The stratified random sample method not only allows a researcher to assure representation of specific groups, but it also makes it possible to analyze data by subgroups (for example, to examine responses from seniors only) as well as for the whole sample.

Systematic Selection

Systematic selection is easier to do, but somewhat less valid than random sampling. When using systematic selection researchers count down a list of names, taking every 3rd or 10th or 25th person, depending on the sample size needed. More precisely, they'll first need to determine the size of sample they want to use and the proportion of the total population that it represents. For example, if they had a middle school population of 600 and wanted to sample 60 students, they would need to choose 10% or one out of every ten students.

Their next step is to get a list of all members of the population from which they are sampling. They would close their eyes and randomly choose a name near the top of the list. They would circle or check that name as one of the sample. Then they would count down from that name whatever number they determined for the proportion they needed. In the example above, they need one in ten, so they should count down ten names and circle/check that name. (If they needed one of every seven, they would count down seven names and select that person.) They would continue counting down the same number and selecting every -nth name until they have the correct number needed for the sample. When all the names have been selected, they should also be near the bottom of the list. If not, their math and/or counting may be off.

This method is clearly easier than writing out names and pulling them from a box, so why isn't it better than random sampling? In systematic sampling, all subjects don't have an equal chance of being chosen, because the interval between names is fixed. Perhaps the list is in alphabetical order. If the population includes people from diverse ethnic groups, the sample may end up with some groups underrepresented because their names may tend to cluster in certain parts of the alphabet. If the list is organized in another way, (homerooms, test scores, etc.), other types of subjects may be underrepresented simply because of the way the names clustered. Despite these difficulties, systematic sampling can often provide a reasonably representative sample in a manner that is manageable by most students.

Cluster Sampling

Cluster sampling is the easiest method to use and, unfortunately, the least valid. When using cluster sampling, researchers choose an existing group or cluster as their sample, for example, a classroom of students, a block in a neighborhood, members of a single club, customers in a single store, etc. That the subjects in a single cluster may be there for a reason, having something in common that is not true of the population as a whole, causes cluster sampling to lose validity. For example, a researcher takes the members of a particular class to be the sample. Even if the school does not formally group students by ability, there are often systematic differences between classes (participation in band, special education placements, foreign language classes, etc.) that could affect student responses to data gathering. The same types of differences present among classrooms also exist in other types of clusters. Although the Chamber of Commerce might provide a ready sample to survey, would its members' views be representative of the community as a whole?

Cluster sampling may turn out to be the reasonable choice for novice researchers if their focus is on practicing gathering and analyzing data or if the research project is fairly small or unsophisticated. In truth, many researchers working in schools have had to use cluster sampling because school officials were unwilling to disrupt the school routine to accommodate data gathering from a random sample across the student body. If students decide to use cluster sampling, it is important that teachers talk with them about the disadvantages and encourage them to consider whether there are likely to be systematic differences between their cluster sample and the population that might affect their results. If so, they should be sure to analyze it in the discussion section when reporting the results of their research.

Choosing a Sampling Method

The students' goals are to balance the need for a representative sample with their experience with research studies. Cluster sampling of a colleague's classroom may be the best option for 6th graders in their first data gathering activity. More experienced students should be involved in selecting a sampling technique after teachers have helped them understand the validity and ease-of-use limitations of various sampling strategies. Whatever strategy students select, the most important thing is for them to understand the implications of their sampling method for data analysis and conclusions.

Sampling Activity 1

MMMMMM Good!

First, find a partner and talk with him or her. Do you think there are the same number of all the colors of M&M®'s? Yes ___ No ___ Why?

If you said "no," do you have a hypothesis about which color will be found the most? Which do you think? ____________ Why do you think that?

You will be given a small amount of M&M®'s to count. Working with your partner, first separate them by color, then carefully count and record the number of each color in the spaces provided. Do not eat any yet! Scientists do not destroy their data until the research is finished! Report your data in order to create a data base for the whole class.

Red ____________ Green ____________

Yellow ____________ Orange ____________

Light Brown ____________ Blue ____________

Dark Brown ____________

Just looking at your data, was your hypothesis confirmed?

Look at the data from the whole class. How is it the same as your data? How is it different? Based on all the data, was your hypothesis confirmed?

Sampling Activity 2

Favorite Subjects

Researchers are seldom able to gather data from all the subjects in a population, so they need to select a sample. A good way to choose a sample is by random selection. You may choose randomly by drawing from a hat or using a table of random numbers. For this activity, you will choose a random sample of students in your class and see how it compares to the whole class. First choose a random sample of five students. Count the number of boys and girls in the group and ask them to tell you their favorite school subject. Next, choose a sample of ten and do the same thing. (Don't forget to put your first sample back. If you want a random sample, every name must be available for selection.) Finally, count the number of boys and girls in the class and tally favorite subject for the whole class. Were your samples representative with respect to gender? Favorite subject? Why or why not?

	Sample of 5	Sample of 10	Population (Whole Class)
Boys			
Girls			
Math			
Science			
Social Studies			
Language Arts			
Physical Education			
Other			
Other			
Other			

Sampling Activity 3

Tables Are More Than Furniture

Imagine that you are a pollster, seeking information about how people feel about a controversial issue in your community. Find a list of names from which you might like to draw a sample—students in your school might be a good one. You might also want to sample opinions of people in a group in which you or your parents participate—athletic league, church/synagogue/mosque, or civic or service organization (such as the Rotary Club, Women's Club, 100 Black Men, Chamber of Commerce, etc.).

Work with your teacher to determine the sample size that you want. Consider the kind of data gathering you will be doing, possible expense involved (postage or printing costs), how much time you will have to analyze data, expected rate of return, etc. If you are not currently doing research and just want to practice selecting a sample using a table of random numbers, choose a sample that represents 20% of your population if the total number of names on your list is 200 or less. Choose 10% of your population if it's larger than 200.

The first step in using a table of random numbers to select a random sample is to sequentially number each name on the list. If you chose a large list, you can divide up the task and have several people number the list. Just be sure each person knows what number to start with! You can number the whole list in sequence or number each page sequentially, starting with a different hundred for the first name on each page (e.g., 100, 101 . . . on the first page; 200, 201 . . . on the second page and so on).

Once the names are all numbered, you can work in pairs. One person should start at the top of a column in the table of random numbers (Appendix A) and read off the relevant part of the number. (To find the relevant part of a number, first determine how many digits there are in the largest number on your list of subjects. For example, if you have a list of 750 subjects, you will be concerned with only the last three digits of the numbers on the table. You will then look at the last three digits of the first number in the table. If the first number is 23198, we will look for subject number 198 and select him/her for our sample.) The other person should find the subject on the list with that same number and circle or check the name to indicate that he/she will be part of the sample. If the number your partner reads is larger than the number of names in your population, simply skip it and go on to the next number in the table. Continue in this fashion until you have selected the number of subjects needed.

Sampling Activity 4

Groups Within Groups

Suppose you had a research question on which you thought subgroups of people might have different opinions. It could relate to preferred extracurricular activities at your school, where kids involved in sports might have different views than those not participating. On a question about privileges for honor roll students, you might find differences in the opinions of students who do well academically and those who do less well. You not only want to make sure that the subgroups are accurately represented in your sample, but you also want to be able to separate their answers to report information by subgroup. This activity will give you a chance to select such a sample.

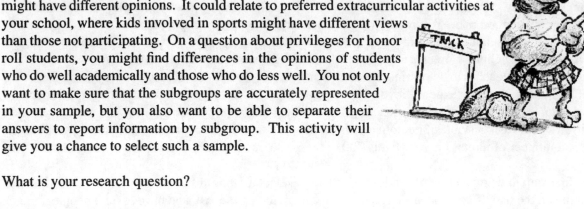

What is your research question?

What subgroup variable seems most relevant to your research question?

Grade level _______ Gender _______ Bus rider/not? _______

Participant in extracurricular activities? _______ Honor roll student? _______

Other: ____

Why do you think the variable you picked is relevant to your research question?

Discuss your reasons with a partner and your teacher. Once you agree, use the questions on the next page to choose a stratified sample.

(continued on next page)

Sampling Activity 4

1. What is the total number of students in the school? _______ Put this number below in the space for school population on the chart.

2. Now decide on the total size of the sample you wish to select. From how many students do you wish to collect data? _______ Put this number in the space for sample size.

3. Once you have decided on which variable to stratify, list the different categories of that variable in the first column. (For example, if you choose the variable "gender," the categories are male and female.) Next, determine how many actual students there are in each category and record this in the second column.

4. Decide what percentage of the population (the whole school) each category represents by dividing the number in that category by the total population. For example, if you decide to use "grade level" as your variable, find out how many students are freshmen, sophomores, juniors, and seniors. Divide each number by the total number of students in the school to find out the percentage in each grade.

5. Once you know how large your total sample will be, you can decide how many students from each category will be in your sample by multiplying the number in the sample by the percentage of students in each category (see Column 4 below). Look at the following example, then record your categories, numbers, and percentages on the chart below.

Example: *School population = 1200* *Sample size = 150*

Categories	Actual number in school	Percent of total school	Number of each group in the sample
Freshmen	360	30% = (360/1200)	45 = (150 X .30)
Sophomores	336	28% = (336/1200)	42 = (150 X .28)
Juniors	264	22% = (264/1200)	33 = (150 X .22)
Seniors	240	20% = (240/1200)	30 = (150 X .20)

YOUR SAMPLE: *School population =* _______ *Sample size =* _______

Categories	Actual number in school	Percent of total school	Number of each group in the sample

The last step is to select the number of people for the sample from each category of names. Use the "names-in-the-hat" method or a table of random numbers to randomly select the necessary number of names from each subgroup of your population. In the example, this would mean pulling the names of 30 seniors randomly from a "hat" with the names of all 240 seniors in the school, then repeating the same for each grade level.

Analyzing and Interpreting Data

Chapter 6

After students have used their interpersonal intelligence to gather data, they must tap into their logical-mathematical intelligence in order to analyze the data and arrive at valid conclusions. There are two basic approaches to data analysis: quantitative and qualitative. The first, quantitative, involves data that can be counted: the number of hours a person works each week, number of middle school students preferring roller skating parties to dances, or the number of people choosing a particular response on a survey. This form of data analysis is the easiest to analyze and has been the backbone of traditional research methodology. For these reasons, it will be the focus of most of the data analysis chapter.

There are many ways to deal with quantitative data. *Descriptive analyses* (or *descriptive statistics*) simply describe the data and include percentages, averages, and various types of graphs. Other types of quantitative analysis attempt to go beyond describing the data that was actually collected to make inferences about a larger population. They attempt to answer questions such as "If this group of 8th graders prefers high-top to low-cut athletic shoes, what can we infer about the preferences of the rest of the 8th grade?" This type of analysis is called *inferential statistics* because it makes inferences beyond the data at hand. Probably most of the images that spring to your mind at the mention of the word "statistics" have to do with inferential statistics.

In thumbing through this chapter, you may have noticed that we have included mathematical formulas for some inferential statistics. The formulas are often complex-looking and may appear daunting. If you are hesitant to try your hand at the formulas, do not despair. However complicated they may appear, the formulas are really just a series of computations (+, –, x, ÷,) that can be done on almost any calculator. Some of your mathematically inclined students may enjoy the challenge of calculating the formulas by hand. If not, you can always do what professional researchers do—learn the purpose of each statistic, then use a statistics program to let your computer do the calculating!

There are other important data that can't be counted, data for which neither descriptive nor inferential statistics are appropriate. How can anyone quantify the experiences of a Vietnam War veteran or the complexity of a day spent observing a middle school teacher? This type of data is called qualitative because interpreting it entails understanding the qualities of a particular experience, rather than counting or calculating variables. Toward the end of this chapter, we will describe some simple techniques for systematically analyzing qualitative data. While a sophisticated treatment is beyond the scope of this book, basic strategies for identifying patterns in qualitative data can allow secondary students an opportunity to analyze qualitative data in ways that parallel those of professional researchers.

Quantitative Analysis

The intent of quantitative data analysis is to help organize numerical data so it is easier to understand. While the thought of doing statistics with middle and high school students may not seem consistent with "easier to understand," there are many forms of quantitative analysis that are both manageable and interesting. Indeed, more and more mathematics courses include statistics, often starting in elementary school. Teaching statistics is recommended in the standards of the National Council of Teachers of Mathematics (NCTM). Since some statistics can only be used with certain types of data, this section will start with a brief discussion about types of data. We will also explain the two basic types of quantitative analysis (descriptive and inferential), the power and limits of each, and how to use several kinds of statistics, from the basic to the more sophisticated. Each will include an explanation, a step-by-step example for you to follow, and an activity in which students can use each statistical technique. Start with the ones with which you are comfortable. If you'd like, you can invite students who are particularly interested in mathematics to study the more complex formulas and explain them to the class.

Types of Data

In the world of quantitative data analysis, there are four types of data that represent different scales of measurement: nominal, ordinal, interval, and ratio. Because different statistics are appropriate for different scales of measurement, it is important to be able to identify which type of data you will be analyzing.

Nominal data is the lowest level, classifying people or objects into two or more categories. Nominal categories have no numerical value—one is not higher or lower than the other. The categories must be discrete, that is, a person or object can only fit into one category in a set. Examples include gender (male, female), religion, school attended, learning style, etc. Categories can be ones that are naturally occurring (gender) or those created by the researcher (tall vs. short).

Ordinal data ranks people in order, based on the amount of some characteristic they possess. In an ordinal scale, subjects are rank-ordered from most to least or highest to lowest on some measure of interest. Ordinal rankings do not indicate how much higher the subject is than the next subject, only that one is higher than the next. Examples include ranking students by height, grade point average in their graduating class, first chair in a band, and fastest to slowest in the 50-yard dash on the track team.

Interval scales are based on equal intervals between measures. The difference between a score of 80 and 90 on a test would be the same as the difference between scores of 50 and 60. Using measurements from an achievement test (an interval scale), you not only know which nominal group (high vs. average) or what ordinal rank (higher score than Sam) Sue is, but also that she scored 10 more points than Lester and seven less than Marcus. You can add and subtract interval scores, as we did with Sue, Lester, and Marcus' scores, but you cannot multiply or divide them in order to compare scores. It's not accurate to say that a person who scores 80 is twice as knowledgeable as one who scores 40. Many educational measurements are of the interval type.

The *ratio scale* is the highest, most precise level of measurement. It has all the characteristics of the other three types, but the added bonus of a true zero point. A true zero means it is possible for there to be none of what is being measured, for example height, speed, distance, weight, and time. In contrast, getting a zero score on a history test (interval scale) does not mean that a person has no history knowledge. Because of the true zero, you can say that a person six feet tall is twice as tall as one who stands three feet tall or that two hundred pounds is twice as heavy as one hundred pounds.

Gay (1992) cleverly summarized these types of data, explaining, "Thus with a ratio scale we can say that Frankenstein is tall and Igor is short (nominal scale), Frankenstein is taller than Igor (ordinal scale), Frankenstein is seven feet tall and Igor is five feet tall (interval scale), *and* Frankenstein is seven-fifths as tall as Igor."

While level of measurement of data may seem an abstract and remote concept, it is important to understand because it helps researchers select an appropriate statistic with which to analyze quantitative data. A statistic appropriate for a lower level of measurement can be used with higher levels, but a statistic designed for a higher level of measurement cannot be used with lower levels of data. For example, chi square, a method which can be used with nominal data, can also be used with ordinal, interval, and ratio level data. On the other hand, a *t*-test, which requires interval or ratio level data, cannot be used with nominal or ordinal level data. We'll indicate the level of data for which each statistic is applicable.

Descriptive Analysis

As with descriptive research, descriptive statistics merely describe the data. They can not be used to generalize to a larger population or to draw grand conclusions, but they can be used to summarize the data that have been gathered.

Frequency Charts

The simplest form of descriptive analysis is frequencies or frequency counts. This analysis tells researchers how many times a given response occurred, whether it is an answer to a survey question, an object being observed, or the number of references made to a particular topic in a document. For example, students surveying 130 people about their preferences in grocery bags might have used the following question:

What type of grocery bag do you prefer?

a. plastic b. paper c. cloth (reusable) d. don't care

The students can count responses to a written survey or tally marks they made to record verbal answers. They can then do a frequency count to determine the number of responses to each preference. Their data summary can be presented in a chart like the one below:

Frequencies of Preferences in Grocery Bags

Plastic	49
Paper	28
Cloth	6
Don't care	47
Total responses	**130**

Frequencies can also be illustrated by a histogram (a bar graph representing frequencies) as in Figure 6.1.

Percentages

Percentages are another easy way to describe quantitative data. Continuing the example above, students can report the percentage of people preferring each type of grocery bag rather than the actual number. This form of data reporting might be even more meaningful to the audience than frequency counts of raw data. The responses are easier to compare and almost everyone is familiar with percentages. Students figure percentages by dividing the number of a given response by the total number of responses in the sample (49 preferred plastic divided by 130 total responses yields 37%). Results expressed as percentages can be displayed on a chart or pie graph, as in Figure 6.2. Many computer programs can create these data displays for researchers when they enter the percentages and response titles. For the do-it-yourselfers out there, most mathematics books have directions for creating pie graphs. Following is a brief refresher:

1. Remember that a circle has a total of 360 degrees.
2. Multiply 360 by the percentage needed, expressed as a decimal. If 50% of the subjects always recycled, multiply 360 x 0.50 = 180. Use an angle of 180 degrees to express 50 percent.
3. Using a protractor, mark off a piece of the circle bounded by the angle. Since a 180 degree angle is a straight line, draw a line through the middle of the pie.
4. Repeat until circle is complete.

Grocery Bag Preference	Number Responding	Percent of Responses
Plastic	49	37%
Paper	28	22%
Cloth	6	5%
Don't Care	47	36%
TOTAL	**130**	**100%**

Measures of Central Tendency (Mean, Mode, Median)

While percentages and frequencies provide some information, there are other times when it is helpful to know the average or middle point of the data in order to interpret it. There are three important measures of central

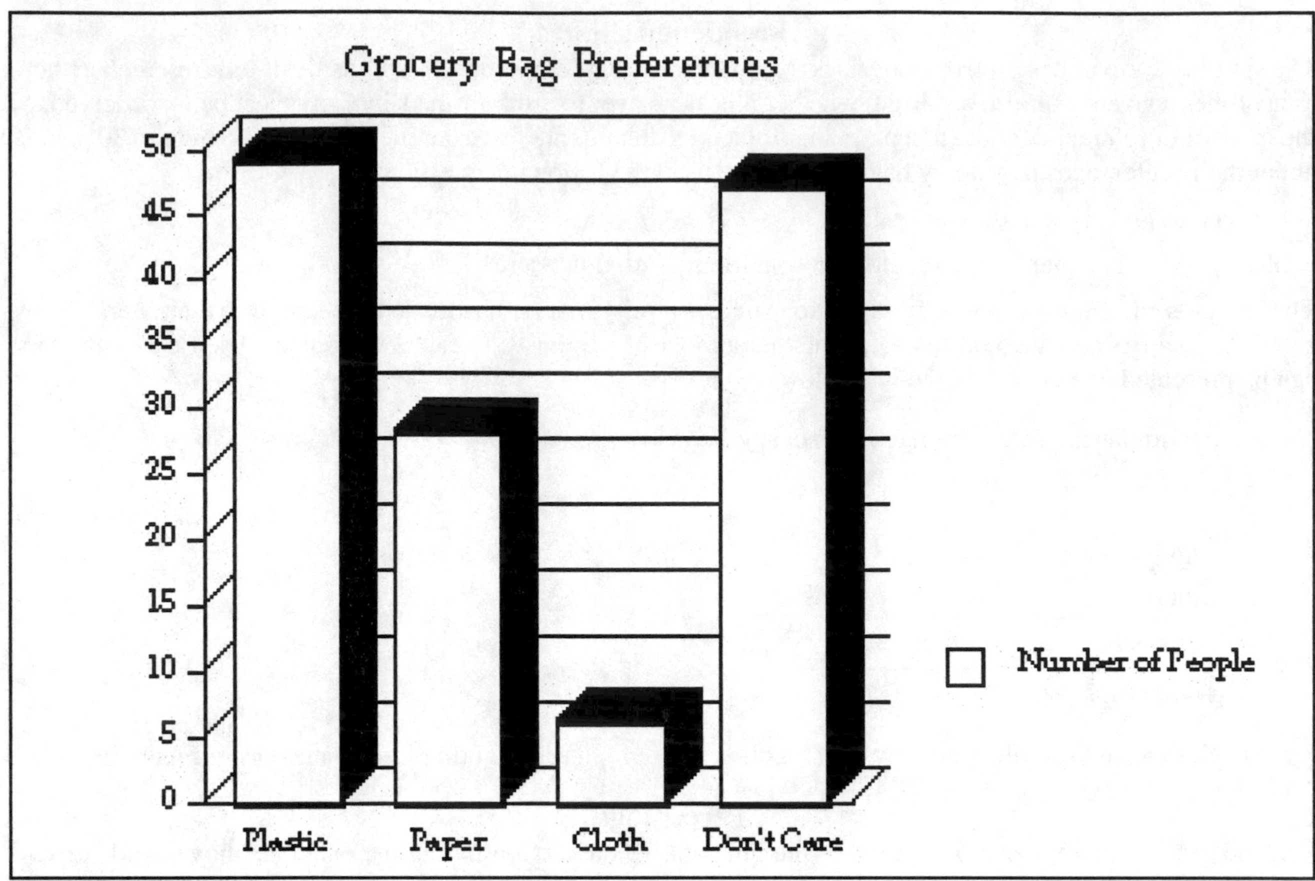

Figure 6.1. Histogram.

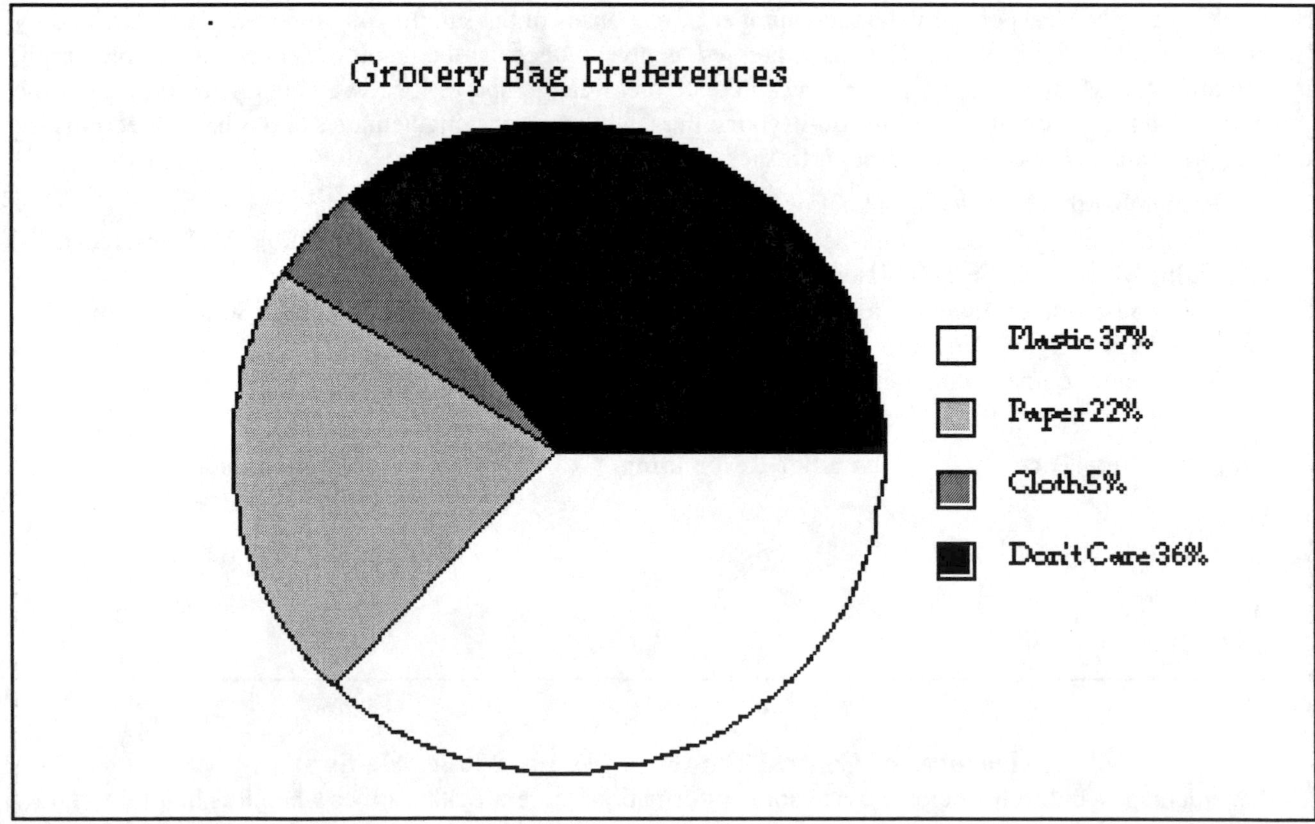

Figure 6.2. Percentage chart and pie graph.

tendency—mean, median, and mode—and there are times when each one is more appropriate to use than the others.

Teachers are probably quite familiar with calculating the mean. Any time you add a group of scores and divide by the number of scores (a very common activity around report card time), the resulting average is the mean score. It's easy and most students are familiar with the mean. So why use another method to calculate central tendency? One reason is that the mean is greatly affected by extreme scores. You've probably had at least one student who flunked a test or didn't turn in an assignment and was astounded that his/her average dropped a whole letter grade.

Imagine that you had heard that the average price of a new home in your neighborhood was $221,154. You'd probably assume most homes were worth $221,154, give or take a few thousand dollars. What if the actual data were represented in Figure 6.3? Is $221,154 an accurate representation of the "average" home price? Don Johnson, with his $950,000 home, has raised the mean to more than the price of most homes in the neighborhood. In cases with extreme scores, either the median or mode is a more helpful representation of central tendency; indeed the median is used to report home prices.

The most frequently occurring score is called the mode. In the home example, the mode is $145,000, since there were two houses sold at this price and only one at each of the other prices.

The median is the middle score. Arrange the house prices in Figure 6.3 from highest to lowest: $950,000, $395,000, $275,000, $176,000, $145,00, $145,000, $137,000, etc. After the thirteen numbers are in order, find the midpoint by counting up or down to the 7th price. The median is $137,000. (If you have an even number of scores, take a mean of the two middle scores.) In this sample, with Don's extreme home, both the mode and the median come closer to accurately describing the price of homes in the neighborhood than does the mean.

Measures of Variability (Range, Standard Deviation)

In addition to central tendency, some researchers want to describe the variability of the data—how spread out the scores are from the mean. They want to know if the scores tend to cluster around the mid-point or if they are spread widely from high to low. The easiest measure of variability is range—a simple report of the highest and lowest scores. It is possible to have samples with the same mean, mode, or median but with very different ranges. This information can be very important. Imagine you are interested in knowing the average amount of computer use by boys and girls in one semester. If the mean for girls was 36 and the mean for boys was 37, you might conclude that computer use was about the same for boys and girls. But what if you knew that the range for girls was 0 to 87 hours and the range for boys was 29 to 47 hours? Those ranges might suggest that computer use by gender was more different than you had originally thought. Applying measures of range and central tendency together for the home price sample would read as follows:

Thirteen homes were sold in the neighborhood in the first quarter of 1996. The range in home price was $95,000 to $950,000. The median selling price of a home was $137,000; the mode was $145,000.

Selling prices of homes in a particular neighborhood:

$950,000	$110,000	$395,000	$145,000
$145,000	$95,000	$107,000	$275,000
$123,000	$176,000	$99,000	$137,000
$118,000			

Frequencies

95,000	118,000	176,000
99,000	123,000	275,000
107,000	137,000	395,000
110,000	145,000	950,000
	145,000	

Figure 6.3. Frequency table.

A more sophisticated way to measure variability in a sample is standard deviation, a statistical examination of the average distance of scores from the mean. Knowing the mean and standard deviation of a set of measures tells researchers a lot about the characteristics of the data under study. For example, if students in your first period class had a mean score of 80 on a recent 100-point test with a standard deviation of 2, you would know that 99% of the students scored between 74 and 86. This range is true because if the distribution is relatively normal (standard curve), 99% of the scores will fall within three standard deviations above and below the mean. In the test example, adding and subtracting three standard deviations (2 x 3 = 6) to/from the mean of 80 gives you the range within which most students' scores fell. If, on the other hand, the test mean in your 6th period class was also 80, but the standard deviation was 7, it is likely that 99% of the scores fell between 59 and 100 [80 – (3 x 7); 80 + 21], indicating a much greater variability in students' performance.

High school students might want to relate their SAT scores to the normal curve. Each section of the SAT is calibrated so that the mean is 500 and the standard deviation is 100. Students scoring 600 are one standard deviation above the mean, 700 represents two standard deviations, and 800 three standard deviations. Since scores are always between 200 and 800 (three standard deviations above and below the mean), the range represents 99% of a normal distribution.

It is possible to calculate standard deviations by hand and that would provide students with a thorough understanding of the calculation. However, virtually no professional researcher would dream of figuring standard deviation by hand in this age of computers. If you have a student who really enjoys complex computation, by all means encourage him/her to work through the standard deviation formula by hand. Explaining the derivation of the standard deviation formula can also be an interesting enrichment topic that can increase understanding of the concept for students with particular interest or ability in mathematics. On the other hand, if students just want to know the standard deviation in order to better interpret their data, by all means show them how to do it on a calculator or on one of the many computer statistics packages (e.g., Statistics With Finesse or StatView). New software is developed almost daily, so check to see what is available through your school, library, or local college.

For those who are interested, below is a step-by-step explanation of the standard deviation formula. While it may initially look complex, it is simply a series of arithmetic computations that students have been doing since elementary school.

$$SD = \sqrt{\frac{SS}{N-1}} \quad \text{where} \quad SS = \sum x^2 - \frac{\left(\sum x\right)^2}{N}$$

SD is standard deviation; *SS* stands for "sum of squares"; *N* is the number of scores; Σ means "sum of"; Σx^2 is found by squaring all the x's, then adding those numbers; $(\Sigma x)^2$ is found by adding all the x's, then squaring the sum. As an example, analyze the quiz scores of ten students. Using the following chart makes computation of the formula easier:

Student	x (score)	x^2		
Amy	10	100		
Maria	8	64		
Derek	9	81		
Joshua	4	16		
Jeremy	6	36		
Tiffany	8	64		
Kenisha	9	81		
Eva	3	9		
Willie	7	49		
Jacob	9	81		
	$\Sigma x = 73$	$\Sigma x^2 = 581$	$N = 10$	$N - 1 = 9$

The first step is to find *SS*. Using the formula for *SS*, substitute in values from the chart on the previous page:

$$SS = \sum x^2 - \frac{(\sum x)^2}{N} \qquad SS = 581 - \frac{(73)^2}{10}$$

Multiply 73 by itself to find $(\Sigma x)^2$ and substitute it in the formula:

$$SS = 581 - \frac{5329}{10}$$

Divide the numerator by the denominator: $SS = 581 - 532.9$

Subtract to find *SS*: $SS = 48.1$

Substitute the values for *SS* and *N* into the standard deviation (*SD*) formula:

$$SD = \sqrt{\frac{SS}{N-1}} \qquad SD = \sqrt{\frac{48.1}{10-1}}$$

Subtract 1 from 10 in the denominator:

$$SD = \sqrt{\frac{48.1}{9}}$$

Divide the numerator by the denominator:

$$SD = \sqrt{5.34}$$

Then use a calculator to find the square root:

$$SD = 2.3$$

There is another opportunity for students to compute standard deviation in Data Analysis Activity 3.

Measures of Relationship (Correlation)

As discussed in Chapter 3, correlation describes how strongly and in what direction two variables are related. The correlation coefficient is the statistical way researchers measure the degree of a relationship. If two variables are strongly related, researchers can predict one by knowing the other. For example, if age and speed running the 50 yard dash are strongly correlated (in children under the age of 18), a researcher can make a reasonable prediction about a child's age just by knowing her sprinting time. The direction of a relationship refers to whether two variables rise and fall together or in opposite directions. When one variable goes up, does the other generally go up (as in calories eaten and body weight)? When one variable goes up, does the other go down (as in number of hours practicing a musical instrument and number of mistakes)? Or does there seem to be no systematic relationship between the variables (as in popularity and shoe size)?

Correlations are reported numerically in a range from -1.0 to +1.0. Either a negative or positive 1.0 indicates a perfect correlation, while zero represents no correlation between the variables. In a perfect 1.0 correlation, each time one variable goes up, the other increases in exactly the same proportion. For example, the number of cans of soda consumed and the number of calories added to the diet would be represented by a correlation of 1.0, assuming each can of soda had the same number of calories.

Though most people have been conditioned to believe that negative numbers represent less of something (and indeed most of the time they do), in the case of a correlation it is not true. A correlation of -1.0 represents just as strong a relationship as a correlation of 1.0. The difference represented by the negative sign is in the direction of the relationship. In a perfect negative correlation there is a decrease in one variable for every increase in the other. For example, if you had two piles of sand and shoveled sand from one to the other, the number of cups of sand in each pile would have a correlation of -1.0. For each cup of sand added to pile A, pile B would decrease—assuming you didn't spill any.

In the real world, very few variables are perfectly correlated. In almost all cases, the correlation coefficient will be somewhere between -1.0 and 1.0. If the correlation is positive, it represents a relationship in which one variable goes up as the other goes up, for example, number of books read in a month and enjoyment of reading. If the correlation is negative, however, one variable generally goes up as the other goes down (amount of time practicing and word processing errors).

The closer the correlation coefficient is to either 1.0 or -1.0, the stronger a relationship it represents. A moderate correlation lies between .3 to .5 or -.3 to -.5. A correlation of .1 to .2 or -.1 to -.2 would be very weak, indicating practically no relationship. A correlation of .8 or -.8 is considered strong. It is critical to remember, however, that even a very strong correlation does not imply that one variable causes the other, just that there is a relationship between the two. Researchers can't tell if variable A caused B, B caused A, or both A and B were caused by C. They can only tell that they vary together.

The correlation between variables can be expressed formally or informally. If you or one of your students want to know the exact strength of the relationship between two variables, you should use the formula described below or consult a statistics package. If you do use statistical software, be sure to read the accompanying documentation carefully. There are several different correlation formulas, each appropriate for a specific type or types of data. The computer will do the calculations as instructed, but the results will be meaningless unless the user has chosen the correct formula for the type of data being analyzed.

Without using statistics, you can estimate and display correlation relationships through graphs. By plotting one variable on each axis, it is possible to make some generalizations about the direction and strength of the correlation. A perfect positive correlation (1.0) is represented by a diagonal line as seen in Figure 6.4. A perfect negative correlation (-1.0) is also a straight diagonal line, only slanting in the opposite direction. Generally positive or negative correlations form graphs of various "football" shapes. These graphs are called scatterplots or scattergrams. The stronger the correlation, the closer the scatterplot approximates a line and the more narrow the football shape. A circular scatterplot would represent a zero correlation or no relationship.

If students choose to indicate a correlation using a scatterplot without including statistics, they might create a scatterplot like the one in Figure 6.5 and express their conclusions as follows:

> We examined the relationship between reported sense of belonging in school and attendance at inter-school athletic games. The shape and slant of the scatterplot indicate a low to moderate positive correlation between students' sense of belonging and attendance at interscholastic athletic events.

More sophisticated researchers will want the more exact information given by a correlation coefficient. Several computer programs can do this calculation, but we encourage you to consider working through the formula with your students so they can see its derivation. While the formula looks daunting, it consists of simple multiplication, subtraction, and square root, all of which can be obtained using a calculator. The example below takes you through it step by step, and there is an additional example for your students in Data Analysis Activity 6.

There are two main formulas used to calculate correlation: the Spearman rho and the Pearson *r*. The Spearman rho formula is used with ordinal data, representing a rank order rather than an amount of something. For example, if you were curious about the relationship between graduation rank in high school and another variable, you would use the Spearman rho formula. You need to do this because graduation rank is an ordinal relationship, with the numbers representing the order in which students rank or line up. To use the Spearman rho formula, when one variable in the correlational relationship is expressed in rank order, the other must also be expressed ordinally. So if you were looking at the correlation between graduation rank and SAT scores, you would need to rank the students ordinally (highest, next highest, etc.) on SAT scores rather than using the scores themselves in the correlation formula. Consult any good statistics text for this formula.

Most data students analyze will be expressed in interval or ratio scales, where the numbers represent amounts of a variable. For these data, the appropriate correlation formula is the Pearson Product Moment Correlation, better known as the Pearson *r*. It is this formula we will explain in detail. The formula is

$$r = \frac{N\sum xy - \sum x \sum y}{\sqrt{\left[N\sum x^2 - \left(\sum x\right)^2\right]\left[N\sum y^2 - \left(\sum y\right)^2\right]}}$$

where x and y represent two measures from each subject, N is the number of subjects, Σ means "sum of," and r is the Pearson Product Moment Correlation. In the following example, assume that you have collected data from ten students on their grades (using a 0-4 scale, with 4 equaling an A, 3 a B, etc.) and liking for an academic subject (using a 1-5 scale, taken from a survey they completed). You are curious about whether there is a correlation between grade in a subject and interest in that subject. Following are the data collected.

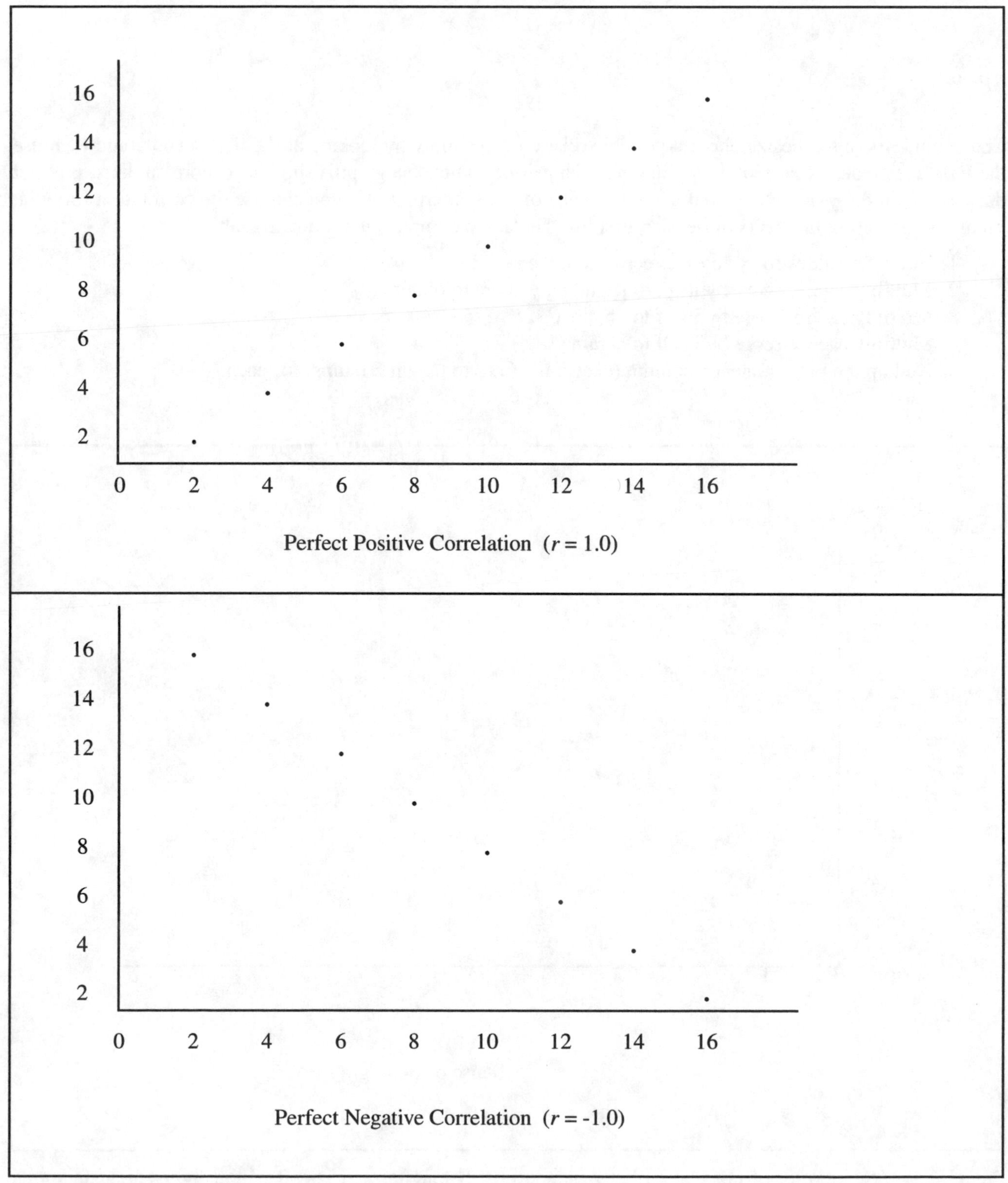

Figure 6.4. Correlation graphs.

Student #	Grade (x)	Liking (y)
1	4	5
2	2	3
3	1	2
4	1	3
5	3	4
6	4	3
7	2	3
8	3	4
9	0	1
10	3	5

You should first hypothesize about a possible relationship simply by looking at the data. You could then use these data to create a scatterplot by graphing each pair of points on a graph, using the x score on the x-axis and the y score on the y-axis, then analyzing the shape of the scatterplot. Or you can use the correlation formula. To make computing the Pearson *r* easier, first use the data to complete the following table.

1. Enter the values for x and y directly from the raw data.
2. Multiply each x-score by its corresponding y-score to obtain xy.
3. Multiply each x-score by itself to obtain x^2.
4. Multiply each y-score by itself to obtain y^2.
5. Add up the values in each column (except the first) to obtain Σ (sums) for each.

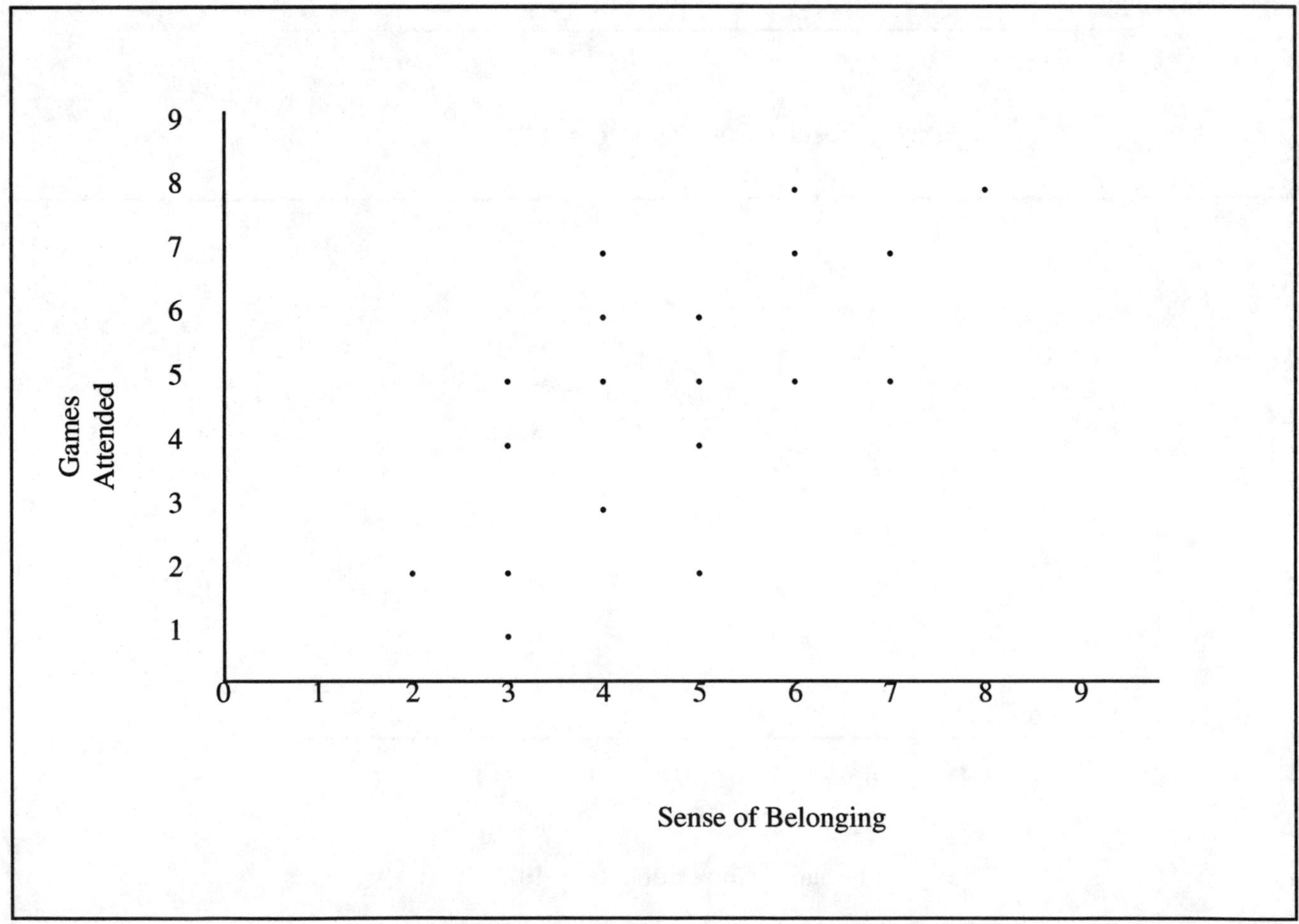

Figure 6.5. Scatterplot of correlation between sense of belonging and attendance at interscholastic sports events.

Subject number	x (grade)	y (liking)	xy	x^2	y^2
1	4	5	20	16	25
2	2	3	6	4	9
3	1	2	2	1	4
4	1	3	3	1	9
5	3	4	12	9	16
6	4	3	12	16	9
7	2	3	6	4	9
8	3	4	12	9	16
9	0	1	0	0	1
10	3	5	15	9	25
Σ (sigma-total of each column)	$\Sigma x = 23$	$\Sigma y = 33$	$\Sigma xy = 88$	$\Sigma x^2 = 69$	$\Sigma y^2 = 123$

In the first step, simply substitute the values for the symbols without doing any calculations. (Remember that "*N*" stands for the total number of subjects, in this case 10.) NOTE: Σx^2 is 69, the sum of all the x-squared values (5th column above). To obtain $(\Sigma x)^2$ first find the sum of x (23, from the 2nd column above), then square it (23 x 23 = 529). Do the same for Σy^2 and $(\Sigma y)^2$

Formula
$$r = \frac{N\sum xy - \sum x \sum y}{\sqrt{\left[N\sum x^2 - \left(\sum x\right)^2\right]\left[N\sum y^2 - \left(\sum y\right)^2\right]}}$$

$$r = \frac{(10)(88) - (23)(33)}{\sqrt{[(10)(69) - 529][(10)(123) - (1089)]}}$$

Using order of operations, first multiply all the expressions next to each other, for example (10)(88), and substitute these results into the formula.

$$r = \frac{880 - 759}{\sqrt{[690 - 529][1230 - 1089]}}$$

Subtract the values within the brackets and above the line and rewrite the equation.

$$r = \frac{121}{\sqrt{[161][141]}}$$

Multiply the numbers within brackets and rewrite the equation.

$$r = \frac{121}{\sqrt{22701}}$$

Next obtain the square root of 22701 and substitute that into the equation. (Most calculators can easily compute square root.)

$$r = \frac{121}{150.67}$$

To obtain the correlation coefficient (*r*), divide the numerator by the denominator. This number may be positive or negative, but should have an absolute value less than 1.0

$$r = .8031$$

Your final step is to compare the correlation coefficient for the data to the critical value in the correlation table (Appendix C). This comparison will allow you to determine if the correlation coefficient you find is strong enough to have statistical significance or if it could have occurred by chance. (Statistical significance is discussed in detail at the beginning of the next section on inferential statistics.) To compare the correlation coefficient you obtained from the data with the critical values in the correlation table, first calculate the degrees of freedom (df) for the data. Subtract two from the number of paired observations. In the example above, there are ten pairs of data (observations), so the degrees of freedom would be eight (10 – 2 = 8). Locate that number in the df column of the correlation table and follow it across to the column representing the level of significance you have chosen for your analysis (usually .05; also explained below).

Computed correlation coefficient (*r*): .8031
Degrees of Freedom (10 – 2): 8
Critical value at .05 from the correlation table: .6319

Since the correlation coefficient obtained from the data (.8031) was greater than the critical value in the table (.6319), you can assume that there is a statistically significant relationship between interest in the subject and grades received for the students and subjects in the sample. Because the correlation is positive, you know that grades rise as interest rises. (If the *r* you obtained was a negative value, it means that one variable rises as the other falls.)

Remember that correlation does not mean causation. It is equally possible that: (a) greater interest leads to higher grades, (b) high grades lead to increased interest in a subject, or (c) some other variable(s) (e.g., good teacher, self-concept, interested parents, school culture, etc.) independently influence both grades and interest in the subject. The only conclusion that can be justified by these data might read, "In a sample of ten sophomore world history students, there was a statistically significant positive relationship between grades and interest in that subject. Students with higher grades tended to have a higher interest in the subject, while students with lower grades indicated lower interest in response to a survey."

If an analysis includes nominal data (discrete categories such as gender, employment status, type of job, etc.), you'll need to use a different correlation formula—the rank biserial correlation. While the formula reaches beyond the scope of the book, some statistics computer programs include that formula and most college level statistics books will show the formula.

Inferential Statistics

Most quantitative data can be expressed using descriptive analyses. However, middle and high school students should take on the more sophisticated analyses made possible by inferential statistics. Where descriptive statistics can only describe the particular situation in which the data were gathered, inferential statistics can be used to make inferences about a larger population beyond the one that was sampled. Inferential statistics allow researchers to answer the questions "How likely is it that the rest of the population is about the same as the sample?" "If we chose another sample, would we get about the same results or are these results simply a matter of chance?" For example, if researchers asked a random sample of 15 6th graders to select their favorite chewing gum and 12 chose Bubble-O brand, could we assume that most of the rest of the 6th graders in the population also prefer that brand? Or, is it likely that the researchers happened to select the only 12 students who prefer Bubble-O and the other students they did not pick all prefer something else?

Inferential statistics answer such questions through the use of probability levels, also called significance levels. When selecting a probability level, researchers decide how sure they want to be that these results were not a result of chance, but would happen again with another sample from the same population. How sure do researchers want to be that their results are "real" before labeling them statistically significant? Professional researchers set probability levels to describe the level of significance they hope to attain. A probability level of $p < .05$ indicates that there would be only five chances out of 100 that these results were due to chance and it is highly likely that another sample would obtain similar results. A probability level $p < .01$ indicates that there is only one chance in 100 that the results were due to chance. These two, $p < .05$ and $p < .01$, are the most common probability levels used by researchers. In setting a probability level, the researcher declares ahead of time, "This is the level I need to attain before I will call my results statistically significant." Occasionally a researcher may set a liberal probability level of $p < .1$ (one chance in ten) for an exploratory study and your students may certainly do the same.

In practical terms, students will choose the appropriate statistical formula for their research question and level of data, then use the formula to calculate a statistic. The correlation formula gives you *r*, the *t*-test yields a *t* score, chi square statistics results in a chi square. The values you obtain from applying the formula to your data are then compared to values in probability tables that correspond to the statistic used. If the value you obtained from your data is higher than the critical value in the probability table, you can assume that your results are not due to chance alone, but are statistically significant at the level you chose to test them.

Chi Square

Chi square is one of the easier inferential statistics to understand and involves just the use of a calculator. It provides a good vehicle for teaching the basic concepts of inference and probability level without involving complex calculations. While chi square can be used in more complicated research designs, we will discuss it in the context of a single sample design.

Chi square is considered a nonparametric statistic, meaning it can only be used to analyze nominal data where the various choices do not represent amounts of something. While that restriction may at first seem limiting, chi square is an excellent tool for analyzing survey data that does not represent amounts. If, for example, a student asks, "Which candidate do you prefer for president? (1) Clinton, (2) Dole, or (3) Perot," the choices are numbered, but choice #3 is not greater than choice #1 in the way that 3 yards is greater than 3 feet. These answers produce nominal data, where the choices do not have numerical value and thus can be analyzed using the chi square statistic. Other types of nominal data include hair or eye color, gender, race/ethnic group, religion, political party, and preferences (food, music, clothing brands, books, sports, hobbies, etc.).

Chi square determines whether the pattern of responses represents true differences between the choices by comparing the actual or observed responses to the responses that would be expected if there were no differences. Suppose a researcher had surveyed 30 people regarding their choice for president. If there were no real differences in preference in the population, the researcher would expect 10 people to select Clinton, 10 to select Dole, and 10 to select Perot. These are the *expected* responses. However, in the sample, only 3 people chose Perot, 10 chose Dole, and 17 chose Clinton. These answers are the *observed* responses. Chi square (X) uses a formula to compare the observed and expected levels for each response. The chi square for each possible response is added together to yield the total chi square. The formula is

$$X = \frac{(O - E)^2}{E}$$

where X represents chi square, O is the number of responses observed, and E is the number of expected responses. E is typically calculated by dividing the number of responses by the number of choices. (If there were no differences you would expect an equal number of responses for each choice.) The observed responses come from your data—survey results, observations, or other kinds of data. To calculate chi square, create a chart like the one below (which uses data from the presidential survey mentioned above). List the data of observed and expected results for each choice. Next, subtract the number expected from the number observed and place those numbers in the third column. Be sure to indicate when the answer is negative. Square this number to find $(O–E)^2$ in the 4th column. The final column represents the previous column divided by the number expected. (Calculators will increase the ease and accuracy of these computations.) The last step is to add the values in the final column for all choices to obtain the chi square value.

	O	E	O–E	$(O–E)^2$	$\frac{(O–E)^2}{E}$
Clinton	17	10	7	49	4.9
Dole	10	10	0	0	0
Perot	3	10	-7	49	4.9
Total X					9.8

The chi square for this sample is 9.8. Is it statistically significant? Determine significance by comparing the chi square value you calculated from the data to the value corresponding to the probability level you chose before beginning data analysis. Look at the chi square probability table in Appendix B. Use the probability level selected (assume it's $p < .05$) and the degrees of freedom (df) for this question. The degrees of freedom is $N - 1$, where N is the number of possible choices. In this case, there were 3 choices for president, so the degrees of freedom is 3-1 or 2. To find out if the calculated chi square is significant, look for the row for df = 2 and follow across the table until you reach the column marked .05 (the pre-chosen probability level). If the chi square value computed is greater than the number determined by the chart, the results can be said to be significant at the $p < .05$ level. If the chi square is lower than the number in the table, the results are not significant at that level. Are the differences in choices for president significant at the $p < .05$ level? The critical level for .05 with two degrees of freedom is 5.99. Since 9.8 is greater than 5.99, it is significant.

It is important to note that the chi square statistic can't tell you which part of the results have led to the significant difference, only that the overall pattern is significantly different from what was expected. You'll need additional statistical procedures to determine which responses were significantly different from expected. Results from the presidential survey can be summarized as follows:

> Thirty subjects were surveyed as to preferences for candidates Clinton, Dole, and Perot. Chi square analysis indicated statistically significant differences in the patterns of response ($p < .05$), with Perot preferred by 10% of the subjects, Dole by 33%, and Clinton by 57%.

By looking at the chi square table in Appendix B, you can see that the number of choices available affects the significance level. It is also affected by the sample size. It is easier to get a statistically significant result if sample size is large because the differences between observed and expected responses tend to be larger numbers, even if the proportion of responses is the same. If your students will be doing research for which chi square is an appropriate form of data analysis, be sure their sample size is large enough that they have a chance of finding significant differences if they exist. As an absolute minimum, the number of subjects should be at least five times the number of choices. Below that level the calculations have little meaning.

t-Test

In many experimental and quasi-experimental designs researchers need to compare mean scores of two groups to see if their treatment made a difference. The *t*-test provides a statistical way to see if the difference between the two sample means is greater than what would be found by chance alone if there were no real difference in the larger population. Data must be on an interval or ratio scale—that is, it must represent an amount of something. The *t*-test cannot be used with nominal data (categories such as political party or gender) or ordinal data (rank order). There are other assumptions about the data that must be satisfied for the *t*-test to be valid, but those are beyond the scope of this book. (Consult any statistics book if you and/or your students want to know more about these assumptions.)

There are two slightly different *t*-test formulas, depending on whether the samples are independent or nonindependent. Independent samples are those in which members of one group are not related in any systematic way to members of the other group. Examples include two different sections of a civics class, two randomly formed groups of students, or two different teams for which members were chosen randomly. Nonindependent samples are ones formed by some kind of matching. The most common type is comparing pre-test and post-test scores from the same group of people. These samples are definitely matched since the pre-test and post-test scores are from the same people. If samples are nonindependent, you can expect some kind of correlation between them, so you must use the *t*-test formula for nonindependent samples.

t-Test for Independent Samples

Following is an example appropriate for using the independent *t*-test. Assume you have tried using simulations as an instructional strategy in one of your classes and taught without simulations in the other. Students may have been randomly assigned to the sections (great!), but even if they haven't, there will be no problem as long as there are no systematic differences between the two classes. (Some factors that might cause systematic differences include ability grouping of the classes, inclusion of a group of special needs students or poor readers in one class, radically different times of the day when the classes meet, for example 1st and 6th period, etc.) After a six week unit in which you used simulations each week in one section and not at all in the other, you want to compare the unit grades of the students to see if simulations improved learning. You find the mean of each class by adding all the unit grades and dividing by the number of students in that class. Assume the means of the two classes were 78 and 84 on a 100-point scale. Use the *t*-test for independent samples to see if this is a statistically significant difference.

$$t = \frac{X_1 - X_2}{\sqrt{\left(\frac{SS_1 + SS_2}{N_1 + N_2 - 2}\right)\left(\frac{1}{N_1} + \frac{1}{N_2}\right)}}$$

In the *t*-test formula, X_1 represents the mean of the first group, X_2 is the mean of the second group, SS_1 and SS_2 are the sum of squares for groups 1 and 2 respectively, and N_1 and N_2 are the number of people in group 1 and 2 respectively. Again, this formula looks a whole lot more complicated than it is. Hang in there and take it step by step!

Start by finding *SS* just as you did when computing standard deviation. First construct a chart for the data. This example requires a chart for both group 1 and 2. To make this example easier and save space, consider that each class has just fifteen students. The unit grade is the letter grade received by the student, converted to a four point scale (A=4, B=3, C=2, D=1, F=0).

(If you're feeling confident, cover up the computations for one group and do them yourself as you follow our example for the other group. Then compare to see how you did.)

Class 1	x (grade)	x^2
Amy	2	4
Maria	3	9
Derek	3	9
Joshua	1	1
Jeremy	2	4
Tiffany	4	16
Kenisha	3	9
Eva	4	16
Willie	3	9
Jacob	4	16
Sharla	4	16
Michael	3	9
Celine	3	9
Jessie	3	9
Tran	3	9
$N = 15$	$\Sigma x = 45$	$\Sigma x^2 = 145$

Class 2	x (grade)	x^2
William	3	9
Eric	2	4
Jeanette	3	9
Tamara	4	16
Elena	3	9
Jan	2	4
Pat	1	1
Crystal	2	4
Mark	4	16
Keith	0	0
Craig	0	0
Shaun	3	9
Carla	1	1
David	2	4
Brittany	1	1
$N = 15$	$\Sigma x = 31$	$\Sigma x^2 = 87$

Using the formula, substitute values from the chart:

Class 1

$$SS = \sum x^2 - \frac{(\sum x)^2}{N}$$

$$SS = 145 - \frac{(45)^2}{15}$$

Class 2

$$SS = \sum x^2 - \frac{(\sum x)^2}{N}$$

$$SS = 87 - \frac{(31)^2}{15}$$

Multiply Σx by itself to find Σx^2 and substitute it in the formula:

$$SS = 145 - \frac{2025}{15}$$

$$SS = 87 - \frac{961}{15}$$

Divide the numerator by the denominator:

$$SS = 145 - 135 \qquad\qquad SS = 87 - 64.1$$

Subtract to find *SS*:

$$SS = 10 \qquad\qquad SS = 22.9$$

WHEW! In the next step find the mean for each group by adding all the grades and dividing by the number of students in each group (15). Then substitute SS, N, and the means in the *t*-test formula:

$$t = \frac{X_1 - X_2}{\sqrt{\left(\frac{SS_1 + SS_2}{N_1 + N_2 - 2}\right)\left(\frac{1}{N_1} + \frac{1}{N_2}\right)}}$$

For the first step, just substitute values for symbols; don't do any computation:

$$t = \frac{3 - 2.1}{\sqrt{\left(\frac{10 + 22.9}{15 + 15 - 2}\right)\left(\frac{1}{15} + \frac{1}{15}\right)}}$$

Now do the addition and subtraction called for:

$$t = \frac{.9}{\sqrt{\left(\frac{32.9}{28}\right)\left(\frac{2}{15}\right)}}$$

Work out the division in the denominator:

$$t = \frac{.9}{\sqrt{(1.175)(0.133)}}$$

Multiply the numbers in the denominator:

$$t = \frac{.9}{\sqrt{0.1563}}$$

Find the square root of the denominator:

$$t = \frac{.9}{0.3953}$$

The final computation is dividing the numerator by the denominator:

$$t = 2.277$$

The last step is to compare the *t* value you computed with the critical value in a table. Using the level of significance you chose at the start of your research (usually .05) and the degrees of freedom (df = $N_1 + N_2 - 2$), look up the critical values in Appendix D.

Critical value of *t* at the .05 level: 2.048
Degrees of freedom: 28
t for the data: 2.277

Since the *t* for the data is greater than the critical value for *t* at the .05 level, you have found a statistically significant difference in the average grades for the two classes. This means that if there were no difference in the classes, you would not get a mean difference of $X_1 - X_2 = .9$ by chance alone. You can say with 95% certainty (derived from the critical value you chose for your research) that there is a difference between the two classes. If your groups were equivalent to start with, it is likely that the use of simulations in group 1 explains the better grades of that group.

t-Test for Nonindependent Samples

Another way that students might conduct experimental or quasi-experimental research is using a pre-test/post-test design to evaluate the value of a treatment. Since the data come from the same subjects with scores from before and after the intervention, the samples are nonindependent. Therefore, students will need to use the t-test for nonindependent samples. A possible research study might have students keep track of the amount of exercise in which they participate for a week. The teacher might then show a video, teach a unit, or implement some intervention intended to increase the amount of exercise in which students participate. About two weeks after the treatment (to allow immediate effects to wear off), students again log the amount of exercise in which they participate for one week. Using the t-test for nonindependent samples, they can see if the difference in amounts of exercise is statistically significant different in order to test the effectiveness of the intervention.

$$t = \frac{\text{mean of D}}{\sqrt{\dfrac{\sum D^2 - \dfrac{(\sum D)^2}{N}}{N(N-1)}}}$$

In the formula, D represents the difference between the matched pairs (pre-test and post-test scores), ΣD^2 is the sum of all the squared differences, and $(\Sigma D)^2$ is the square of the sum of the differences. Your success computing the first t-test formula should have left you feeling quite confident about this one!

Class	x_1 (pre-test)	x_2 (post-test)	D ($x_2 - x_1$)	D^2
Ardra	0	1	1	1
Martina	0	2	2	4
Duane	5	7	2	4
Tim	1	4	3	9
Tracy	0	0	0	0
Tenisha	1	4	3	9
Ella	1	3	2	4
Bill	1	1	0	0
John	2	4	2	4
Marta	0	2	2	4
Terry	6	8	2	4
Chrissie	1	3	2	4
Helena	0	4	4	16
Shawn	0	0	0	0
Neal	0	5	5	25
$N = 15$	$\Sigma x_1 = 18$	$\Sigma x_2 = 48$	$SD = 30$	$SD^2 = 88$

Remember that the mean of D is calculated by dividing the sum of D by the number of subjects:

$$\text{mean of D} = \frac{\sum D}{N} = \frac{30}{15} = 2$$

Using the formula, substitute values from the chart we just completed:

$$t = \frac{2}{\sqrt{\dfrac{88 - \dfrac{(30)^2}{15}}{15(15-1)}}}$$

Multiply ΣD by itself to find $(\Sigma D)^2$, subtract $N - 1$, and substitute both in the formula:

$$t = \frac{2}{\sqrt{\frac{88 - \frac{900}{15}}{15(14)}}}$$

Divide $(\Sigma D)^2$ by N:

$$t = \frac{2}{\sqrt{\frac{88 - 60}{15(14)}}}$$

Then subtract the numbers in the numerator:

$$t = \frac{2}{\sqrt{\frac{28}{15(14)}}}$$

Multiply the numbers in the denominator:

$$t = \frac{2}{\sqrt{\frac{28}{210}}}$$

Divide the numbers in the denominator:

$$t = \frac{2}{\sqrt{0.133}}$$

Now use a calculator to find the square root of the denominator:

$$t = \frac{2}{0.3647}$$

And finally, divide the numerator by the denominator:

$$t = 5.48$$

The last step is to compare the t value you computed with the critical value in a table. Use the level of significance we chose at the start of our research (usually .05) and the degrees of freedom, which is found using the formula, df $= N - 1$.

> Critical value of t at the .05 level: 2.145
> Degrees of freedom: 14
> t for the data: 5.48

Since the t for the data is greater than the critical value for t at the .05 level, you have found a statistically significant difference in the amount of exercise engaged in by the sample before and after the treatment. If there were no real difference in amount of exercise before and after the treatment, you would not see a difference of 2 between pre-exercise hours and post-exercise hours by chance alone. You can say with 95% certainty (derived from the critical value you chose for the research) that there is a difference in amount of exercise before and after the treatment.

Qualitative Analysis

Analyzing qualitative data is a very different process from that of analyzing quantitative data. Remember that a qualitative approach to data involves interpretation in order to understand the qualities of an experience rather than counting or calculating variables. These experiences studied can include events (Pearl Harbor), cultures (Vietnamese residents in the U.S.), and institutions (your school). The purpose of analyzing qualitative data is to uncover the system of meanings that people use—in other words, how your informants (people you observe or interview) make sense of the experience you are researching.

Qualitative data can be analyzed by describing the main ideas, trends, or themes that appear, with particular attention to the point of view of the data source. Qualitative data analysis is attuned to variables that are specific to a given situation or individual. Students analyzing such data should be on the lookout for how the information and experiences shared are unique to that situation, as well as how they may fit into a larger pattern. For example, if students were to interview three veterans of Pearl Harbor, some information (such as an account of the weather) may be fairly consistent and add to the general knowledge of the event. Other data (feelings at the time of the attack) may vary widely among individuals. In such cases, qualitative research looks for patterns. Did those with families report different feelings than those who were single? Did experienced sailors report different feelings than those who were less experienced? Such descriptions are reasonable for middle and high school students. In fact, they may reach conclusions not far distant from those attained through more sophisticated qualitative methodology.

The key to analyzing qualitative data is to figure out what things mean *to the people being studied.* The same behavior can have different meanings to different people and in different cultures. In one culture it may be a sign of respect to look someone in the eye when he/she talks to you, while in another culture, that same gesture may be considered a sign of disrespect.

One way to keep track of trends and themes is to use different colors to highlight sections of the data. Students first should read through the notes they've taken and think about what ideas come through most powerfully. Do some ideas evoke strong emotions? Do some themes arise several times? They should get a set of markers or colored pencils in several different colors and begin their second read-through. Have students use different colors to circle or underline words that relate to the same general topic or theme. Professional researchers don't start with pre-set themes. Instead, they let them "jump out" at them from their notes. As beginners, students might want to start with a few ideas for categories, but they should be open to other themes as they read through their notes and listen to their tapes.

Imagine that your students were analyzing data about the culture of Vietnamese people living in your town in the U.S. They might first think about elements present in most cultures in order to create starting categories. Below is one possible coding system for such a study.

blue - education
red - religion
green - work
orange - food
yellow - family
brown - clothing
purple - spare time
pink - language

After students have gone through their whole set of notes from observations and/or interviews and coded them for categories using different colors, they should go back and check over them again. This time they may notice new themes or new examples of existing themes.

Their next task is to gather together all the examples of a given theme on one sheet of paper. Students should start a new piece of paper for each theme/color used and put the name of the theme at the top of the paper. Students should go through their notes once more, looking for additional examples of each theme and starting new theme pages if necessary. For example, they should list everything anyone said about education on the sheet headed "Education." The list might include comments such as "very important," "way to get ahead," "want kids to go to the university," "expensive but worth the sacrifice," "important," "better do well," etc. Within each of the themes, students should then see if there are phrases or ideas that seem to go together. In the example just given, several comments relate to the importance of education. Students also can use different colored markers to show items that go together *within* each category page as well. Sometimes qualitative researchers will count the number of comments or the number of people who shared a particular point of view. Your students can do this as well.

Once students have looked over their notes and lists of phrases and ideas, they need to think about what they have read, seen, and heard. Starting with one of the individual theme pages (education, religion, etc.), have them read through it again and think about one or more summary statements they can make about how that theme is expressed in the culture and its importance to the culture they are studying. They should do the same for each of the theme pages extracted from their notes. Students can then arrange the theme pages on a desk, putting those that seem related closer to each other. Invite them to create a visual picture of how the themes relate to each other. They can indicate the importance of various themes to the culture being studied by the distance the sheets are placed from the researcher.

Drawing and verifying conclusions in qualitative research is where the final making of meaning takes place. Miles and Huberman (1984) describe twelve tactics for generating meaning. *Counting* helps the researcher see "what's there;" *noting patterns and themes, seeing plausibility*, and *clustering* help illuminate "what goes with what;" *making metaphors* allows for more integration; and *splitting variables* is a way to differentiate when necessary. One can see items and their relationships more abstractly by *subsuming particulars into the general, factoring, noting relations between variables,* and *finding intervening variables*. Finally, the researcher assembles a coherent understanding of the data by *building a logical chain of evidence* and *making conceptual and theoretical coherence* of what has been found.

Because the making of meaning is filtered through the researcher and the data is less precise and objective than numbers, it is especially important to test or confirm the findings of qualitative data analysis. Miles and Huberman (1984) believe that data quality can be assessed through *checking for representativeness* ; *checking for researcher effects* on the site (and the site on the researcher); and *triangulating* across data sources and methods. Triangulation supports a finding with independent measures that agree with it or, at the very least, do not contradict it. For example, if two people observe family members helping children with homework and hear in several interviews that doing well in school is important, these findings confirm the importance of education in the culture being studied. A final strategy for assessing the quality of the data is *weighing the evidence* by deciding which kinds of data should be trusted the most.

Contrasting the data can test a conclusion about a theme or pattern by saying what it is not. One tactic is *contrasting and comparing* two people, groups, roles, activities, etc. that differ in some other respect (for example, a Vietnamese family and a Bosnian family) to see if similarities and differences are what researchers would have expected. *Checking the meaning of outliers* or discrepant sites, people, etc., allows researchers to see how they differ from more typical examples. *Using extreme cases* consists of asking questions of the person who has the most to gain or lose by affirming or denying a theory. Finally, the researcher can test his/her explanations in three ways: (1) he/she can consider whether a third variable might be influencing two variables that appear to influence each other in order to rule out *spurious relations;* (2) he/she can *replicate a finding* by collecting new information from new informants or in new settings to see if it supports or contradicts earlier conclusions; and (3) he/she can *check out rival explanations* and *look for negative evidence* by actively seeking data that contradicts conclusions. Researchers can obtain a final check on data through *feedback from informants* in the group being studied. Do they think the researcher has accurately described the group, institution, or event?

Drawing Conclusions

Research is not over once the calculator has been turned off. The researcher's next task is to determine and communicate conclusions with respect to the initial hypothesis. The teacher's most important role when helping students draw conclusions is guiding them as they determine what the data do and do not say. Teachers should remind students about the limitations of the data and types of data analysis. Descriptive data and analyses can do only that—describe. Even if 95% of the students in an 11th grade sample plan to attend college, a researcher can't conclude that 95% of all 11th graders plan to do so. If a researcher has randomly selected our sample from all juniors in the school, he/she can say it is likely that a large number of 11th grade students in the school plan to attend college, but percentages alone do not allow him/her to predict how many others have similar intentions.

If a researcher has used chi square or other inferential statistics, he/she can conclude that the results are statistically significant and that it is likely that more 11th graders than expected in the school plan to attend college. The researcher must then consider the differences between statistical significance and practical significance. While statistical significance has to do with calculations and probability levels, practical significance asks the question, "Who cares?" Remember that a large sample size makes it easier to get statistically significant results. If an extraordinarily ambitious student surveys 600 students and finds statistically significant differences in a chi square analysis of their preferences for four brands of canned corn, but the number of students preferring each brand ranges from 145-155, is that enough difference to be worth the expense a cafeteria would incur in buying the preferred brand? Are the differences big enough to have practical significance? You also may want to discuss with your students the statistical versus practical significance of research reported on television, news magazines, or advertisements.

A simple approach to drawing conclusions involves examining results with two questions in mind: (1) Can we say this is true for everyone? and (2) What might have affected our results? In Observation Activity 1, students observing preferences in grocery bags could be asked, "Could we say all people would choose the type of bags our sample did? Why or why not?" "What might have made the people in our sample choose the type of bags they did?" (Maybe they use paper bags to recycle newspapers, maybe it was raining that day and they chose plastic to protect their groceries from the rain, maybe there are lots of dog owners and they use the plastic bags to pick up after their dogs.) Often this kind of discussion leads to new hypotheses which can generate another round of data gathering. What matters is that students appreciate the tentative nature of research conclusions and the ways they may be affected by choice of subjects, particular circumstances, and other variables. Hopefully, as students develop this perspective, they will begin to challenge claims that "Research says . . . ." with questions such as "What questions were asked?" "How were the subjects chosen?" "Under what circumstances did the interviews take place?" Only after they are satisfied that the research was conducted appropriately, should students accept the conclusions.

When researchers present their conclusions formally, they describe the problem addressed, the methodology followed, and the findings. Based on the data analysis, they tentatively accept or reject original hypotheses. They describe possible sources of error and raise new questions. If appropriate, they can make suggestions for the use of data. For example, if a student surveyed a random sample of 7th graders on their feelings about choices in elective classes and found that art was the most preferred class, the limitations discussed might include the single grade level surveyed and the recently hired art teacher. The researcher might suggest that additional data be gathered from other grade levels or that the requests for elective classes be examined. As discussed in Chapter 7, these conclusions may be presented in a formal report or through another creative vehicle.

Data Analysis Activity 1

Frequency and Range: Compact Disc Ownership

You have gathered data about the number of compact discs owned by students in your class and now want to make some sense of the data. These are the results of your survey.

Chris	0	LeRoy	6	Cindy	2	Kenisha	8	Rosa	4
Nathan	4	Jean	0	Eduardo	11	Larry	5	Rashad	12
Jared	3	Katie	0	Matthew	0	Ben	0	John	4
Kaylynn	9	Dora	84	Martha	0	Keena	0	Abraham	8

To begin, tally the frequency of each response. Next to each number, use one tally mark for each student who owns that number of CDs. When you are done, add up the tally marks and indicate the frequency of each response using a numeral.

0

1

2

3

4

5

6

7

8

9

10

11

12

.

.

.

84

To find the range or variability of responses, subtract the lowest response (0) from the highest (84), then add one.

Data Analysis Activity 2

Averages: Number of Compact Discs

Someone might wonder about the average number of compact discs owned by adolescents. Use the data from the previous activity to find the mean, median, and mode of the sample. Imagine you wanted to know the average number of CDs owned by students in your class.

Chris	0	LeRoy	6	Cindy	2	Kenisha	8	Rosa	4
Nathan	4	Jean	0	Eduardo	11	Larry	5	Rashad	12
Jared	3	Katie	0	Matthew	0	Ben	0	John	4
Kaylynn	9	Dora	84*	Martha	0	Keena	0	Abraham	8

*Why might Dora have so many?

The mean is one kind of average. You find the mean by adding all the responses (total number of CDs) and dividing by the number of responses (number of students = 20). What is the mean number of CDs for this sample? __________

The mode is the most frequently occurring response. What is the mode for this sample? __________
_

The median is the middle score. Arrange all 20 scores in order from lowest to highest. If more than one student has the same number of CDs, list each one separately. Count from either end of your list to find the middle score. (Because there are an even number of scores, you'll have to find the average of the 10th and 11th score.) What is the median number of CDs in this sample? __________

Which average do you think is best to describe the results of this survey? Why?

Would it be the best for all surveys?

Why or why not?

Data Analysis Activity 3

Standard Deviation: Musical Variability

Here is a chance to practice finding the standard deviation of a set of scores or measures. Use the data given, a set of data you have collected, or one that your teacher will provide (your class's last test scores?). As a quick reminder, in the formulas below

$$SD = \sqrt{\frac{SS}{N-1}} \quad \text{where} \quad SS = \sum x^2 - \frac{(\sum x)^2}{N}$$

SD is standard deviation; *SS* stands for "sum of squares"; *N* is the number of scores; Σx^2 is found by squaring all the x's, then adding those numbers; $(\Sigma x)^2$ is found by adding all the x's, then squaring that number.

In this activity, compute the standard deviation of the number of errors made by clarinet players in your band during a recent dress rehearsal. The standard deviation will help you quantify the degree of variability in the performance of the twelve clarinet players. Complete the following chart to make computing the formula easier.

Student	x (errors)	x^2
Arianna	11	
Lupe	3	
Darla	2	
Joanna	4	
John	3	
Tenisha	2	
Kerry	9	
Eva	3	
Pat	1	
Elena	2	
Terry	7	
Jan	1	

$\Sigma x =$ $\Sigma x^2 =$ $N =$ $N - 1 =$

First find *SS* by substituting Σx^2 after the equal sign, Σx in the parentheses in the numerator, and *N* in the denominator using values from the chart you just completed:

$$SS = \sum x^2 - \frac{(\sum x)^2}{N}$$

$$SS = \quad - \frac{(\quad)^2}{\quad}$$

Multiply Σx by itself to find $(\Sigma x)^2$ and substitute it in the numerator:

$$SS = \quad - \frac{\quad}{\quad}$$

(continued on next page)

Data Analysis Activity 3

Divide the numerator by the denominator: *SS* = –

And subtract to find *SS*: *SS* =

Now substitute the values for SS and *N* into the standard deviation formula:

$$SD = \sqrt{\frac{SS}{N - 1}} \qquad SD = \sqrt{\frac{\quad}{\quad - 1}}$$

Subtract 1 from *N* in the denominator:

$$SD = \sqrt{\frac{\quad}{\quad}}$$

Divide the numerator by the denominator:

$$SD = \sqrt{\quad}$$

Use a calculator to find the square root: *SD* =

Data Analysis Activity 4

Graphing Correlation: Does Video Game Experience Pay Off?

You can express the correlation between two variables by graphing. Imagine you want to examine the relationship between the number of previous video games played and the number of points scored in a new video game. Using graph paper, or the chart below, create a scattergram to represent the data.

Subject number	x (previous games)	y (points)
1	1	2
2	3	2
3	4	2
4	2	2
5	3	3
6	4	4
7	2	3
8	3	4
9	4	6
10	2	4
11	3	5
12	5	4
13	2	5
14	3	6
15	5	6

Use the slant and shape of your scattergram to estimate the correlation.

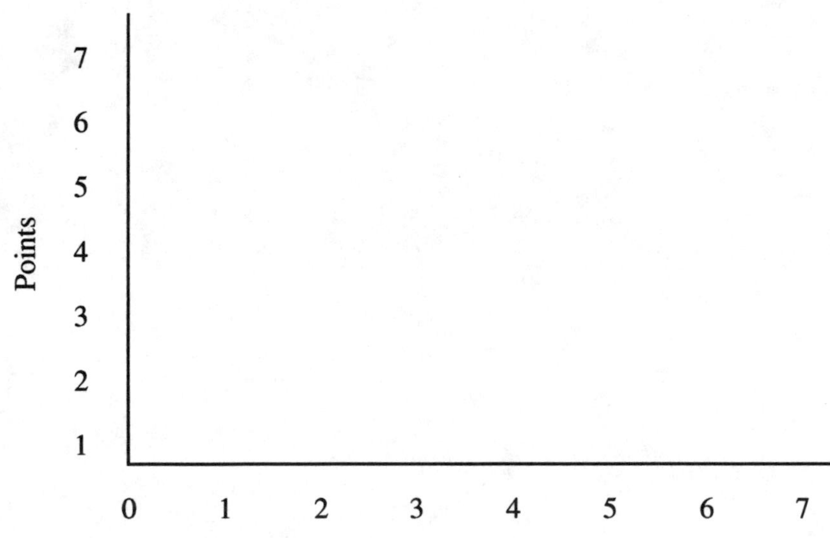

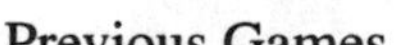

Write a statement summarizing your findings.

Data Analysis Activity 5

Correlation Formula: Video Game Experience II

In this activity, you will analyze the correlational data from Activity 4 more precisely. Instead of graphing and estimating the correlation from the width of the football shape of the scattergram, use the correlation formula to compute an exact value. The table below displays the data indicating number of previous games played and the number points scored in a new video game. Use that information to complete the table.

Subject number	x (previous games)	y (points)	xy	x^2	y^2
1	1	2	2	1	4
2	3	2	6	9	4
3	4	2			
4	2	2			
5	3	3			
6	4	4			
7	2	3			
8	3	4			
9	4	6			
10	2	4			
11	3	5			
12	5	4			
13	2	5			
14	3	6			
15	5	6			
Σ (sigma-total of each column)	$\Sigma x=$	$\Sigma y=$	$\Sigma xy=$	$\Sigma x^2=$	$\Sigma y^2=$

Place the values in the appropriate place in the formula that follows these directions.

1. In the first step, simply substitute the values for the symbols, without doing any calculations. (Remember that "*N*" stands for the total number of subjects.) NOTE: Σx^2 is the sum of all the x-squared values (5th column above). To find $(\Sigma x)^2$, multiply Σx (from column two) by itself.

2. Using order of operations, first multiply expressions next to each other (N times Σxy; Σx times Σy; *N* times Σx^2; N times Σy^2). Then substitute the answer in the formula.

$$r = \frac{N\sum xy - \sum x \sum y}{\sqrt{[N\sum x^2 - (\sum x)^2][N\sum y^2 - (\sum y)^2]}}$$

(continued on next page)

Data Analysis Activity 5

3. Subtract the values within the brackets and above the line and rewrite the equation.

4. Multiply the numbers within brackets and rewrite the equation.

5. Find the square root of the denominator. (Most calculators will do this.)

6. Divide the numerator by the denominator. This number may be positive or negative, but should have an absolute value less than 1.0.

For the final step, compare the correlation coefficient you obtained from your calculations to the critical values in the correlation table (Appendix C). First calculate the degrees of freedom (df) for your data by subtracting two from the number of paired observations. Locate that number in the df column of the correlation table and follow it across to the column representing the level of significance you have chosen for your analysis (assume .05 for this example).

Computed correlation coefficient (r): __________
Degrees of freedom ($N - 2$): __________
Critical value at .05 from the correlation table: __________

Was the correlation you found statistically significant? __________
Write a statement describing your findings.

Data Analysis Activity 6

Chi Square: Cola Preferences

Which type of cola do middle school students like best? Sally used a taste test to compare three brands of cola. She asked 60 students to taste three brands of cola and tell her which they preferred. Below are her results.

Pepsi®	22
Coke®	28
Shazam	10

Use chi square to see if these results indicate statistically significant differences. You will need the probability table for chi square (Appendix B).

	O	E	(O–E)	$(O–E)^2$	$\frac{(O–E)^2}{E}$
Pepsi®					
Coke®					
Shazam					
Total					

Degrees of freedom ($N - 1$): __________

Significance level (.05) from the probability table: __________

Chi square from your data: __________

Is your chi square significant? __________

Write a statement summarizing your results.

Data Analysis Activity 7

t-Test (Independent Samples): How Is School?

For this activity, assume you have gathered data from randomly sampled students in Grades 11 and 9. You asked them to rate how much they liked your school, using a 1-5 rating scale (with 1 being the lowest rating and 5 being the highest). The results are listed below.

Grade 11	x (rating)	x^2
St 1	3	
St 2	5	
St 3	3	
St 4	4	
St 5	4	
St 6	2	
St 7	5	
St 8	2	
St 9	4	
St 10	5	
N =	Σx =	Σx^2 =

Grade 9	x (rating)	x^2
St 1	2	
St 2	3	
St 3	3	
St 4	1	
St 5	2	
St 6	4	
St 7	3	
St 8	4	
St 9	3	
St 10	3	
N =	Σx =	Σx^2 =

Start by finding *SS* and complete the chart above. Using the *SS* formula, substitute values from the chart:

Grade 11 $$SS = \sum x - \frac{(\sum x)^2}{N}$$ Grade 9 $$SS = \sum x - \frac{(\sum x)^2}{N}$$

$SS = \quad - \frac{(\quad)^2}{\quad}$ $SS = \quad - \frac{(\quad)^2}{\quad}$

Multiply Σx by itself to find $(\Sigma x)^2$ and substitute it in the formula:

$SS = \quad - \frac{\quad}{\quad}$ $SS = \quad - \frac{\quad}{\quad}$

Now divide the numerator by the denominator:

SS = – *SS* = –

Subtract to find *SS*:

SS = *SS* =

Now that you know *SS*, you need to find the mean for each grade. Within each grade, add all the scores and divide by the number of students in each grade. Then substitute *SS*, *N*, and the means in the *t*-test formula. Let X_1 equal the mean of Grade 11 and X_2 equal the mean of Grade 9.

$$t = \frac{X_1 - X_2}{\sqrt{\left(\frac{SS_1 + SS_2}{N_1 + N_2 - 2}\right)\left(\frac{1}{N_1} + \frac{1}{N_2}\right)}}$$

(continued on next page)

Data Analysis Activity 7

For the first step, just substitute values for symbols; don't do any computation:

$$t = \frac{\quad - \quad}{\sqrt{\left(\frac{\quad + \quad}{\quad + \quad - 2}\right)\left(\frac{1}{\quad} + \frac{1}{\quad}\right)}}$$

Do the addition and subtraction:

$$t = \frac{\quad}{\sqrt{\left(\frac{\quad}{\quad}\right)\left(\frac{\quad}{\quad}\right)}}$$

Do the division in the denominator:

$$t = \frac{\quad}{\sqrt{(\quad)(\quad)}}$$

Multiply the numbers in the denominator:

$$t = \frac{\quad}{\sqrt{\quad}}$$

Find the square root of the denominator. (Many calculators can do this.)

$$t = \frac{\quad}{\quad}$$

Divide the numerator by the denominator:

$$t =$$

Finally, compare the *t* value you computed with the critical value in the table. Assume you set the significance level at .05 at the start of your research. Compute the degrees of freedom, using the formula, df = $N_1 + N_2 - 2$.

Critical value of *t* at the .05 level: __________

Degrees of freedom: __________

t for the data: __________

Given this sample, was the difference between freshmen and junior opinions of school significantly different? __________

Write a sentence summarizing your conclusions.

Data Analysis Activity 8

t-Test (Nonindependent Samples): Conflict Resolution

In this example, assume your school has problems with verbal and physical conflicts between students and wants to implement a conflict resolution program in the 9th grade. The school district is quite interested in the results of this quasi-experiment. If it works in your school sample, they will consider adopting it in the other secondary schools in the district. You are in charge of making that recommendation. You asked 9th grade teachers to tally the number of conflicts in their classes for one week before and another week after implementation of the conflict resolution program. x_2 represents number of conflicts before your conflict intervention program, x_1 the number of conflicts after the program; *D* is the difference between the two (subtract x_1 from x_2); and D^2 is the difference times itself. You have gathered the following data concerning verbal conflicts among students:

Teacher #	x_2 (pre)	x_1 (post)	D (x_2 - x_1)	D^2
1	10	8	2	4
2	5	3	2	4
3	18	15	3	9
4	21	18	3	9
5	18	14	4	16
6	20	15	5	25
7	33	35	-2	4
8	28	25	3	9
9	15	10	5	25
10	42	43	-1	1
$N = 10$	$\Sigma x_2 = 210$	$\Sigma x_1 = 186$	$\Sigma D = 24$	$\Sigma D^2 = 106$

Remember that Σ means "sum of," and that the mean of *D* is calculated by dividing the sum of *D* by the number of subjects:

$$\text{mean of D} = \frac{\sum D}{N} = \frac{24}{10} = 2.4$$

Remember: In the formula, *D* represents the difference between the matched pairs (pre-test score minus post-test score), ΣD^2 is the sum of all the squared differences, and $(\Sigma D)^2$ is the square of the sum of the differences.

Using the formula, substitute values from the chart you just completed:

$$t = \frac{\text{mean of D}}{\sqrt{\dfrac{\sum D^2 - \dfrac{(\sum D)^2}{N}}{N(N-1)}}}$$

$$t = \frac{\quad}{\sqrt{\dfrac{\quad - \dfrac{(\quad)^2}{\quad}}{(\quad - 1)}}}$$

(continued on next page)

Data Analysis Activity 8

Multiply ΣD by itself to find ΣD^2, subtract $N - 1$, and substitute both in the formula:

$$t = \frac{\quad}{\sqrt{\frac{\quad - \frac{\quad}{\quad}}{\quad(\quad)}}}$$

Divide ΣD^2 by N:

$$t = \frac{\quad}{\sqrt{\frac{\quad - \quad}{\quad(\quad)}}}$$

Then subtract those numbers:

$$t = \frac{\quad}{\sqrt{\frac{\quad}{\quad(\quad)}}}$$

Multiply the numbers in the denominator:

$$t = \frac{\quad}{\sqrt{\frac{\quad}{\quad}}}$$

Divide the numbers in the denominator:

$$t = \frac{\quad}{\sqrt{\quad}}$$

Using a calculator, find the square root of the denominator:

$$t = \frac{\quad}{\quad}$$

Divide the numerator by the denominator:

$t =$

Finally compare the t value you computed with the critical value in the table. Assume you set the significance level at .05 at the start of your research. Compute the degrees of freedom, using the formula, df = $N - 1$.

Critical value of t at the .05 level: __________

Degrees of freedom: __________

t for the data: __________

Given this sample, was the average number of verbal conflicts before and after the conflict resolution treatment significantly different? __________

Write a sentence summarizing your conclusions.

Data Analysis Activity 9

Qualitative Analysis: Club Membership

Below are notes from a student's observation of the first Computer Club meeting of the year at the high school. Using the strategies outlined in the section about Qualitative Data Analysis, develop a list of themes that emerge from the following data. Include themes you are fairly sure about, as well as hypotheses you would want more data to confirm. Remember that in an actual qualitative study, you would be analyzing much more data (additional observation notes, interviews with a variety of people, possibly surveys, etc.).

Tuesday, September, 15; 2:45 p.m.

First meeting of the year of the Computer Club at Zion High School. Club has been in existence before this year; not sure how long ago or how it started (need to find out). Meeting takes place in computer lab. Computer teacher, Mr. Marks, is moving from computer to computer, doing something to each one. Students stand around the room in small groups, some stand by themselves. One group of eight boys talks in an animated fashion; seem to know each other. No one speaks to me or the others who are standing alone. The ones who are talking with each other seem dressed in the latest fashions, with name brand athletic shoes and clothes. Some of the people standing alone also seem fashionably dressed, while about six others are less so.

At 2:50 p.m. a boy asks people to sit down so they can get started. The girls sit together on the left side of the room. John Martin, who says he is the president, welcomes people. I count 20 students in the room; 16 boys and 4 girls. John introduces Mr. Marks as the club sponsor. Mr. Marks waves, says "Hi," and goes back to what he was doing. John then says how glad he is to see so many members from last year back, naming nine of the boys. He asks how many people now have their own computers at home and eleven raise their hands. He asks how many of those have modems and nine raise their hands. He then invites any of the old members who upgraded hardware or got new software over the summer to tell everyone about what they got. Several members speak about this for about ten minutes.

John then asks what kinds of things people want to do in the coming year in the club. As students start to call out ideas, he asks one of the girls to write them on the board. Several of the boys who had talked earlier contribute ideas. One or two of the people who had not talked previously made suggestions. To one, John said, "We already did that last year." To the other, several of the members said, "We already know how to do that." These ideas were not listed on the board. One boy talked about some things they had done in the computer club at the school he transferred from. No one commented or asked questions about his ideas. The girl at the front wrote the ideas on the board.

Ideas on the board were: surf the net; create a home page; upgrade to a TCP link; create a bulletin board for other high school students in the town; find interactive games that members could play in real time; compare several computers and make recommendations in several price categories to the student body (from the transfer student). Several of the students who had not participated looked puzzled and a few whispered to each other. One finally asked what WWW meant and several other students laughed. One said, "If you don't know that, you probably don't belong here."

John then asked if people would form committees to work on some of the ideas. He said he wanted to head the home page committee and asked George to look into the upgrade, Jason to head the bulletin board group, and Jeremy to start finding out about interactive games. He then asked who wanted to work on what group. About six boys volunteered, including the students who had been actively involved in the meeting. John asked two others what they wanted to do and

(continued on next page)

Data Analysis Activity 9

encouraged them to choose one of the committees. The girls and the four boys who had not participated did not volunteer for a committee and were not asked to join one. The transfer student was among those not asked to join a committee. In fact, a committee was never formed for his idea.

John said they were trying to get a time for the Club members to work in the computer lab before school two days per week. One of the new students pointed out that the busses did not arrive until ten minutes before school started. John and several of the others said that wasn't a problem since they all drove to school. Two of the new students muttered, "Well, I ride the bus," but did not say anything out loud.

John said that was enough for the first meeting. He again welcomed back the previous members of the club and said he was looking forward to another great year like last year. The meeting ended at 3:15. Several of the boys who had spoken at the meeting stayed around talking. All the girls and the new people waited a minute or so, then left when no one talked to them.

As you develop your list of themes, keep in mind the steps in qualitative data analysis:

1. Read through all the notes.
2. Think about themes or hypotheses that emerge. Start a list of them, along with the color you will mark that theme.
3. Read through notes again, underlining words representing each theme or set of ideas with the corresponding color marker, crayon, or pencil. Note any words that don't seem to fit your existing categories, starting new themes as necessary.
4. List words or phrases connected to each theme on a separate piece of paper with the theme at the top.
5. Move words to more appropriate categories as needed, collapse smaller categories or themes into broader ones, divide larger categories into smaller ones as needed.
6. Look back over your notes for additional data to fit or challenge your tentative themes and for additional data or themes you might have missed.
7. Look at your category sheets and decide which themes you are fairly sure about and which would need more data to confirm.
8. State your findings in a few sentences, written on a summary sheet. Share findings with other students, discussing themes and your evidence in support of each.
9. Decide what further data could help confirm or challenge your themes and hypotheses.

ANSWERS FOR DATA ANALYSIS ACTIVITIES

Data Analysis Activity 1—**Frequency and Range: Compact Disc Ownership**

Chris	0	LeRoy	6	Cindy	2	Kenisha	8	Rosa	4
Nathan	4	Jean	0	Eduardo	11	Larry	5	Rashad	12
Jared	3	Katie	0	Matthew	0	Ben	0	John	4
Kaylynn	9	Dora	84*	Martha	0	Keena	0	Abraham	8

0									7
2			1
3			1
4					3
5			1
6			1
8				2
9			1
11			1
12			1
84			1

Range: 0 to 84; 85

Data Analysis Activity 2—**Averages: Number of Compact Discs**

*Why might Dora have so many? (She or one of her relatives works in a music store, she really likes music and can afford that many, other answers possible)

The mean number of CDs for this sample is 8.

The mode is the most frequently occurring response. The mode for this sample is 0.

The median number of CDs in this sample is 3.

Which average do you think is best to describe the results of this survey? Median

Why: Extreme score (Dora's 84) distorts the mean. Median gives a better idea of average when there are extreme scores.

Would it be the best for all surveys? No.

Why or why not? Not all surveys have extreme scores. Sometimes you do need to know the mean.

(continued on next page)

Answers for Data Analysis Activities

Data Analysis Activity 3—**Standard Deviation: Musical Variability**

Student	x (errors)	x^2
Arianna	11	121
Lupe	3	9
Darla	2	4
Joanna	4	16
John	3	9
Tenisha	2	4
Kerry	9	81
Eva	3	9
Pat	1	1
Elena	2	4
Terry	7	49
Jan	1	1
	$\Sigma x = 48$	$\Sigma x^2 = 308$

$N = 12$ $\quad N - 1 = 11$

$$SS = \sum x - \frac{(\sum x)^2}{N}$$

$$SS = 308 - \frac{(48)^2}{12}$$

$$SS = 308 - \frac{2304}{12}$$

$$SS = 308 - 192$$

$$SS = 116$$

Now substitute the values for *SS* and *N* into the standard deviation formula:

$$SD = \sqrt{\frac{SS}{N-1}} \qquad SD = \sqrt{\frac{116}{12-1}}$$

Subtract 1 from *N* in the denominator:

$$SD = \sqrt{\frac{116}{11}}$$

Divide the numerator by the denominator:

$$SD = \sqrt{10.545}$$

Use a calculator to find the square root:

$$SD = 3.247$$

What conclusions can you make about variability in the number of errors committed by players in this clarinet section? Summarize your conclusion in a sentence below. The statement should include the following information: "The mean number of errors committed by clarinet players in the dress rehearsal was 4.0. The range of errors was 11, from one to 11, with a standard deviation of 3.2, indicating large variability in number of errors."

(continued on next page)

Answers for Data Analysis Activities

Data Analysis Activity 4—**Graphing Correlation: Does Video Game Experience Pay Off?**

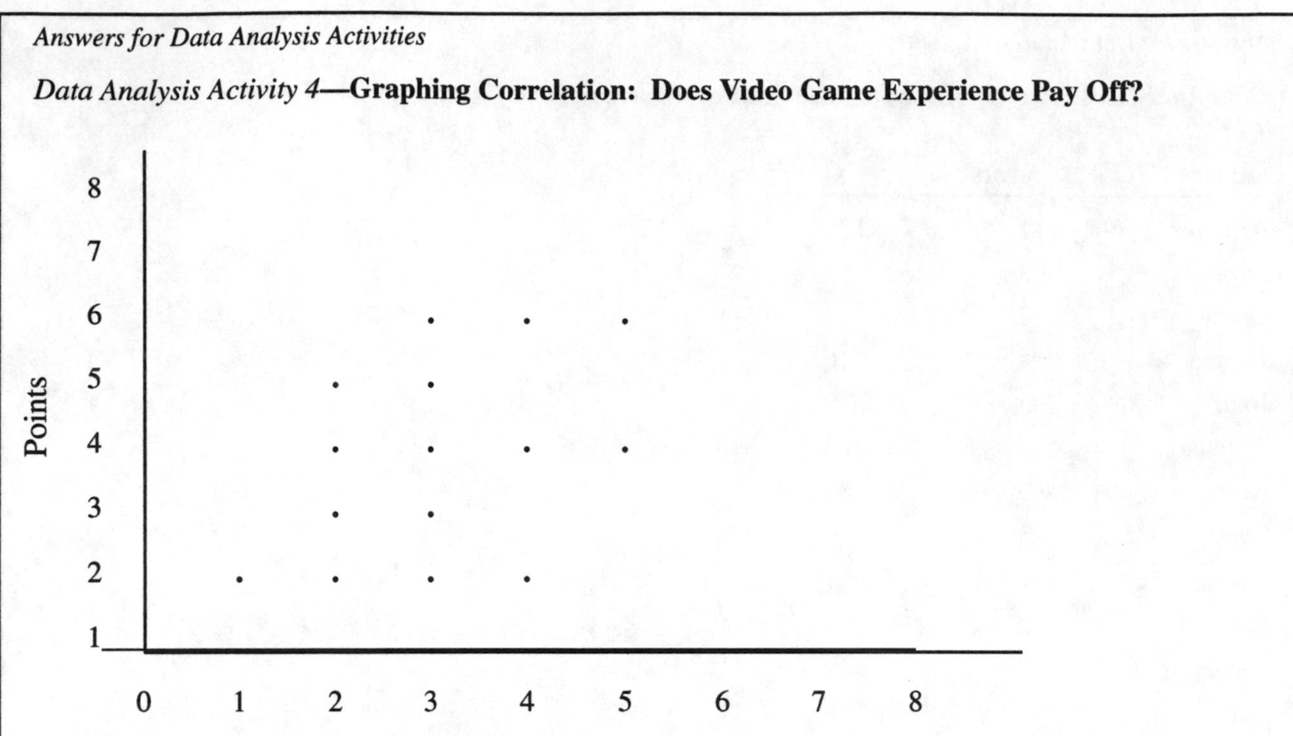

The graph indicates a moderate positive correlation between previous video games played and number of points scored in the new video game.

Data Analysis Activity 5—**Correlation Formula: Video Game Experience II**

Subject number	x (previous games)	y (points)	xy	x^2	y^2
1	1	2	2	1	4
2	3	2	6	9	4
3	4	2	8	16	4
4	2	2	4	4	4
5	3	3	9	9	9
6	4	4	16	16	16
7	2	3	6	4	9
8	3	4	12	9	16
9	4	6	24	16	36
10	2	4	8	4	16
11	3	5	15	9	25
12	5	4	20	25	16
13	2	5	10	4	25
14	3	6	18	9	36
15	5	6	30	25	36
Σ (sigma-total	$\Sigma x = 46$	$\Sigma y = 58$	$\Sigma xy = 188$	$\Sigma x^2 = 160$	$\Sigma y^2 = 256$

(continued on next page)

of each column)

Answers for Data Analysis Activities

$$r = \frac{N\sum xy - \sum x \sum y}{\sqrt{[N\sum x^2 - (\sum x)^2][N\sum y^2 - (\sum y)^2]}}$$

$$r = \frac{(15)(188) - (46)(58)}{\sqrt{[(15)(160) - (46)^2][(15)(256) - (58)^2]}}$$

$$r = \frac{(2820) - (2668)}{\sqrt{[2400 - 2116][3840 - 3364]}}$$

$$r = \frac{152}{\sqrt{[284][476]}}$$

$$r = \frac{152}{\sqrt{135184}}$$

$$r = 0.4134$$

Computed correlation coefficient (r): 0.4134

Degrees of Freedom ($N - 2$): 13

Critical value at .05 from the correlation table: 0.5139

Write a statement describing the significance of your findings. The statement should include the following information: "There was not a significant correlation between the number of video games previously played and the number of points scored in the new video game."

Data Analysis Activity 6—**Chi Square: Cola Preferences**

	O	E	(O–E)	$(O–E)^2$	$\frac{(O–E)^2}{E}$
Pepsi®	22	20	2	4	.2
Coke®	28	20	8	64	3.2
Shazam	10	20	-10	100	5.0
Total					8.4

Degrees of freedom ($N - 1$): 2

Significance level (.05) from the probability table: 5.99

Chi square from your data: 8.4

Is your chi square significant? yes

Write a statement summarizing your results. The statement should include the following information: "Sixty students who sampled three brands of cola (Pepsi®, Coke®, and Shazam) had the following preferences: Pepsi® 36.6%; Coke® 46.6%; Shazam 16.6%. The chi square statistic indicated that there were significant differences in students' cola preferences."

(continued on next page)

Answers for Data Analysis Activities

Data Analysis Activity 7—*t*-Test (Independent Samples): How is School?

Grade 11	x (rating)	x^2
St 1	3	9
St 2	5	25
St 3	3	9
St 4	4	16
St 5	4	16
St 6	2	4
St 7	5	25
St 8	2	4
St 9	4	16
St 10	5	25
$N = 10$	$\Sigma x = 37$	$\Sigma x^2 = 149$

Grade 9	x (rating)	x^2
St 1	2	4
St 2	3	9
St 3	3	9
St 4	1	1
St 5	2	4
St 6	4	16
St 7	3	9
St 8	4	16
St 9	3	9
St 10	3	9
$N = 10$	$\Sigma x = 28$	$\Sigma x^2 = 86$

Using the *SS* formula, substitute values from the chart:

Grade 11

$$SS = \sum x - \frac{(\sum x)^2}{N}$$

$$SS = 149 - \frac{(37)^2}{10}$$

$$SS = 149 - \frac{1369}{10}$$

$$SS = 149 - 136.9$$

$$SS = 12.1$$

Grade 9

$$SS = \sum x - \frac{(\sum x)^2}{N}$$

$$SS = 86 - \frac{(28)^2}{10}$$

$$SS = 86 - \frac{784}{10}$$

$$SS = 86 - 78.4$$

$$SS = 7.6$$

The mean for Grade 11 is 3.7; the mean for Grade 9 is 2.8. Substitute the values for the symbols in the *t*-test formula:

$$t = \frac{X_1 - X_2}{\sqrt{\left(\frac{SS_1 + SS_2}{N_1 + N_2 - 2}\right)\left(\frac{1}{N_1} + \frac{1}{N_2}\right)}}$$

For the first step, just substitute values for symbols; don't do any computation:

$$t = \frac{3.7 - 2.8}{\sqrt{\left(\frac{12.1 + 7.6}{10 + 10 - 2}\right)\left(\frac{1}{10} + \frac{1}{10}\right)}}$$

Do the addition and subtraction:

$$t = \frac{0.9}{\sqrt{\left(\frac{19.7}{18}\right)\left(\frac{2}{10}\right)}}$$

(continued on next page)

Answers for Data Analysis Activities

$$t = \frac{0.9}{\sqrt{\left(\frac{19.7}{18}\right)\left(\frac{2}{10}\right)}}$$

$$t = \frac{0.9}{\sqrt{(1.09)(0.2)}}$$

$$t = \frac{0.9}{\sqrt{0.218}}$$

$$t = \frac{0.9}{0.4669}$$

$$t = 1.9276$$

Critical value of *t* at the .05 level: 2.101

Degrees of freedom: 18

t for the data: 1.9276

Was the difference between freshmen and sophomore opinions of school significantly different, given this sample? No

Write a sentence summarizing your conclusions. The statement should include the following information: "When the ratings of our school by ten freshmen and ten sophomores were compared using the *t*-test for independent samples, no significant difference was found."

*Data Analysis Activity 8—**t*-Test (Nonindependent Samples): Conflict Resolution**

Teacher #	x_2 (pre)	x_1 (post)	D	D^2
1	10	8	2	4
2	5	3	2	4
3	18	15	3	9
4	21	18	3	9
5	18	14	4	16
6	20	15	5	25
7	33	35	-2	4
8	28	25	3	9
9	15	10	5	25
10	42	43	-1	1
$N = 10$	$\Sigma x_2 = 210$	$\Sigma x_1 = 186$	$\Sigma D = 24$	$\Sigma D^2 = 106$

$$\text{mean of D} = \frac{\sum D}{N} = \frac{24}{10} = 2.4$$

(continued on next page)

Answers for Data Analysis Activities

Using the formula, substitute values from the chart you just completed:

$$t = \frac{\text{mean of D}}{\sqrt{\frac{\sum D^2 - \frac{(\sum D)^2}{N}}{N(N-1)}}}$$

$$t = \frac{2.4}{\sqrt{\frac{106 - \frac{(24)^2}{10}}{10(10-1)}}}$$

Multiply ΣD by itself to find ΣD^2, subtract $N - 1$, and substitute both in the formula:

$$t = \frac{2.4}{\sqrt{\frac{106 - \frac{576}{10}}{10(9)}}}$$

Divide ΣD^2 by N:

$$t = \frac{2.4}{\sqrt{\frac{106 - 57.6}{10(9)}}}$$

Subtract numbers in the numerator:

$$t = \frac{2.4}{\sqrt{\frac{48.4}{10(9)}}}$$

Multiply the numbers in the denominator:

$$t = \frac{2.4}{\sqrt{\frac{48.4}{90}}}$$

Divide the numbers in the denominator:

$$t = \frac{2.4}{\sqrt{0.5378}}$$

Using a calculator, find the square root of the denominator:

$$t = \frac{2.4}{0.7333}$$

Divide the numerator by the denominator:

$$t = 3.273$$

Critical value of t at the .05 level: 2.262

Degrees of freedom ($N - 1$): 9

t for the data: 3.273

(continued on next page)

Answers for Data Analysis Activities

Was the average number of verbal conflicts before and after the conflict resolution treatment significantly different, given this sample? Yes

Write a sentence summarizing your conclusions. The statement should include the following information: "After implementing a conflict resolution program in 9th grade classes, a significant difference was noted in the average number of verbal conflicts per week before the treatment (21) and after the treatment (18.6).

Data Analysis Activity 9—**Qualitative Analysis: Club Membership**

Possible themes:

- High level of computer knowledge and sophistication among previous club members (ideas for club projects involve Internet, sophisticated uses of computers).
- High cohesion among previous members (informal talk before meeting began, active participation during meeting, informal talk after meeting ended).
- Not welcoming to new members (did not talk with them before meeting started; did not welcome or introduce them during the meeting; did not ask them anything before or during the meeting; did not ask them to be on committees; did not form a committee around the idea of the transfer student).

Hunches to be explored further:

- Sexism? Few girls in club; those there not included much; one was asked to record information on the board (secretarial role).
- Socio-economic or class bias? Most previous members own their own computers and have modems; most previous members drive their own cars to school; little concern for students who ride the bus and would not be able to participate in before-school computer lab time; members who participated most seemed well-dressed, possibly indicating wealth.

Sharing Results

Chapter 7

As we mentioned in the introduction, professional researchers do what they do in order to make the world a better place. To accomplish this goal, they need to find out or create something of value and share this information with a real-world audience using appropriate communication vehicles. Like professional researchers, student researchers should also share the results of their endeavors with an interested audience. Real-world researchers share their results with colleagues through a variety of professional meetings, conferences, and publications. We believe that sharing information is an important aspect of research for students as well. In our experience, students who work toward sharing with a real-world audience show greater task commitment, focus, and care in their research.

While most professional researchers are limited to formal reports, student researchers may have greater flexibility in the format and circumstances through which their research results are shared. Students may choose to write a research report to submit for publication, but they also may elect to share research results through a speech, letter to the editor, graphic image, skit, song, or poem—options seldom available to traditional research scientists. While formal oral and written reports may not be the most effective communication vehicles for professionals, they are locked into these by the standards of the professions. Fortunately, students are not bound by such traditions and are freer to choose a communication vehicle that is most appropriate for their intended audience. We want you to encourage your students be as professional as possible in framing problems, designing research, and collecting and analyzing data. We believe that the creativity and motivation that are encouraged through a variety of research products are a valuable asset to a school research program.

In this chapter, we will discuss existing authentic audiences for student products, strategies for generating additional audiences, descriptions of various product possibilities, and the components of a traditional research report. We hope these ideas will present many options for research products that share your students' results with professionalism, clarity, and enjoyment.

Identifying Authentic Audiences

If professional researchers simply wrote reports, turned them in to supervisors, and got them back with a grade, we doubt whether much quality work would ever be produced. Creative producers do what they do to bring about change, add to knowledge in their field, contribute to the aesthetic enjoyment of others, influence policy—in other words, to make a difference! Specific examples include market researchers who decide if a product or service is needed in a particular area, researchers who want to help teachers find more effective ways to teach increasingly diverse groups of students, traffic specialists who want to know how traffic volume and patterns would be affected by a new bridge in a particular location, or historians who want to help people better understand the historical roots of current world conflicts.

Our experience with student research supports our belief that there is no substitute for a real-world audience. Students spend much more time and energy re-working, polishing, and refining their efforts when the audience is a professional publication, presentation to the School Board, or letter to the community newspaper. Like all of us, students work harder, dig deeper, and expend extra amounts of effort in order to prepare materials for someone who genuinely cares about what they have to say.

The writing process approach focuses a great deal of attention on the idea of audience, being aware of who will read a person's writing and the kind of impact the writer would like to have upon that audience. This same awareness of audience and impact will greatly increase the power of students' communication about their research. Sometimes students are clear about their audience and intent; indeed, the audience may have been the impetus for the research in the first place. Amy investigated the effects of gelatin on plant growth in order to tell her mother (audience) whether it was worthwhile to continue that practice (impact). Eric surveyed other students' food preferences in order to convince the cafeteria manager (audience) to alter the school lunch menu (impact).

There are times when students don't initially have an audience in mind; their interest lies in finding out answers for themselves. For example, middle school students might survey their peers to determine their favorite types of music just because it is an interesting topic. While we would never discourage the pursuit of knowledge for its own sake, students should consider sharing what they found out with others who might also be interested. Asking students to identify potential interested audiences might help focus their research and determine the most appropriate format for the final product. When Erin wondered which books her fellow 8th graders enjoyed reading, she decided that other students who were looking for new books to read might also be interested in the information. The resulting product was an annotated bibliography of recommended books placed in the middle school library.

Where might middle and high school students find potential audiences for their research? The answer will depend a great deal on the nature of the research question. Research about student behaviors, opinions, and preferences might be of interest to Student Council, school administrators, the school newspaper, the PTA, school governing council, etc. Students can share information about current issues in the community with councils, organizations, or task forces empowered to make recommendations or decisions about the particular issue. They can also share results with the community at large to spur a campaign to support a particular position through letters to the editor, displays, leaflets, or door-to-door informational campaigns. This approach is particularly appropriate if research results suggest action projects that are necessary for community well-being. For instance, if students find that very few people know basic first aid techniques, they may decide to create some kind of education program in the form of an instructional unit, pamphlet, poster, or skit.

Regardless of the particular approach taken, it is critical that you help students identify authentic audiences (outside of the school whenever possible) with whom to share their results. You may be dubious about the value of adolescents' research in the real world, but we urge you not to underestimate the possibilities. Secondary students have documented pollution in area streams, charted acid rain statewide, written stories and books, and researched and started businesses. All of these ideas and products were shared with interested audiences beyond the school.

Creating Product Outlets

Sometimes it just isn't possible or realistic to submit all students' research to professional journals or other outside audiences. While it is important not to lose sight of real professional opportunities for students, it is also useful to think about how to create audiences for student research that will allow novice researchers an opportunity to share their efforts in a more limited, but still "professional" arena. In the next sections, we will discuss five outlet vehicles teachers can help create: student journals; science, social studies, and research fairs; history days; invention conventions; and student research conferences. Any of these, alone or in combination, can be established at a school, district, county, or state level. These are only a few of the possible outlet vehicles for student researchers. Teachers may be able to build on local resources, link up with other organizations in their area, or create new ways to share results with audiences that meet their students' needs.

Student Journal

Adult researchers in a variety of fields from education and psychology to chemistry and medicine publish in a wide variety of professional journals. While the standards of these journals are probably too high for any but the most advanced student, teachers might want to create one or more local student journals that can serve the same function for their students. These student journals can be general in nature, with subsections for biological sciences, physical sciences, and social sciences or can be more narrowly focused, such as a journal devoted to community problems or local historical research. Literary magazines provide a similar opportunity for students working in the humanities.

When starting a student journal, teachers will first need to decide on its scope. Will it include submissions just from their school or the entire district, county, or state? What types of material will they include? How will they solicit manuscripts and select pieces that will be published? What process will they use for printing and binding? How will they finance the journal—individual sales, subscriptions, advertisements, business sponsorships, etc.? How will they publicize its existence in order to generate submissions and sales? The smaller the scope of the publication, the easier some of these logistics will be. However, teachers may find that printing costs for a very small number of journals may be significantly higher than those for a larger print run or that students are anxious to share their results with an audience beyond the school. If they choose to create a journal at the district, county, or state level, they may be able to find colleagues in other schools or districts willing to assist them. Once the publication involves more than just one school, it would be advisable to create an editorial board to coordinate efforts and maintain communication. This board should include at least one adult from each building or district involved in the project. In addition, we recommend also including students from participating units.

One of the first major decisions facing a teacher is whether his/her journal will be competitive or inclusive. Will he/she print everything that is submitted or review submissions and publish only the best? There are advantages to both positions. Inclusive journals that publish all submissions encourage students to participate, provide recognition, and are probably most appropriate for younger students and/or single schools. Journals that include entire districts or larger areas will not be able to publish all submissions and will need some type of review process. Teachers can also argue that competitive publication guidelines are more typical of the "real world." Professional publications typically send each submission to two or three reviewers who evaluate it and recommend acceptance, revision, or rejection. We encourage teachers to do the same and to include some students among the reviewers and the review board. Adolescents, particularly those with expertise in the content of the articles, would gain much from reviewing and editing their peers' work. Indeed, with the growing popularity of the writing process, many students have had years of experience with peer editing. Review forms typical of student journals and literary magazines are included in Figures 7.1 and 7.2.

A timeline will determine whether it is feasible to ask students to revise and resubmit manuscripts. If the journal will only be publishing one issue per year, a teacher's only decision may be either to publish or reject the manuscript. While rejection of any kind is never pleasant, even to professional adults, acceptance by a competitive journal is a meaningful goal for a student researcher and includes greater validation because of its competitiveness.

Having made all these decisions about the scope and nature of the journal, the next step is letting students know about the journal and the process for submitting manuscripts. It is important that all students receive this information. Students who show little interest in traditional library research may be just the ones to get excited about original research with professional-type outlets. Distributing information through teachers will reach some students, but a teacher might also want to consider school-wide publicity through school newspapers, posters, announcements, and word-of-mouth. If students are involved in the production of the journal, the students responsible for publicizing its sale might also be involved in soliciting manuscripts.

Once the journal is set into motion, a teacher must also consider the details of how the journal will be printed. Is the school copy machine sufficient or does he/she want professional printing and binding? To what extent can his/her school's computer technology be used to produce the journal? (We have seen schools where entire yearbooks and newspapers are written, laid out, and sent to the printer by students using computers and desktop publishing programs.) If a teacher will be selling the journals, how many copies can he/she reasonably expect to sell? Who will handle the sales? How will orders be taken and money collected? Teachers who are experienced in producing newspapers, literary magazines, or yearbooks can be valuable resources for this type of information. Almost every high school has some professionally produced publications. Faculty members who have been involved in such endeavors may provide valuable input regarding local printers, successful distribution strategies, or staff organization. Whatever the size and scope of journal a teacher chooses, a student research journal can provide an audience for research reports that parallels those of adults and adds an element of professionalism to student research endeavors.

Literary magazines can serve many of the same purposes and be completed in the same way as research journals. In addition to being an outlet for students interested in more literary types of writing, it is important to highlight and validate the research that goes into successful literary writing. Professional authors of both fiction and

District Research Journal Review Form

Student Number ______ Reviewer Number ______

Grade Level ___ K-3 ___ 4-6 ___ 6-9 ___ 9-12

Elements	Weak		Moderate			Strong
Research Question • clear, unambiguous • important	1	2	3	4	5	6
Data Gathering • appropriate to question • primary sources used • appropriate sampling	1	2	3	4	5	6
Data Analysis • appropriate to question/data • correctly used	1	2	3	4	5	6
Conclusions, Discussion • clear • supported by data	1	2	3	4	5	6
Format • well organized • communicates clearly	1	2	3	4	5	6
Originality • unique question • original methodology	1	2	3	4	5	6

Total Score ____________

Comments/Concerns if selected for publication:

Figure 7.1. Research journal review form.

District Literary Journal Review Form

Student Number _______ Reviewer Number _______

Grade Level ___ K-3 ___ 4-6 ___ 6-9 ___ 9-12

Elements	Weak		Moderate		Strong	
Organization • unity, development, clarity	1	2	3	4	5	6
Structure, Grammar	1	2	3	4	5	6
Originality • imagination, tone, theme, style	1	2	3	4	5	6
Unusual or Other Elements • e.g., dialogue, special format, mood, character development, etc.	1	2	3	4	5	6
Sense of Audience	1	2	3	4	5	6

Total Score _____________

Comments/Concerns if selected for publication:

Figure 7.2. Literary journal review form.

nonfiction do significant research in preparation for writing. While the research involved in nonfiction writing may be more obvious, it is important that we teach students interested in fiction how to do research that increases the sophistication of their writing about characters, locations, dialect, and specialized information contained in the stories. These often involve the data gathering strategies of observation, interviews, and document analysis. Conversely, students whose main focus is research may choose a literary form to communicate their results because it may have a more powerful impact on their chosen audience.

Science, Social Studies, and Research Fairs

For most schools, the only research outlet has been the traditional science fair. If a school does not currently have a science fair, teachers may want to consider establishing one or its social science counterpart—a social studies fair. A third possibility is a research fair that welcomes and celebrates original research on any topic. The latter might be more appropriate for a middle school or a high school just starting to emphasize original research. As with student journals, science, social studies, and research fairs can be organized at a school, district, or county level. State or county organizations may already exist in your area. Your district science or social studies curriculum coordinator should be able to provide information and support.

Unlike many journals, school-level science, social studies, and research fairs are generally inclusive—that is, all projects submitted are displayed. Teachers will need to decide if they want to add an element of competition to their fair by giving prizes. If students will be selected for more limited state or county competitions, it may be necessary to identify a specific number of prize winners. Students, teachers, and judges may find it frustrating to have a fixed number of winners in each category. Some years the number is insufficient, while in other years there are not enough projects worthy of ribbons. An alternative approach to recognizing excellence is a "Certificate of Merit" that can be awarded to as many participants as desired. Other students can be presented with a "Certificate of Participation" as a recognition of their efforts and a souvenir of the fair. Teachers can also identify other specific award categories: best research design, most intriguing research question, best data gathering/analysis, etc.

Judges at a science, social studies, or research fair should be knowledgeable about research techniques and should give awards to projects that demonstrate excellence in research question, design, and data analysis rather than interesting graphics, computer-produced charts, or a colorful display. Developing a rubric for assessing entries should help judges, teachers, and students know what criteria are important. (See Chapter 8 for suggested rubrics and procedures.)

Students, too, should be aware that the goal of the fair is to conduct research, and they should understand the differences among displays, demonstrations, and research. Even the most careful dissection of a frog is still a demonstration and the best diagram of the human body is still a display. Demonstrations and displays have a place at science and social studies fairs, but they are not the chief goal of such endeavors. Teachers may also find that some of their colleagues need clarification regarding these distinctions. A brief brochure on preparing materials and products for a fair or recommendations for reference books (see Resource List) can help students and teachers transform a science, social studies, and/or research fair from a collection of ordinary school reports mounted on poster board to a celebration of data gathering and the production of knowledge. Multiple copies of the reference books should be made available to teachers and students.

History Day

Closely related to a social studies fair is a history day. National History Day is an event that is organized and sponsored in several states. If it does not exist in your area, you can create a local version in which students share the results of their historical research. Although some students may be interested in eras of history in which primary data gathering is very difficult (e.g., ancient Egypt), many students will become interested in conducting true historical research about local people, events, or institutions. Whatever type of research is involved (true historical or secondary research), a history day provides students with a chance to share their interests in history with an audience beyond the classroom. History day projects can include written reports, displays (life-size replica of a room from an Egyptian tomb), demonstrations of historic crafts, skits, readers' theater, original stories, or any other format that helps history come to life. The same considerations about inclusion versus competition considered for science, social studies, or research fairs should also apply to a history day.

One way history days are different from science, social science, or research fairs is that they often include performances, thus necessitating a more careful consideration of the scheduling and placement of various exhibits. Will performances and demonstrations be ongoing? Will they occur on the hour or half-hour? When and where will students perform plays and readers' theater? If teachers decide to use programs or signs, someone needs to prepare them. They'll also need to consider the intended audience when deciding whether the program will be presented during the school day, after school, or during evenings and weekends. This format requires a bit more organization and assistance than a science fair in order to keep things running smoothly. We think teachers will find all the work meaningful when they see history come alive for both presenters and audience at a history day. It will encourage students to see history in a whole new light.

Invention Convention

Strictly speaking, invention conventions are not displays of research as we have traditionally thought of them. They can, however, be valuable outlets for researchers of a different type. An invention convention looks a lot like a science, social studies, or research fair, but instead of research projects, displays, or demonstrations, students enter original inventions designed to solve identified problems.

Commercial materials on inventions and invention conventions are becoming more available every day. Many states have state conventions with guidelines and materials to help teachers get started. If you are not familiar with materials on inventions, **Steven Caney's Invention Book** (1985) and **Using Creative Problem Solving in Inventing** (Treffinger, McEwen & Wittig, 1989) are excellent starting places. Check with teachers in your district's gifted and talented program, particularly those working with elementary students. They are often familiar with the invention process and may have materials that can be adapted for your students. Middle and high school technology teachers may also be valuable resources.

While the organization of an invention convention closely parallels that of a science, social studies, or research fair, there is one important difference. Teachers need to make sure that they indicate on the application materials that all inventions must be self-contained—that is, they cannot demand outside electricity or running water. While they may want to impose similar restrictions in any type of fair, inventions, more than science fair projects, are likely to need such a power source. Teachers might find themselves the morning of the invention convention with thirty projects needing electricity and five needing running water, all in the midst of the school gym with three electrical outlets!

Student Research Conference

The final outlet we will discuss may be new to teachers. It is a student research conference, a parallel to the professional conferences at which adult researchers present their findings. Most teachers have attended a state, regional, or national conference of a professional educational organization. At the conference they probably received a program and selected from a variety of sessions in which presenters spoke about current research or new teaching techniques.

A student research conference parallels such an event. At these conferences, student researchers submit proposals of research projects to be presented. After acceptance by a program committee, presentations are scheduled for specific times and locations with several presentations occurring simultaneously. Those attending the research conference receive a program and decide which presentation to attend in each given time period. Presentations may be repeated, if desired. When students are not presenting their own research, they attend other sessions.

Professional conferences usually have a keynote speaker and teachers may want to replicate this feature at their student conference. They should avoid scheduling any other sessions at the same time to allow all participants to attend the keynote. We know of one student conference in New Orleans where the keynote speaker was an accomplished twelve-year-old researcher! If such a student is not available, teachers should consider inviting a professional researcher, particularly a female and/or member of an ethnic group that is under-represented in the ranks of professional research. Such a speaker would not only present an important message about research, but also serve as a good role model.

Whether students present at a research conference, fair, or history day within the school or with audiences outside the school, they will need to select an appropriate product format. What works for one audience will be a disaster with another even if the research being shared is the same.

Choosing a Product: Impact on Audience

When considering a product format to communicate research results, students should consider two factors—the nature of the audience and the impact one desires to have. A scholarly, well-documented book about the Civil War would probably be the most effective way to communicate with professional historians, but may not be nearly as effective with the general public. The success of Ken Burns' PBS photo-essay "The Civil War" is testimony to the effectiveness of the product format he chose. One product is not inherently better than another. It is only better if it has the desired impact upon the intended audience.

Some factors to consider regarding the nature of the audience include age, reading ability, preferred mode of information acquisition (words, images, sounds, movement, etc.), sophistication regarding the topic, and current interest in the topic. One speaks quite differently about pollution in a neighborhood stream when talking to people who live along its banks than to members of the county pollution control agency. Similarly, trying to convince early adolescents not to smoke would require a different communication medium than if that message were targeted at adults.

In addition to using an appropriate medium for the particular audience, students also need to consider the impact they wish to have on that audience. Informing may call for more detailed information than persuading. Motivating people to take action may require emotional as well as intellectual appeal in addition to an understanding of the current state of mind of the audience.

Students also need to consider the interaction between the audience and the desired impact they wish to have upon it. In the example of students sharing results of their water quality analysis of the local stream, they wanted to have an impact on both neighbors and government officials. Their presentation to the neighbors involved a more emotional tone, one in which they used pictures of belly-up fish along the shores of the stream to motivate the neighbors to influence the appropriate government agency. Pollution Board officials however, with their greater knowledge about fish, quickly realized there were many reasons fish died. To be persuaded about the need to regulate discharges into the stream, they needed to see scientific data regarding parts-per-million concentrations of various pollutants taken upstream and downstream of the companies being targeted for regulation. In each case, the communication vehicle needed to fit both the audience and the action the students wanted them to take.

Teachers can help students analyze these factors by having them first focus on what they want the particular audience to do in response to their research. Is it enough for them to simply hear and understand the results? Do students want them to have a particular emotional response? Take a particular action? Students need to consider the people they are addressing. What motivates them? Is the motivation more emotional or logical? To what extent do other factors such as cost, pleasing constituents or superiors, or other factors come into play? How does this audience normally take in information? What communication vehicles and styles will have credibility for them? Which will hold their interest? These are some of the questions students should consider when choosing a communication vehicle. This process will not only make the sharing of their research results more effective, but will also serve students well in life beyond school.

Much as we think schools emphasize library research at the expense of primary research, we also think they overemphasize reports as a format for sharing research results. Not all research should be shared through a formal research report. For reasons described above, reports are not the most effective way to have the desired impact on many audiences. Short term projects or research conducted by novice researchers may not warrant a formal report. A never-ending series of research reports can be wearing even to motivated adults, so you can imagine what it would do to students who have not chosen research as part of their life's work. Adolescents need more variety, flexibility, and creativity in the dissemination of their research findings, just as they need variety in their classroom endeavors. Imagine how a song could communicate soldiers' experiences during the Vietnam War, a poster could show student preferences for elective courses, or a skit could share the results of interviews with people about ethical dilemmas they face in various careers. In addition to nurturing students' creativity, these alternative formats are likely to be more effective than reports in bringing about the desired impact on the students' chosen audience.

We encourage teachers to be flexible, use their imaginations, and enjoy this opportunity to encourage their students to communicate in a variety of ways. They might involve students by having them brainstorm all the possible ways a study might be shared, break into groups to plan different ways to share the same results, or give special recognition to a student who devises a unique way to communicate results. Students need to see that it is acceptable to choose an alternate communication vehicle. It will take much persuasion to overcome six to ten years of being told they have to write a report.

However, teachers need to be sure that students have had enough instruction in how to create effective and high quality skits, songs, posters, videos, Hypercard stacks, or other forms of communication before expecting them to use such means to share research results. It is easy for teachers to assign students "creative" endeavors without providing them with the skills necessary to be successful. If teachers want their students to create a variety of products to communicate research results or any other information, they'll need to set a long term goal to provide instruction in product development. We encourage teachers to enlist the help of others in their school with expertise. Art, music, technology, and drama teachers might be willing to teach teachers or students how to present professional products in their field of specialization. Instead of, or in addition to, the human resources in a school, teachers can use "how-to" books that will show them and/or their students how-to create quality products in a variety of modes. Several useful book titles and descriptions are included in the Resource List. Figure 7.3 lists alternative communication vehicles and may prove helpful as teachers brainstorm project alternatives. Sharing Results Activity 1 can also be used to help students practice generating product ideas.

Writing a Research Report

After all we've said about alternative communication vehicles, we do acknowledge that, for some projects, the most appropriate vehicle for communicating results is still the traditional research report. Research reports are particularly suitable for projects that involve an extensive review of literature, numerous or complex variables, or a degree of professionalism that may allow them to be submitted for professional publication. A typical research report will contain the following components: title page and abstract, introduction and review of the literature, method, results, and discussion. We will review each component briefly in this book. For a more detailed discussion of report formats, see one of the many available texts on research design or publication manuals of professional organizations such as the American Psychological Association. If the report is to be submitted for publication, teachers will need to find out which guidelines are used by the particular publication and follow those specific references.

Alternative Communication Vehicles

map	diagram	sculpture
discussion	demonstration	poem
profile	dance	chart
campaign	audiocassette	skit
play	quiz show	banner
brochure	debate	flow chart
puppet show	tour	flag
scrapbook	graph	almanac
museum	learning center	advertisement
photo essay	computer program	terrarium
petition	lesson	book list
calendar	game	rap
television show	song	video
collection	living graph	trial
recipe	diary	club
speech	overhead	prototype
biography	mural	test

Figure 7.3. Alternative communication vehicles.

Title Page and Abstract

Any research report should begin with a title that clearly and concisely identifies the main topic and variables of the research. A title should not contain unnecessary words such as "A Study of" or "An Experiment" and should be limited to approximately 8-15 words. Although some research titles may appear daunting to one unfamiliar with the variables ("Adenovirus-Induced Inhibition of Cellular DNase"), titles should clearly convey the topic of the research to those familiar with the general area of study. Examples of clearly stated titles of student projects include "Effects of Gelatin, Sugar, and Salt on the Growth of House Plants," "Ethnic and Racial Changes in the Population of Miami between 1960 and 1995," and "Factors in Novel Selections of 8th Grade Students in Jefferson Middle School." The title page of a research report should include the title, author's name and affiliation (Lincoln High School), and the date.

A professional research report usually includes an abstract, a brief (100-150 words) summary of the research that immediately follows the title page. This summary allows the reader to quickly get an idea about the contents of the report. An abstract may not be necessary for some research reports (especially if it is as long as the report itself), but may be suitable for advanced students or those desiring an extra measure of professionalism.

Introduction and Review of Literature

The body of a research paper begins with an introduction explaining the nature of the problem, why it was important to study, and the background literature that was reviewed. In this part of the report, students present their research question and any information concerning the variables that has been gathered through library research. While beginning student researchers may conduct short term projects without doing any secondary research, more sophisticated students should recognize that original research is not conducted in a vacuum. In a professional research report, investigators find out what others have discovered about their topic before designing research and gathering data. Such a review of literature saves needless replication of effort and allows researchers to identify potentially important variables.

The next element of a research report, the review of literature, helps the reader understand how the current research fits with previous discoveries and why it is important. Such a review may not always be appropriate (or necessary) for some secondary students. Not only might it entail reading complex material, but the questions asked by adolescents (What are the musical preferences of 7th graders?) may not have a prominent place in the research literature. If, however, a student has conducted a particularly sophisticated project, he or she may wish to include a review of literature in the report. For example, a student who surveyed working practices of high school peers could begin her research report by discussing previous studies of the amount and nature of students' work outside of school. She might argue that her study is important because economic conditions and student values have changed since previous studies were conducted.

The introduction and review of literature typically ends with a formal statement of the research question and/or hypotheses such as "The following research question was investigated: In what ways do study habits and school subject preferences of 7th grade students in Jefferson Middle School differ from those of 10th grade students at Lincoln High School?"

Method

The method section of a research report describes how the research was conducted. It should include how subjects (if any) were selected, forms and materials used to gather data, and the procedure used for gathering data. If any instruments (surveys or interview protocols) were created, the report should describe how they were developed and field tested. This section should also include a description of how the data were analyzed. It might include statements such as,

> Fifty subjects were randomly selected from the 208 8th graders in Fields Middle School. Each student completed a twelve-item questionnaire about the amount and type of television shows they watch in a typical week. The questionnaire was field tested with ten 8th graders not in the sample. After the field test, one question was changed to make it clearer. The questionnaire can be found in Appendix A. Questionnaires were analyzed by calculating the average number of hours spent watching television and a frequency count of the types of shows watched.

Results

The results section summarizes the data collected and reports the results of any statistical analyses. While it is inappropriate to include individual scores, many reports are clearer if they include tables that break down the data into relevant categories. For example, the study described above might include a table that describes the percentage of students giving each response to the twelve items. This section should clearly indicate the answer to the original research question(s), possibly restating them for clarity.

Discussion

In the discussion section of the report, the researcher explains how the results support or conflict with the original hypothesis and information included in the review of literature, how the results might be used, and makes suggestions for further research. The discussion section of a report on the student work survey might discuss the fact that the types of work students do has not changed much in the last twenty years but that the number of hours worked has. It might suggest that the results of the survey be communicated to teachers so they are aware of the extent of students' out of school commitments. The discussion section might also recommend that further research be conducted on the possible relationship between hours worked outside of school and academic success. A list of references (in consistent bibliographic form) and any appendices, such as questionnaires, sample release forms, or other relevant documents, should be included at the end of a research report.

Sharing Results Activity 1

Who Cares?

Most researchers hope that their research will make a difference—that it will have a meaningful impact on an audience. It is important to choose a research product to share results in a way that can have an impact on your audience of choice. For each research study below, think of the audiences, products, and impacts that would be most appropriate for the gathered data.

Data	Audience	Desired Impact	Possible Products
Number of hours of TV watched by 7th graders	PTA, students	better supervision, alternative activities	charts of statistics, skit about activities, poster campaign
Foods liked most and least by students			
Percentage of adults voting in the last school board election			
Pounds of paper thrown away by school			
History of a local industry			
Number of students who work, number of hours they work			

Procedures for Assessing Original Research

Chapter 8

It would be nice if students involved in original research only had to deal with authentic feedback from the real-world audiences with whom they shared their results, as do professional researchers. Unfortunately, our educational system, and sometimes the students themselves, insist on an accounting of student work through grades. Meeting this requirement clearly calls for a different approach to assessment than the one used for school assignments or even traditional library research papers. To be useful, these assessments should not only give students feedback upon completion of the project (summative assessment), but should also guide their work along the way (formative assessment). They should deal with both content and process, as well as respond to the multiple dimensions of the research process. Traditional tests and grades certainly haven't been effective in meeting these goals.

One promising method for assessing authentic research that works as both formative and summative assessment is the use of rubrics. A rubric includes criteria to evaluate the work and defines multiple levels of performance (e.g., novice, apprentice, proficient, and distinguished). It can be used for assessing products, performances, portfolio entries, and other kinds of student work. Rubrics make clear the criteria being used for assessment and should be given to students ahead of time so they know what is expected of them. Teachers should also include *benchmarks*, actual examples of work at each of the performance levels, so students can see what is meant by the criteria descriptions.

In a university class one of us taught about original research, the participants developed a rubric for original research projects. After learning about original research and planning to teach it to their students, participants felt a need for a more appropriate way to assess their students' research efforts. Most of the teachers worked with primary students (grades K-3) and the rubric was developed for that age group. When we later adapted the rubric for secondary students, we were somewhat surprised to find that we made very few changes. The criteria for good research are clear, even when it is done at varying levels of sophistication. The remainder of this chapter will describe a rubric for assessing secondary students' research, along with examples and explanations of how to use it. (If you are interested in developing your own rubrics, we highly recommend **Open-ended Questioning** (Freedman, 1994), which explains the process of rubric development and gives numerous examples, and **Assessing Student Outcomes** (Marzano, Pickering, & McTighe, 1993), which includes multiple examples of rubrics for assessing high-level thinking activities.)

Research Rubric

The first step in designing a rubric is the enumeration of criteria, those elements of the project a teacher feels should be assessed. In our example (Figure 8.1), we listed steps for conducting and presenting research down the left side of the chart. Across the page are listed levels of performance. Our research rubric includes the four levels used in Kentucky's state-wide assessment process (Novice, Apprentice, Proficient, and Distinguished). Teachers may want to use different descriptors for the levels. We have seen rubrics with two levels (Acceptable and Not Yet), three levels (Above and Beyond/WOW, Expected Performance, and Improvement Needed/Not Yet) and six levels (numbered 1-6, in Freedman, 1994). Generally the next-to-highest level represents what you expect/hope all students to attain as a result of instruction, with the highest level representing performance that goes beyond in sophistication, depth, creativity, or other relevant dimension. Levels below "Proficient" indicate various degrees of progress toward, but not yet at, the desired level.

CRITERIA	NOVICE	APPRENTICE	PROFICIENT	DISTINGUISHED
Research Question	No question Topic, not question	In question form; question not answerable by data and/ or answer easily known	In question form; answer not readily found and can be answered with data	In question form; answer not readily found; can be answered with data; generalizable **
Hypothesis	None given	Hypothesis is unrelated to research question; should be stated more clearly	Hypothesis is clear, logical, and related to the research question	Hypothesis is clear, logical, and related to the research question; reasons for hypothesis are stated
Sample Selection	No evidence of sample selection	Chooses a sample that is unrepresentative of the population **	Chooses a representative sample of appropriate size**	Chooses a representative sample of appropriate size using random sampling methods**
Data Gathering Techniques	Has data but it is unrelated to the research question	Inappropriate data gathering strategies; biased, unclear, vague questions/observations	Data gathering appropriate for research question; objective, unbiased	Multiple sources of data; uses more sophisticated data gathering methods than peers
Representation and Analysis of Data	Data not represented, no data; no analysis	Data represented/analyzed using inappropriate methods; data represented/analyzed inaccurately	Uses descriptive statistics and/or qualitative data analysis accurately and appropriately	Uses inferential statistics** and/or makes inferences from qualitative data accurately and appropriately
Conclusions	No conclusion	Conclusion unrelated or weakly related to research or results	Conclusion directly related to research; clearly stated	Conclusions directly related to research; clearly stated; implications beyond research stated
Report of Findings	Findings not presented or presentation is inaccurate or unclear	Findings communicated with some clarity	Findings communicated clearly and accurately; appropriate format	Creative format or content; multiple ways of reporting (graphic, writing, kinesthetic)
Surface Features	Errors seriously interfere with comprehension	Errors distract the reader	Errors exist but are not overly distracting	Few or no errors in surface features

* Adapted from: Rubric for Primary Research Projects, developed by M. Buttermann, J. Curry, M. Knight, L. Lowrey, G. Moore, D. Raible, L. Ricketts, G. Schack, B. Schott, J. Shanahan, P. Underwood, & V. Wheatley

** If appropriate. Some may not be applicable to qualitative and case/field research studies; use of inferential statistics depends on question.

Figure 8.1. Rubric for secondary research projects.

The final step in rubric development is filling in the boxes, i.e. describing elements of performance for each criterion at each level. It is best to state these positively, in terms of what the student did rather than what he/she did not do (though this can be difficult for the lowest level of performance). Most rubric developers also say that descriptions should be discrete, i.e. the same description should not appear in more than one column. Descriptors should also indicate qualitatively different performances, rather than quantitatively different ones.

Benchmarks

In addition to descriptions of what is expected for each criterion, it is useful to provide students with concrete examples at various performance levels. Using a holistic approach, you can display entire research products completed by students (with names removed) representing each of the performance levels. These displays can be accompanied by the appropriate level-of-performance column from the rubric itself and/or additional explanations of why each example represents that particular performance level. A student can look at a "Proficient" level research product and compare it with the rubric to see more clearly what made it proficient. The student can also compare his/her product to ones at each level to get a better feel for his/her current level of performance as well as see concrete examples of how to make it better.

A more analytic approach to benchmarks involves creating actual examples for each criterion at each performance level. These examples can be shared and discussed with students so they can see why or how each is representative of the level of performance for individual criteria. We have used the analytical approach to create sample benchmarks for the research rubric shared on Figure 8.1. Compare each set to the rubric to see why each represents the descriptions of work at each level for each criterion. This example describes experimental research about the effect of listening to music while completing school work. Comments in parentheses explain how certain examples vary from the "Proficient" response.

Research Question

Novice: No question or "Listening to the radio." (topic, not a question)

Apprentice: "Should kids listen to the radio?" (doesn't really address the research question of the effect of listening to music on quality of homework)

Proficient: "Does listening to music when doing homework affect the accuracy of high school students' homework?"

Distinguished: "When 9th grade students listen to music, does the type of music or degree of loudness affect the quality of homework?" (goes beyond effect of music in general to examine additional variables)

Hypothesis

Novice: No hypothesis.

Apprentice: "Kids should be able to listen to whatever type of music they like." (does not address the question of effect on homework)

Proficient: "Listening to music will not affect the accuracy of homework."

Distinguished: "Listening to music will not affect the accuracy of homework because students are used to listening to music. If they are more relaxed by the music they are likely to do better on their homework." (includes an explanation for why they chose the hypothesis)

Sample Selection

Novice: No explanation is given for source of data.

Apprentice: "I surveyed ten of my friends." "I did my experiment in the freshman General Math class." (likely to be a biased sample)

Proficient: "My experiment was done in four heterogeneous math classes."

Distinguished: "My experiment was done in four heterogeneously grouped math classes in grades 9-12. Within each class students' names were drawn blindly from a hat to determine if they were in the treatment or control group." (explained how random sampling procedures were used)

Data Gathering Techniques

Novice: "I surveyed students to see if they listened to music when they did homework." (does not address effect on homework)

Apprentice: "I asked kids if they thought listening to music made them mess up on their homework. Based on asking them, I made a list of kids who said they did and did not listen to music while doing homework. Then I asked the teacher how many from each list had good homework grades." (opinion rather than actual results; some attempt to match music listening with homework grades, but measures are very general)

Proficient: "In class I had students work math problems with and without music and compared the accuracy of their answers."

Distinguished: "In class I randomly selected groups of students to do math problems and read a story, then answer questions. Each group was given the same task and the same amount of time to do it, but in a different order. During one part of the period, the groups worked in silence doing math and/or reading. During the other part of the period, they worked while listening to rock music. The treatment group listened to music at a level they agreed was usual for them, which was fairly loud. The control group worked in silence." (extensive description of experimental procedures; indicates sophisticated use of this research design)

Representation and Analysis of Data

Novice: Presents no data or presents two lists of scores for kids who listen to music while doing homework and those who do not. (data have not been manipulated in any way)

Apprentice: Presents mean scores for the groups (computed inaccurately) or presents a frequency distribution of scores for the total group. (some data analysis, but using less-sophisticated techniques)

Proficient: Presents a chart indicating number of subjects and average scores for treatment and control group. (appropriate use of descriptive statistics)

Distinguished: "Below I have indicated number of subjects and mean scores for each groups. A series of *t*-tests indicate that some differences between the groups are statistically significant while some are not." (appropriate use of inferential statistics)

Conclusions

Novice: No conclusion presented.

Apprentice: "I think listening to music is okay cause it didn't bother some people." (not related to effect of music on homework or not clear if "bother" relates to effect on homework)

Proficient: "Students who listened to music while doing math problems had lower average accuracy scores than those doing them without music. This suggests that music might distract students and that they would probably do a better job if they did not play music while doing homework."

Distinguished: "Students listening to rock music at loud levels had significantly lower scores in reading comprehension. There were no significant differences in math computation. These results suggest that listening to music might interfere with higher order thinking skills and might have little or no effect on lower order thinking. Based on this research, students (and possibly adults as well) should not listen to loud music when doing tasks involving higher order thinking." (detailed explanation of conclusion with implications beyond the research explored)

Report of Findings

Novice: (written report to the teacher) "I asked kids if they liked music or not. Most kids did but some didn't, so I had them do some math problems and played music, but some kids didn't like the kind I played and spent the whole time complaining and didn't get any problems done. But some kids did good on the problems, so I don't know what to say." (presentation somewhat unclear in content; writing style distracts from understanding)

Apprentice: (report to the teacher) "I had kids in four math classes do problems first with music, then without. I graded their papers and looked at how they did and the group with music did worse than the group without. From this I guess you'd have to say kids shouldn't listen to music but it does not bother me. Maybe the problems were harder that they did with the music." (explanation somewhat understandable but not thorough; some distraction from writing style)

Proficient: (speech to the Parent Teacher Association) "Students in four math classes at my high school took part in my experiment. I wanted to know if listening to music interfered with doing homework. After getting the teacher's permission, I had half of each class do ten math problems, while the others read a book. It was quiet in the room. When they were done I gave the same problems to the other group, but I played songs from the latest Pearl Jam CD. They both got the same amount of time to work. Then I went off and graded the papers and averaged the grades. I found that the group who listened to music got an average of 66 percent right while the group that didn't get to listen to music got 75 percent right. From this I think the music did interfere and even though I hate to say this and my classmates will kill me, you probably shouldn't let your kids listen to rock music while they do their homework."

Distinguished: (speech to the Parent Teacher Association, enhanced by playing a sample of the music used in the experiment, displaying charts of the statistical findings, and reading sample student comments) "Students in four heterogeneously grouped math classes at John Jones High School took part in my experiment. My research question was, 'Does listening to rock music affect the accuracy of homework for high school students?' After getting the teachers' permission, I randomly selected half of each class to do ten math computation problems (long division and three-number multiplication) while the other half read a book. It was quiet in the room. When the first half was done, I gave the same problems to the second group. They worked for the same amount of time, but listened to songs from the latest Pearl Jam CD at a volume typical for high school students. (Play a few bars of the song at the volume used in the experiment.) Then I graded the papers and averaged the grades. I found that the group who listened to music got an average score of 66 out of 100 points while the group that didn't listen to music got an average of 75. I used the *t*-test statistic to see if this difference could have happened by chance alone and it came out significant. This means the results would probably be the same if we tested all the kids in my high school. Based on these results, I think the music did interfere with students' performance. Even though it did not confirm my hypothesis and my classmates will be disappointed, you probably shouldn't let your kids listen to rock music while they do their homework." (very clear and thorough communication of process and outcome; used music and charts in addition to oral communication; articulate communication with few or no errors)

We must acknowledge the difficulty of creating one set of benchmarks that will apply to all nine kinds of research. While using inferential statistics is the mark of a distinguished experiment, it is inappropriate in a case study. Teachers will probably need to develop different benchmarks for the various types of research done by their students. One way to develop benchmarks is to wait until one set of students has completed research and choose benchmarks from that body of work. Another is to make up sample benchmarks ahead of time so the first set of students has examples from which to work. These benchmarks can then be modified or supplemented by actual products once students have completed their research.

Using Rubrics With Students

When using rubrics in class, teachers can use an existing one or develop their own. We strongly recommend that teachers consider a third alternative—involving students in the process of developing rubrics. Involving students not only builds student ownership in the assessment process, but also serves an instructional purpose by clarifying the process for which they are designing the rubric. Once students understand the task to be done, in this case original research, teachers can ask them to identify important elements of a quality product. Through discussion, teachers and their students can jointly develop the criteria to be used. A teacher colleague of ours has had great success asking students, "What would quality look like with respect to (the focus of the rubric)?"

Once teachers have a complete list of the criteria or dimensions that describe a product, the next step is to decide how many levels of performance they wish to include and to name them. Initially they might want to use only two (Acceptable/Not Yet) or three levels (WOW, Acceptable, Not Yet) until they and their students feel more comfortable with the process of rubric development. To complete the descriptors for each criterion at each level, we recommend first working as a large group to describe all levels of performance for one criterion in order to model the process. Teachers can then invite subgroups of students to draft ideas for "filling in the boxes" for the remaining criteria. After working in subgroups, they can share their ideas with the whole class for revision and final decision making. We have found it helpful to start with the equivalent of the "Proficient" or "Expected Performance" column by asking students to describe what quality would look like with respect to that criterion. Students can then describe performance at the lowest level of the rubric and then explain any intermediary levels representing growth that are still not completely adequate performances. Finally, students can describe

"Distinguished" performance, considering ways students might go above and beyond the expected performance. This level should include evidence of greater depth, sophistication, and creativity, rather than greater quantities of the same behavior expected at the "Proficient" level.

If students are to be involved in rubric development, we recommend that teachers develop the rubric before students have started working on the product. The process not only reinforces their teaching of the research process and allows students to use the rubric as a guideline as they work, but it also increases the likelihood that students will consider levels of performance objectively. When working on rubric development after students have started their projects, we have experienced instances where some students appeared to be skewing the descriptions so their product would be described as "Distinguished."

We recommend asking students to use the rubric for self-assessment at various points during the development of the project as a way to keep students on target and mindful of quality work. They should also complete the rubric when they have finished their project for summative self-evaluation. Students can also help themselves and each other by using the rubric for peer assessment. They can provide feedback during project development to help peers refine their work. They should also assess others' projects upon completion. Serving as an evaluator will refine students' sense of and use of criteria. Teachers and others familiar with research and the area being studied should also complete the rubric. To make the process more mutual, they can invite students to comment or write about the ways in which they agree and disagree with the teachers assessment.

If teachers are sponsoring a research fair, rubrics can be of great assistance. They let students know what elements of research are important and communicate expectations about what constitutes quality work. They provide consistent information to educators about the kinds of skills and performances they should be helping students develop. Finally, rubrics contribute to validity and reliability in the judging process by spelling out criteria and levels of performance. Through specification of criteria, teachers can also make sure judges focus on the substantive elements of research that they wish to acknowledge in students' work.

To be most effective, anyone using a rubric should first examine the overall project to see its goals, methods, and results. After getting a holistic picture of the project, the assessor can then look more closely for evidence of each criterion in the rubric. After making a judgment about level of performance based on descriptions in the rubric, he/she can mark the descriptor that best fits that student's work on each criterion. Rubrics that provide space for written comments will allow for even more effective feedback.

Grading

While rubrics are an effective vehicle for communicating expectations and giving feedback, teachers are still left with the question of how to turn a multidimensional rubric into a number or letter in the grade book. One method is to assign weights to each criterion based on its relative importance to the overall project. Teachers can assign a series of grades based on the level achieved for each criterion with each criterion worth a different amount of points or by double-counting the more important elements. The association of grades with columns in a rubric is controversial among experts in authentic assessment, who prefer to separate the assessment/feedback process from that of grading and evaluating. While that position is admirable, many teachers who are still left with the requirement of giving grades feel a need for consistency and find ways to connect grades to rubrics. They have come up with several ways to make that connection.

In the example in Figure 8.2, the teacher has made a correlation between letter grades and columns, choosing to let the "Proficient" or "Expected Performance" column represent a B, the "Distinguished" or "Above and Beyond" column an A, and the other columns C's, D's, and F's, depending on the quality of work. For this assignment, the teacher decided to weigh research question, data gathering, data representation/analysis, and drawing conclusions more heavily than hypothesis, sample selection, report of findings, and surface features. Her students had just started their study of research and she saw the latter four features as less important elements at this point in their learning. Therefore, she chose to double count the grades assigned for the four categories she wished to emphasize. The teacher assigned grades based on the quality of work within each criterion, using pluses and minuses to reflect the range of responses within a level.

CRITERIA	NOVICE	APPRENTICE	PROFICIENT	DISTINGUISHED
Research Question	No question Topic, not question	In question form; question not answerable by data and/ or answer easily known	In question form; answer not readily found and can be answered with data ✔	In question form; answer not readily found; can be answered with data; generalizable**
Hypothesis	None given	Hypothesis is unrelated to research question; should be stated more clearly ✔	Hypothesis is clear, logical, and related to the research question	Hypothesis is clear, logical, and related to the research question; reasons for hypothesis are stated
Sample Selection	No evidence of sample selection	Chooses a sample that is unrepresentative of the population **	Chooses a representative sample of appropriate size** ✔	Chooses a representative sample of appropriate size using random sampling methods**
Data Gathering Techniques	Has data but it is unrelated to the research question	Inappropriate data gathering strategies; biased, unclear, vague questions/observations	Data gathering appropriate for research question; objective, unbiased ✔	Multiple sources of data; uses more sophisticated data gathering methods than peers
Representation and Analysis of Data	Data not represented, no data; no analysis	Data represented/analyzed using inappropriate methods; data represented/analyzed inaccurately	Uses descriptive statistics and/or qualitative data analysis accurately and appropriately	Uses inferential statistics** and/or makes inferences from qualitative data accurately and appropriately ✔
Conclusions	No conclusion	Conclusion unrelated or weakly related to research or results	Conclusion directly related to research; clearly stated ✔	Conclusions directly related to research; clearly stated; implications beyond research stated
Report of Findings	Findings not presented or presentation is inaccurate or unclear	Findings communicated with some clarity ✔	Findings communicated clearly & accurately; appropriate format	Creative format or content; multiple ways of reporting (graphic, writing, kinesthetic)
Surface Features	Errors seriously interfere with comprehension	Errors distract the reader	Errors exist but are not overly distracting ✔	Few or no errors in surface features

* Adapted from: Rubric for Primary Research Projects, developed by M. Buttermann, J. Curry, M. Knight, L. Lowrey, G. Moore, D. Raible, L. Ricketts, G. Schack, B. Schott, J. Shanahan, P. Underwood, & V. Wheatley

** If appropriate. Some may not be applicable to qualitative and case/field research studies; use of inferential statistics depends on question.

Figure 8.2. Rubric scoring example.

The student whose work is represented by the rubric in Figure 8.2 received the following grades for his project:

Research Question	B+, B+
Hypothesis	C
Sample Selection	B
Data Gathering Techniques	B+, B+
Represent/Analyze Data	A+, A+
Draw Conclusions	B, B
Report of Findings	C-
Surface Features	B

As an alternative, teachers can assign weights or points to each criterion, decide how many points to award within each criterion and then add them up for a total number of points for the project. Using the rubric in Figure 8.2, a different teacher could have apportioned the points available for the total project (60) among the criteria, based on his/her sense of their relative worth. The appropriate points are indicated in parentheses after each criterion. He/she could have assigned points for each criterion based on his assessment of how well he/she felt the work represented each one.

Criterion (possible points)	Actual points assigned
Research Question (10)	9
Hypothesis (5)	3
Sample Selection (5)	4
Data Gathering Techniques (10)	9
Represent/Analyze Data (10)	10
Draw Conclusions (10)	8
Report of Findings (5)	3
Surface Features (5)	4

The teacher would then add up the points and enter them in his/her grade book as the grade for that project. In this case, the student would receive 50 out of 60 possible points for the research project.

A more holistic approach involves looking at the pattern of circles or checks on the rubric, then awarding a grade based on the column in which most fall. In this example, the teacher looked at the rubric in Figure 8.2, saw that five of the eight checks fell in the "Proficient" column, and assigned an overall rating of proficient to the research project. If she had previously decided that a "Proficient" rating would result in a grade of B, that is the grade she would assign for the project.

Rubrics provide enormous flexibility in assessment through choice of criteria, decisions about levels, and specification of what performance exemplifies each level of each criterion. Their structure encourages teachers to consider criteria important in the real world, thereby providing a more authentic approach to assessment than more unidimensional assessment methods such as tests, essays, or notebooks. Original research involves several distinct dimensions, making rubrics an ideal way to give students guidance beforehand and feedback afterwards. Rubrics can be adapted for a variety of projects and differentiated for differing levels of sophistication. In addition, by involving students in the development of rubrics and benchmarks, teachers help clarify learning goals, build ownership in the assessment system, and provide guidelines that actually help improve the quality

Assessment Activity 1

Exercising Judgment Using Rubrics

Here's your chance to use a rubric to assess someone else's research project. What follows is a shortened description of a research project that might have been carried out by a middle or high school student. Use the rubric in Figure 8.1 to see how well this represents experimental research.

1. First read through the whole research report to get the idea of what was done.
2. Go back and look for each element listed on the left side of the research rubric. Consider each one separately. Put a large check in the box you think best represents the level of performance for that element.
3. When you have finished scoring each element, look at the pattern of checks. In which column do most of them fall? ____________________ Are you comfortable assigning that overall rating to this research project? _______________ Why or why not?

4. Be ready to explain why you made the assessments you did.

EXERCISE AND SCHOOL SUCCESS

What I set out to find out is whether kids who exercise do better in school. I think they would, cause exercise takes discipline and kids who have the discipline to exercise on a regular basis probably have the discipline to do their homework and study too.

I made a survey asking kids if they exercised regularly (at least four times a week) and what their grades on their report cards were the last recording period. To try to make sure kids told thc truth I told them not to put their names on the papers. My teacher said he would pass out and collect the surveys in his English (one honors, two regular) and drama (beginning and advanced) classes. The English classes are mostly 10th graders. The drama classes have kids in all grades, with mostly 9th and 10th in the beginning one and mostly 11th and 12th in the advanced class.

Then I divided the surveys into 2 groups: one pile the kids who did exercise regularly, the other pile of ones who didn't. I averaged all their report card grades separately to get a grade average for each student. Then I found the average grade for each group. The exercisers had a average of 2.0 and the non-exercisers had a 2.2.

It didn't turn out the way I thought it would, so I had to think about why. Maybe people who exercise also do sports and don't spend much time on their school work. Maybe students who take drama exercise more cause it helps with their drama, and lots of the drama kids don't do well in school. I guess it's possible that the difference between 2.0 and 2.2 isn't big enough to say that exercise is related to doing good in school.

(continued on next page)

Assessment Activity 1

If you'd like to take this a little further:
How could you help this person improve his/her research report? First consider elements that you rated lower than "Proficient" and make some suggestions for improvement. Once you've done that, consider suggestions that would help the person move from "Proficient" to "Distinguished." Write down specific suggestions in at least three areas.

To prepare to participate in peer assessment in a helpful and supportive manner, you might want to role-play how you would talk with the author of this research report. Have one person volunteer to play the part of the author and others take turns talking with him/her about what he/she did well and how to make it better. Be sure to give honest and specific feedback while being sensitive to the person's feelings. Think about how you would like someone to give you feedback.

Assessment Activity 2

Designing Pizza Rubrics

Before you attempt to develop a rubric for an activity or assignment in your class, try to create one for something more familiar and less threatening . . . a pizza. Think about good pizzas and bad pizzas you have tasted in your life. What distinguished the good from the bad?

What elements or dimensions of pizza did you consider (crust, sauce, toppings, price, etc.)? List those down the left side of the blank rubric on the next page.

For this activity use three levels of performance, though rubrics can include more or less than that. Consider what you want to label each level. The middle one should represent acceptable (not great, but not awful). The lower label should indicate unacceptable quality, while the higher one should indicate that the pizza is much better than most. Discuss your suggestions for labels, then write the ones to which you have agreed on at the top of each column.

Fill in the boxes and describe three levels of quality for each of the elements or dimensions down the left side. You may want to divide the task and have different small groups work on each of the dimensions. They can then share their ideas and the whole class can give feedback, make suggestions, and come to consensus.

Good rubrics are clear enough that several people rating the same item should come up with pretty similar ratings. When that happens, you have inter-rater reliability. If you want to see if your rubric is clear enough to ensure inter-rater reliability, see if your class can order a pizza (or use the rubric the day the cafeteria serves pizza). Make sure everyone evaluating the pizza gets a big enough piece to taste crust, topping, and sauce. Using the rubric your class developed, have each person rate the pizza independently, then compare your assessments. Was your rubric clear enough that most people gave similar ratings to the same pizza? If not, examine areas where there was the most disagreement to see if you can write descriptions with less ambiguity.

(continued on next page)

Assessment Activity 2

PIZZA RUBRIC

Elements of Pizza	Levels		
Crust	Soggy or too crisp Too thin/thick Breaks/tears easily Doughy taste Burned taste	Okay texture Right thickness Holds fairly well Little/no taste	Good texture Right thickness Holds together well Flavor complements the pizza
Sauce			
Toppings			
Cost			

Data Gathering: Methodologies of the Disciplines

Chapter 9

We've dealt so far with general research strategies that apply across many disciplines and research questions. In this chapter we'll get a little more specific by looking at more specialized research methodologies used within academic disciplines. If your intent is to help students become more sophisticated researchers, it makes sense to teach them the research methodologies used by practicing professionals.

Let's consider two students who both are investigating substance abuse among teenagers. One student reads books and pamphlets, uses the **Reader's Guide to Periodical Literature** to identify relevant magazine and journal articles, reads them on her school's CD-ROM collection, then writes a ten page report. The other locates members of her school's drug subculture and interviews them about their lives, values, attitudes, and behaviors, then organizes a group of interested participants and develops a substance abuse program based on her findings.

What's the difference between these two investigations? An obvious and important one is the authentic dimension of the latter project. That student not only researched real-world substance abusers in her school, but also used that information to make a positive difference by developing a substance abuse program tailored to her school. This difference was possible because she used primary sources, ethnographic interviews, and qualitative data analysis, as sociologists do. While both students have found out about substance abuse, the quality of the latter student's process and product is clearly superior, displaying both authentic research skills and evidence of advanced mastery of content in the social sciences. It is the teaching of these research methodologies of the specific disciplines that can escalate both the ambitions and abilities of our students in their research pursuits.

What Are the Research Methodologies of the Disciplines?

We spend much time in school teaching students *knowledge of* (that a particular topic or discipline exists) and *knowledge about* (what has been previously learned in the discipline or area). Very little time is spent on *knowledge how*—(how professionals learn or work in their particular discipline). It is this *knowledge how* that not only will enable students to better understand the content and workings of the discipline, but will also teach them the means to become original researchers in their own right. For this reason, teaching students the methodologies and research strategies of a discipline can result in more sophisticated understanding of the discipline, greater challenge, and the development of the attitudes and skills of research professionals in the various disciplines.

Methodologies of the disciplines are the specific ways professionals gather, analyze, and use data to create new knowledge. Starko (1995) feels it is important to teach students the methodologies and habits of practicing professionals if teachers are to help them become creative in authentic ways.

> If individuals are creative in an effort to find and solve problems and find and express ideas, teaching that supports creativity must allow them to do those things in school . . . . First, students must gain enough understanding of the major concepts, generalizations, and "big ideas" of the discipline to be able to ask reasonable questions. Second, they must learn the techniques and methodologies (as well as habits of mind) of creative individuals in the field. Students of science must learn not just facts and rules but how science "works." Whatever the content area, students must learn what kinds of problems are explored in that area, how they are addressed, and how information is shared. Students of social studies must learn how social scientists view their fields, what they explore, and how they proceed. (pp. 140-141)

Below is a look at how these methodologies can be taught in the four core academic disciplines: social studies, science, mathematics, and language arts.

Social Studies

Students rarely learn the methodologies underlying what they study in social studies. "It's in the book" is how you know where a country is located or that an event happened. But how did the book's author figure that out in the first place? Without knowing how such knowledge was created, students are left to take it on faith, hardly an appropriate basis for a discipline that prepares students to become thinking, active citizens.

Students need to understand not just facts, but also the broad concepts that organize the social sciences, including interdependence and systems; cause, effect, and change; and conflict, power, rights, and justice. They also need to know how to use the methodologies of social scientists. Chapter 3 provides an explanation of historical research, including distinguishing between primary and secondary sources, establishing the validity and reliability of sources, creating fine-tuned research questions, analyzing print and non-print sources, and drawing reasonable conclusions from data. Beyond historiography, students should also learn the methodologies of the other social sciences including trend analysis, mapping, sociograms, ethnographic interviewing, card sorts, economic analysis, etc.

Social science also deals with researching and solving social problems. Students who engage in community problem solving model the behaviors of involved, informed citizens. Their efforts will be aided by knowledge of survey design, sampling options, interview techniques, participant observation strategies, ethnographic interviewing, and other methodologies used by sociologists and anthropologists.

Science

In addition to using the scientific method when appropriate, students will benefit from experiencing science as scientists do, starting with the problem identification stage. Scientists start with hypotheses or questions, something students rarely do in school. After the many years students spend reading the results of scientific research presented as facts in textbooks and doing canned experiments with predetermined answers, it is no wonder that many of them are unaware of the problem finding and problem focusing strategies that jump-start scientific investigation. Teaching students to raise questions and design ways to test hypotheses brings them in touch with both the techniques and the "habits of mind" of scientists. We also venture that it will increase the likelihood that students see science as interesting, challenging, and ever-changing.

To aid in their exploration, students can benefit from learning the specialized observation strategies of scientists. These include using instruments such as microscopes, telescopes, binoculars, night vision goggles, and seeing high technology equipment such as electron microscopes. Students can learn to design controlled experiments using a variety of research designs and master several types of measurement techniques (volume, length, number—metric and English) used in science. They can use observation strategies such as field census, regular and microphotography, and specimen collection and preservation. Finally, they should also learn the "habits of mind" necessary for scientists: curiosity, seeking logic and consistency, looking at a problem from multiple perspectives, and persistence in the face of confusion.

Mathematics

At first, the study of mathematics seems to consist entirely of methodology: how to count, measure, and represent information quantitatively. Indeed, this is true when mathematics is used to gather data, do creative things, and solve practical problems. Examples include tallying and analyzing a survey, calculating the total volume of trash produced in the school in one day, and designing an aluminum foil boat with maximum cargo area. This aspect of mathematics parallels the real-world use with which most of us are familiar.

Methodologies that facilitate this aspect of mathematics include descriptive and inferential statistics (to analyze data); sampling theory and practice; representing data using graphs, charts, and other products; recording and making sense of observational data; etc. What remains is making the real-world connections clear to students by using real data when teaching data analysis skills and showing how statistics can help them conduct research in a variety of disciplines.

A second aspect of mathematics is "mathematical questions." Unlike those described above, where mathematics is used to accomplish a task, mathematical questions constitute original research in the field of mathematics. Rather than performing calculations, professional mathematicians look at our current understanding of numerical relationships and wonder what might logically follow, whether that is true in all cases, or what would happen if one aspect of the problem was changed.

The investigation of mathematical questions does not rely on formulas and prescribed algorithms, as does the data gathering, problem solving aspect. Instead, mathematicians must use a variety of problem solving strategies, trying to decide which one(s) seem most appropriate for the given problem. Challenges that invite students to discover patterns, series, or relationships stimulate this kind of mathematical thinking.

Language Arts

In teaching language arts, content and process are closely interwoven, but specific research skills involved are rarely highlighted and taught. One of the most evident places for research is in the writing of nonfiction—books, articles, pamphlets, reports, project proposals, technical writing, etc. In order to accurately describe an event, topic, or process, one must understand it and be able to describe it. Numerous observation, interviewing, and document analysis strategies can be used, depending on the subject being investigated.

Fiction writing also involves research, which will surprise many students who think fiction is entirely fabricated without any basis in reality. This research takes place in the early stages of idea-finding and story-creation, as well as in the actual writing of the piece—book, story, script, speech, or cartoon. Prospective writers must learn to pay attention to things they care enough about to communicate to others, then closely observe their experiences and attitudes about the topic, as well as how others feel about it.

Another strategy for budding authors and speakers involves examining the ideas and emotions behind stories they hear and read. This can include listing words that evoke various feelings, experimenting with writing to evoke a feeling, discussing why authors write happy or sad stories, etc. They also can learn how different authors get ideas for their writing by talking with local authors or reading biographies. They might start keeping a writer's notebook, jotting down ideas, phrases, questions they wonder about, etc.

Once students have chosen an idea to communicate, they should be encouraged to focus more clearly by identifying an audience for their communication, choosing relevant observations, narrowing their goals for the piece, and determining a point of view from which to communicate. They then need to write the piece, a process which will require another kind of research. In order to clearly communicate, writers and speakers must convey powerful images of the setting, characters, action, and dialogue through words. Research about these elements (using secondary sources, observation, interviewing, etc.) will help students create more vivid and accurate descriptions. Observation (in the form of listening) will help writers create realistic dialogue, especially if that involves capturing dialects or other ways of speaking that differ from the author's.

Why Teach Research Methodologies of the Disciplines?

We see two different, yet related reasons to teach students how to be original researchers and how to use the research methodologies of practicing professionals. We believe that students who are actively engaged in the process of original research will develop greater interest in and sophistication with both the content and processes of the academic disciplines in which they work, advancing the goal of greater school learning. We also believe involvement in original research will help students develop the skills, self-concept, and desire to continue as authentic researchers in areas of interest.

Advanced Mastery of Content

All teachers want to help students develop a more sophisticated understanding of content. We believe teaching them the methodologies of the disciplines can advance this goal. An emphasis on *knowledge how* allows the student to be more actively involved with his or her learning, where emphasis on greater *knowledge about* keeps the student in the more passive role of consumer of information.

Methodologies can be tools for critical understanding. Just as people can better evaluate and appreciate an article of clothing if they know how to sew, students can better understand disciplines when they know how that knowledge came to be. For example, an understanding of primary and secondary source material and the issues of authenticity, credibility, and bias in the gathering of information would go a long way toward helping students understand both the process and content of history. In addition to different criteria for source material, historians also differ in their underlying perspectives: Economic History, the Great Man Theory, Psychohistory, Marxist Interpretations, etc. An awareness of how historians analyze data and use underlying theories of history would give students the tools to analyze a given historical event in a variety of ways and, in the process, gain a greater appreciation for both the discipline of history and the content being studied.

In addition, students would have a more accurate understanding of the nature of the discipline. They would see that much of the content they are learning is work in progress, rather than final answers. A scientific theorem is only good until a better one comes along. History is always being refined, based on new evidence or new interpretations. Periodically, a new prime number is discovered. By approaching the curriculum in this way, students can see that knowledge is a constant refining of understanding, advanced by on-going research. It is also important that they understand that what is known today may be supplanted tomorrow by a more comprehensive understanding gained through research.

Methodologies can lead to greater interest in the discipline. Students often complain about the sterility and irrelevance of what they are taught in school. They feel no personal connection or identification with the content and hence may exhibit low levels of motivation. It has been our experience that when students understand *how* knowledge came to be and when they are actively involved in their learning, they show much greater levels of interest, motivation, and commitment.

Many years ago, one of us sat semi-awake through the first several weeks of a university history course about the Near East in the Modern World. The professor talked on about the Israeli claim to the land of Israel, citing original sources and logical arguments while students dutifully took notes. Sometime around the midterm, he started doing the same thing from the Palestinian viewpoint, also citing original sources (sometimes the same ones!) and logical arguments. Needless to say, the conclusions were quite different. Just before raising my hand to ask which version was right, the professor said, "And that's what makes history so interesting—that people can examine a series of sources, using different analysis strategies, and come up with such different conclusions. We'll never know what really happened back then. History is our attempt to recreate what occurred as accurately as possible, all the while having no way to know for sure if we are right." Seeing history as questions instead of answers upped my interest 500%, and I wondered why I had gotten all the way to college before anyone ever shared the *how* of history along with the *what*.

Original Research and Creative Productivity

We celebrate the inventors, writers, scientists, composers, artists, leaders, and others who have made valuable contributions to our society. On a junior level we do this through science and social studies fairs, invention conventions, problem solving competitions, writing contests and magazines that feature student work, and local and national recognition of students' accomplishments in the arts. It seems clear that our society values those who, in fulfilling themselves, make original, authentic contributions. Therefore it makes sense to ask how schools and teachers can help more students become original researchers/contributors.

Inspiration: Where do students get ideas? One of the unfortunate side-effects of the limited curriculum taught in schools is that students are seldom exposed to many of the subdisciplines within the larger field. When students are taught the methodologies of sociologists, botanists, statisticians, or poll-takers, for example, they also gain an introduction to new fields of inquiry, new questions, and new ways to approach problems. Because such teaching is involving and action-oriented, students are invited to act like authentic researchers by the very nature of the instruction. Debriefing discussions help students generate new ideas for potential exploration and see connections with current interests.

In addition, investigations are often begun when students see how particular methodologies make it possible for them to pursue a previous area of interest. One of us experienced this in a 6th grade class during a lesson about controlled experiments as a way to test hypotheses. One group within the class had been given written directions about visual imagery in addition to the general directions for remembering 20 words the teacher read aloud slowly (Bunker, Pearlson, & Schulz, 1975). Afterward the correct number of words recalled by the two groups was compared to determine if imagery directions improved recall.

Following this class, one of the students excitedly told the teacher that she now saw how she could successfully win the argument with her mother about listening to music while doing homework. If she designed an experiment where the class did academic work under conditions of both music and silence and they didn't do any worse during the music, that would prove her contention that it was okay to play the radio while doing homework. As a result of the methodological lesson, the student knew that all conditions except music had to be held constant—the students, length of time, difficulty of task, setting, etc. If this were done and no significant differences were found in the quality of student work, she would have found support for her hypothesis.

She did indeed pursue her investigation (and provided the basis for Quasi-Experimental Activity 1). After deciding on an appropriate academic task and choosing the music, she enlisted her classmates in the experiment. To her disappointment, the results were not what she had hoped. The positive outcome, however, was that the student initiated an experience in which she served as an authentic researcher in an area of interest and that the project was stimulated by instruction in research methodology.

Escalating the sophistication of student work. The research methodologies of the disciplines give students new tools that can escalate the level of their work and understanding. The old saying goes, "If all you have is a hammer, everything looks like a nail." If the only research tool students have is note-taking from secondary sources, every investigation looks like a library report. Developing skills in research methodologies of the disciplines can make the difference between gathering raw data or using secondary sources, between being original researchers or synthesizers of others' research.

Teaching the Methodologies of the Disciplines

For middle and high school content area teachers, the first step in teaching methodologies of the disciplines is identifying the disciplines within the subject being taught, the -ologies and -ographies of the field. Some examples are provided in Figure 9.1.

-Ologies and -Ographies in the Disciplines

SOCIAL SCIENCES	NATURAL SCIENCES	
Archaeology	Entomology	Botany
Anthropology	Paleontology	Physics
Psychology	Oceanography	Chemistry
Geography	Ornithology	Geology
Oral History	Meteorology	Biology
Political Science	Herpetology	Ecology
History	Astronomy	Chronobiology
Sociology	Biochemistry	Pathology
Economics	Microbiology	Ichthyology

MATHEMATICS	LANGUAGE ARTS	
Statistics	Forensics	Playwriting
Probability	Etymology	Speed Reading
Logic	Debate	Linguistics
Number Theory	Proofreading	Editing
Set Theory	Video Production	Poetry Writing
Calculus	Technical Writing	Journalism
Geometry	Song Writing	Screen Writing
Mathematical Modeling	Cinematography	Film Animation
Packaging	Science Fiction	Story Telling
Computer Programming	Pantomime	Cartooning
Algebra	Literary Criticism	Short Stories

Figure 9.1. -Ologies and -ographies in the disciplines.

Once the areas or subdisciplines have been chosen, teachers will need to identify the methodologies within the particular discipline. While they may be familiar with some methodologies in areas of their specialization or interest, there are probably others with which they are less familiar. How can teachers learn about these methodologies? One possibility is to become experts themselves, taking courses or working with experts for periods of time. Another would be to interview or shadow experts as they work, but these ideas don't seem feasible for most teachers we know.

Fortunately, there is another way! How-to books explain the methodologies of practicing professionals in terms that students and/or teachers can understand. These books provide a practical, inexpensive, and effective way to learn about unfamiliar methodologies. (A list of exemplary how-to books is located in the Resources section near the end of the book.) A few how-to books are texts, but most are published as trade books, intended for a general audience. Characteristics of a good how-to book include:

- Information about the structure of the field
- Procedures for problem finding and focusing
- Specific methodological skills of the discipline
- Suggestions for independent investigations students can pursue
- Suggestions for format/communication of findings

While it is a rare book that covers all five areas well, there are many that do an excellent job in several areas. The most important area that should be included is the third, specific methodological skills described in enough detail to enable students to actually carry out the techniques. The teacher often can provide procedures for problem finding and focusing and suggestions for investigations students might pursue, so these items are less critical when choosing how-to books.

How-to books can be used in a variety of ways depending on the goals, setting, and present level of student involvement in original research. In explaining these uses, we will proceed from a broad inclusion in teacher instruction to more specific instances of independent investigations undertaken by individuals or small groups of students. When teachers use approaches simultaneously, the potential for benefits is magnified through mutual reinforcement.

Inclusion in the Regular Curriculum

One way for teachers to enrich their teaching as they advance the cause of original research is to incorporate the teaching of research methodologies into the regular content curriculum. As a part of teaching each unit, teachers could share with students how that particular knowledge came to be. They can do this in a discussion, a one period introduction, a multi-session mini-course or anything in between. Examples include

History—Lessons on determining the authenticity and validity of historical documents, choosing a subject for historical studies, or analyzing different aspects of history and how a variety of points of view might give a different perspective on the topic of study.

Chemistry—Lessons on how to develop hypotheses, research questions, and research designs in order to test an individual's theories rather than merely replicating the work of others.

Mathematics—Lessons on some of the less-complicated statistical procedures as well as the principles of inferential statistics.

Language Arts—Lessons about observing for detail with respect to settings as well as people (character, description, language, etc.).

By including *knowledge how* in their teaching of *knowledge about* and *knowledge of*, teachers remind students that knowledge production is an on-going process, that what they are learning in school is the product of someone's research, and that they, too, can be authentic researchers.

Introductory Lesson/Mini-Course

Teachers can also use methodological lessons or mini-courses to introduce students to new topics and processes in order to generate interest in original research. As an example, a series of lessons about public opinion polling including sample selection, poll construction, interviewing techniques, and data analysis can spark interest in a variety of questions about past legislative and presidential elections, size and effect of interest groups, opinions of peers or the general population about a topic of interest, the effect of polls on local elections, market research for a business venture, etc.

If a teacher's goal is to help students devise research questions they would like to pursue independently or in small groups, then it is important for him/her to conduct debriefing discussions with students to help them see the relationship between the methodologies they are learning and personal interests, real-world problems, and areas of potential investigation. Questions to stimulate interest in further exploration might include:

1. How does this field relate to something in which you are already interested? (Use forced connections to see the relationship of the methodology to students' personal interests, no matter how remote they may seem at first.)
2. What are some unsolved problems in this area? What are some issues currently being considered by professionals in this field?
3. If you were interested in solving a problem in this area, what kinds of things could you do?
4. Are there some problems in our school or community that relate to this field?
5. How could you use these methodologies to solve a problem of interest to you?

Mentor-in-Print for Individual Investigations

Teachers can use how-to books as mentors-in-print for students who have already identified a potential area for research. Depending on the ability of the student and the readability of the book, teachers may choose to teach the techniques, using the book as a resource, or have the student read the book independently. The book might provide additional suggestions for research questions as well. Once the student has focused on his/her research question, the book should provide guidance and instruction in authentic research methodologies that the student can use in carrying out the investigation. Finally, the book might have information about appropriate audiences and formats for communicating findings.

Teachers have struggled with the balance between teaching process and content for a long time. If one of our goals is to encourage and nurture students as original researchers, it is important to teach them the research methodologies involved in the academic disciplines. We believe this will further both the content and process goals of teaching as well as facilitate student interest in and ability to do original research.

Conclusion

Regardless of the topic, research method, or communication format chosen, students will benefit from sharing their original research with an authentic audience. An interested audience sends a message that research efforts are valuable, that research makes a contribution to the world, and that secondary students can do things in school that add knowledge to the world and provide adults with interest, challenge, and enjoyment. The power of such a message makes the proofreading, paper filing, table juggling, and assistance recruiting all worthwhile.

Research teaches adolescents valuable lessons beyond critical thinking, organization, and problem solving. Finding, focusing, and investigating issues of personal interest teaches adolescents that their thoughts and ideas are important. Sharing results with an authentic audience teaches them that they are powerful and that they can use their ideas to change the world.

It is interesting, exciting, and sometimes frightening to think about the world in which our students will live. For generations teachers have struggled with the task of preparing students for problems and opportunities different from those the teachers have known and often different from anything currently existing. As the pace of technology and social change accelerates, the responsibility to prepare students for the unknown and the currently unknowable increases. We see the ideas in this book as one way to deal with that challenge.

We hope that teachers in middle and secondary schools will be able to find a comfortable balance between teaching students the important concepts, principles and generalizations that make up the content of the disciplines and helping them learn the research methodologies that will allow them to become investigators and producers in those disciplines. We hope they will be able to use research skills to identify and solve problems that are meaningful to them, both within the traditional curriculum and in other areas of interest. It is exciting to envision classrooms of students, curious and questioning, seeking out interests and challenges, analyzing information, and drawing new conclusions to share with teachers, peers, and real-world audiences. We believe that as students become questioners and investigators of their lives and interests today, they become better prepared to investigate the dilemmas of tomorrow. If the ideas we have presented help them do that, we can ask no greater reward.

References

American heritage electronic dictionary. (1992). New York: Houghton Mifflin.

Bunker, B., Pearlson, H., & Schulz, J. (1975). *The student's guide to conducting social science research.* New York: Human Sciences Press.

Burns,D.E. (1990). *Pathways to investigative skills: Instructional lessons for guiding students from problem finding to final product.* Mansfield Center, CT: Creative Learning Press.

Caney, S. (1985). *Steven Caney's invention book.* New York: Workman.

Freedman, R. L. H. (1994). *Open-ended questions: A handbook for educators.* Menlo Park, CA: Addison-Wesley Publishing.

Gay, L. R. (1992). *Educational research: Competencies for analysis and application* (4th Ed.). New York: Macmillan Publishing.

Isaac, S., & Michael, W. B. (1981). *Handbook in research and evaluation* (2nd ed.). San Diego, CA: EdITS.

Katz, B., & Katz, L. S. (1985). *How-to: 1400 best books on doing almost everything*. New York: R. R. Bowker Company.

Maker, C. J. (1992). *Curriculum development for the gifted.* Rockville, MD: Aspen Publishers.

Marzano, R. J., Pickering, D., & McTighe, J. (1993). *Assessing student outcomes: Performance assessment using the dimensions of learning model.* Alexandria, VA: Association for Supervision and Curriculum Development.

Miles, M. B., & Huberman, A. M. (1984). *Qualitative data analysis: A sourcebook of new methods.* Beverly Hills, CA: Sage Publications.

Merriam Webster Dictionary. (1974). New York: Pocket.

New York Historical Society. (1985). *Antique advertising postcards*. Mineola, NY: Dover Publications.

Renzulli, J. S. (1977a). *The enrichment triad model.* Mansfield Center, CT: Creative Learning Press.

Renzulli, J. S. (1977b). *The interest-a-lyzer.* Mansfield Center, CT: Creative Learning Press.

Starko, A. J. (1995). *Creativity in the classroom: Schools of curious delight.* New York: Longman Publishers.

Starko, A. J., Schack, G. D. (1992). *Looking for data in all the right places.* Mansfield Center, CT: Creative Learning Press.

Treffinger, D. J., McEwen, P., & Wittig, C. (1989). *Using creative problem solving in inventing.* Honeoye, NY: Center for Creative Learning.

Resource List

The following list of resources contains books that we think can help students and teachers further develop research skills. The collection, which includes books that have a wide range of reading and conceptual levels, offers approximate grade level recommendations for bright students. Many of the books listed for high school students are also excellent background and reference sources for teachers. Books do periodically go out of print, so there's no guarantee that you'll be able to order all of these books from publishers years after this book has been published. Check your school and public libraries for copies—they have more than you think.

General Research Methodology

How to Do a Science Fair Project by David Webster, Franklin Watts, 1974. This book is a good introduction to the field of scientific investigation. It includes suggestions for reports, demonstrations, and research projects and gives directions for all the steps between planning and presenting results. Photographs of actual student projects provide examples and inspiration. Grades 3-7

How to Do a Science Project and Report by Martin Gutnik, Franklin Watts, 1980. This book makes scientific investigations as easy as ABC. The author describes the scientific method in eight clearly written chapters and includes everything the young scientist needs to achieve results, from observation, making inferences, and testing hypotheses to drawing conclusions and writing reports. Grades 5-9

Nuts & Bolts: A Matter of Fact Guide to Science Fair Projects by Barry Van Deman and Ed McDonald, The Science Man Press (Division of TSM Marketing), 1980. Using cute illustrations, this book introduces intermediate students to the process of scientific investigation. Chapters cover project selection, library research, other sources of help, materials, data gathering, conclusion drawing, and communicating results. Appendices list awardwinning titles, unusual sources of information, glossary, and bibliography. Grades 4-9

A Student's Guide to Conducting Social Science Research by Barbara Bunker, Howard Pearlson & Justin Schulz, Human Sciences Press, 1975. The introduction relates research to real-life experience, then gives a nine-step approach to research. Later chapters present information about research design, testing hypotheses, surveys, observation, and experiments and provide hands-on experience with data gathering methods through ready-to-use activities. Grades 5-10

Data Gathering and Analysis

The Ethnographic Interview by James P. Spradley, Holt, Rinehart and Winston, 1979. Did you ever wish you could see the world through another's eyes or understand what it is like to be a vagrant or a bar waitress? This book shows readers how to do ethnographic research and learn about other cultures by interviewing informants. It includes techniques for locating informants, asking questions, making a variety of analyses, discovering cultural themes, and writing up results. Grades 9-adult

How to Analyze Data by Carol Fitz-Gibbin and Lyn Morris, Sage Publications, 1987. This book makes sense of statistics and allows readers to analyze data in a sophisticated way. Included are instructions, examples, and worksheets for examining a single set of scores, differences between groups, and relationships between variables as well as test-construction and questionnaire analysis. Each chapter includes notes for SPSSX (mainframe) computer users and a final chapter discusses meta-analysis. Grade 9-adult

How to Calculate Statistics by Carol Fitz-Gibbin and Lyn Morris, Sage Publications, 1978. This book includes clear instructions for calculating mean, standard deviation, t-tests, and correlation coefficients, along with explanations of when to use each. This book is perfect for teachers who don't have access to a microcomputer statistics program or like doing statistics the old-fashioned way. Grade 9-adult

How to Conduct Surveys: A Step-by-Step Guide by Arlene Fink and Jaqueline Kosecoff, Sage Publications, 1985. A thorough resource for planning and conducting surveys, this book contains information about survey design, data analysis, and presentation of results. Many positive and negative examples clearly illustrate the points being made, making this the ideal book for those wanting a more sophisticated understanding of surveys. Grade 9-adult

How to Use Your Community as a Resource by Helen Cary and Deborah Hanka, Franklin Watts, 1983. This book gives excellent advice for preparing and conducting interviews and surveys, developing and organizing a community resource file, and using community resources to research a variety of topics. There are especially good suggestions for writing appropriate interview and survey items and for identifying researchable questions and possible community resources. Grades 5-10

Making Metric Measurements by Neil Ardley, Franklin Watts, 1983. This neat book consists of a variety of investigations students can do using everyday equipment. They involve the metric measurement of weight, time, height, speed, pressure, and volume. Activities involving the making of predictions and a variety of calculations are also included along with formulas and conversion tables. Grades 3-7

Participant Observation by James P. Spradley, Holt, Rinehart and Winston, 1980. In this book, Spradley shows readers how to learn about another culture by becoming a participant observer, learning as they take part in the situation, whether it is a job, subgroup in a school, or a religious or cultural group. Excellent instruction in systematic observation and recording, as well as analyzing data, making a cultural inventory, and writing up the results. Grades 9-adult

The Craft of Interviewing by John Brady, Vintage Books (Random House), 1977. With humor and many interesting anecdotes, Brady gives insider tips about interviewing. Along with the traditional suggestions about background research, taping, and note-taking, he also tells how to get interviews, develop rapport, ask interesting questions, get tough nicely, hurdle hazards, and verify and write the final product. Grades 8-12

Tell Me About Yourself: How to Interview Anyone From Your Friends to Famous People by D. L. Mabery, Lerner Publications, 1985. This resource shows learners how to decide who to interview, how to arrange and prepare the interview, and how to find useful materials. Other chapters explain how to turn information into a final product and give students ideas for interview projects. Anecdotes from the author's experiences will provide good examples and a personal touch for students. Grades 4-8

Social Sciences

After the Fact: The Art of Historical Detection (Vols. 1 and 2) by James W. Davidson & Mark H. Lytle, Alfred A. Knopf, 1986. The authors of these volumes introduce readers to a variety of historical methodologies as they are applied to several events in U.S. history. Approaches include social history, document analysis, history and grand theory, pictorial evidence, psychohistory, oral history, photographic evidence, the Great Man theory, and others. This book is a must-have both for aspiring historians and teachers of history, because understanding how history is written helps us to better understand both the process and the content. Grade 8-adult

How to Tape Instant Oral Biographies by William Zimmerman, Guarionex Press, Ltd., 198 1. This guide can enable students to create a family library of spoken histories. It contains sections that explain audio and videotape techniques, interviewing suggestions and questions to ask. Forms to record family names, dates, and other data provide an organized way to create a family tree. Grades 4-12

How to Trace Your Family Tree by The American Genealogical Research Institute Staff, Bantam, Doubleday, Dell Publications, 1975. Written by a knowledgeable research team, this book explains how to conduct a family history project. The authors discuss different genealogical records found in libraries, local and state agencies, federal government sources, churches, newspapers, and organizations. Additional chapters highlight how to organize findings and use relatives as sources of information. Grades 7-12

Like It Was: A Complete Guide to Writing Oral History by Cynthia Stokes Brown, Teachers and Writers Collaborative, 1988. Septima Clark's oral history of the civil rights movement begins this book with a real-life example. The author then moves into the n itty-gritty-using a recorder, conducting the interview, transcribing, and writing from the transcript. The book also provides directions for creative final products such as short articles and full-length biographies. Grades 6-12

My Backyard History Book by David Weitzman, Little, Brown and Company, 1975. This amusing book makes the study of history both interesting and personally relevant. Ample photographs and illustrations introduce the wonders of family trees, fads, artifacts, history in the yellow pages and at the cemetery, oral history, old photographs, and much more. It's loaded with ideas for primary data sources and projects that are designed to interest students in historical studies. Grades 3-7

Oral History: A Guide for Teachers (and Others) by Thad Sitton, George Mehaffy, and 0. L. Davis, Jr., University of Texas Press, 1983. If a teacher's goal is to help students preserve the recollections of people about the past, this book will provide information about research methodology, interviewing techniques, photography, note-taking, legal forms, and more. The authors suggest a wide range of student products, including media productions, archive development, and the research of current community problems. Grade 8-adult

Pursuing the Past: Oral History, Photographs, Family History, and Cemeteries by Eugene and Asterie Provenzo and Peter Zorn, Jr., Addison Wesley, 1984. Focusing on primary sources, the authors teach readers how to gather data from various sources and organize information using several forms and charts. Issues of authenticity, credibility, and interpretation are clearly explained and illustrated with numerous examples from the authors' own family histories. A Teacher's Guide also accompanies this text. Grades 6-12.

Unpuzzling Your Past: A Basic Guide to Genealogy (2nd Ed.) by Emily Anne Croom, Betterways Publications, 1989. This excellent how-to for more sophisticated genealogists provides very informative explanations and includes annotated lists of information sources, a glossary, relationship chart, examples, and many forms. In addition, the book offers a list of libraries and archives (by state), alternate forms of common names, and a guide to reading 18th and 19th century cursive writing. Grade 8-adult

Who Put the Cannon in the Courthouse Square? by Kay Cooper, Walker & Co., 1985. Using as an example the question posed in the title, this book helps children uncover the past. An opening chapter suggests many starting points for historical investigation, while subsequent chapters explain how to answer those questions. In addition to the usual library sources, Cooper explains the data sources of vertical files, news media, state historical libraries, museums, cemeteries, historical societies, state archives, interviews, and more. Grades 4-8

Writing Family Histories and Memoirs by Kirk Polking, F & W Publications, 1995. This comprehensive book teaches readers how to turn sterile dates into exciting, vibrant stories that can be passed on to future generations. Topics include locating information from courthouse records, interviewing techniques, making genealogical charts, handling legal issues, and knowing how much research is enough. Samples of written histories and tips on good writing techniques ensure that family biographers can produce interesting family histories and memoirs. Grades 7-12

Natural and Physical Sciences

The Amateur Naturalist's Handbook by Vinson Brown, Prentice-Hall, 1980. This resource contains information about investigating animals, plants, rocks, and minerals; starting nature collections; and learning about climate and ecology. The last section deals with classification and special studies of animals, plants, rocks and minerals, ecosystems, and ethology. Excellent illustrations and a final chapter suggesting investigations are an added bonus. Grades 6-12

Ecology by Richard Spurgeon, Usborne/EDC, 1988. This resource presents information about ecosystems, cycles in nature, adaptation, urban ecosystems, tropical rain forests, the future, and more. In addition to colorful illustrations, almost every page contains a hands-on project or experiment that is related to the environment, from making recycled paper to organizing a group for social action. Grades 5-9

A Field Manual for the Amateur Geologist by Alan M. Cvancara, Prentice Hall, 1985. Much of this book is devoted to explaining a wide variety of landforms, minerals, rocks and fossils as well as explaining how geologists reconstruct past events and mentally attack problems. The author provides methodological information on reading and constructing geological maps, making collections, and reading rock weathering. Appendices list museums, parks, and other geological resources. Grades 7-12

Microscope: How to Use It and Enjoy It by Eve and Albert Stwertka, Julian Messner, 1988. After a brief explanation and history, the authors clearly explain how to set up and use a microscope. Later chapters suggest investigations involving water, plants, animal cells, and insects, with illustrations of what learners should see. Along the way, students will learn such skills as preparing and staining slide specimens and recording observations. A list of scientific supply houses will launch students into a study of the invisible world. Grades 4-8

Tom Brown's Field Guide to Nature Observation and Tracking by Tom Brown, Jr., Berkley Books, 1983. The author takes readers on an adventure, sharing what he learned from an Apache elder about understanding nature in all its wonder. Beginning with attitudes and habits that increase awareness through all the senses, he goes on to explain how to recognize, follow, and read a variety of animal tracks and recognize animal highways. Grades 6-12

Weather and Forecasting by Storm Dunlop & Francis Wilson, Collier Books (Macmillan Publishing), 1982. Through clear explanations, drawings, and color pictures, the reader first learns to recognize a variety of weather conditions and how they are produced. Later chapters discuss weather forecasting and include information about instruments, symbols, and language used by professionals. Grades 8-12

The World of the Microscope by Chris Oxlade and Corrine Stockley, Usborne/EDC, 1989. An illustrated explanation of how to use a microscope leads directly into descriptions of many projects in addition to directions and drawings about finding and mounting specimens. Investigations include cells, bacteria, fungi, water, plants, insects, crystals, rocks, and minerals. Readers will also learn about staining, mounting, measuring, and making sections. Grades 7-12

The Young Naturalist by Andrew Mitchell, Usborne/EDC, 1982. This book contains suggestions and instructions for observing and experimenting with plants, birds, insects, mammals, ecosystems, and wildlife. It also includes excellent ideas for making collections that involve evidence of living things (bones, shells, sounds, plaster casts, etc.) rather than the creatures themselves. Grades 2-7

Modes of Communication/Alternative Products

The Art of Cartooning by Syd Hoff, Stravon Educational Press, 1984. Hoff uses simple language to express what he knows best: faces, expressions, figures, composition, perspective, and technique. He also includes how to get ideas, how to sell cartoons to publications, how to sell cartoons to advertisers, and how to sell a comic strip, political cartoons, and children's story illustrations. This book is a must for any aspiring cartoonist! Grades 8-12

The Game Inventor's Handbook by Stephen Peek, Betterway Publications, 1993. The author, a game designer himself, provides a realistic view of creating, developing, manufacturing, and marketing board and computer games, including stories about his ventures. The book includes an analysis of a game presentation, and, if no one will buy the idea, the author includes information about self-publishing, marketing, and publicity. Grade 8-adult

How to Debate by Robert Dunbar, Franklin Watts, 1987. Debate provides another way for students to share the results of their research, particularly for issues involving controversy. Included in this book are chapters about methods of argument, how the affirmative and negative sides work, listening and responding effectively, and how formal debates are operated and judged. Ile book also presents information about debate topics, information sources, and national debate competitions. Grades 5-9

How to Make Visual Presentations by Dennis McBride, Art Direction Book Company, 1985. In addition to helping readers decide which visual presentations to use under different circumstances, this book includes information about overhead projectors, charts, slides, movies, and video. General tips about charts, graphs, diagrams, illustrations, and lettering apply to all media. A list of suppliers and other reference books extends its usefulness. Grades 7-12

How to Paint and Draw What You See by Ray Smith, Alfred A. Knopf, 1984. In this book the aspiring artist is taken step-by-step through a variety of projects. The author gives precise directions for pre-selected projects, so the reader can concentrate on a particular technique. Later chapters introduce students to several subjects and styles (landscapes, still life, portraits) using the same process. Grades 7-12

How to Write and Give a Speech by Joan Detz, St. Martin Press, 1992. Written in a casual but competent style, this book includes both the formal and informal advice people need to give effective speeches. Included are sections on assessing the audience, researching and writing speeches, style, humor, delivery, speeches for special occasions, and nitty-gritty details such as preparing the room, using audiovisual aids, and mental preparation. Grades 7-12

KidVid: Fun-Damentals of Video Instruction by Kaye Black, Zephyr Press, 1989. With clear illustrations and entertaining cartoons, this book introduces students to the basic equipment and production techniques of video production. Nine easy lessons take readers through scripts, storyboards, program treatment, production, editing, and evaluation, with project suggestions throughout. Several appendices provide such useful items as sample script and storyboard sheets, blank script, storyboard, edit log forms, a video production proposal, materials for the classroom, and even suggestions for positive feedback. Grades 4-12

Usborne Guide to Drawing by Patience Foster, Usborne/EDC, 1981. Whether to record observations, illustrate findings, or persuade people about a point of view, drawing can be a useful skill for young researchers. Through numerous illustrations readers will learn about choosing and buying materials and using pencils, charcoal, pastels, crayons, and pen and ink to achieve a variety of effects. There are also useful sections about using color, planning pictures, and drawing people, animals, landscapes, and other subjects. Grades 6-12

Usborne Guide to Photography: From Beginner to Expert by Moira Butterfield and Susan Beach, Usborne/EDC, 1987. A picture speaks a thousand words and this book will show readers how to take those pictures and illustrate research findings. Some of the many topics covered in this book are cameras, lighting, composition, printing, and specialty photos. Positive and negative examples along with drawings clearly illustrate both introductory and advanced aspects of photography. Grades 3-8

Usborne Guide to Technical Drawing by Susan Peach, Usborne/EDC, 1987. Prospective inventors and artists alike will benefit from this beginner's guide to technical drawing and illustration. Using just a ruler and pencils, young artists can create professional drawings that use orthographic projections, isometric perspective, and architectural drawing techniques. The author provides additional information about sketching, modeling, displaying work, and using equipment along with suggestions for projects. Grades 5-12

Where Do You Get Your Ideas? by Sandy Asher, Walker & Co., 1987. The author shares many of her strategies (poetry, journals, writing to discover, and playing with ideas) and some examples of her writing that resulted from using these techniques. She also includes brief stories-behind-the- stories from 25 other successful authors as well as twelve ideas in search of a writer. A chapter on choosing characters, problems, and solutions helps readers develop their ideas. Grades 3-9

Inventing

Stephen Caney's Invention Book by Stephen Caney, Workman Publishing, 1985. Here readers will learn everything prospective inventors need to know, from inspiration to marketing. The author highlights steps in the invention process such as getting started, the inventor's workshop, keeping a notebook, planning, prototypes, names, patents, and marketing. Each section includes an interesting and relevant anecdote about a successful invention. Also included are 25 great invention stories that illustrate inventors' maxims. Grades 4-12

Out of Print (but may be found in libraries)

The Amateur Archaeologist's Handbook (3rd Ed.) by Maurice Robbins and Mary Irving, Harper & Row, 1981. This book provides a step-by-step how-to in archaeology, from pre-dig planning to writing a site report. It includes several pictures and illustrations of techniques and further reference material about artifacts and soil. Information about museums, organizations, and antiquities laws add to the book's value for the aspiring archaeologist. Grades 6-adult

Creative Word Processing by Vivian Dubrovin, Franklin Watts, 1987. This book would be useful for students who are writing research reports, starting a school newspaper, or editing a student journal. In addition to learning how to use word processors, readers also get excellent ideas for writing projects. Great examples, a glossary, a bibliography, and a section on desktop publishing add the finishing touches. Grades 5-12

Ecology in Your Community by D. F. Wentworth et al., Holt, Rinehart and Winston of Canada, 1975. This outstanding book introduces students to the study of ecology through hands-on investigations and data collection. Many suggestions and examples of observation and record-keeping are provided, with questions to help students analyze what they find. Topics include habitats, communities, interdependence, and adaptation. Grades 3-8

How to Use Primary Sources by Helen Carey and Judith Greenberg, Franklin Watts, 1983. This book helps students go beyond the usual library sources by explaining how to gather information from interviews, paintings, monuments, photographs, legal documents, diaries, journals, and museums. Ideas about creating museum collections and discovery boxes help students not only gather information in more diverse ways, but also share it using different formats. Grades 5-10

Making and Using Your Own Weather Station by Beulah and Harold E. Tannenbaum, Franklin Watts, 1989. Along with information about air, moisture, winds, clouds, and storms, chapters include suggested activities and directions for making a barometer, thermometer, sling psychrometer, rain/snow gauge, wind vane, and anemometer. Using tips in the final chapter, youngsters can record and predict the weather. Grades 4-12

Mapping Small Places by D. F. Wentworth et al., Holt, Rinehart and Winston of Canada, 1976. This is the only book we've seen that actually teaches children how to make maps. Through activities children learn how to make floor plans and two-dimensional maps, measure angles on the ground and in the air, and make contour maps. The author provides directions for making and using inexpensive versions of professional equipment and tools. Illustrations and photographs of kids in action fill the pages. Grades 4-8

Planning and Producing Instructional Media (6th Ed.) by Jerrold Kemp et al., Harper & Row, 1989. The book begins with a section on planning audiovisual productions, including objectives, script development, materials, storyboard, editing, and post-production work. It then details skills for photography, graphics, sound recording, slide show production, filmstrips, tape recordings, overhead transparencies, motion pictures, videotapes, and multi-media productions. Drawings and photographs illustrate the text. Grade 9-adult

Roots for Kids: A Genealogy Guide for Young People by Susan Provost Beller, Betterway Publications, 1989. This how-to guide for beginning genealogists was developed and field-tested as a mini-course for bright students. Clear explanations of terms and methodologies and wonderful examples throughout also make it suitable for students working independently. Several simplified forms containing information on where and how to find information provide icing on the cake. Grades 5-10

Running a School Newspaper by Vivian Dubrovin, Franklin Watts, 1985. It's not exactly original research, but a school newspaper can provide an excellent outlet for student work. In addition, one could regard reporters as researchers, so starting a newspaper might encourage further research on the part of students. Book chapters deal with writing stories, features, and editorials; interviewing; headlines; layout; advertising; and many other skills. The book is strengthened by numerous examples, a sample style sheet, and a listing of proofreaders' marks. Grades 4-8

Speak Up! A Guide to Public Speaking by Patricia Sternberg, Julian Messner, 1984. Often a speech to decision-makers or those in a position to influence policy is the most effective outlet for students' research. This author addresses both professional techniques of speaking and the concerns of students. The book discusses topic selection, organizing the speech, voice and diction, controlling stage fright, making friends with the audience, and working with microphones and cameras. Grades 5-12

Understanding and Collecting Rocks and Fossils by M. Branwell. This book is full of interesting and informative illustrations explaining the forces continually changing the earth's surface. Many experimental activities are included to challenge the young geologist, such as identifying minerals and fossils, making time charts, showing how geological processes work, and establishing collections. Grades 6-12

Understanding History: A Primer of Historical Method by Louis Gottschalk, Alfred Knopf, 1950. This is the definitive how-to-do-history book. Topics include problem finding and focusing, sources of historical information, authenticity, credibility, historical techniques, writing, and some of the problems involved in historical writing (selection, arrangement, emphasis, cause, motive, etc.). Grade 9-adult

The Young Cartoonist by Syd Hoff, Stravon, 1983. Editorial cartoonists have known for years the power of the visual image to communicate and now students can, too. The author uses numerous examples and illustrations to show readers the techniques of cartoonists. He covers heads and faces, expressions, animals, figures, sports, captions, and drawing a comic strip. Many techniques such as angle and speed can be generalized to anything students might draw. Grades 4-12

Additional Resources for Adults

General Research Methodology

Chi Square, Pie Charts, and Me by Susan Baum, Robert Gable, and Karen List, Royal Fireworks Press, 1987. Topics include the research process, types of research, management plans, presentation of studies, and an excellent section explaining statistical techniques. This book offers a clear explanation of how to calculate the correlation coefficient and t-tests using a calculator. Examples of research done by students demonstrate the potential they have for hands-on research.

Handbook in Research and Evaluation by Stephen Isaac and William B. Michael, EDITS Publishers, 1981. This book presents a sophisticated overview of the research and evaluation process. Chapters cover planning, research designs, instrumentation and measurement, statistical techniques and data analysis, and guidelines for preparing, writing, and evaluating research proposals or reports. If adults feel the need for more information about research design, this book will provide greater depth.

Looking for Data in All the Right Places by Alane Starko and Gina Schack, Creative Learning Press, 1992. The elementary counterpart to Research Comes Alive!, this book provides teachers with explanations, examples, and activities to involve elementary-age children in original research. The book will help students get out of the library and into the real world, gathering and analyzing data about their research questions.

Data Gathering and Analysis

A Teacher's Guide to Classroom Research by David Hopkins, Open University Press, 1985. While written for classroom teachers interested in doing action research about their practice, this small book provides useful information about several aspects of action research, such as problem formation, data gathering, observation, analysis, and maintaining the action. Readers can easily translate the recommendations into a more general form to help students conduct their own action research.

An Introduction to Survey Research and Data Analysis by Herbert Weisberg and Bruce Bowen, W. H. Freeman, 1977. While the data analysis section is probably more than teachers will need with middle and high school students, the background they'll gain about survey design is useful. Specific topics include sampling procedures, questionnaire design, interviewing techniques, coding, and problems in interpreting surveys.

Educational Research by L. R. Gay, Macmillan Publishing, 1992. Believe it or not, this book about quantitative research contains lots of laughs! Gay uses a conversational style in much of the book and includes sections about choosing a research problem, designing a plan, choosing subjects and instruments, using research methods and procedures, analyzing and interpreting data, and preparing research reports and critiques of research.

Qualitative Data Analysis by Matthew B. Miles and A. Michael Huberman, SAGE Publications, 1984. This comprehensive book about qualitative data analysis includes sections about focusing data collection, analysis during data collection, within-site analysis, cross-site analysis, suggestions for matrix displays, and drawing and verifying conclusions. Examples from actual research supplement the sophisticated explanations in the book.

Questionnaires: Design and Use (2nd Ed.) by Doug Berdie, John Anderson, and Marsha Niebuhr, The Scarecrow Press, 1986. In a readable style, this book provides further information about reliability and validity, sampling, study design, interview or mail format, questionnaire design, and ideas for stimulating response and analyzing the results. Samples are included.

Social Science Research Methods by B. A. Chadwick, H. M. Bahr, & S. L. Albrecht, Prentice-Hall, 1984. This book provides readers with greater background about sample selection, observation methods, surveys and interviews, experimental research, and qualitative research, including content and secondary analysis techniques.

Inventing

Using Creative Problem Solving in Inventing by Donald Treffinger, Patricia McEwen, & Carol Wittig, Center for Creative Learning, 1989. Here teachers will find the instruction and activities for applying the creative problem solving (CPS) process to the process of inventing. Students can use this book as a new approach to problem solving for problems identified by their research or can start with an invention and later research its effectiveness. Explanations are clear enough for those not already familiar with CPS.

Appendix A—Table of Random Numbers

Table of Random Numbers

	00-04	05-09	10-14	15-19	20-24	25-29	30-34	35-39	40-44	45-49
00	54463	22662	65905	70639	79365	67382	29085	69831	47058	08186
01	15389	85205	18850	39226	42249	90669	96325	23248	60933	26927
02	85941	40756	82414	02015	13858	78030	16269	65978	01385	15345
03	61149	69440	11286	88218	58925	03638	52862	62733	33451	77455
04	05219	81619	19651	67079	92511	59888	84502	72095	83463	75577
05	41417	98326	87719	92294	46614	50948	64886	20002	97365	30976
06	28357	94070	20652	35774	16249	75019	21145	05217	47286	76305
07	17783	00015	10806	83091	91530	36466	39981	62481	49177	75779
08	40950	84820	29881	85966	62800	70326	84740	62660	77379	90279
09	82995	64157	66164	41180	10089	41757	78258	94688	88629	37231
10	96754	17676	53659	44105	47361	34833	86679	23930	53249	27083
11	34357	88040	53364	71726	45690	66334	60332	22554	90660	71113
12	06318	37403	49927	57715	50423	67372	63116	48888	21505	80182
13	62111	52820	07243	79931	89292	84767	85693	73947	22278	11551
14	47534	09243	67879	00544	23410	12740	02540	54440	32949	13491
15	98614	75993	84460	62846	59844	14922	48730	73443	48167	34770
16	24856	03648	44898	09351	98795	18644	39765	71058	90368	44104
17	96887	12479	80621	66223	86085	78285	02432	53342	42846	94771
18	90801	21472	42815	77408	37390	76766	52615	21141	30268	18106
19	55165	77312	83666	36028	28420	70219	81369	41943	47366	41067
20	75884	12952	84318	95108	72305	64620	91318	89872	45375	85436
21	16777	37116	58550	42958	21460	43910	01175	87894	81378	10620
22	46230	43877	80207	88877	89380	32992	91380	03164	98656	59337
23	42902	66892	46134	01432	94710	23474	20423	60137	60609	13119
24	81007	00333	39693	28039	10154	95425	39220	19774	31782	49037
25	68089	01122	51111	72373	06902	74373	96199	97017	41273	21546
26	20411	67081	89950	16944	93054	87687	96693	87236	77054	33848
27	58212	13160	06468	15718	82627	76999	05999	58680	96739	63700
28	70577	42866	24969	61210	76046	76799	42054	12696	93758	03283
29	94522	74358	71659	62038	79643	79169	44741	05437	39038	13163
30	42626	86819	85651	88678	17401	03252	99547	32404	17918	62880
31	16051	33763	57194	16752	54450	19031	58580	47629	54132	60631
32	08244	27647	33851	44705	94211	46716	11738	55784	95374	72655
33	59497	04392	09419	89964	51211	04894	72882	17805	21896	83864
34	97155	13428	40293	09985	58434	01412	69124	82171	59058	82859
35	98049	66162	95763	47420	20793	61527	20441	39435	11859	41567
36	45476	84882	65109	06597	25930	66790	65706	61203	53634	22557
37	89300	69700	50741	30329	11658	23166	05400	66669	48708	03887
38	50051	95137	91631	66315	91428	12275	24816	68091	71710	33258
39	31753	85178	31310	89642	98364	02306	24617	09609	83942	22716
40	79452	53829	77250	20190	56535	18760	69942	77448	33278	48805
41	44560	38750	83635	56540	64900	42912	13953	79149	18710	68618
42	68328	83378	63369	71381	39564	05615	43451	64559	97501	65747
43	46939	38689	58625	08342	30459	85863	20781	09284	26333	91777
44	83544	86141	15707	96256	23068	13782	08467	89469	93842	55349
45	91621	00881	04900	54224	46177	53309	17852	27491	89415	23466
46	94896	67126	04151	03795	59077	11848	12630	98376	52068	60142
47	53751	62515	21108	80830	02263	29303	37204	96926	30506	09808
48	85156	87689	95493	88842	00664	55017	55539	17771	69448	87530
49	07521	56898	12236	60277	39‘02	62315	12239	07105	11844	01117

Appendix B—Critical Values for the Chi Square Distribution

Upper Percentage Points of the χ^2 Distribution

1 - a

a

0 x_a^2

df	*.99*	*.98*	*.95*	*.90*	*.80*	*.70*	*.50*	*.30*	*.20*	*.10*	*.05*	*.02*	*.01*	*.001*
1	.03157	.03638	.00393	.0158	.0642	.148	.455	1.074	1.642	2.706	3.841	5.412	6.635	10.827
2	.0201	.0404	.103	.211	.446	.713	1.386	2.408	3.219	4.605	5.991	7.824	9.210	13.815
3	.115	.185	.352	.584	1.005	1.424	2.366	3.665	4.462	6.251	7.815	9.837	11.345	16.266
4	.297	.429	.711	1.064	1.649	2.195	3.357	4.878	5.989	7.779	9.448	11.668	13.277	18.467
5	.554	.752	1.145	1.610	2.343	3.000	4.351	6.064	7.289	9.236	11.070	13.388	15.086	20.515
6	.872	1.134	1.635	2.204	3.070	3.828	5.348	7.231	8.558	10.645	12.592	15.033	17.812	22.457
7	1.239	1.564	2.167	2.883	3.822	4.671	6.346	8.383	9.803	12.017	14.067	16.622	18.475	34.322
8	1.646	2.032	2.733	3.490	4.594	5.527	7.344	9.524	11.030	13.362	15.507	18.168	20.090	26.125
9	2.088	2.532	3.325	4.168	5.380	6.393	8.343	10.656	12.242	14.684	16.919	19.679	21.666	27.877
10	2.558	3.059	3.940	4.865	6.179	7.267	9.342	11.781	13.442	15.987	18.307	21.161	23.209	29.588
11	3.053	3.609	4.575	5.578	6.989	8.148	10.341	12.899	14.631	17.275	19.675	22.618	24.725	31.264
12	3.571	4.178	5.226	6.304	7.807	9.034	11.340	14.011	15.812	18.549	21.026	24.054	26.217	32.909
13	4.107	4.765	5.892	7.042	8.634	9.926	12.340	15.119	16.985	19.812	22.362	25.472	27.688	34.528
14	4.660	5.368	6.571	7.790	9.467	10.821	13.339	16.222	18.151	21.064	23.685	26.873	29.141	36.123
15	5.229	5.985	7.261	8.547	10.307	11.721	14.339	17.332	19.311	22.307	24.996	28.259	30.578	37.697
16	5.812	6.614	7.692	9.312	11.152	12.624	15.338	18.418	20.465	23.542	26.296	29.633	32.000	39.252
17	6.408	7.255	8.672	10.085	12.002	13.531	16.338	19.511	21.615	24.769	27.587	30.995	33.409	40.790
18	7.015	7.906	9.390	10.865	12.857	14.440	17.338	20.601	22.760	25.989	28.869	32.346	34.805	42.312
19	7.633	8.567	10.117	11.651	13.716	15.532	18.338	21.689	23.900	27.204	30.144	33.687	36.191	43.820
20	8.260	9.237	10.851	12.443	14.578	16.266	19.337	22.775	25.038	28.412	31.410	35.020	37.566	45.315
21	8.897	9.915	11.591	13.240	15.445	17.182	20.337	23.858	26.171	29.615	32.671	36.343	38.932	46.797
22	9.542	10.600	12.338	14.041	16.314	18.101	21.337	24.939	27.301	30.813	33.924	37.659	40.289	48.268
23	10.196	11.293	13.091	14.848	17.187	19.021	22.337	26.018	28.429	32.007	35.712	38.968	41.638	49.728
24	10.856	11.992	13.848	15.659	18.062	19.943	23.337	27.096	29.553	33.196	36.415	40.270	42.980	51.179
25	11.524	12.697	14.611	16.473	18.940	20.867	24.337	28.172	30.675	34.382	37.652	41.566	44.314	52.620
26	12.198	13.409	15.379	17.292	19.820	21.792	25.336	29.246	31.795	35.563	38.885	42.856	45.642	54.052
27	12.879	14.125	16.151	18.114	20.703	22.719	26.336	30.319	32.912	36.741	40.113	44.140	46.963	55.476
28	13.565	14.847	16.928	18.939	21.588	23.647	27.336	31.391	34.027	37.916	41.337	45.419	43.278	56.893
29	14.256	15.574	17.708	19.768	22.475	24.577	28.336	32.461	35.139	39.087	42.557	46.693	49.588	58.302
30	14.953	16.306	18.493	20.599	23.364	25.508	29.336	33.530	36.250	40.256	43.773	47.962	50.892	59.703

Taken from table IV, p. 47 of Fisher and Yates, *Statistical Tables for Biological, Agricultural and Medical Research*, published by Longman Group, Ltd., London.
Reprinted by permission of Addison Wesley Longman Ltd.

Appendix C—Critical Values for the Correlation Coefficient

Values of the Correlation Coefficient for Different Levels of Significance

	p			
df	.10	.05	.01	.001
1	.98769	.99692	.99988	.99999
2	.90000	.95000	.99000	.99900
3	.8054	.8783	.95873	.99116
4	.7293	.8114	.9172	.97406
5	.6694	.7545	.8745	.95074
6	.6215	.7067	.8343	.92493
7	.5822	.6664	.7977	.8982
8	.5494	.6319	.7646	.8721
9	.5214	.6021	.7348	.8471
10	.4973	.5760	.7079	.8233
11	.4762	.5529	.6835	.8010
12	.4575	.5324	.6614	.7800
13	.4409	.5139	.6411	.7603
14	.4259	.4973	.6226	.7429
15	.4124	.4821	.6055	.7246
16	.4000	.4683	.5897	.7084
17	.3887	.4555	.5751	.6932
18	.3783	.4438	.5614	.6787
19	.3687	.4329	.5487	.6652
20	.3598	.4227	.5368	.6524
25	.3233	.3809	.4869	.5974
30	.2960	.3494	.4487	.5541
35	.2746	.3246	.4182	.5189
40	.2573	.3044	.3932	.4896
45	.2428	.2875	.3721	.4648
50	.2306	.2732	.3541	.4433
60	.2108	.2500	.3248	.4078
70	.1954	.2319	.3017	.3799
80	.1829	.2172	.2830	.3568
90	.1726	.2050	.2673	.3375
100	.1638	.1946	.2540	.3211

Taken from table VII of Fisher and Yates, *Statistical Tables for Biological, Agricultural and Medical Research*, published by Longman Group, Ltd., London.
Reprinted by permission of Addison Wesley Longman Ltd.

Appendix D—Critical Values for the *t* Distribution

Distribution of t

	p			
df	.10	.05	.01	.001
1	6.314	12.706	63.657	636.619
2	2.290	4.303	9.925	31.598
3	2.353	3.182	5.841	12.924
4	2.132	2.776	4.604	8.610
5	2.015	2.571	4.032	6.869
6	1.943	2.447	3.707	5.959
7	1.895	2.365	3.499	5.408
8	1.860	2.306	3.355	5.041
9	1.833	2.262	3.250	4.781
10	1.812	2.228	3.169	4.587
11	1.796	2.201	3.106	4.437
12	1.782	2.179	3.055	4.318
13	1.771	2.160	3.012	4.221
14	1.761	2.145	2.977	4.140
15	1.753	2.131	2.947	4.073
16	1.746	2.120	2.921	4.015
17	1.740	2.110	2.898	3.965
18	1.734	2.101	2.878	3.922
19	1.729	2.093	2.861	3.883
20	1.725	2.086	2.845	3.850
21	1.721	2.080	2.831	3.819
22	1.717	2.074	2.819	3.792
23	1.714	2.069	2.807	3.767
24	1.711	2.064	2.797	3.745
25	1.708	2.060	2.787	3.725
26	1.706	2.056	2.779	3.707
27	1.703	2.062	2.771	3.690
28	1.701	2.048	2.763	3.674
29	1.699	2.045	2.756	3.659
30	1.697	2.042	2.750	3.646
40	1.684	2.021	2.704	3.551
60	1.671	2.000	2.660	3.460
120	1.658	1.980	2.617	3.373
∞	1.645	1.960	2.576	3.291

Taken from table III of Fisher and Yates, *Statistical Tables for Biological, Agricultural and Medical Research*, published by Longman Group, Ltd., London.
Reprinted by permission of Addison Wesley Longman Ltd.

Appendix E—Creating a How-to Library

Creating a How-to Library

Locating How-to Books

The best place to start your search for how-to books is on the shelves of your school and community library. There are probably several excellent examples already awaiting your discovery. Having "how-to" as part of the title is a good clue, but most good ones don't. You will have to go beyond the "H" drawer of the card catalog in your search. How-to books are often found within the first section of any given 100 in the Dewey Decimal system (800-815, for example). One effective method for finding books is to scan the nonfiction shelves looking for promising-sounding titles. Once you've located a likely candidate, examine the table of contents and scan the pages, using the criteria for analyzing how-to books explained in Chapter 9.

This same method can be used in book stores, though books in the children's section are often not sophisticated enough for middle and high school students. You should scan the shelves in the section of nonfiction books that correspond to the discipline in which you are working, since the how-to shelves are often limited to hobby-type activities. In good book stores where employees know their stock, consider asking them for guidance in finding how-to books. University book stores are particularly good sources of books for older students or teachers. A few undergraduate texts make excellent how-to books as well.

If you attend educational conferences, take time to browse the exhibit area. Look for how-to books among the ones on display and ask publishers' representatives about others that might be available or forthcoming. Look through the books critically, however. Many books published specifically for classrooms involve practice and application or deal superficially with topics, in contrast to how to books which provide sufficient information for a student to independently carry out an investigation.

In addition to conducting the search yourself, enlist the help of experts. Talk with subject matter teachers, graduate students, professors, hobbyists, or amateur practitioners. The latter offer particular promise because they are more likely to be familiar with books aimed at beginners in the field. Other possible sources of recommendations are professionals in the book business—librarians, bookstore owners, and publishers' representatives.

Organizations also can be excellent sources of how-to books. Hobby and amateur clubs can recommend books for beginners and may even publish books or pamphlets themselves. Junior Achievement is an excellent source for business and economic topics and Boy Scout manuals provide information about a wide variety of topics.

Teachers might look at **How-to: 1400 Best Books on Doing Almost Everything** (Katz & Katz, 1985), which should be available in the reference section of larger libraries. This book contains bibliographic information and brief descriptions of approximately 1,400 books, arranged by alphabetically-ordered topics. While most of the entries are about hobbies and crafts and target an adult audience, teachers can still find many books that will support and extend students' interests and learning.

Finally, Creative Learning Press, (P. O. Box 320, Mansfield Center, CT 06250) serves as a distributor of how-to books for elementary and secondary students and teachers. Their catalog contains brief descriptions and grade level recommendations for over 150 how-to books that are currently available.

Unfortunately, books often don't stay in print for more than a few years. One place to check availability is **Books in Print**, located in most libraries and book stores. Updated annually and organized by title, author, and subject, the entries contain title, author, publication date, publisher, paper and/or hardcover format, number of pages, price, and the ISBN number. If the book isn't listed in the most recent **Books in Print**, it probably is not currently being published.

Building a How-to Library

Because students have a wide variety of interests, it would be ideal to have a complete library of how-to books available in a resource room, library, or school. While establishing a collection may not be accomplished overnight, there are several ways you can start building it.

The first step is locating those books to which you already have access, those in their school library, in the libraries of other schools in the district, and in the community library. You can augment this search with a survey of books that are in departmental offices of secondary schools and personal books that teachers might be willing to lend.

To further expand the collection, ask school and community librarians to consider how-to books as part of their regular library purchases. Supplying a list of titles and publishers will make their task easier and increase the likelihood that you will get the ones you want. In addition, academic departments in junior and senior high schools and teams in middle schools sometimes have money for book and equipment purchases. Teachers should let these groups know that how-to books would be valuable resources for both students and teachers.

Because books are relatively inexpensive, they are good items to suggest as possible donations. A school's parent organization or gifted education support group may be persuaded to donate $50 to $100 a year to build a how-to library or students may want to plan a fund-raiser to purchase books. If school policy permits, teachers can circulate a wish list of books for those who want to support the schools with individual donations.

Building on the idea of bridal showers, perhaps teachers could register at a local book store which, in turn, might be willing to give a discount to people who purchase books for their school's collection. Teachers might also be able to arrange an in-school book sale, with a percentage of the sales earmarked for the how-to collection.

Because it is likely that the available how-to books will be scattered in a variety of locations, it is important to create a system by which teachers and students can locate books of interest. A loose-leaf notebook containing information about the content and location of books would be ideal. Notebooks can be located in each school's library and resource room and can be easily updated when new books are acquired. At the very least, title, topic, and book location should be available. Ideally a form like that in Figure E.1 would be completed for each book, allowing the user to decide if the book is appropriate and to use it more efficiently once it is obtained.

General Field ______________________ Specific Area ______________________

Title ____

Author ______________________ Publication Date______________________

Location ______________________ Call Number______________________

Approximate Grade Level ______________

1. Information about Structure of the Field _____ Yes _____ No
   Pages:

   Description:

2. Procedures for Problem Finding and Focusing _____ Yes _____ No
   Pages:

   Description:

3. Specific Methodological Skills _____ Yes _____ No
   Pages:

   Description:

4. Studies/Investigations Students Can Pursue _____ Yes _____ No
   Pages:

   Description:

5. Format/Communication of Findings/Products _____ Yes _____ No
   Pages:

   Description:

Figure E.1. Summary form about how-to books found in school and/or district libraries.